A CENTURY OF FRENCH PAINTING
1400–1500

BY GRETE RING

PHAIDON

ST. JOHN AND THE DONOR
DETAIL FROM THE » PIETÀ OF VILLENEUVE-LÈS-AVIGNON «
⟨ Cat. No. 206 ⟩

A CENTURY OF FRENCH PAINTING 1400–1500

BY GRETE RING

PHAIDON PRESS LTD · LONDON

MADE IN GREAT BRITAIN
1949

PRINTED IN GREAT BRITAIN BY ROBERT MACLEHOSE AND CO. LTD
THE UNIVERSITY PRESS, GLASGOW

CONTENTS

PAGE

INTRODUCTION 7

 GENERAL

 SURVEY OF LITERATURE

 PATRONS AND SITTERS

 ARTISTS AND THEIR WORK

PLATES 41

LIST OF ABBREVIATIONS 188

CATALOGUE 191

BIOGRAPHICAL NOTES ON THE PAINTERS 244

INDEX OF PLACES

TABLE OF PATRONS AND THEIR ARTISTS

⟨ Cat. No. 101 ⟩

A CENTURY OF FRENCH PAINTING
1400–1500

EARLY French art is essentially Gothic art. Its great period was in the twelfth and thirteenth centuries, its main manifestations architecture and sculpture, its material was stone, 'la matière du grand moyen-âge'. French painting began when Gothic art was on the wane; its early monuments are scarcer than those in almost any other country, and many of them have given rise to controversy. It is the ill fortune of this book to be concerned with painting alone, and to start at the moment when France was about to lose the undisputed artistic hegemony in Europe which she was not to regain fully until the nineteenth century.

To the scholars of former days, accustomed to taking the sovereign art of Italy as measure, the hundred years from 1400 to 1500 stood for 'Quattrocento', and Quattrocento meant Early Renaissance—headings that convey the idea of a certain style. Neither of these headings applies to France. About 1400, French art underwent a slight change, but only in so far as pure 'Isle de France Gothic' merged into 'le style international', or 'International Gothic', whose centres, beside Paris, were Prague and Vienna, Verona and Milan, Barcelona, Cologne, and the Hanseatic towns. Since the line separating Late Gothic from Early Renaissance has now become less rigid, the question how to term the period can be approached in a different way. We have learnt that all the cultural and artistic currents previously regarded as typical Renaissance innovations had, in fact, originated in the Middle Ages. Man—homo—is not an invention of the Renaissance; he is present in medieval art, as its centre, although still bound by his relations to the universe and to God, who Himself is the image of humanity. Even the revival of classical antiquity, long attributed exclusively to the Renaissance and hailed as its great 'modern' discovery, has now been found to have originated during the twelfth and thirteenth centuries, in science, literature, and in the visual arts, particularly in sculpture.

Nor is this all. The idea of a continual evolution, so dear to our forefathers, has lost its hold on us. We feel no longer in a position to believe indiscriminately in progress, 'ce fanal obscur', as Baudelaire, its great opponent, has called it, we do not necessarily see an improvement in the transition from one period to the next, the change from one style to another. We are therefore not surprised to find the most perfect specimen of a type rather at the beginning than at the end of the line.

This already precludes the use of the term 'primitive art' for early French painting. The masters of the fifteenth century are, in the words of Huizinga, 'primitive in a purely chronological sense, in so far as they are the first to come and no older painting is known to us'. But neither their art nor their spirit is primitive in the accepted sense of the word.

All these points, which sound like so many truisms, must be remembered if we wish to deal fairly with the subject. If, in this survey, we take pains to look for medieval traits throughout the fifteenth century, we are prompted not by nostalgic predilection for a romantic past, but by the wish to seek the indigenous roots of French painting instead of patching it together from so many foreign 'influences'.

There is, of course, no means to avoid discussing these influences. The Sienese masters working in Avignon for the Popes brought something of their native style with them as early as in the Trecento, and during the whole of

PRESENTATION OF THE VIRGIN.

FIG. 1. Drawing by Taddeo Gaddi, Louvre   FIG. 2. Miniature by Paul de Limbourg ⟨ Cat. No. 65 ⟩

the Quattrocento, Italy and Flanders, the powerful neighbours of France, made themselves felt. The relations of France to the adjacent countries were, however, not quite as unilateral as art history is inclined to present them. Not only are the roots of Eyckian painting to be sought in French miniatures—though this raises at once the point of the partly Flemish origin of the miniaturists—but the schools of Verona and of Milan were greatly indebted to France. While it is known that the Franco-Fleming Paul de Limbourg borrowed the model for a page in his *Hours* in Chantilly from a fresco by Taddeo Gaddi,[1] it has also been noted that the sketch-book attributed to the Lombard artist Giovannino de' Grassi[2] shows a copy after the same Limbourg *Hours*.[3] Pisanello's profile portraits, his landscapes and his animals are based on French models. Above all, the Neapolitan Colantonio, the teacher of Antonello da Messina, was so closely dependent upon Franco-Flemish painting that one of the masterpieces of Southern France could be ascribed to him.[4]

The so-called dualism of early French painting, traditionally derived from these two sources, Italy and Flanders, has more recently been explained in another way, particularly since the illuminating interpretations of Focillon. Instead of believing that French painting owes its grandeur and monumentality to Italy, its alertness of observation, precise characterization, delight in detail and early interest in landscape to Flanders, we are now inclined to look upon the former qualities as a heritage of French medieval sculpture and to attribute the latter to a descent from Parisian miniatures.

I have already hinted at the argument that can be raised against the second part of this thesis. But if Jacquemart de Hesdin, André Beauneveu, Jacques Coëne, and the Brothers de Limbourg—nearly all the glories of late medieval book illumination in France—were born 'Flemings', it is no less true that these artists were com-

---

[1] Taddeo Gaddi, *Presentation of the Virgin in the Temple*. Santa Croce, Florence, Cappella Baroncelli (Drawing in the Louvre, Fig. 1).

[2] Bergamo, Biblioteca Civica.   [3] Hunting group in the calendar picture 'December'; both probably based on an older French model.

[4] Altarpiece of the Annunciation of Aix, Cat. 91–94, pl. 43–52; cf. Colantonio, Cat. 97–98, Fig. 29 and 33.

pletely gallicized once they had settled in France, where a great original tradition was able to meet and absorb them. Their works on French soil are entirely different from those of their countrymen who remained at home, and it can be assumed, without forestalling history, that their own art would have taken a different course had they not gone to France.

The genius of France is to a large extent a genius of assimilation. It is part of its greatness that from time to time it is capable and willing to regenerate itself by adopting foreign contributions, and to incorporate the contributors so successfully that a wholly homogeneous 'esthétique' is the result. French painting has practised this method again and again during its long history. We have an obvious example in the 'École de Paris' of our own time, where painters from all parts of the globe have been accepted and assimilated with ease and generosity, not only by the art-loving public, but by their fellow artists—by France herself. It seems just as impossible to cut off the Flemings Malouel, Limbourg or Coëne from the early School of Paris as it would be to deprive the present one of the Spaniards Picasso, Juan Gris and Miro, the Russian Chagall, the Pole Soutine, the Bulgarian Pascin, the Italians Modigliani and the early Chirico. The designation 'style international' can be applied to both periods for equally good reasons.

It is this genius for assimilating foreign talent—or the talent for assimilating foreign genius—which, among other achievements, has helped to keep French art alive throughout the ages up to the present day. The flow of French production was always constant, with hardly any interruptions, and it had this distinctive feature that it culminated at a time when other schools of painting—with a still greater past—had long been experiencing a gradual or abrupt decline. To treat of the early period of painting in France is not an antiquarian's task: since French art is still a living organism, everyone dealing with it deals with 'art vivant'. There should, however, be no misconception about the way we look at French fifteenth-century art: it is not just a light hors d'œuvre to a solid meal, nor even the socle of a huge monument; it has enough substance of its own to be valued independently, without constant reference to the future. The French 'Quattrocento' had no summits of gigantic proportions, no counterparts to a Jan van Eyck, a Masaccio or Piero della Francesca, but from the beginning it showed the features that were to distinguish it throughout its later history: a universal high level of civilization and a reasonable use of tradition.

It seems in keeping with the spirit of tradition that French artists cannot be represented as detached phenomena, owing nothing to their historical and social surroundings. The setting of their background must be built up in order to get the right approach to their work. Fouquet must be set before the Court of Charles VII, the Master of Moulins before the Court of the Bourbons. This again marks a difference between France and her neighbours. It is quite possible to understand the art of, say, Gruenewald, without tackling the problem whether he was in fact Mathis Nithart, court painter to the Archbishop of Mayence, and in spite of recent attempts to present Italian art under a strictly sociological angle, one can hardly imagine social conditions in Arezzo to be the decisive factor for Piero della Francesca's frescoes in San Francesco. French art is never ageless, it is always embedded in the general circumstances of the epoch and the country. These may be limitations, but they are at the same time reasons for the famous 'continuité'. I have therefore taken special pains to present the artists of this survey not as cut flowers against the walls of a botanist's study, but to give something of the garden where they grew, the weather in which they blossomed, in a chapter devoted to their historical and social environment.

It has always been maintained that early French painting lacks all homogeneity, and most books dealing with it, obsessed by the 'déterminisme géographique', have chosen a regional partition, thereby further stressing the differences between the various centres of art within France. Here the other alternative has been tried and the illustrative material has been arranged chronologically, taking local variations into account as little as possible. It seems that this arrangement has brought out a greater coherence than might have been expected. The painting of Provence—which has often been treated as a perfectly autonomous school, or at least as a kind of local milieu —does not clash with the rest, although we have freely interspersed its documents among those of the other regions. On the other hand, in order not to test the unity too severely, we have confined the representation of the School of Nice to one illustration, as we believe its painters to fit better into the Italian than into the French context. Pl. 149

On the whole we have aimed rather at keeping the image of French art pure than at attaining completeness. We have accordingly been very strict in all borderline cases, particularly in those pointing to the Spanish and *Pl. 91* Catalan frontiers. If we have included the much-discussed *Portrait of a Man* of 1456 we did so in order to show that we consider this a French and not a 'Portuguese' painting. Among the examples of the early period, we have eliminated everything that might rather be listed under the headings 'Verona', 'Bohemia', or 'Austria', *Cat. 26, 25,* thereby depriving French art of such charming specimens as the tiny *Madonna* in Boston, the two panels in *29, 22, 58* the Morgan Library, the *Trinity* in Berlin, the *Polyptique Cardon* in the Louvre, the *Shutters of Heiligenkreuz* in *Cat. 31* Vienna and a number of drawings. We have even ventured, with due caution, to restore the *Wilton Diptych* to English art. All these discriminations are no easy task in view of the many crosscurrents of the 'style international'; and the possibility, even the desirability, of future amendments must be anticipated.

This holds good in particular for works having almost equal claims to French and Flemish origin; here, following the trends of history, we have adopted a more lenient course. In the early period, we have taken care to include only those works by Flemings that were executed in France, and we have not even illustrated the famous *Cat. 18* *Broederlam Altarpiece*, which was executed in Dijon and is, therefore, 'Burgundian' in the stricter sense. But we realize that the question of the 'Franco-Flemish' or 'Franco-Burgundian' style is still a controversial matter and apt to be solved in a controversial way. Hence our attitude in regard to the later period of this school and to the provinces of the half-Flemish North—Artois, Hainault and Picardie—might not seem perfectly consistent. We have, perhaps more out of practical than of purely logical considerations, included Simon Marmion and the Master of St. Giles, whose 'œuvres' have not yet been completely catalogued, while we have omitted the hardly less eligible Jean Bellegambe, who has been fully treated in M. J. Friedlaender's *Altniederländische Malerei*—a work on whose classical authority we cannot venture to improve.

The main subject of this book is *easel painting*. We should, however, not be fair to French art if we confined ourselves to panels. Some of the most remarkable figures of French pictorial art are miniaturists as well as panel painters, others have left evidence of their work in book illumination exclusively. This alone makes the inclusion of *miniatures* a necessity, quite apart from the fact that early French painting showed itself bolder and more progressive on parchment than on panel. *Drawings* of the fifteenth century are exceedingly rare—the more reason *Pl. 33, 34,* to reproduce as many as were available. *Mural paintings* will be shown in a few specimens only, as they are mostly *172, Fig.* in a poor state and difficult to photograph, while the fresco 'relevé'—or copy—remains a substitute, including the *4, 20, 21* excellent new type that has been practised in France during the last ten years. But even if the condition of French murals were more favourable, they could still not claim the place of primary importance which they hold in Italy. This place in France is reserved to *tapestries*, the supreme transalpine contribution to monumental art, *Pl. 11, Fig. 3* France's challenge to the otherwise unsurpassed Italian wall decoration. Here again, we shall offer only a few examples in our plates, if only because so many special publications have lately been dedicated to the subject. The fact that a great French master—Jean Fouquet himself—has worked in a kind of enamel technique has been *Pl. 89–90* known for a long time, and the close stylistic connection of the best French *enamels* with easel painting makes it plausible that more 'finds' might be made in this field, once the problem is tackled seriously. The recent attribution of miniatures to a master hitherto only known as an enameller seems a welcome advance on this road.[1]

It has been said—somewhat paradoxically—that 'all art in the Middle Ages was applied art' (Huizinga). Reversing the paradox, one may say that all art in those times was free art. The masters who illuminated manuscripts and painted pictures were the same who drew the cartoons for tapestries, designed stained glass windows, painted shields and gilded statues.

It would be the ideal solution to treat the whole of early French art as an entirety, disregarding technique and material, so grossly overrated by a materialistic age, and uniting, in one conspectus, panels, drawings, miniatures, tapestries, stained glass, enamels, stone and wood carvings, ivories, and works in gold and silver. But art history seems, alas, still far from this ultimate goal.

---

[1] M. C. Ross: *The Master of the Orléans Triptych*, Journal of the Walters Art Gallery, IV, 1941.

LITERATURE

'Gothic Art', the word used in the depreciatory sense, as a synonym for barbaric, was neglected and despised during the seventeenth and eighteenth centuries, in France as much as in any other country or perhaps even more so in view of the exceptional brilliance and self-confidence of the French dix-huitième siècle. 'Neither the fury of the iconoclasts of protestantism nor the stupid vandalism of the revolution has left such deplorable marks on our monuments as the bad taste of the eighteenth and nineteenth centuries' laments Prosper Mérimée, the romantic 'Inspecteur général des monuments'[1]; and, in 'Notre-Dame de Paris', Victor Hugo joins in: 'In this manner has the marvellous art of the Middle Ages been treated in all countries, particularly in France. One can distinguish three kinds of violations: the time . . . the religious and political revolutions . . . the taste, more and more silly and grotesque. . . .' The credit of having been the first champions of the great and sacred relics of the past does thus not go to the professional antiquarians but to the poets and writers whose vision was ahead of the pedestrian pundits.

The same remark applies to Germany, where the romantic poets, Tieck and Wackenroder, showed the way to a national Gothic revival. But while in France the revision of taste was for some time confined to the official care given, in the first instance, to the monuments of architecture and sculpture, the stimulus of the German writers was quickly taken up by the individual romantic amateurs, whose interest turned to painting just as much as to stone. The Boisserée and Wallraf, the romantic collectors par excellence, illustrated the new message in a practical way, by gathering as many samples from the highly praised bygone times as they could obtain. Thereby they not only saved numerous 'Gothic' pictures from destruction but also established nuclei for the knowledge and propagation of this kind of art, which were the more effective as their collections afterwards entered public galleries. The public recognition of early French painting was less fortunate; only occasionally was a 'Gothic' specimen allowed to enter a French museum. One of the first acquisitions of the Louvre in this line, Fouquet's *Portrait of Charles VII*, was bought in 1838 as 'un ouvrage grec'—incidentally by Louis-Philippe, *Pl. 69* who made it part of his policy to glorify the monuments of the past.

The German romantic circles did not confine themselves to the discovery of their own early school. Sulpiz Boisserée acquired the *Portrait of Charles de Bourbon*, now ascribed to the Master of Moulins, as early as 1815.[2] *Pl. 170* By a rare combination of good luck and understanding, Fouquet's *Portrait of Etienne Chevalier* had come into the *Pl. 73* possession of a collector who already owned forty Fouquet miniatures (now in Chantilly), Herr Georg Bren- *Cat. 130* tano-Laroche, a half-brother of the poet Clemens Brentano. The late-romantic—or post-romantic—writers G. F. Waagen[3] and Carl Schnaase[4] were the first connoisseurs to define and to group Fouquet's œuvre, and Schnaase's characterization of French fifteenth-century painting still holds good.

It was not until 1904 that France presented the incunabula of her pictorial art as a whole, but then it was done with force and élan and in the grandest manner. The famous exhibition of that year 'Les Primitifs Français' was a turning point for the appreciation of early French art. It still remains the chief source of all information on the subject. This supreme effort, which has never been repeated, was due in the first place to the energy and enthusiasm of Henri Bouchot, then Conservateur du Département des Estampes. He was assisted by a team of equally keen co-operators, of whom we should like to mention MM. L. Delisle, J. Guiffrey, P. Vitry and that great connoisseur of illuminated manuscripts, Comte Paul Durrieu. The show gave rise to a manifold literature on 'French Primitives', the most constructive criticism coming from the eminent Belgian scholar Georges Hulin de Loo. It is an astonishing fact that since the 'heroic' times of 1904, the corpus of early French painting has not been noticeably altered and has in any case scarcely been enlarged. Some obvious aberrations which the generation of the great 'conquistadori' made in their first explorer's passion, like the annexation of the Maître de Flémalle, were quickly remedied, but little new material has come to light to make up for the losses.

---

[1] *Études sur les Arts au Moyen-Âge,* 1875.   [2] Sulpiz Boisserée, *Lebensbeschreibung, Briefwechsel,* 1862, I, p. 270.
[3] G. F. Waagen, *Kunstwerke und Künstler in England und Paris,* 1838, III, p. 369 ff.
[4] Carl Schnaase, *Geschichte der bildenden Künste im 15. Jahrhundert,* 1879, VIII, 3, p. 298 ff.

The question has often been asked, more recently again by P. A. Lemoisne, himself a veteran of the 1904 show, why the study of the origins of painting in France has advanced so slowly. One of the reasons has already been mentioned: the absence of early methodical collecting. Another point is the lack of a contemporary historiographer and commentator; France had no Vasari or Karel van Mander. A further and perhaps more decisive factor is the general French outlook on the history of art. There are, in fact, three different types of French art history proceeding on separate lines which never seem to converge: firstly, research—done in the archives—on the lives of artists and their families, on commissions by clients, on records of lost works in inventories; secondly, designation and classification of paintings—done, at least partly, before the originals in the museums; and thirdly, the study of illuminated manuscripts, confined to the libraries. All these activities are hardly ever blended, their representatives seldom combine their results, as has been done in other countries with considerable success. Indeed, the first type —archival research—has from the start carried decisive weight, owing to the eminence of the French archivists, who can proudly point to such authorities as L. de Laborde, Requin, Prost, Delisle. Even those French art historians who profess style criticism are traditionally suspicious of every new attribution that lacks the backing of a document, and prefer to exclude fresh material from the jealously guarded sanctuary of their 'Primitives'. Unluckily it so happens that a number of French fifteenth-century pictures safely supported by entries in the archives or, what

Pl. 118–124 is more, by signatures, are in no way characteristic of French art. If the famous *Froment Triptych* in Florence had not been signed and documented beyond the shadow of a doubt, the keepers of the flame of 'l'esthétique française' would have expelled it from the temple of their art long ago. The numerous altarpieces of the School of Nice,

Cat. 83 signed 'Mirailhet', 'Durandi', 'Bréa'—the *Triptych* signed 'Jacques Iverny', which is an obligatory feature of every book on French painting, convey hardly anything that goes beyond the achievements of Italian provincial art, while many important and truly French examples remain unsupported either by signatures or by documents. A critic like Louis Dimier, who made a point of relying solely on 'ascertained' pictures, has arrived at a sadly unrepresentative aspect of early French painting, stripping it of many of its greatest and most legitimate glories. Dimier, the Frenchman, has shown himself far more critical than foreign scholars, even those whose judgement may have been biassed by national prejudice.

Just as the 'Primitifs Français' of 1904 were followed by a torrential output of literature so the general exhibitions of French paintings in London (1932) and Paris (1937) with their extensive 'primitive' sections gave rise to a new literary surge. Already in 1931, shortly before the London show, all the material known at the time had been assembled and critically commented on by P. A. Lemoisne in his sound and comprehensive work, *Gothic Painting in France*. In the same year, A. C. Barnes, with V. de Mazia, published a highly personal book, *French Primitives and their Forms*, whose most unorthodox and outspoken remarks often blow like a breath of fresh air into the generally subdued atmosphere of the specialists. It was also in 1931 that the first momentous find since

Pl. 85–88 1904 was made and published with cautious modesty by P. Vitry: Fouquet's large *Pietà*, dug out, as it were, from a little village church. This picture formed the chief topic of the papers reviewing the 1932 show, together

Pl. 43–52 with the *Altarpiece of the Aix Annunciation*, whose importance became newly evident since its dismembered parts had found themselves—at least temporarily—reunited. In 1937 Jacques Dupont, to whom the students of early French painting already owed several valuable contributions, published a slender, well-chosen volume, *Les Primitifs français*, and in 1938 Charles Sterling contributed the section *Les Primitifs* to the series *La Peinture française*, noticeable for its abundance of illustrations and the many references to previous literature. Surveys of the whole range of French Painting, in direct connection with the Paris 1937 show, were given by G. Bazin and G. Jedlicka, both showing particular understanding for the origins of French art. Bazin also introduced the handsome booklet, *La Peinture française des origines au XVIe siècle* (1937). More recent publications dealing only with early French painting are those by L. Réau (1939) and by L. Gillet (1941). In the same year, 1941, Charles Jacques (Sterling) set out to compile the entire material then available, arranging it for the first time in the form of a catalogue raisonné. This huge book certainly means an extraordinary effort; final judgement on it should, however, be postponed, following the author's own 'captatio benevolentiae' in his excellent review on the newest Fouquet literature (*Art Bulletin,* June 1946) where he promises a revised edition 'with many additions and corrections'. An abbreviated study on *L'Art Gothique* in France, combining architecture, sculpture, painting and the applied arts, each section being treated separately, was published by Réau, in 1945.

The renewed interest in French fifteenth-century painting has during the last years been focussed on the central figure of Fouquet. A monograph on *Jean Fouquet* by K. Perls (1940), copiously illustrated, with a singularly unprepossessing text, proves useful if one reduces many of its seemingly unquestionable statements to their real value as so many hypotheses. Paul Wescher's *Fouquet und seine Zeit* (1940), standing altogether on a different level of erudition, has its chief merit in the vivid portraiture of the artist's time and society. An extensive study on Fouquet's style by Otto Paecht, hidden in the learned pages of the *Warburg Journal* (1940–41), has found less attention than should have been its due in view of the numerous stimulating suggestions and observations which it offers. The paper, however, that in my opinion gives the clue to the whole Fouquet problem—and on this point I fully agree with Sterling—is the essay by Henri Focillon, *Le style monumental dans l'art de Jean Fouquet* (*GBA*, 1936). It is a beautiful piece of writing in the best tradition of the French 'littérateurs' and conveys a rare artistic vision. Involuntarily one is reminded of Baudelaire, the prototype, as it were, of this manner of interpretation, and of his words, 'Je crois sincèrement que la meilleur critique est celle qui est amusante et poétique, non pas . . . froide . . . et algébrique . . . Ainsi, le meilleur compte-rendu d'un tableau pourra être un sonnet ou une élégie'. It is indeed a sobering experience to realize that from this side comes the real elucidation, even in questions which seem to be the specialist's domain.

But since not everybody concerned with art history can be a writer or poet, style criticism with its plain and factual statements must retain its place and I want to make it quite clear that I do not consider stylistic designations as 'guesswork', after the manner sometimes adopted of late. Style criticism is, however, not a purely critical device, and a silent agreement should be passed, under which pictures, formerly given with good reason to certain artists or schools, may be written off by those scholars only who have proved their ability by making at least one fruitful and convincing new attribution.

PATRONS AND SITTERS

French Art of the twelfth and thirteenth centuries—architecture, sculpture and the early forms of two-dimensional art: mural paintings, stained glass and tapestry—addressed itself to the community; it was to be understood and enjoyed by everybody.

In accordance with the collective thinking of the Middle Ages, the ordering of works of art was not left to the personal taste of the patron, even if there should happen to be a single donor. Such works were chosen by the large congregations which represented the tendencies of the general public. It was only during the fourteenth century that the particular donor made himself felt. An exception has, of course, to be made for miniature painting, which was a 'one man's art' from the beginning. French easel painting, on the other hand, which began in the fourteenth century, owed its very existence to the private amateurs who desired to own these precious and daring tokens of a new spirit.

King Jean II le Bon, of the house of Valois, can be recorded as the first client in this fresh branch of art. His portrait of about 1360, in strict profile, is the earliest example of an independent easel painting in France and *Fig. 11* the first single portrait in history. We wish to point to the precedence of France in this domain and to the fact that French painting began with a portrait. It seems beyond doubt that the King commissioned the picture and approved of his not too flattering likeness.

The royal patronage of the arts was taken up in an enhanced degree by John's sons. The eldest, King Charles V, was by his whole disposition a lover of books. One can visualize him, after Michelet's[1] description, as 'le sage', 'le lettré'—the first king who used to be represented not on horseback, but sitting, often reading or being presented with an illuminated manuscript. Inventories are preserved of his magnificent library which was placed in a tower of the Louvre, forming the germ, as it were, of the 'Bibliothèque du Roi'. He also collected pictures,

---

[1] J. Michelet, *Histoire de France au Moyen-Âge,* vol. V.

among them small panels, their frames mostly ornamented with precious stones. Charles sponsored yet another
Cat. 2, new type of painting, the 'grisaille', of which a sample, with the portraits of the King and his spouse, Jeanne de
Fig. 26 Bourbon, has luckily been preserved in the famous *Parement de Narbonne*.

It requires indeed a good deal of imagination to reconstruct a flourishing 'École de Paris' of that time from
written records and a few relics, all pictorial documents on a larger scale having been destroyed. The best way to
Fig. 3 get an idea of the lost pictures may be to look carefully at the tapestries of the *Apocalypse d'Angers* (based on a
volume in Charles V's library), which convey the finest flavour of the period, although in another medium.
Tapestries must also take the place to-day of the many mural paintings ordered by Charles V, the loss of which is
the more deplorable as they chiefly represented profane subjects, scenes of court life, etc., and would have provided
a telling—if not adequate—counterpart to the religious frescoes of Italy.

The King's brothers, Philippe le Hardi, Duke of Burgundy, and Louis I, Duke of Anjou (who commissioned
the *Apocalypse*), set up art centres of their own; their residences at Dijon and at Angers were to become the
nuclei of important and more or less independent schools of painting. Luckily we are in a somewhat better
Cat. 18 position to judge Philippe's activity as a patron than that of his royal brother; the wings of the *altarpiece* made at
his order by the court painter Melchior Broederlam for the Chartreuse de Champmol are still in Dijon, documented back without interruption to their year of origin, 1399.

The most passionate lover of art among the Valois brothers was Jean, Duke of Berri, one of the greatest collectors of all times, ancestor and prototype of the true 'creative' patron. Not content to order and to keep works of art,
he co-operated with his artists, stimulating them to their highest exertions. He was apparently the first to set the
fashion of importing not only works of art, but also artists from the neighbouring Flanders: André Beauneveu,
Jacquemart de Hesdin, Henri Bellechose, Jacques Coëne, the Brothers de Limbourg, all practised for him
their 'métier de Flamands' at his residences in Bourges, Poitiers, etc. The designation of a 'Berri Master' has since
become an art-historical term, accepted from the time of Robertet, who used it in his famous note to
Cat. 129 Fouquet's *Antiquités Judaïques* (about 1500) down to our days. It seems, by the way, to have been quite usual for

FIG. 3. THE ANGEL SHOWS TO ST. JOHN THE WORLD'S HARLOT WHO COMBS HER HAIR TO SEDUCE THE KINGS OF THE EARTH.
Tapestry, part of the 'Apocalypse of Angers' ⟨ Cat. No. 5 ⟩

these princely enthusiasts to snatch a particularly able immigrant painter from each other: Beauneveu was employed by the king before he entered the service of Berri; Jean Malouel worked for Philippe le Hardi after having been painter to Isabelle de Bavière, Charles V's foreign daughter-in-law, who, whatever her other shortcomings, was an art-lover worthy of the best traditions of the court of Paris.

It was the Duke of Berri's fortune and merit to attach to his entourage, for a long period according to the archives, one of the ablest and most progressive painter-miniaturists of his time, Jacquemart de Hesdin (since 1384) and, as Jacquemart's successors (from 1411 to 1416), the Brothers de Limbourg. The three brothers had started in the service of Jean sans Peur, Duke of Burgundy, with some already rather remarkable work, but *Fig. 9* it must be put to the Duc de Berri's everlasting credit that he inspired the great Paul de Limbourg's genius to the supreme achievement of the *Book of Hours*, now in Chantilly. The atmosphere of the 'Berri' court, the late *Pl. 27–29,* and all the more glorious flowering of the spirit of chivalry, all this knightly poetry come to life, seems to have *31–32* been needed to create the book, which has so appropriately been called 'Les très riches Heures'. An intense and at the same time subtle 'joie de vivre', a sublimated luxury, pervades the world of these Hours. It is a world where noble ladies and gallant gentlemen are forever absorbed in leisurely, vaguely amorous games and sports, where working people look like princesses and courtiers in disguise. We can assume that the more 'advanced' features of the *Heures,* the introduction of contemporary costumes in the Biblical scenes, the representation of nudes, the exact rendering of buildings, also go back to the wishes of the enlightened patron. Jean de Berri has often been portrayed by his miniaturists. We have selected two examples, one by Jacquemart, showing the *Pl. 21* prince in profound devotion, the other by Paul de Limbourg, representing him at his well-laid table in all his *Pl. 28* worldliness—the two inescapably contrasted and combined aspects of medieval man.

It is thus largely due to the activities of his famous 'uncles' that the reign of Charles VI, the 'poor mad king', was to go down in history as one of the summits of artistic glory. If the 'uncles' mismanaged their regency in every other way, they certainly did their best in this domain. As a result, the period from 1380 to 1422, which otherwise would have left a rather sad mark on French history, lives on for ever, brilliant beyond others. It is not always the lucky and prosperous period that coincides with a blossoming of art; art now and again likes to shine on decay.

Only towards the end of Charles VI's reign, when external circumstances became too overwhelming, did French art succumb to the general strain. The violent death of Jean sans Peur in 1419 turned Burgundy from a *Fig. 9* friendly vassal state, however powerful, into an openly hostile competitor. The struggles between Armagnacs and Bourguignons devastated the country. Worst of all, the disaster of Agincourt had occurred in 1415 and, to quote the beautiful phrase of Michelet, 'not the king but the kingdom itself, France was made a prisoner'. About 1420, after the Treaty of Troyes, the royal court had to relinquish the capital, which until then had still been the centre of the 'École de Paris' around which the ducal courts with their painters had circled. Paris was now left to the occupying forces. Their regent, the Duke of Bedford (brother of the victorious King Henry V *Fig. 10* of England), who seems to have run France as yet on the lines of a British protectorate, took over the legacy of art patronage with the best of wills. Only one studio of importance had remained in Paris and this studio worked for the regent; hence its 'chef d'atelier' is known as the 'Master of the Duke of Bedford'. It was the unfortunate *Cat. 76–79* constellation of this period in France which gave the Burgundian branch of the house of Valois its great chance. The court of Burgundy, the centre of this 'improvisation monstrueuse', as the profound French legitimist Michelet calls it, was also the centre of a new art. When Philippe le Bon—son and successor to the murdered Duke Jean—chose Jan van Eyck as his court painter, a blow was dealt to the superiority of French painting from which it did not wholly recover for centuries.

Meanwhile, the 'royal domain' had been transferred to Bourges. Charles VII, Duke of Touraine, reigned there as 'roi de Bourges' from 1422, his territory still comprising Le Berry, Tours, Mehun-sur-Yèvre, etc. It was at his court that the role of art patron passed, at least in some measure, from the exclusive ranks of the old nobility to the new 'upstart' holders of office and fortune. Jacques Cœur, Chancellor of the Exchequer and financial adviser to the king, certainly one of the first men of bourgeois extraction to assume the political lead of a state,

FIG. 4. 'LES ANGES DE BOURGES'. Detail of a Mural Painting, about 1450. Bourges, Hôtel Jacques Cœur ⟨ Cat. No. 114 ⟩

erected in Bourges his magnificent Hôtel, luckily still standing. The mural paintings on the Chapel vault of the
Fig. 4 Hôtel—*Les Anges de Bourges*—could, as an 'immovable object' never be exhibited, nor have they been ade-
quately photographed. They are a masterpiece of early French art and bear full testimony to Jacques Cœur's
patronship. No single portrait of him has been preserved, but we find him, demurely praying, on a miniature in a
Book of Hours (Munich, State Library, Cod. lat. 10103). Portraits of other dignitaries of the king's surroundings
give a good survey of this society, which is remarkable for its stateliness, its formal seriousness approaching the
verge of pomposity—indeed a contrast to the unreal grace, the easy casual manners, that the genuinely aristocratic
Pl. 72 Berri world could afford. *Guillaume Jouvenel des Ursins*, Chancellor of France, who was less a pure upstart
than the eternal type of the high civil servant, is set before a richly coloured and gilded architectural background,
Pl. 73 which emphasizes his rank and fortune. *Maître Étienne Chevalier*, secretary to the King (later treasurer and
ambassador), appears as a pious self-confident donor, on a panel with his patron Saint St. Stephen (in Berlin)
Pl. 75 and in his famous *Book of Hours* (Chantilly) on two religious scenes, which look like state ceremonies.

The painter to whom we owe these works is Jean Fouquet, a native of Tours. It seems as if the innate forces of
France had combined to make this reign, which had started so unluckily, a success: to Jeanne d'Arc, the spirit
of the peasantry, who saved Charles's throne, and to Jacques Cœur, the embodiment of the bourgeoisie who
provided the economic basis to his rule, may be added Jean Fouquet, the representative of the artisans who lifted
French art from sterility and degeneration and gave a lasting form to the period. No authentic portrait of the
'Pucelle' has been preserved; we may visualize her after the beautiful Fouquet miniature of a saintly shepherdess
Pl. 82 among her flock (*St. Margaret*).

THE ANNUNCIATION TO THE SHEPHERDS

MINIATURE FROM THE » GRANDES HEURES DE ROHAN «

〈 Cat. No. 86 〉

B

Although the painter's services to the king did not lead up to the same disasters that befell Joan of Arc and Jacques Cœur—the financier's career ended with a trial for murder, a narrow acquittal and subsequent exile—Fouquet also seems to have met with a certain lack of gratitude; the title 'painter to the king' was not bestowed on *Pl. 69* him until after Charles's death. The *Portrait of Charles VII* is preserved, a queer human document showing the monarch with his long nose, small eyes and thick sensual lips, his sad and sulky expression contrasting with the inscription 'Le très Victorieux' on the picture frame. He is segregated from the outside world by the barrier of an only temporarily lifted curtain. We possess also, in all probability, a portrait by Fouquet of the king's mistress, Agnes Sorel, 'La dame de beauté' (an appropriate double meaning: she resided at the Castle Beauté-sur-Marne), in the guise of the Holy Virgin. The donor of this painting was not the king, but again Étienne Chevalier, the *Pl. 74* *Virgin and Child* combining with his own portrait to form a diptych. 'The madonna is, in fact, represented here according to the canons of contemporary fashion. There is the bulging shaven forehead, the rounded breasts, placed high and wide apart, the high and slender waist . . . there is a flavour of blasphemous boldness about the whole' (Huizinga, *Waning of the Middle Ages*). Be that as it may, 'la belle Agnès' was a true child of her times, believing in the new ruling power, wealth. Étienne Chevalier and Jacques Cœur were her confidants and the executors of her will; the moralizing historiographer Jean Jouvenel brands her as 'cette reine des nouveautés et du luxe'. She collected jewels and other precious things, and she also supported the arts: a gilded statue of Mary Magdalen, the patroness Saint of the sinners, was given by her to Loches Cathedral (1444).

Art patronage of still another type than that of the Court of Tours had in the meantime been established in the East of France. Louis I, Duke of Anjou, the tapestry lover, was succeeded in 1384 by his son Louis II, whose *Pl. 26* likeness has come down to us in a portrait continuing the severe profile type of his grandfather's image. His profile leads in a direct line to the Italian Quattrocento profiles, giving an early instance of the close connection between Italy and the rulers of Anjou-Naples-Sicily. But it was René, called the Good, that great romantic figure, who gave to the art of this court its distinctive flavour and physiognomy. René is in fact the first among the princely amateurs who was himself a professional artist, a painter as well as a writer. Princely poets and writers were not unknown to the time. René's kinsman and friend, Charles d'Orléans, was certainly a great poet, in spite of his descent; but a royal Sunday painter had hitherto been unheard of. The considerable 'œuvre' with which earlier literature had endowed René—he had been named as the master of the *Burning Bush* of Aix—could not stand up to more recent criticism. Nevertheless we should like to imagine that his relations to the artists around him were different from those of the non-professional patrons, and of a more direct approach. He may have passed on to them the technical knowledge of foreign methods: Pietro Summonte, in his letter to Marcantonio Michiel, of *Cat. 97* 1524, mentions as the king's pupil 'a certain Colantonio, who between 1438 and 1442 had learned from René the art of painting in the Flemish manner'—an art which Colantonio on his part transmitted to Antonello da Messina. But what is more, René could have conveyed to his entourage something of the new artistic spirit beyond the frontiers, a notion of which he might have captured on his many voluntary and involuntary travels.

René's life reads like a romance. Born in Angers in 1409, the second son of Louis II and Yolande of Aragon, married to the heiress of Lorraine, brother-in-law of Charles VII, he had from the start an equivocal position among the powers, and he sided now with one party now with the other. Lacking as he did the political instinct of his much less brilliant brother-in-law, he met with many set-backs. On the other hand, countries and fortunes seemed to fall into his lap, and at one moment of his career, about 1434, he was not only Duke of Anjou, Bar, Lorraine and Count of Provence, but also King of Sicily and Naples, and—a prisoner of war. René's is a transitory type in every respect; he stands between the different countries, France, Burgundy, and Italy, between the different ranks, as a king and an artist, and also between the ages; he is in one way essentially modern and he has the romantic's leaning towards the past. We are therefore not surprised to find his early portrait (the costume *Fig. 5* suggests a date shortly after 1437) inserted in a manuscript from the workshop of the 'Maître des Heures de Rohan'. It is at least possible that this great anonymous master—'ce grand isolé' as Focillon calls him—was active in the orbit of an outsider such as René, the more so as the artist also combines a topical and far-sighted vision with a certain archaism. I do not hereby venture to solve the mystery surrounding the Rohan Master, indeed, I am

FIG. 5. KING RENÉ AS A YOUNG MAN. Miniature 〈 Cat. No. 87 〉. FIG. 6. KING RENÉ IN HIS STUDY. Miniature from the
MS. 10308 in the Bibliothèque Royale, Brussels. FIG. 7. KING RENÉ AS AN OLD MAN 〈 Cat. No. 217 〉
FIG. 8. KING RENÉ AS A CROWNED SKELETON. Miniature 〈 Cat. No. 101 〉

not even certain whether to locate him in Angers at all, but I do want to point once more to the fact that he worked for the house of Anjou.

Pl. 54–58   We are on more solid ground in dealing with another group of illuminated manuscripts, foremost among which is the *Le Livre au Cuer d'Amours espris* of the Vienna State Library. The text of the manuscript, the typical idyllic allegory of the period and in itself not too inspiring, is written by René, and his influence on the illuminations can be assumed as fairly certain. Here again we have an instance of productive co-operation between artist and client, which stimulated the artist to give his very best. The illuminator, to whom other works can be assigned, all with texts by René, is now usually called 'The René Master'—a well-deserved posthumous 'hommage' to the royal script writer.

Cat. 91–94   Returning to conjectures we should like to remark that the painter of the famous *Altarpiece of Aix* (1442) can also best be imagined in René's entourage. The mixture of styles which has puzzled the critics, the Burgundian influence, the connection with Conrat Witz, the affinity to Antonello, all might be explained by giving the work to an itinerant artist who took the widely travelled king's advice, or even followed him on some of his wanderings. The fact that the Aix Altarpiece was actually a donation by the draper Corpici, a member of the new bourgeois client class, is in no way contrary to such an order of thought.

Pl. 126–130   The only work that documents prove to have been commissioned by René is the *Burning Bush*, still to be seen in Aix Cathedral. Here we may again test the truism that facts are often less right than feasible conceptions: the classical, in no way daring altarpiece, painted by Nicolas Froment in his later years (1476), seems hardly as characteristic for the crowned eccentric as the wonders which strike us in the works of the 'Rohan' and 'Aix' Masters. The wings of the *Burning Bush* give the portraits of René, a tired and very pious man, far remote from the *Fig. 5* pugnacious vivacity of his youthful likeness in the *Anjou Hours*, and of his second wife, Jeanne de Laval, *Fig. 22* who looks astonishingly plain and prim, considering the bucolic poems which her elderly husband-lover showered upon her. To complete the image of René in all its complexity, which is in fact the complexity of the late

FIG. 9. DUKE JOHN THE FEARLESS OF BURGUNDY BEING PRESENTED WITH A BOOK BY JOHN HAYTON. Miniature
⟨ Cat. No. 38 ⟩

FIG. 10. THE DUKE JOHN OF BEDFORD IN ADORATION BEFORE HIS PATRON SAINT. Detail of a miniature
⟨ Cat. No. 78 ⟩

FIG. 11. PORTRAIT OF KING JOHN II THE GOOD, Paris, about 1360.
⟨ Cat. No. 1 ⟩

FIG. 12. PORTRAIT OF KING LOUIS XI, about 1475.
⟨ Cat. No. 318 ⟩

Middle Ages, we show him in one of his *Books of Hours* as 'le roi mort', a crowned skeleton, a fantastic and *Fig.* 8
bizarre vision of the 'macabre'.   UGH!

With the *Altarpiece of Aix* we have entered the zone of Provence. This Southern province, with Aix
and Avignon as its principal towns, had the oldest tradition of artistic patronship in France. The original
foundation of its school of painting was not due to temporal lords, but to the popes who had resided in the Palace
of Avignon since 1305 and ordered the walls to be decorated with large frescoes. As the papal residence was
transferred back to Rome in 1378, the whole period does not fall within the limits of this book. But in view of the
universal fame of the 'first style of Avignon', it should be mentioned that it comprised not only religious paintings,
believed to be by Italian (Sienese) artists, but also representations of profane subjects, such as hunting, fishing, etc.
These are by common assent attributed to French artists both for stylistic reasons and because their contents
correspond to the lost frescoes commissioned by the Valois kings (p. 14).

Deprived of papal patronage, art in Avignon lost its main impulse. Only some scattered relics remain of a
'second style of Avignon', about 1400-1410. We illustrate an extremely 'Sienese' specimen, the *Madonna adored
by a Donor* who looks small and inconspicuous beside his guardian Saint, even allowing for the general use of *Pl.* 10
the age. After 1410, Avignon experienced the break of a few decades found in all French production until,
about 1445, the 'third style' sets in gloriously. Its two great anonymous examples, the *Pietà de Villeneuve* and the
Retable de Boulbon, were commissioned by clerical donors, neither of whom has so far been identified. Both *Pl.* 111-112
donors are strong Southern types, obviously of peasant origin, which hold their own next to the holy figures.

Pl. 63–68 In dealing with the central work of the province, the *Coronation of the Virgin* of the Chartreuse de Villeneuve-lès-Avignon, which has been called the French 'Altarpiece of Ghent', we have the support of documentary evidence. Not only the painter of the work is known, Enguerrand Charonton, but also the patron who presented
Pl. 68 it, a priest, 'Joannes Montanhaccus presbyter' (i.e. Jean de Montagnac), who is seen kneeling, a solitary frail figure, before the crucifix.

In the royal domain, Louis XI had succeeded to the throne in 1461. Like other problematic heirs-apparent, he made an excellent king, under whose reign France was thriving. He followed and intensified the practical lines his father had taken, protecting commerce and industry and consolidating the position of the 'nouveaux riches' whom he used against the old feudal lords. As a matter of course, he took over Jean Fouquet, whom he at last appoints 'peintre du roi' in 1475.

Fouquet had gone on working for the great 'upstarts'. In the last year of Charles's reign he illustrated
Cat. 131 the *Boccaccio* (Munich) for 'Maître Laurens Gyrard, Controlleur de la recette des finances'. The frontispiece,
Pl. 81 the *Lit de justice* with many contemporary portraits, shows an historical event of Fouquet's own time: the Assembly of Justice held in Vendôme in 1458, where sentence of death was passed on Jean Duke of Alençon, a prince of royal blood. The reports that Fouquet worked for Jean Moreau, 'Valet de chambre du roi', and for the historian Philippe de Commines are now generally disbelieved, as they are found in documents whose authenticity is doubtful.

Towards the end of his career, Fouquet, obviously very famous and 'arrivé', receives a number of commissions
Cat. 129 from patrons of the old princely ranks. He executes (or rather finishes) the *Antiquités Judaïques* for Jacques d'Armagnac, a grandson of Jean de Berri, and a *Book of Hours* (not yet identified) for Marie de Clèves, the widow of Charles d'Orléans (in 1472). For the king, he drafts a cartoon for the royal tomb; in 1476 he designs a daïs for the solemn entry into Tours of Alfonso V, King of Portugal. In 1469, Louis XI had founded the 'Ordre de S. Michel' and Fouquet painted a number of pictures for the order ('certains tableaux que ledit seigneur lui a chargé faire pour servir aux chevaliers de l'Ordre de Saint-Michel'). None of these pictures has survived, but the
Pl. 84 *Frontispiece for the statutes of the Order,* illuminated by Fouquet, is preserved. It shows the sovereign, attended by the knights of St. Michael, in full frontal view, his extraordinary features rather toned down. No single portrait of the king by Fouquet's hand is known. He lives for posterity under the form which minor followers have created: in full or three-quarter profile, sly eyes looking down an unending nose, the grin of the bigoted hypocrite on a
Fig. 12 bland face. The picture that shows the type most clearly has been attributed (without certainty) to Jean Bourdichon, who worked for the court after Fouquet's death, being appointed 'peintre du roi et valet' in 1484. 'L'aimable Bourdichon' apparently did not suffer from the fate of being a second-rate artist succeeding a great master. His sound clearness, pleasantly presented, seems well suited to his royal patron's matter-of-fact mind, and he must have also satisfied Louis's successors. Four different kings made use of Bourdichon's efficient talent, his richest and best-known work being the *Book of Hours* executed for Queen Anne de Bretagne, the wife of Charles VIII.

The merit of having secured the services of the outstanding figure after Fouquet, and the one equal to him in artistic calibre, does not belong to the royal court, but to the Bourbon family, which was then ruled by Anne de Beaujeu, Louis XI's daughter and female counterpart. From the connection with this ducal house, the painter was called 'Le peintre des Bourbons', when his personality first took shape. He is now known as the 'Maître de Moulins', a designation we should like to preserve, the identification with Jean Perréal having been definitely rejected by recent research and the identification with Jean Hay, although more plausible, not yet perfectly
Pl. 159–163 established. The master's chief work is the *Altarpiece of Moulins Cathedral,* commissioned by Pierre II de
Fig. 23 Beaujeu, Duke of Bourbon, and 'la grande madame', who is seen presented by her patroness St. Anne, and accompanied by her young daughter Suzanne (later to be married to her famous kinsman, the Connétable de Bourbon). The portraits of the ducal couple correspond faithfully to the historical tradition describing the formidable lady and her mild partner, who was 'less her husband than her humble servant' (Michelet). The portrait of another Bourbon recalls still more popular historical reminiscences; the young ecclesiastic who is

represented on the picture in Munich is *Charles*, Pierre de Beaujeu's brother, the 'Monsieur le Cardinal' of Victor   *Pl. 170*
Hugo's *Notre-Dame de Paris*. His figure lives after the poet's image: a good man of good looks, wearing his
purple robe in the proper manner, distributing alms more liberally to comely girls than to old women. The
Munich picture is supposed to portray the Cardinal in 1485, the date of his official entry into Lyon. A less handsome
ecclesiastic, also of cardinal's rank, appears as the donor of the *Nativity* of Autun. It is Jean Rolin, a great dig-   *Pl. 157*
nitary of the church, 'Confessor to the Dauphin' since Louis XI. From his father, Nicolas Rolin, the chancellor
of Philippe le Bon, Jean had taken over the part of a patron of the arts. Although he devoted himself faithfully
to rebuilding and adorning the cathedral of his native Autun, he could not equal the record of his father, who
incidentally was the donor of Jan van Eyck's *Madonna* in the Louvre and of Rogier van der Weyden's *Altarpiece* in
Beaune. Cardinal Jean was born in 1408, he died in 1483, his age dating the *Nativity* about 1480. This makes it
the earliest work by the Master, who thus appears to have owed his start, not to princely amateurs, but to a
prominent member of the 'new clientèle'. The sitters of further works by the master have not been fully identified;
for the knight of the Glasgow picture, various names have been proposed, none of them convincing; the charming
girl at one time thought to be Suzanne de Bourbon is now tentatively called Marguerite d'Autriche (then   *Pl. 169*
betrothed to Charles VIII). Of the few direct commissions given to the Moulins Master by the king, we
mention a *miniature for the Ordre de St. Michel*, and the rather touching specimen of a sad baby—the *Dauphin*   *Pl. 156*
Charles Orland, son of Charles VIII and Anne de Bretagne, doomed to die at the age of three.   *Cat. 306*

Looking back on French art, since Charles VII set up in Bourges the 'first modern court in history', we have
to realize that it was by no means a bourgeois art which was practised there, although it was largely supported by
commoners. The employers of Fouquet and his followers, irrespective of their origin, gravitated to the court. The
famous 'upstarts' did not remain true to the class of their birth, not even under Louis XI, who has been termed the
'roi bourgeois'. They formed instead a new nobility, backed by high office and fortune, which was less concerned
with opposing the hereditary nobility than with slowly merging into it. The sitters and clients of this epoch,
laymen and priests alike, were not members of a fresh society borne by something like a popular movement, but
they all belonged to the very rich and powerful. There was no popular French painting during the fifteenth and the
following centuries. After Louis XI had crushed the feudal lords and unrestricted monarchy had been established
in France, the idea of absolutism passed on to the arts. The richness and many-sidedness of artistic production,
nourished by the variety of 'local milieux', gave way to centralization, with the inevitable consequence of uni-
formity. Of all the branches of French painting which had flourished until 1500, portraiture was the one which
survived best but it became the strict servant of the 'absolute' Government in Paris. Clouet was a 'peintre du roi'
in yet another sense and degree than Fouquet because he was nothing but a court painter.

THE ARTISTS AND THEIR WORK

It should not prove impossible to define the essence of Early French Painting. Indeed, one is constantly faced
with this problem when compiling a *catalogue raisonné*, accepting one picture and rejecting the next. It is, however,
one thing to sort and group pictures, as one has done more or less unconsciously for a lifetime, and another to
come into the open and be articulate about them.

So much is certain: the spirit of fifteenth-century art cannot be caught by enumerating details and adding
them up. Nor will a solution be found by trying to visualize an 'ideal' image of this art to be used as a kind of
tuning fork by which each work could be tested. This method (if one may call it a method) as applied with
spectacular results by Max J. Friedlaender in regard to single artists, would hardly work when dealing with an
entire country and epoch. Neither the art of a country nor that of a century can be wholly homogeneous: the
country has its regional variations, the century its periods, its youth, its ripe and old age. Above all, each work of
art is made by an individual who should not be solely assessed as the representative of his nation and epoch—
one might even say that the only artists worth treating are those who sometimes defy the limits of time and origin.

Instead of losing ourselves in generalizations, it will therefore be better to follow the path of French painting from 1400 to 1500, singling out the more definite personalities, trying to throw some spotlights on the essential features of their art. There again, a double danger must be evaded: the danger of first deducing certain qualities from a picture whose author is known or presumed to be French and afterwards declaring the picture as a typical product of France because it shows those qualities.

The works that correspond best to the usual idea of 'French Primitives' are the paintings of the School of Paris about 1400. The observation should make us careful: this art is still to a great extent embedded in the universal trend of 'le style international', differentiating itself from the other centres of 'international Gothic' rather by subtle degrees and nuances than by fundamental principles. Keeping these nuances in mind, we can state that the early 'École de Paris' is graceful and pleasant, precious and refined. It is nimble, with a nimbleness of mind as well as of forms, always tending to elegance, often to luxury, sometimes to splendour, but to a restrained, highly civilized splendour; and it never gives way to gorgeousness. Its figures are of slender build, the heads softly rounded, the curves of drapery concave, swinging inward, the outlines undulating, forming a kind of pattern, which in the finer specimens is not merely ornamental but the bearer of feeling and emotion. The palette is delicate, with frequent use of broken tones, but the colour of preference is still the clear blue—'bleu ciel'—which is taken over from the thirteenth century, and which was to remain the favourite of French artists for many centuries—pervading the paintings of Poussin, turning up again as 'bleu Nattier', scintillating in the pastels of Perronneau, of
Cat. 2, Quentin de La Tour and Degas, sparkling through Manet's landscapes, until it culminates in Cézanne's water
Fig. 26 colours. Of the works of the early Paris School, I shall cite: the *Parement de Narbonne* (which sets the tune), the
Pl. 1–5, two Bargello *Diptychs*, the 'Sachs' *Annunciation*, the Louvre *Entombments*.
16–17
If this art marks the youth of the fifteenth century, it is indeed a most precocious youth, which could equally well be defined as the old age of the fourteenth, pervaded as it is by a kind of 'fin de siècle' atmosphere. The refinement soon threatens to become affected, the loveliness stereotyped, the decorative tendency mechanical, and it obviously needed the fortifying blood transfusion which it received from the imported 'Flemings'. Jacquemart de Hesdin, while keeping the old forms, starts with a new vitality; the 'Maître du Maréchal de Boucicaut' —whom we may safely call Jacques Coëne—apparently also traditional, even retrograde, with his soft boneless figures—introduces a new sense of spatial relations between these figures and their surroundings, relinquishing the ornamental plane. Jean Malouel, Bellechose, or whoever may finally be recognized as the painter of the group of
Fig. 28, panels comprising the beautiful (damaged) *Pietà* of Troyes, the large circular *Pietà* and the *St. Dionysius* in the
Pl. 18, 20 Louvre, shows a new sense of the volume of the human body. And to Malouel's nephews, the great Pol de Limbourg and his brothers, it was given to make this art shine most brilliantly, as must once more be repeated, in the *Heures de Chantilly*. However, lest there be a misunderstanding, let me add: none of these artists, not even the great brothers, should be regarded as initiators of the 'modern' age. It is true that the Limbourgs erected actual buildings in their landscape backgrounds, but these famous landscapes were more dreamlike than real, the whole of this art essentially romantic. Pol de Limbourg when he created his masterpiece was an elderly man, the representative of a bygone generation. His work marks an end, not a beginning. It is at this point that the new era sets in, but its centre was, alas, not to be France. The van Eyck pages of the *Heures de Turin/Milan* are only separated by about one year from the Limbourg *Hours*, but here the decisive step is made. Jan van Eyck was a young man and a revolutionary; his art is no longer romantic or idealistic, it is in the first line pledged to nature, and it was to be—for better or worse—the art of the future.

It is one of the most telling tests of the tenacity, the praised 'continuité' of French painting that at this crucial moment it carried on while other exponents of the 'style international'—I think of the school of Bohemia—had long given up. Looking at the matter from a different angle, one might even say that French art started only now, at the moment when it broke away from the international context. While its centre was shifted from the borders of the Seine to those of the Loire and the Rhône, it became national, even local. And it is to its everlasting credit that it achieved this change without becoming provincial.

There is no danger of going wrong if we first let the art of Jean Fouquet speak for French art as a whole, since Fouquet is in fact a piece of France personified. He is the embodiment of measure, of reason, of order, of poise

MASTER OF ST. GILES: ST. REMI GIVING BENEDICTION ⟨ Cat. No. 240 ⟩

He is simple, with the self-chosen simplicity born of richness, not of want. He is strong without being brutal, healthy without being insensitive, sane without being banal. His art has neither the exuberance of youth nor the tiredness of old age, it is eminently adult. He is nearly always serious, always factual and objective, the born historiographer in images, the interpreter of action and men of action. It is by a queer whim of fate that one of the greatest history painters of all times has realized his historical conceptions in miniatures only, or that these alone have survived. Thrown on the screen by the magnifying projector Fouquet's miniatures regain at once their inherent monumental quality and assume the stature of frescoes.

Fig. 34   The portraits of Fouquet will be best understood by comparing them to the portraits of Jan van Eyck. Focillon has coined a telling phrase, establishing the antithesis between the 'portrait monumental' and the 'portrait d'analyse': Jan van Eyck, the analytical mind, is possessed by the uniqueness of his sitter, whose likeness he catches without mercy. 'His eye becomes a magnifying glass, his brush nearly an engraver's burin'. Fouquet sees his models in simple masses, in large planes. His images have the monumentality of carved and coloured stones. They are motionless, silent, impenetrable. They are very real, perhaps realistic, never naturalistic.

His landscapes partake of the same grandeur and simplicity. Clearly planned, cut down to the essentials, they seem an early instance of the twentieth-century doctrine that 'art consists in leaving out'.

Seen against the Flemish background, Fouquet is more of a line-draughtsman, less an explorer of light and atmosphere. His colours retain the peculiarities of the illuminator even when applied to panels: they are clean and neat, not too variegated, the flesh tones of the women very white, those of the men very brown. Being singularly free from mannerisms, Fouquet's art is not easy to dissect for the eager adept of 'morellian' style criticism. One may give as a 'clue' the shape of the noses which are round and protruding. The types of Fouquet's elderly bearded men are also unmistakable. The finger nails, of oblong oval form, are each marked by a shiny lengthwise stroke. But, on the whole, convenient prescriptions to identify his work are bound to fail.

Most of Fouquet's commentators have stressed the Italian influence on his art. He was in Italy, and there is no doubt that he brought home with him the knowledge of linear perspective. His outlook on the world, however, was not changed by this cognition, as the world of, say, Duerer or Lucas van Leyden was changed by their collision with the South. Fouquet was too deeply rooted in his native artisan's tradition to overrate the new technical experience. He casually made use of the 'costruzzione legittima', only to come back again to the habitual 'empirical' perspective. If it should be deemed imperative to place Fouquet within a transalpine context, he ought not to be coupled indefinitely with Fra Angelico. There certainly are similarities with the 'Beato' but they remain more or less superficial, whereas there is a deep and real affinity to Piero della Francesca. It is with good reasons that Roberto Longhi has suggested, in an illuminating passage of his book on Piero: 'One should enquire closely into the full historical significance attributable to Piero's stay in Rome' and into 'the consequences to be drawn from this fact and Fouquet's Italian journey'.

Pl. 36–42   The work of Fouquet is not the only facet through which to see French fifteenth-century art. Another current can be detected besides the main stream of classical purity. We have stressed the 'irreality' of the Limbourgs—the last flowering of the rhetorical poetry of French fourteenth-century art. We have now the sensation of watching a new unreal art appear, in full fifteenth century, a generation after the Limbourgs and hardly a generation earlier than Fouquet, in the work of the 'Maître des Heures de Rohan'. Here is the great counterpart to Fouquet, the only near contemporary of equal stature. If Fouquet, the champion of measure, is himself measurable, the Anonymous is unmeasurable, and hence perhaps the only early French artist who corresponds to the conception of genius in the more Northern sense. Although some of his compositions can be derived from previous miniaturists, particularly from the Limbourgs, and although he is akin to them 'in romanticis', he is too different in spirit to be regarded as their successor. His is the spirit of a visionary, an ascetic and a mystic, tragic, bitter and austere, far from the pleasant hedonism of the Berri artists. The Rohan Master is at his most grandiose when representing scenes of suffering and death, the corpse and its putrefaction, the lost causes and the last judgement. He is at his comparatively weakest when trying his hand at courtly and worldly subjects. If he has no contemporary companion in the world of the visual arts, he has his parallels in poetry: Pierre de Nesson, 'le poète de la

FIG. 13. PAUL DE LIMBOURG: ST. JEROME IN HIS STUDIO. Drawing.
⟨ Cat. No. 67 ⟩

FIG. 14. Pulpit from the 'ANNUNCIATION OF AIX'.
⟨Detail from Plate 43⟩

mort', not to mention Villon's 'Poésie funèbre' of a later generation.[1] In spite of his archaizing tendencies, the Rohan Master is by no means backward in regard to his forms: they are excellently constructed, with a keen sense of reality, which breaks through in details. The draughtsmanship is of the highest level of the period, the sweeping lines never simply decorative but subservient to the one major aim: expression. Louis Gillet has aptly called the master 'an astonishing mixture of Blake and Gruenewald', and it is in particular the analogy to the other great solitary and 'expressionist', Nithart-Gruenewald, which imposes itself.

If the figure of the 'Maître de Rohan' seems to upset considerably the balance of French fifteenth-century painting, he fits into the French context when seen under a wider aspect. He had in fact no immediate following—neither had Fouquet, since the poor imitators of the master of Tours, including Bourdichon, can hardly be regarded as such, And just as Fouquet's art has its legitimate 'suite' in the 'Maîtres de la réalité' of the seventeenth century, in Ingres and the early Degas, the line from the Rohan Master may be traced over Callot and Bellange to, say, Daumier, Redon or Toulouse Lautrec.

The popularity of the 'Maître des Heures de Rohan' suffers under two grave handicaps: he has to carry the load of his long and not even pertinent 'temporary name', and he has been known as a miniaturist only. A panel is here cautiously ascribed to him, and it is to be hoped that more suggestions in this direction will follow, since *Pl.* 41–42 easel painting seems well suited to the master's disposition.

[1] Heimann, p. 39.

The number of artists able to match the standard set by the two great figures is restricted. We pass on to another Anonymous[1], this time a panel painter, known by one work, which luckily consists of various parts.

Cat. 91–94, Pl. 43–52 Even allowing for the controversies bound to be aroused by a single and unconnected mid-fifteenth-century work of the greatest importance, the 'Altarpiece of the Annunciation of Aix' has become the battlefield for the most diverging theories in a particularly high degree. All possible origins, from pure Flemish to South Italian have been proposed—the more reason to see in the perfect blending of North and South a product of France. This seemingly chance statement may be supported by the facts that the interior of the 'Annunciation' shows a French *Fig. 13–14* Cathedral, that the Virgin's pulpit can be traced back to a French drawing and that the figures are again derived from French monumental statues. They are of a high reality like Fouquet's figures, but in contrast to the Master of Tours' laconic sobriety, figures and draperies of the Master of Aix are more ample, more exuberant, more voluble as it were. The affinities to the Netherlands cannot be denied: the 'Maître d'Aix' has the 'Fleming's' loving eye for the inanimate objects of nature, his assemblages of books, pots and papers being among *Colour Plate p. 29* the foremost incunabula of still-life painting. But while the still-life on early religious pictures in Flanders is often liable to become an end in itself, on the *Retable of Aix* it always remains subordinate to the essential issue. Within the Flemish school it is Jan van Eyck who sets the model—not the masters of Tournai—that fixes the 'Annunciation' to the 'classical' side from the start.

The connection of the master with Claus Sluter has been stressed. However, to put it paradoxically, the professional sculptor Sluter is in a way more 'pictorial' than the painter of Aix, whose forms go back to the severer type of indigenous sculpture. They are cubic or cylindric, more like bossed out of metal than hewn from the stone, thereby connecting the master on the other end of the line with Antonello da Messina. The resemblance of Antonello's *Annunciation* from Palazzolo Acreide with the *Annunciation* of Aix remains evident, in spite of disbelievers, although one must remember that Antonello himself was an adept of Flemish art and that both *Annunciations* may go back to the same prototype which in this case might have been of Eyckian invention.

No other work of importance has as yet been ascribed to the 'Maître d'Aix', but two further groups of Anonymi *Cat. 143, 144 Pl. 54–58* have lately been placed within his orbit: the portraits attributed to the so-called 'Master of 1456', formerly connected with Fouquet, and the miniatures of the 'René Master'. In the first group it is chiefly the Eyckian character which provides the common denominator. The fact that the van Eycks had a more immediate following abroad than in their own country, where the Flémalle-Rogier ascendency soon became preponderant, has been observed. And both portraits ascribed to the 'Master of 1456'—whether belonging together or not—have a close and exclusive bond with Eyckian art—as after all has Nuño Gonçalvez, whose name has been mentioned in connection *Pl. 91* with them. I should in any case like to place the *Portrait of a Man* of 1456 in the Liechtenstein Collection very near to the *Altarpiece of Aix* and perhaps still nearer to the illuminations of the 'Cuer d'amours espris'. The massive 'cubic' form of the head, the strong contrasts of light and shade, the colour of the flesh—all combine to point in this direction. The link that joins the painter of the *Annunciation* to the René Master seems to lie, however, on the side of the Aix Master's mediterranean component. It is another signpost on the not yet sufficiently explored road that leads from Southern France to Antonello da Messina. The resemblance of one of *Pl. 54* the miniatures (*Love getting hold of the heart of Cuer*) to Piero della Francesca's *Dream of Constantine* in Arezzo, which has already been noticed and commented on, is also more than a coincidence: it testifies afresh to the intrinsic kinship between Franceschian, Antonellesque and mid-fifteenth-century French painting.

The René Master has been compared to Fouquet. Both artists have in fact one major trait in common: the faculty to be monumental in the size of miniatures. Otherwise their aims and their achievements differ. The René Master is the born colourist, concerned above all with the sensations of light and tone; he is one of the first to have painted 'the night' and 'the sunset', one of the first to have tried the effects of clair-obscur. Lacking the supreme subtlety and the universality of the master of Tours, he is more robust, more naïve. His compositions

---

[1] The recent identification of the Anonymous with Jean Chapus appears the best suggestion yet made though it is also not completely conclusive.

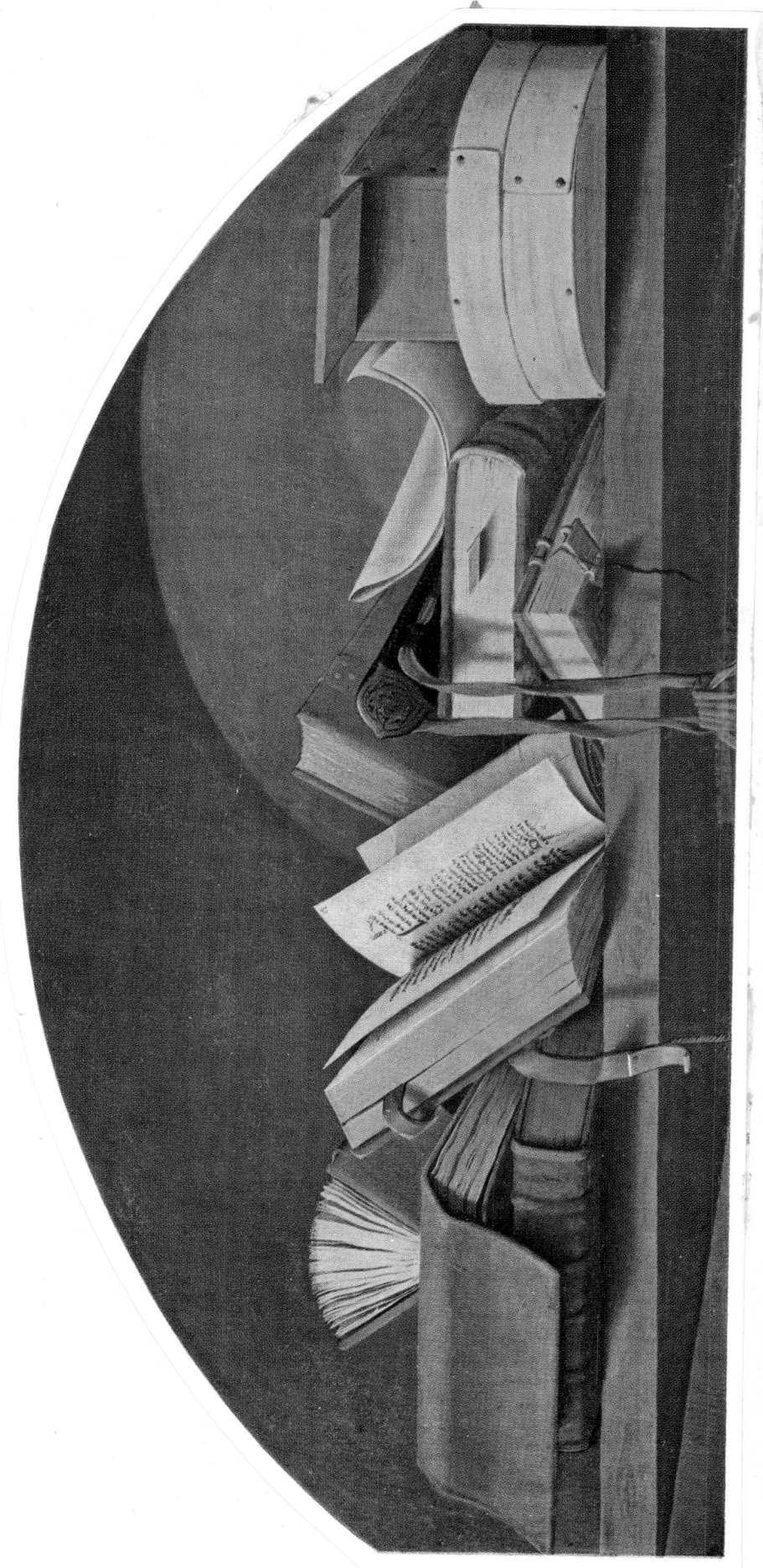

STILL-LIFE FROM THE » ANNUNCIATION OF AIX «
〈 Cat. No. 94 〉

FIG. 15. PIERO DELLA FRANCESCA: MADONNA DELLA MISERICORDIA. Part of the Polyptych of San Sepolcro.

FIG. 16. ENGUERRAND CHARONTON AND PIERRE VILLATTE: VIRGIN OF MERCY. Detail from Plate 62.

are as it were more 'primitive', without intersections and intertwinings; his figures large in relation to the surrounding space. The René Master is, however, not an 'archaïsant', he is in a way extremely advanced, the least 'gothic' painter among those we have treated. His forms have lost the last trace of calligraphic outline, his spirit is free from medieval mysticism, free even from the usual religious bondage of early French art. It is 'a spirit of vigorous antique paganism' (Wescher), a pantheistic worship of nature, which shows itself in a new and entirely 'modern' unity of man and natural phenomena, of human, animal and vegetative forms.

The aspects of the art of Southern France are manifold. It is not far from the place of the 'pagan' René Master's worldly activity that originated the most passionately religious, the most deeply moving realization of the holy *Pl. 108–110,* drama which has become famous under the name of the *Pietà de Villeneuve*. Hulin has characterized the picture *112* from the Flemish point of view as 'une œuvre déconcertante, à la fois archaïque et avancée, maladroite et savante'. It is, indeed, one of the great masterpieces of the epoch, but its author appears to be timeless as well as nameless. The composition has the severe simplicity of great sculpture, the figures arranged on one plane, in the manner of a high relief, their majestic silhouettes standing out from the 'archaic' gold back-ground. All details and accessories are eliminated, the interest focussed on the simple rhythmical movement of the group. The deep and austere colours enhance the effect of suffering and sadness.

FIG. 17. ENGUERRAND CHARONTON: Detail from the 'CORONATION OF THE VIRGIN', Villeneuve-lès-Avignon, Hospice. ⟨ Pl. 63, Cat. No. 116 ⟩

FIG. 18. PAUL CÉZANNE: Detail from the 'MONTAGNE SAINTE-VICTOIRE', William Rockhill Nelson Collection, Kansas City, Missouri.

It has often been noticed that the picture corresponds in feeling, and even to a certain degree in its plastic approach, better to Iberian than to French art—indeed it seems to foreshadow Zurbaran. All attempts, however, to place it in a contemporary Spanish or Portuguese context have so far failed. Perfectly adequate pieces of comparison are also lacking within the range of fifteenth-century painting in France, but it will be of more avail to look for analogies in French sculptured Pietàs and 'Sainte-Tombes'. The nearest painted example is the *Retable de Boulbon*, another work of ingenious conception, whose state of preservation, however, forbids too daring conclusions. *Pl. 107, 111*

We are once again on firm ground when treating one of the latest and grandest achievements of truly medieval French painting: the *Coronation of the Virgin* in Villeneuve-lès-Avignon, which Enguerrand Charonton *Pl. 63–68* executed in strict fulfilment of the terms of a preserved contract. The arrangement of the panel recalls the 'tympanon' of French Cathedrals, and it has been observed that it is nearer to the romanesque than to the gothic type of tympanon. There is a striking discrepancy between the upper and lower parts of the picture. The upper part, representing Heaven and Paradise, is carefully elaborated, its large figures solidly built; it is composed symmetrically in a traditional hieratic way. Even the many portraits in the zone of 'Paradise' are only slightly individualized, all unified by the common thought that nothing is of importance except Heaven and Grace. The lower parts—Earth, Purgatory and Hell—are surprisingly unorthodox and original, and it is these parts which make the picture remarkable. Like Hieronymus Bosch, Charonton seems more at home in Hell than in Heaven. The theme sets his imagination free, and with the spirit the form frees itself from the hieratic stringency of the heavenly zone. The composition becomes loose, the execution quick, bold, cursory, sketchy. The colours are set up in short strokes and dots in an almost pointillist manner. The small figures on Earth and in Hell are two-dimensional, without much weight and substance, the tiny souls flying in the dark-blue sky above the Earth, perfectly diaphanous; Christ on the Cross a vision, the donor nearly more ghostlike than the figures of the artist's invention. The most extraordinary feature, however, is the landscape which envelops figures and buildings, the great 'Latin' landscape of Provence with the classical silhouettes of its mountains, including the 'Montagne Sainte-Victoire', meanwhile immortalized. The ardent and burning luminosity of the Southern *Fig. 17–18* country exhales a pathetic sadness. 'Il y a une tristesse en Provence que personne n'a dite', writes Gasquet, the correspondent of Cézanne, and it is this sadness which pervades the entire Provençal production. It links the *Coronation* with the supreme tragedy of the *Pietà de Villeneuve*, with the *Retable de Boulbon* and the *Pietàs* of the Frick Collection.

Recording Charonton's origin in the diocese of Laon, one might expect to find a Northern tinge in his work. But nothing in the *Coronation* nor in the second documented picture by the Master, the *Virgin of Mercy* *Pl. 62* in Chantilly, can in any way be claimed for Picardie or another school of Northern France. The *Virgin* which Charonton executed in collaboration with the otherwise unknown Pierre Villatte is exclusively mediterranean, and her affinity to the *Madonna della Misericordia* on Piero della Francesca's polyptych of Borgo San Sepolcro *Fig. 15–16* seems more than a casual correspondence of subjects: it shows once again the gigantic figure of Piero looming over the fifteenth century of France.

We have to traverse the entire realm of French painting to find artists who are truly Northern, not only by birth, but also by their work. If the key-note of Fouquet's art was serious and that of Provence sad, Simon Marmion, the master of Valenciennes, whom we shall take as the foremost representative of Northern France, is pleasant and cheerful. Of the two sources of French painting, great sculpture and book illumination, the second alone recurs in his work. Marmion, who has been called 'le prince d'enluminure', is an illuminator before he is a painter, and it is only in close connection with his miniatures that his easel pictures can be assessed.

There is no difficulty in recognizing the differences between the art of the North, as personified by Marmion, and that of the other centres of France. Northern French art is just as remote from the pathetic intensity of the South as from the formal stateliness of Touraine and the amplitude of Burgundy, besides lacking monumentality, the unifying feature of the rest of French painting. The difficulty arises only when this art has to be fitted into the larger French context, in spite of all divergencies. The task may best be attacked by contrasting Marmion with

FIG. 19. CLOISTERS WITH MURAL PAINTINGS, REPRESENTING THE DANCE OF DEATH. Detail from the altarpiece of S. Omer ⟨ Cat. No. 170 ⟩

FIG. 20–21. THE DANCE OF DEATH. Two parts of mural paintings, about 1470 ⟨ Cat. No. 115 ⟩

his nearest relations, the masters of Flanders. Compared to the pure Flemings, the painter of Valenciennes displays a number of qualities which have been marked as typically French from the start, although they do not apply to the whole of French painting. He has wit and elegance, subtlety of spirit and of form, his figures move quickly and gracefully, making gentle gestures; all exaggerations are absent, including excesses of emotion. A tendency to genre-like interpretation of religious subjects is noticeable; even the scenes of monastic life, which is the theme of the master's principal panel paintings—*the Life of St. Bertin*—have a light and worldly undertone. The best *Pl. 103–104,* means of distinguishing between Marmion and his Flemish contemporaries may be the colour: bright and gaily *Fig. 19* sparkling on the French side, deeper and more saturated across the frontier.

The School of Picardie starting propitiously in 1437 with the *Sacerdoce de la Vierge*—the earliest example of the *Pl. 97* 'Puy d'Amiens' and probably the earliest easel painting of Northern France—never surpassed the accomplishments of Marmion, who was himself a native of Amiens. The northern style appears here in a harder, coarser, more provincial variety.

No substantial change took place in the painting of Northern France during the fifteenth century. The 'Maître de S. Gilles', the leading artist in the eighties and nineties, is no less to be derived from miniature painting than Marmion, even if no book illuminations by him are known. Elegance and agility, witty and lively narration remain the distinctive traits; monumentality is missing. M. J. Friedlaender characterizes the master as 'tender, with a liking for intimately human motifs, a predilection for the display of religious splendour and profane luxury, which he presents with a purified taste. . . .' Like Marmion and his entourage, the Master of St. Giles is fond of making experiments with light; one of his pictures, a night scene, treats the clair-obscur in *Pl. 137* a new and bold way, leading in a straight line to the lighting effects of a Georges de La Tour. Parisian views on several of the pictures testify to the master's stay in Paris, but no clue to his origin has yet been found.[1] He has *Fig. 40* sometimes been regarded as a Fleming working in France, sometimes as a Frenchman trained in Flanders. Among *Colour Plate* his most Flemish traits are a 'love for the vegetation which is nearly a botanist's' (Friedlaender) and the highly *p. 33* finished rendering of precious materials, furs and stones, brocades and embroideries. On the whole, the French component predominates, and it seems justified to include the master without reserve in the French School.

We are faced with another borderline art in Burgundy, the province with a great and independent past, which had been reincorporated in the Kingdom of France in 1477 and whose products can therefore not be omitted from the French context although they sometimes seem to fit better into the School of Tournai. Portraits are the principal achievement of this art, standing about midway between the 'portrait monumental' and the 'portrait d'analyse', but nearer to the monumental type. Portraiture predominates even in the religious compositions of the region, the frescoes of Beaune and Autun. We have accordingly reproduced two pairs of portraits to represent Franco-Burgundy: the superb paintings in the Rockefeller Collection closely bound to *Pl. 131–132* the succession of Rogier van der Weyden, and the hardly less impressive examples in Worcester, U.S.A. *Pl. 133–134*

If the painters of the Northern provinces have to be carefully kept apart from their Flemish neighbours, French painting of the South must be separated with equal care from the adjacent art of Italy. As we have mentioned, such a separation is not feasible for the School of Nice which merges imperceptibly into the Italian 'local milieu'. The case is different for the painting of Provence in spite of its Sienese ancestry and many lasting Italian traits. Although Provençal painting may sound sometimes like an artistic 'langue d'oc' beside the general 'langue d'oïl' it always remains essentially French—indeed Provence appears as one of the most vital centres of French production. A picture like the Avignonese *Adoration*, which may be the most 'Italian' specimen of this entire *Pl. 150* survey, cannot be simply discarded as an imitation after the pattern of Milan. It is a complex mixture, transposing Eyckian reminiscences into the idiom of the South—it almost seems as if Lombardy were, at a late date, repaying its debt for some of the gifts it had received from France at the beginning of the century.

Nicolas Froment, who not only worked in Avignon but was a native of this region, has the rare good fortune

---

[1] The evidence of Parisian monuments on a picture is in itself not sufficient proof of a French origin. Neither the author of the *Retable du Parlement de Paris* (Cat. 157) with the view of the Louvre, etc., nor the painter of the *Pietà* (Cat. 251), with the view of S. Germain-des-Près is any longer regarded as a French artist.

c

FIG. 22. QUEEN JEANNE DE LAVAL. Detail from the 'Burning Bush' ⟨ Cat. No. 216 ⟩

FIG. 23. DUCHESS ANNE DE BOURBON. Detail from the Moulins Triptych ⟨ Cat. No. 293 ⟩

Pl. 118–124 of having left two documented altarpieces. The earlier of these, the Triptych of the *Raising of Lazarus*, signed and dated 1461, is by a further stroke of luck preserved at the Uffizi, a fact that has made its author popular at a time when most early French painters were still unnoticed. Apart from this, the Uffizi Triptych cannot be regarded either as a significant or a creditable addition to the corpus of French art. The caricaturesque sharpness of the angular forms, the grimacing faces seem rather to point to Naples or some Spanish provincial school. According to Hulin's unkind commentary 'even the landscape is grimacing'. One asset results from the excesses of expression: the penetrating characterization of the portrait-like faces in the background of the centre panel. Otherwise the triptych is saved mainly by the shutters on the outside, which in the words of Berenson[1] 'display a Madonna with a face of as pure an oval as will be found anywhere in the North and scarcely more lovely in Italy. Indeed it foreshadows Raphael's *Madonna del Granduca*'. In view of the unusual fact that the outside panels of a retable are of a strikingly finer quality than the inside ones it may be noted that it is here the outside which bears the signature.

Recent research has reconstructed two artists who are certainly Southern French and has endowed them with the names of Josse Lieferinxe and Nicolas Dipre. Their personalities emerge clearly, no matter whether we are inclined to accept the names or prefer to call them 'Maître de S. Sébastien' and 'Maître du retable da la Vie de la Vierge' after their principal works. At a first cursory glance the Master of St. Sebastian appears to be an able but not outstanding 'Quattrocentista' of the stature of, say, a Pinturicchio. His types, his architecture, his manner of building up the space and arranging the principal groups of figures is Italian, correct views of the Colosseum and the Arch of Constantine give evidence of his knowledge of Rome. And yet, there are differences, which prove decisive: a less dramatic way of narration, the more reticent and unheroic gestures, some details like the numerous straight parallel folds of the drapery; and above all, a certain gentleness in the expression, even in scenes of cruelty and suffering.

Pl. 139–142 The 'œuvre' of the second artist, less numerous and still less well-known, has here been enriched by three further scenes from the *Life of the Virgin*. Like his previously established works, the newcomers show massive figures of short proportions with large heads. The execution is rustic, even coarse, the expression vigorous. Following these characteristics, the painter can be listed under the heading of 'Alpine Art', a style that was practised on either side of the Alps, in Northern Italy—Savoy and Piedmont—, in Austria, Southern Germany and Switzerland, just as in South Eastern France. In introducing this term, I wish to make it quite clear that it must not be understood in any depreciatory sense. On the Swiss and Austrian sides Alpine painting has among its representatives such
Pl. 114 great artists as Conrat Witz and Laib, Frueauf and Michael Pacher; on the French side the beautiful and myste-
Fig. 37; rious two *Pietàs* of the Frick Collections and—perhaps—the equally mysterious *Adoration of the Child* in Glasgow
Fig. 30 may be explained by their inclusion in this circuit. The Master of the Retable of the Life of the Virgin, while
Pl. 141 showing many Italo-Alpine traits, is distinctly French in his distribution of light and shades—his *Presentation* seems to lead once more to the art of La Tour. In view of these various incunabula of lighting effects in early France one wonders whether French seventeenth-century clair-obscur is really as completely dependent on Caravaggism as art critics generally suppose, or whether it may not be traced back, at least in great part, to indigenous sources.

As the century draws to a close, so its art slowly declines. Two major achievements in the sphere of religious paint-
Pl. 126–130; ing mark the last stage: Froment's *Burning Bush* and the *Triptych of Moulins Cathedral*. Both works keep to the
159–163 traditional Gothic form of the winged altar; in Moulins, the Virgin is still arranged in the manner of the ancient sculptured 'théophanie' with angels at the cornerstones (Focillon). In spite of these external medieval reminiscences, the spirit in both works is the spirit of the 'modern' times. Their first aim is decoration, festive elegance, the perfect rendering of the human form by applying the most recent acquirements of science and technique. As the metaphysical vision which in the Middle Ages had illuminated such worldly things was passing, these things and their glorification alone remained. The Madonna in the centre panel of Moulins is nothing but a beautiful accomplished lady, the angels around her 'so many beautiful children', as Prosper Merimée had already
Fig. 4 called their predecessors, the *Anges de Bourges*. The two altarpieces are as much products of the Renaissance

---

[1] Preface to the Catalogue of the Exhibition of French Painting in Florence, 1945.

as any work could be within the limits of the French fifteenth century. For them the term 'Quattrocento' would be well suited and it is not by accident that in early literature the name of Ghirlandaio has been mentioned in connection with each of them.

It does not seem quite fair to the great masterpiece of Moulins to be thus ranged indiscriminately with the *Burning Bush*, although the parallel is obvious and tempting. Nicolas Froment's second altar, of 1476, shows his *Pl. 126–130* art considerably mellowed and toned down but hardly more inspired than in the *Uffizi Triptych*. The dryness and angularity have remained and so have, fortunately, the chief merits of the earlier work: individualization and characterization. The portraits of King René and his Queen on the wings of the *Burning Bush* are of a precision and a psychological finesse which make it probable that the artist who achieved them has also left single portraits; one example is here tentatively ascribed to his entourage. *No. 220*

Nevertheless, one look at the donor's heads in Moulins is sufficient to make us keenly aware of the abyss that *Pl. 162, 163;* separates the good from the extraordinary artist. With the Maître de Moulins, we return to central France, the *Fig. 23* region of Fouquet. For the last time we return to the standard of the painter of Tours and to the qualities that made him the century's French Master par excellence: clarity, limpidity, dignity. Like Fouquet, the Anonymous constructs his figures with masterly accuracy and makes his forms cohere in a well-balanced system. Like Fouquet he aims rather at defining the form with precision than at displaying it under the varying effects of chiaroscuro. As befits the representative of a younger generation, the Maître de Moulins has a more fully developed sense of space and composes with more liberty and verve. His colouring is stronger and gayer than that of Fouquet, suggesting 'a limpid atmosphere with a positive, almost gaudy effect' (Friedlaender). In his youth the master must have been deeply impressed by Hugo van der Goes; the shepherds on his *Nativity* of about 1480 are derived from the *Portinari Altarpiece*. But already at this early stage, the Moulins Master's adaptation is definitely French, making *Pl. 158* orderly working people of the wild and unbalanced creations of the Flemish genius. In the Master's portraits, van der Goes's influence is also noticeable; the charming *Young Princess* in the Lehman collection seems a more *Pl. 162* conventional sister of Maria Portinari, and the *Donor with his Patron Saint* in Glasgow as well as the *Female Profile Drawing* have long been listed under the Ghent master's name. *Fig. 46*

Portraits stand at the end of this survey just as a single portrait stood at its beginning. But the species 'portrait' has gained a new rank. As in every age when the transient glories of men come to the foreground, the representation of man's individual likeness now assumes the first place. The Middle Ages have waned for ever.

It is gratuitous to ask whether the flow of French painting was deliberately cut off at the beginning of the sixteenth century by the Italian artists summoned to work in Fontainebleau, or whether their arrival led only to another salutary blood transfusion. Be that as it may: the indigenous painting of fifteenth-century France found a beautiful ending in the work of the Maître de Moulins, and—after a short and in itself rather fascinating interval —French painting went on gloriously for many a century to come.

NOTE

If no special material is mentioned, the objects described in the Catalogue are paintings on panel. Very few indications are given with regard to the medium—oil, tempera, etc.,—since early painting technique is still a controversial subject in which I am not prepared to take sides. Drawings, miniatures, frescoes are explicitly distinguished.

In the measurements, height precedes width. For all paintings reproduced here, the sizes are given not only in centimetres, but also in inches, in order to make it easier to visualize the impression of the original. In the drawing-up of the catalogue a number of pictures mentioned in several previous publications on early French painting have been omitted, not because their French origin is contested but because, whether French or not, they are in no way representative of the art whose essence I have here endeavoured to define.

On the other hand, a number of works are included which in my opinion are not French or whose origin is still open to discussion. All these works, however, have definite connections with undoubtedly French paintings and therefore seemed essential for comparison and analogy. They are clearly marked in the Catalogue by being printed in small capitals; their catalogue numbers are put in brackets. None of them appear in the Plates.

The Introductory Essay is meant for the general reader; anything of interest for the specialist is dealt with in the Catalogue.

The Catalogue is not a compilation; with a few exceptions, I have seen in the original all the works which are catalogued here. The pictures which have entered American collections during the last twenty-five years have mostly been available to me for inspection while they were still in Europe, and often in the restorer's studio. Several of the pictures catalogued here have passed through my hands e.g. No. 298, now in the National Gallery, London.

The Catalogue is arranged mainly in chronological order, in particular as far as anonymous works are concerned. Masters and their followers are left together even if this slightly disturbs the strict chronological sequence.

Plate numbers of works reproduced are given in the Catalogue; and catalogue numbers appear in the captions of the Plates. The Biographical Notes on the artists, and the index of collections, both public and private, give further references to plate numbers and catalogue numbers.

As there are Lists of the names of the artists and of the places, I have refrained from drawing up a general Index, which would not have added to the easier use of the book.

Six colour plates have been inserted at the suggestion of the publishers.

No general bibliography is attempted as extensive bibliographies are to be found in nearly all the publications on early French art mentioned in my 'list of abbreviations'. Literature on individual pictures is fully quoted under the respective number in the Catalogue. In the case of pictures which are here catalogued but not illustrated, reproductions in the most easily accessible publications are mentioned.

The map appearing on the last page of this book is reproduced from *Life in Mediaeval France* by Joan Evans, by Courtesy of the Oxford University Press.

Among scholars who have given me valuable advice and have kindly supplied me with photographs, special acknowledgments are due to M. Jacques Dupont, Dr. M. J. Friedländer, Dr. Adelheid Heimann, Dr. Jan Lauts, Dr. Hanns Swarzenski, Dr. Paul Wescher, Prof. F. Winkler. I have to express my gratefulness to various friends who have assisted me in struggling with the English language, which is not my native tongue. First of all I wish to thank Ludwig Goldscheider, who has been an unfailing source of encouragement and help and without whose co-operation this book would never have come into being.

Gr. Rg.

PLATES

1. SCHOOL OF PARIS, ABOUT 1390: TWO ANGELS PLAYING ON STRINGED INSTRUMENTS.

DETAIL FROM THE LEFT SHUTTER ON THE » LARGE BARGELLO DIPTYCH «, UPPER PART.

FLORENCE, BARGELLO, MUSEO NAZIONALE

⟨ Cat. No. 6 ⟩

2. SCHOOL OF PARIS, ABOUT 1390: MADONNA AND CHILD WITH SAINTS.

LEFT SHUTTER OF THE » LARGE BARGELLO DIPTYCH «, LOWER PART.

FLORENCE, BARGELLO, MUSEO NAZIONALE

⟨ Cat. No. 6 ⟩

3. SCHOOL OF PARIS, ABOUT 1390: THE CRUCIFIXION.
RIGHT SHUTTER OF THE » LARGE BARGELLO DIPTYCH «, LOWER PART.
FLORENCE, BARGELLO, MUSEO NAZIONALE
〈 Cat. No. 6 〉

4. FRENCH SCHOOL, ABOUT 1390: » THE SMALL CIRCULAR PIETÀ «.

PARIS, MUSÉE DU LOUVRE

⟨ Cat. No. 8 ⟩

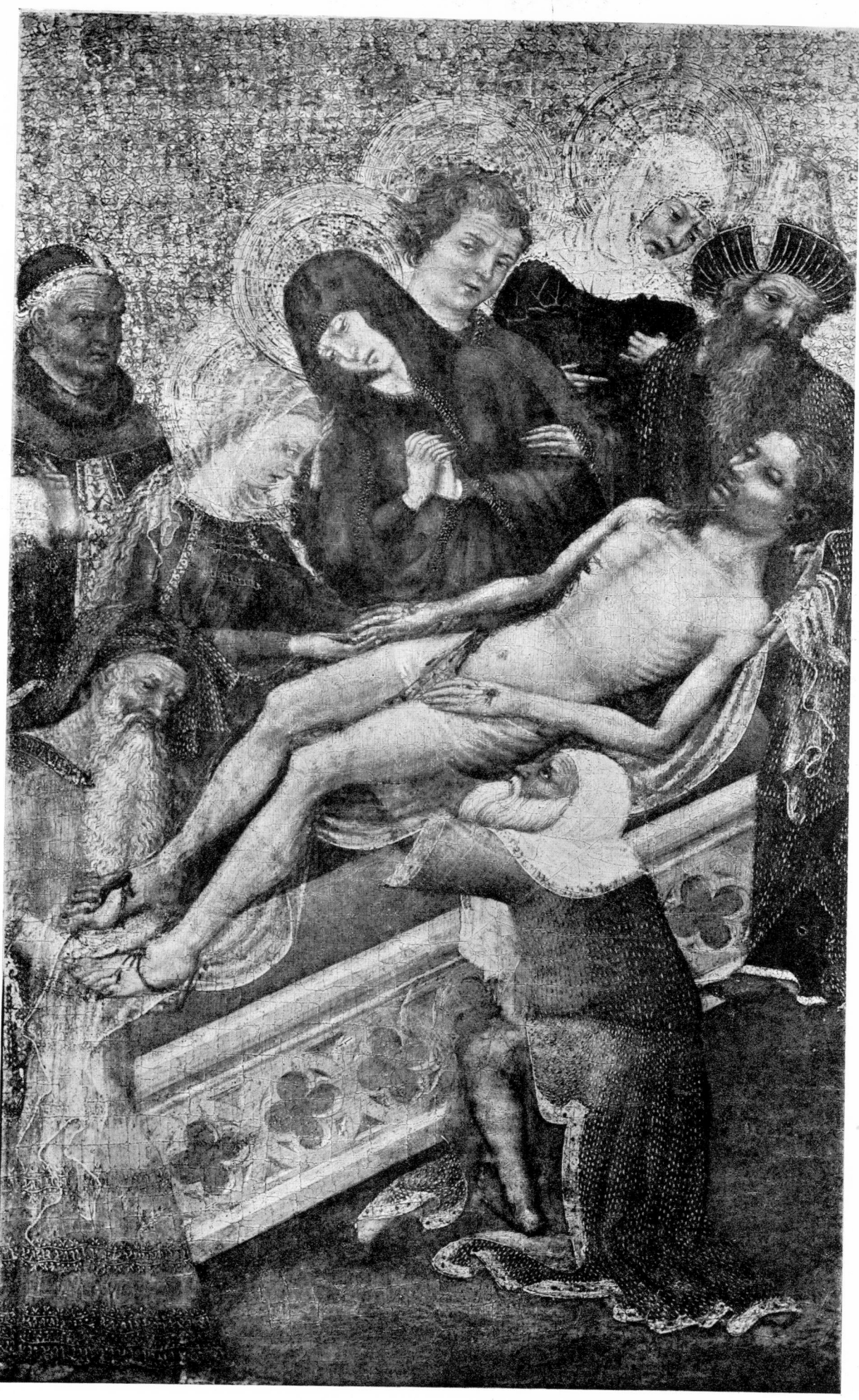

5. FRENCH SCHOOL, ABOUT 1380–90: THE ENTOMBMENT.
PARIS, MUSÉE DU LOUVRE

⟨ Cat. No. 9 ⟩

6. FRENCH SCHOOL, ABOUT 1400-1410 : THE CORONATION OF THE VIRGIN.

BERLIN, DEUTSCHES MUSEUM

〈 Cat. No. 49 〉

7. MASTER OF THE HOURS OF THE MARÉCHAL DE BOUCICAUT:
THE RICH MAN AND THE POOR LAZARUS.

FORMERLY CHATEAU DE RIPAILLE, ENGEL-GROS COLLECTION

〈 Cat. No. 37 〉

8. SCHOOL OF PARIS, ABOUT 1390–1400:
DEATH, ASSUMPTION AND CORONATION OF THE VIRGIN. DRAWING.

PARIS, MUSÉE DU LOUVRE

⟨ Cat. No. 11 ⟩

9. SCHOOL OF AVIGNON, ABOUT 1390: CHRIST CARRYING THE CROSS, WITH TWO DONORS.
PARIS, MUSÉE DU LOUVRE
⟨ Cat. No. 33 ⟩

10. SCHOOL OF PROVENCE, ABOUT 1400:
LE BIENHEUREUX PIERRE DE LUXEMBOURG, PRESENTING A DONOR TO THE VIRGIN.

WORCESTER, U.S.A., ART MUSEUM

⟨ Cat. No. 35 ⟩

11. SCHOOL OF ARRAS, ABOUT 1410: THE OFFERING OF THE HEART. TAPESTRY.

PARIS, MUSÉE DU LOUVRE

⟨ Cat. No. 41 ⟩

12. FRENCH SCHOOL, ABOUT 1400–1410: LADY WITH A DOG AND A FALCON.
WATERCOLOUR DRAWING. PARIS, MUSÉE DU LOUVRE
⟨ Cat. No. 40 ⟩

13-14. ANDRÉ BEAUNEVEU, BEFORE 1402: KING DAVID AND AN APOSTLE.

MINIATURES FROM A PSALTER. PARIS, BIBLIOTHÈQUE NATIONALE

⟨ Cat. No. 42 ⟩

15. SCHOOL OF PARIS, ABOUT 1390: THREE REPRESENTATIONS OF THE VIRGIN AND CHILD.

DRAWING. BASLE, OEFFENTLICHE KUNSTSAMMLUNG, PRINT ROOM

⟨ Cat. No. 17 ⟩

16. SCHOOL OF PARIS, ABOUT 1390: THE ADORATION OF THE MAGI.

LEFT SHUTTER OF THE » SMALL BARGELLO DIPTYCH «.

FLORENCE, BARGELLO, MUSEO NAZIONALE

⟨ Cat. No. 15 ⟩

17. SCHOOL OF PARIS, ABOUT 1390: THE ANNUNCIATION.

SANTA BARBARA, CALIFORNIA, ARTHUR SACHS COLLECTION

⟨ Cat. No. 16 ⟩

18. ATTRIBUTED TO JEAN MALOUEL OR TO HENRI BELLECHOSE, ABOUT 1400–1410:
» THE LARGE CIRCULAR PIETÀ «.

PARIS, MUSÉE DU LOUVRE

⟨ Cat. No. 53 ⟩

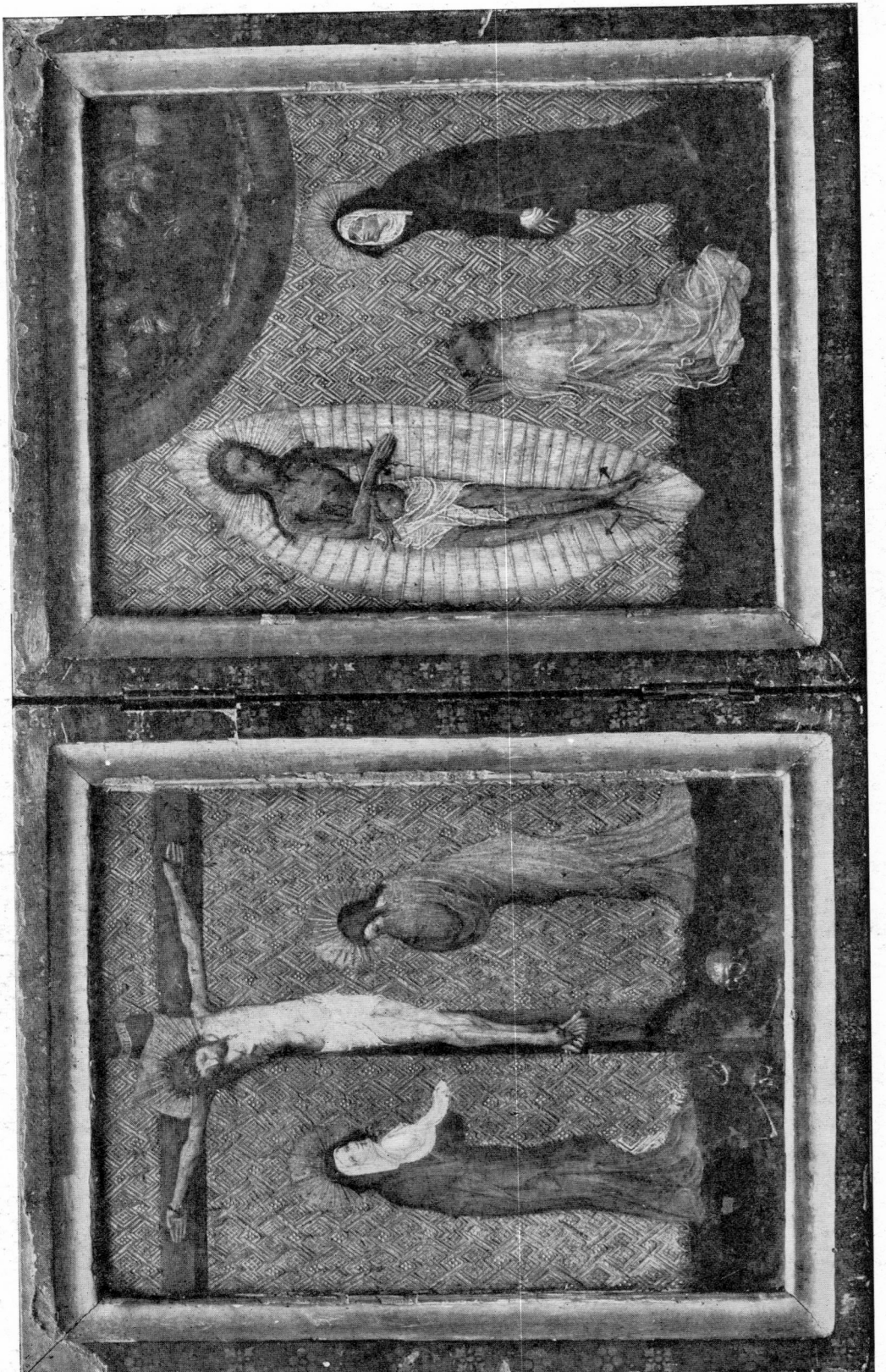

19. FRENCH SCHOOL, ABOUT 1400: DIPTYCH:
CHRIST ON THE CROSS BETWEEN THE VIRGIN AND ST. JOHN (LEFT SHUTTER);
THE VIRGIN PRESENTING A CISTERCIAN MONK TO THE » CHRIST DE PITIÉ « (RIGHT SHUTTER).

BERLIN, DEUTSCHES MUSEUM

⟨ Cat. No. 7 ⟩

20. ATTRIBUTED TO HENRI BELLECHOSE, 1416: THE HOLY COMMUNION AND THE MARTYRDOM OF ST. DIONYSIUS.

PARIS, MUSÉE DU LOUVRE ⟨ Cat. No. 54 ⟩

21. JACQUEMART DE HESDIN, ABOUT 1402: JEAN DE BERRI PRESENTED BY ST. JOHN THE BAPTIST
AND ST. ANDREW. MINIATURE FROM THE » TRÈS BELLES HEURES DU DUC DE BERRI «.
BRUSSELS, BIBLIOTHÈQUE ROYALE
⟨ Cat. No. 46 ⟩

22. JACQUEMART DE HESDIN, ABOUT 1402: THE VIRGIN ENTHRONED.

MINIATURE FROM THE » TRÈS BELLES HEURES DU DUC DE BERRI «.

BRUSSELS, BIBLIOTHÈQUE ROYALE

⟨ Cat. No. 46 ⟩

23. JACQUES DALIWE: THREE HEADS. DRAWING FROM A SKETCH BOOK.
BERLIN, STAATLICHE BIBLIOTHEK
⟨ Cat. No. 75 ⟩

24. JAQUES DALIWE: WOMAN RIDING ON A » HIPPOGRYPH «.
DRAWING FROM A SKETCH BOOK.
BERLIN, STAATLICHE BIBLIOTHEK
⟨ Cat. No. 75 ⟩

25. FRANCO-FLEMISH SCHOOL, ABOUT 1400–1410: VIRGIN AND CHILD.

PARIS, MUSÉE DU LOUVRE (FORMERLY COLLECTION DE BEISTEGUI)

⟨ Cat. No. 51 ⟩

26. FRENCH SCHOOL, ABOUT 1412–15: PORTRAIT OF LOUIS II OF ANJOU. WATERCOLOUR DRAWING

PARIS, BIBLIOTHÈQUE NATIONALE

⟨ Cat. No. 63 ⟩

27. FRENCH SCHOOL, ABOUT 1410–15: PORTRAIT OF A LADY IN PROFILE.

WASHINGTON, NATIONAL GALLERY

⟨ Cat. No 64 ⟩

28. PAUL DE LIMBOURG, ABOUT 1416: THE MONTH OF JANUARY, WITH A PORTRAIT OF JEAN DE BERRI.
MINIATURE FROM THE CALENDAR OF THE » TRÈS RICHES HEURES DU DUC DE BERRI «.
CHANTILLY, MUSÉE CONDÉ

⟨ Cat. No. 65 ⟩

29. PAUL DE LIMBOURG, ABOUT 1416: THE MEETING OF THE THREE HOLY MAGI.

MINIATURE FROM THE » TRÈS RICHES HEURES DU DUC DE BERRI «.

CHANTILLY, MUSÉE CONDÉ

⟨ Cat. No. 65 ⟩

30. FRANCO-BURGUNDIAN SCHOOL, ABOUT 1420: THE PLANET VENUS.

FROM A SERIES OF PLANETS. DRAWING.

DRESDEN, KUPFERSTICHKABINETT

⟨ Cat. No. 70 ⟩

31. PAUL DE LIMBOURG, ABOUT 1416: THE TEMPORAL PARADISE.
MINIATURE FROM THE » TRÈS RICHES HEURES DU DUC DE BERRI «.
CHANTILLY, MUSÉE CONDÉ
⟨ Cat. No. 65 ⟩

32. PAUL DE LIMBOURG, ABOUT 1416: THE MONTH OF APRIL.
MINIATURE FROM THE CALENDAR OF THE » TRÈS RICHES HEURES DU DUC DE BERRI «.
CHANTILLY, MUSÉE CONDÉ
〈 Cat. No. 65 〉

33–34. JACQUES IVERNY, ABOUT 1420–30: SIX HEROINES OF ANTIQUITY.

PARTS OF A FRESCO. CASTELLO DELLA MANTA, PIEDMONT

⟨ Cat. No. 84 ⟩

35. ATTRIBUTED TO PAUL DE LIMBOURG: THE BETRAYAL OF CHRIST.
DRAWING. LONDON, BRITISH MUSEUM (PRINT ROOM)
⟨ Cat. No. 69 ⟩

36. MASTER OF THE HEURES DE ROHAN: THE POOL OF BETHESDA.
DRAWING. BRUNSWICK, HERZOG ANTON ULRICH MUSEUM
⟨ Cat. No. 90 ⟩

37. MASTER OF THE HEURES DE ROHAN: THE LAST JUDGEMENT.

MINIATURE FROM THE » GRANDES HEURES DE ROHAN «.

PARIS, BIBLIOTHÈQUE NATIONALE

⟨ Cat. No. 86 ⟩

38. MASTER OF THE HEURES DE ROHAN: PIETÀ.

MINIATURE FROM THE » GRANDES HEURES DE ROHAN «.

PARIS, BIBLIOTHÈQUE NATIONALE

⟨ Cat. No. 86 ⟩

39. MASTER OF THE HEURES DE ROHAN: MAN BEFORE HIS JUDGE.
MINIATURE FROM THE » GRANDES HEURES DE ROHAN «.
PARIS, BIBLIOTHÈQUE NATIONALE
⟨ Cat. No. 86 ⟩

40. MASTER OF THE HEURES DE ROHAN: THE ANNUNCIATION.

MINIATURE FROM THE » GRANDES HEURES DE ROHAN «.

PARIS, BIBLIOTHÈQUE NATIONALE

⟨ Cat. No. 86 ⟩

41–42. MASTER OF THE HEURES DE ROHAN, OR HIS STUDIO: APOSTLES AND PROPHETS.
THE ANGEL OF THE ANNUNCIATION AND A DONOR PRESENTED BY A FEMALE SAINT.
OBVERSE AND REVERSE OF A SHUTTER.
LAON, MUSEUM ⟨ Cat. No. 89 ⟩

43: MASTER OF THE ANNUNCIATION OF AIX, 1445: THE ANNUNCIATION.

44. MASTER OF THE ANNUNCIATION OF AIX: GOD THE FATHER AND ANGELS.

DETAIL FROM THE PL. 43

45. MASTER OF THE ANNUNCIATION OF AIX: THE ANGEL OF THE ANNUNCIATION.

DETAIL FROM PL. 43

46. MASTER OF THE ANNUNCIATION OF AIX: THE VIRGIN OF THE ANNUNCIATION.

DETAIL FROM PL. 43

47. MASTER OF THE ANNUNCIATION OF AIX: ST. MARY MAGDALEN.

REVERSE OF THE LEFT SHUTTER OF THE ALTARPIECE OF » THE ANNUNCIATION «.

VIERHOUTEN, VAN BEUNINGEN COLLECTION

⟨ Cat. No. 93 ⟩

48. MASTER OF THE ANNUNCIATION OF AIX: NOLI ME TANGERE.
REVERSE OF THE RIGHT SHUTTER OF THE ALTARPIECE OF » THE ANNUNCIATON «.
BRUSSELS, MUSÉES ROYAUX DES BEAUX-ARTS
⟨ Cat. No. 92 ⟩

49–50. MASTER OF THE ANNUNCIATION OF AIX:
THE PROPHET ISAIAH. VIERHOUTEN, VAN BEUNINGEN COLLECTION.
STILL LIFE. AMSTERDAM, RIJKSMUSEUM.
TWO PARTS OF THE LEFT SHUTTER OF THE ALTARPIECE OF » THE ANNUNCIATION «. OBVERSE ⟨ Cat. No. 93–94 ⟩

51. MASTER OF THE ANNUNCIATION OF AIX: THE PROPHET JEREMIAH.

RIGHT SHUTTER OF THE ALTARPIECE OF » THE ANNUNCIATION «. OBVERSE.

BRUSSELS, MUSÉES ROYAUX DES BEAUX-ARTS

⟨ Cat. No. 92 ⟩

52. MASTER OF THE ANNUNCIATION OF AIX: THE PROPHET JEREMIAH.

DETAIL FROM PL. 51

53. ATTRIBUTED TO THE MASTER OF THE ANNUNCIATION OF AIX:
PRAYING MAN. DRAWING.

ROTTERDAM, BOYMANS MUSEUM

⟨ Cat. No. 95 ⟩

54. THE RENÉ MASTER: » AMOUR « COMES TO THE LOVE-SICK KING
AND TAKES HIS HEART AWAY. miniature from the » cuer d'amours espris «
vienna, staatsbibliothek
⟨ Cat. No. 102 ⟩

55. THE RENÉ MASTER: » CUER « AND » DÉSIR «, LED BY » MÉLANCHOLIE «,
COME TO THE BRIDGE » PAS PÉRILLEUX «.

miniature from the » cuer d'amours espris «.

vienna, staatsbibliothek
⟨ Cat. No. 102 ⟩

56. THE RENÉ MASTER: » CUER « AND » DÉSIR « EMBARK FOR THE ISLAND OF THE » OSPITAL D'AMOURS «.
MINIATURE FROM THE » CUER D'AMOURS ESPRIS «. VIENNA, STAATSBIBLIOTHEK
⟨ Cat. No. 102 ⟩

57. THE RENÉ MASTER: » CUER « READING THE INSCRIPTION ON THE MAGIC WELL.
MINIATURE FROM THE » CUER D'AMOURS ESPRIS «. VIENNA, STAATSBIBLIOTHEK
⟨ Cat. No. 102 ⟩

58. THE RENÉ MASTER: » CUER « AND » DÉSIR « MEET THE OLD WOMAN » JALOUSIE «.

MINIATURE FROM THE » CUER D'AMOURS ESPRIS «. VIENNA, STAATSBIBLIOTHEK

⟨ Cat. No. 102 ⟩

59. SCHOOL OF AVIGNON, ABOUT 1450: » LE BIENHEUREUX PIERRE DE LUXEMBOURG « IN ECSTASY.

AVIGNON, MUSÉE CALVET

⟨ Cat. No. 106 ⟩

60. FRENCH SCHOOL, ABOUT 1470: THE VISION OF ST. BERNARDINUS, AND TWO DONORS IN ADORATION.

MARSEILLE, MUSÉE GROBET-LABADIÉ

⟨ Cat. No. 198 ⟩

61. SCHOOL OF PROVENCE, ABOUT 1450: CRUCIFIXION, WITH TWO DONORS AND THEIR PATRON SAINTS SEBASTIAN AND GILES.

AIX-EN-PROVENCE, MUSÉE PAUL ARBAUD ⟨ Cat. No. 110 ⟩

62. ENGUERRAND CHARONTON AND PIERRE VILLATTE, 1452: THE VIRGIN OF MERCY, ADORED BY JEAN CADARD AND HIS WIFE.

CHANTILLY, MUSÉE CONDÉ ⟨ Cat. No. 117 ⟩

92. ENGUERRAND CHARONTON, 1454: THE CORONATION OF THE VIRGIN (VILLENEUVE-LÈS-AVIGNON, LÈS AVIGNON MUSEUM) (Cat. No. 114)

64. ENGUERRAND CHARONTON: CONDEMNED SOULS IN HELL. DETAIL FROM THE » CORONATION OF THE VIRGIN « (PL. 63)

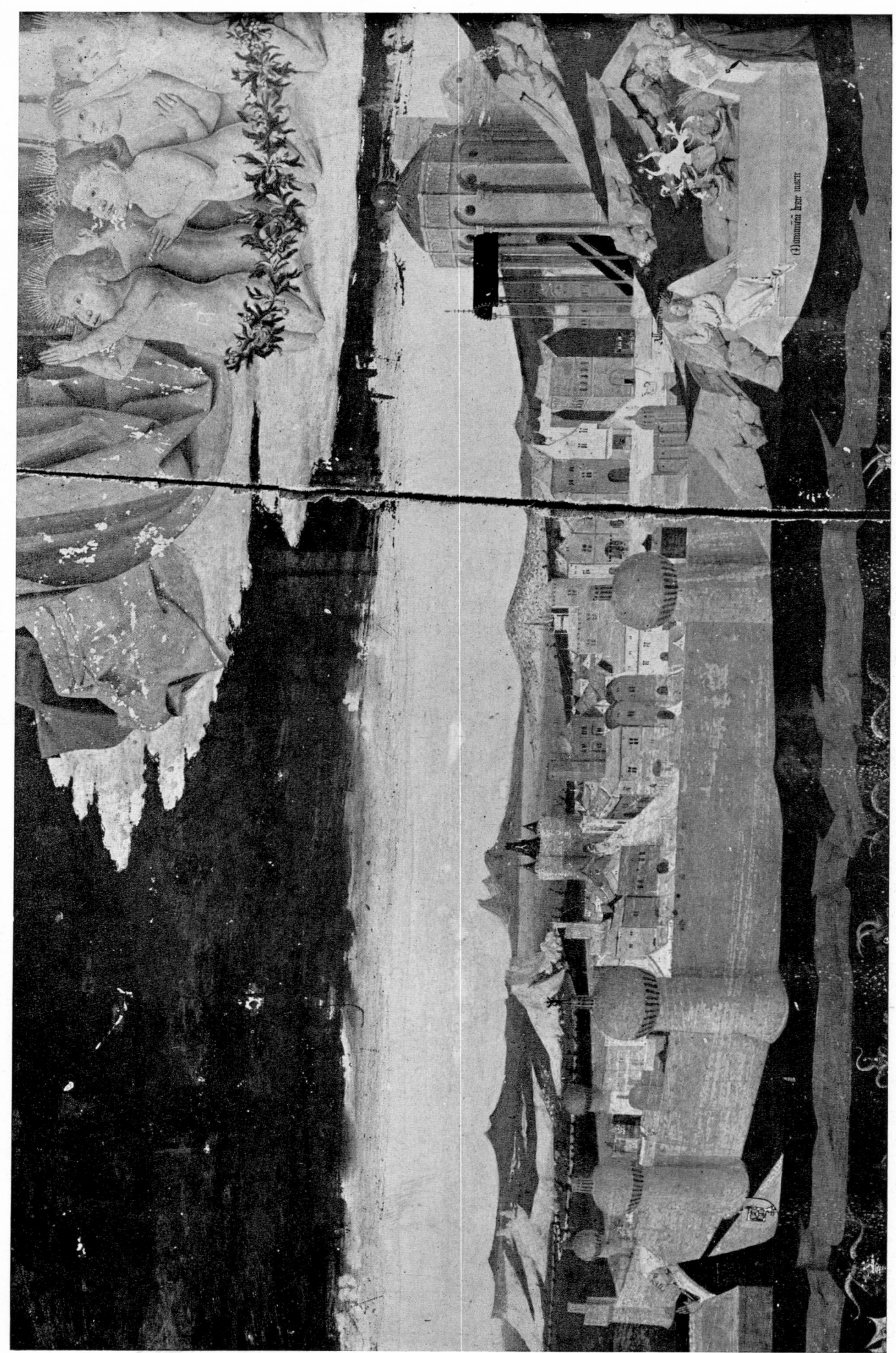

65. ENGUERRAND CHARONTON: JERUSALEM. DETAIL FROM THE » CORONATION OF THE VIRGIN « (PL. 63)

66. ENGUERRAND CHARONTON: ROME. DETAIL FROM THE » CORONATION OF THE VIRGIN « (PL. 63)

67. ENGUERRAND CHARONTON: THE VISION OF MOSES AND THE MASS OF ST. GREGORY.

DETAIL FROM THE » CORONATION OF THE VIRGIN « (PL. 63)

68. ENGUERRAND CHARONTON: CHRIST ON THE CROSS ADORED BY THE DONOR JEAN DE MONTAGNAC.
DETAIL FROM THE » CORONATION OF THE VIRGIN « (PL. 63)

69. JEAN FOUQUET, ABOUT 1445: PORTRAIT OF KING CHARLES VII.

PARIS, MUSÉE DU LOUVRE

⟨ Cat. No. 120 ⟩

70. JEAN FOUQUET: ADORATION OF THE MAGI, WITH A PORTRAIT OF CHARLES VII.

MINIATURE FROM THE HOURS OF ÉTIENNE CHEVALIER.

CHANTILLY, MUSÉE CONDÉ

⟨ Cat. No. 130 ⟩

71. JEAN FOUQUET: HEAD OF GUILLAUME JOUVENEL DES URSINS.
DRAWING. BERLIN, KUPFERSTICHKABINETT
⟨ Cat. No. 127 ⟩

72. JEAN FOUQUET, ABOUT 1455: PORTRAIT OF GUILLAUME JOUVENEL DES URSINS.

PARIS, MUSÉE DU LOUVRE

⟨ Cat. No. 126 ⟩

73. JEAN FOUQUET, ABOUT 1450: ÉTIENNE CHEVALIER PRESENTED BY ST. STEPHEN.
LEFT PART OF THE MELUN DIPTYCH. BERLIN, DEUTSCHES MUSEUM
⟨ Cat. No. 122 ⟩

74. JEAN FOUQUET, ABOUT 1450: VIRGIN AND CHILD.

RIGHT PART OF THE MELUN DIPTYCH. ANTWERP, MUSEUM

⟨ Cat. No. 123 ⟩

75–76. JEAN FOUQUET: ÉTIENNE CHEVALIER AND HIS PATRON SAINT STEPHEN ADORING THE VIRGIN AND CHILD.

TWO MINIATURES FROM THE HOURS OF ÉTIENNE CHEVALIER.

CHANTILLY, MUSÉE CONDÉ ⟨ Cat. No. 130 ⟩

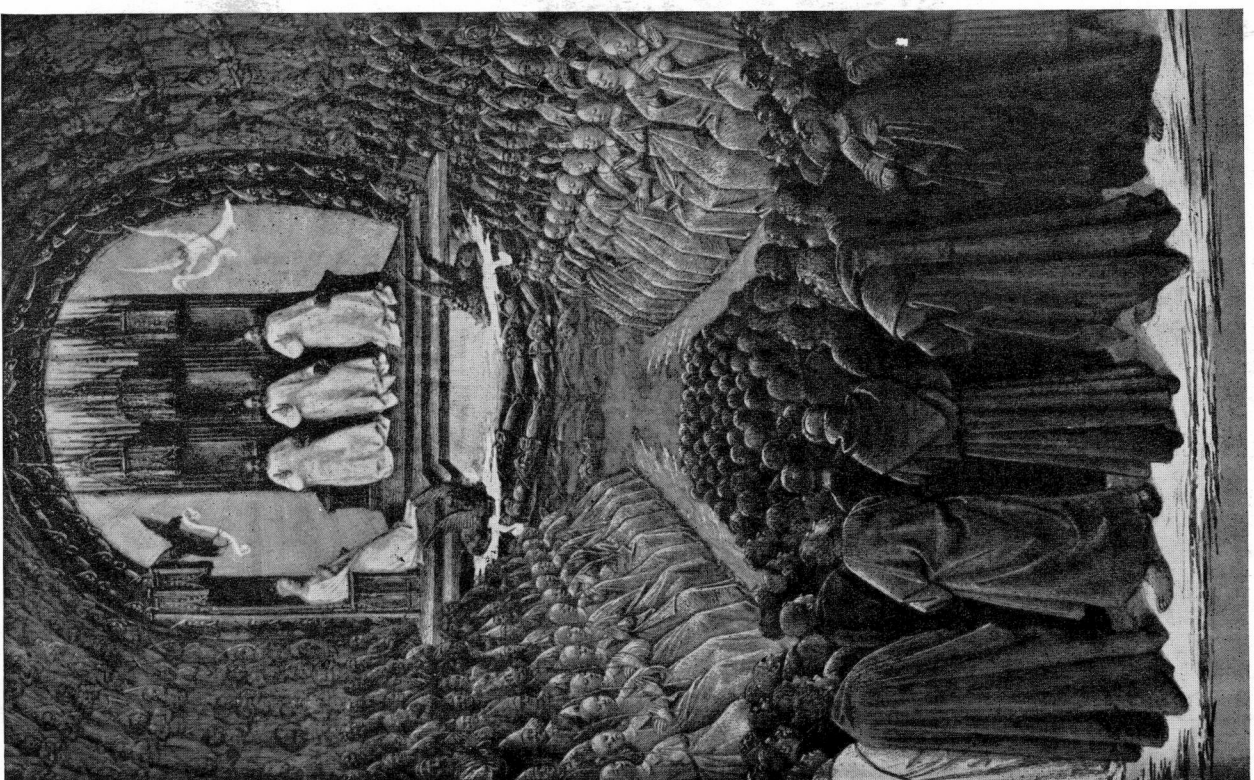

78. JEAN FOUQUET: THE TRINITY IN GLORY.

MINIATURE FROM THE HOURS OF ÉTIENNE CHEVALIER.

CHANTILLY, MUSÉE CONDÉ

⟨ Cat. No. 130 ⟩

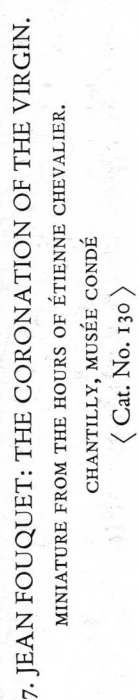

77. JEAN FOUQUET: THE CORONATION OF THE VIRGIN.

MINIATURE FROM THE HOURS OF ÉTIENNE CHEVALIER.

CHANTILLY, MUSÉE CONDÉ

⟨ Cat. No. 130 ⟩

79. JEAN FOUQUET: THE BUILDING OF THE TEMPLE.

MINIATURE FROM THE » ANTIQUITÉS JUDAÏQUES «.

PARIS, BIBLIOTHÈQUE NATIONALE ⟨ Cat. No. 129 ⟩

80. JEAN FOUQUET, OR HIS STUDIO: THE CORONATION OF KING LOUIS VI.

MINIATURE FROM THE » GRANDES CHRONIQUES DE FRANCE «.

PARIS, BIBLIOTHÈQUE NATIONALE ⟨ Cat. No. 134 ⟩

81. JEAN FOUQUET: THE TRIAL OF THE DUKE OF ALENÇON AT VENDÔME IN 1458.
MINIATURE FROM » BOCCACCIO, LES CAS DES NOBLES HOMMES ET FEMMES «.
MUNICH, STAATSBIBLIOTHEK ⟨ Cat. No. 131 ⟩

82. JEAN FOUQUET: ST. MARGARET AS A SHEPHERDESS.
MINIATURE FROM THE HOURS OF ÉTIENNE CHEVALIER.
PARIS, MUSÉE DU LOUVRE ⟨ Cat. No. 130 ⟩

83. JEAN FOUQUET: ENTRANCE OF HEROD INTO JERUSALEM.

MINIATURE FROM THE » ANTIQUITÉS JUDAÏQUES, II «.

PARIS, BIBLIOTHÈQUE NATIONALE

⟨ Cat. No. 129 ⟩

84. JEAN FOUQUET: KING LOUIS XI PRESIDING OVER AN ASSEMBLY OF THE ORDER OF ST. MICHAEL.

MINIATURE. FRONTISPIECE OF THE STATUTES OF THE ORDER OF ST. MICHAEL.

PARIS, BIBLIOTHÈQUE NATIONALE

⟨ Cat. No. 133 ⟩

85. JEAN FOUQUET, ABOUT 1470-75: THE DESCENT FROM THE CROSS, KNOWN AS THE » PIETÀ DE NOUANS «.

NOUANS (INDRE ET LOIRE), PARISH CHURCH ⟨ Cat. No. 136 ⟩

86. JEAN FOUQUET: THREE HOLY WOMEN. DETAIL FROM THE »PIETÀ DE NOUANS « (PL. 85)

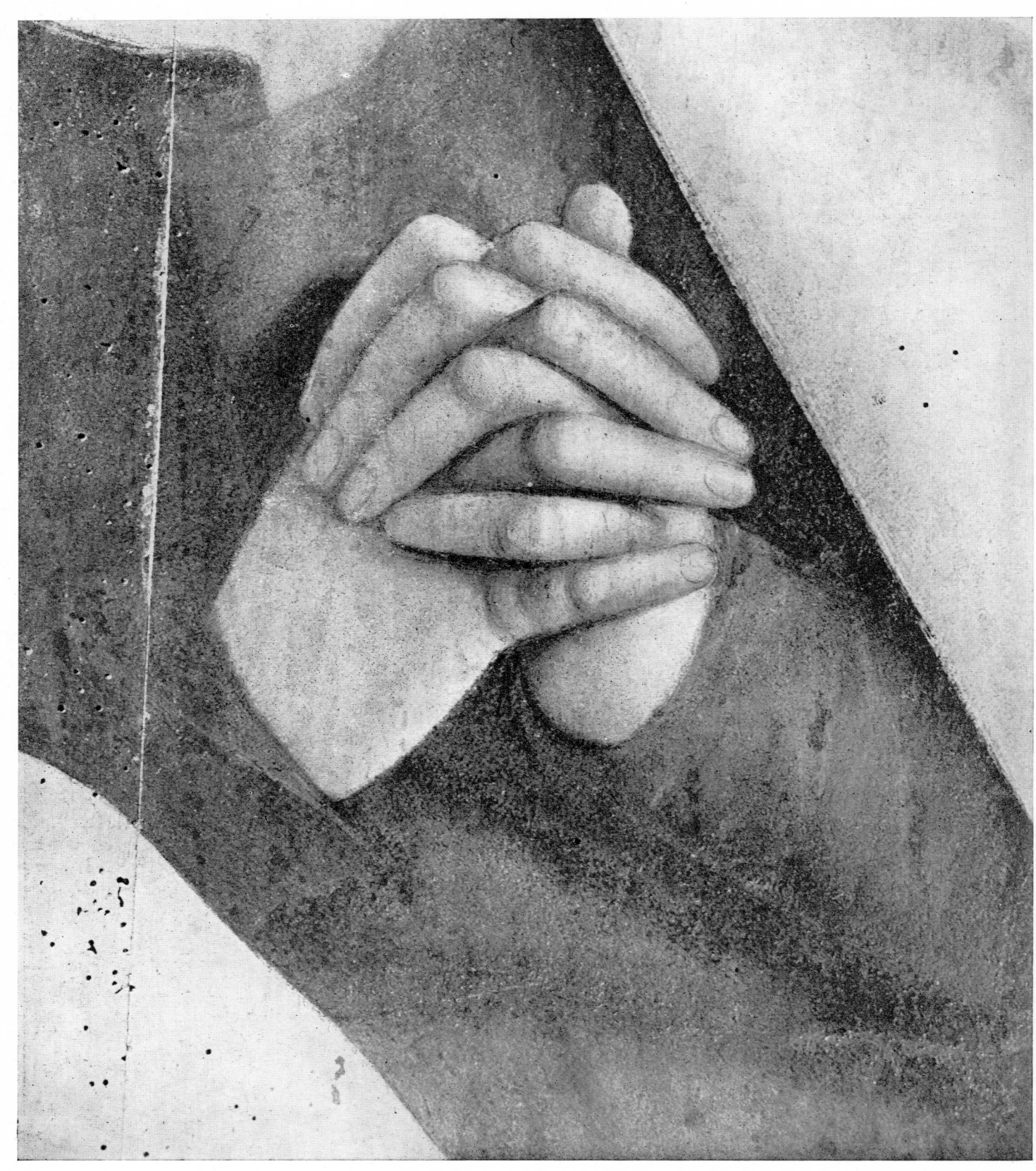

87. JEAN FOUQUET: THE HANDS OF THE VIRGIN.

DETAIL FROM THE » PIETÀ DE NOUANS « (PL. 85)

88. JEAN FOUQUET: THE HEAD OF THE VIRGIN.
DETAIL FROM THE » PIETÀ DE NOUANS « (PL. 85)

89. JEAN FOUQUET: SELF-PORTRAIT.

ENAMEL. PARIS, MUSÉE DU LOUVRE

⟨ Cat. No. 124 ⟩

90. JEAN FOUQUET: BELIEVERS AND UNBELIEVERS.

ENAMEL. FORMERLY BERLIN, SCHLOSSMUSEUM

⟨ Cat. No. 125 ⟩

91. CONTEMPORARY OF FOUQUET, SCHOOL OF SOUTHERN FRANCE, 1456: PORTRAIT OF A MAN.

VADUZ, FUERST OF LIECHTENSTEIN

⟨ Cat. No. 143 ⟩

92. ATTRIBUTED TO FOUQUET, ABOUT 1470: PORTRAIT OF A PAPAL LEGATE.

DRAWING. NEW YORK, COLLECTION OF THE LATE LORD DUVEEN

⟨ Cat. No. 139 ⟩

93. SCHOOL OF TOURAINE, ABOUT 1460: PORTRAIT OF A YOUNG MAN. FRAGMENT.

PARIS, COLLECTION HEUGEL

⟨ Cat. No. 142 ⟩

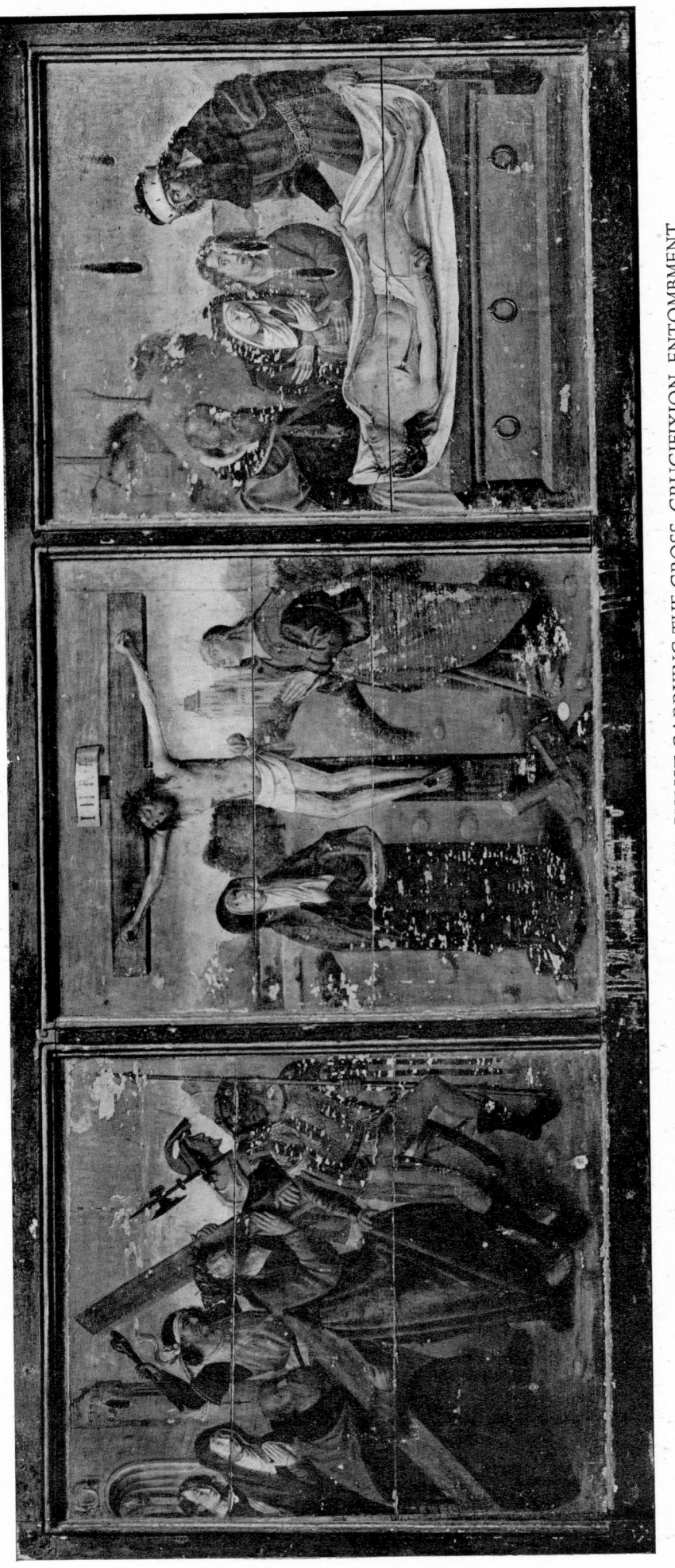

94. SCHOOL OF TOURAINE, ABOUT 1480: TRIPTYCH: CHRIST CARRYING THE CROSS, CRUCIFIXION, ENTOMBMENT.

MOULINS, MUSEUM

⟨ Cat. No. 148 ⟩

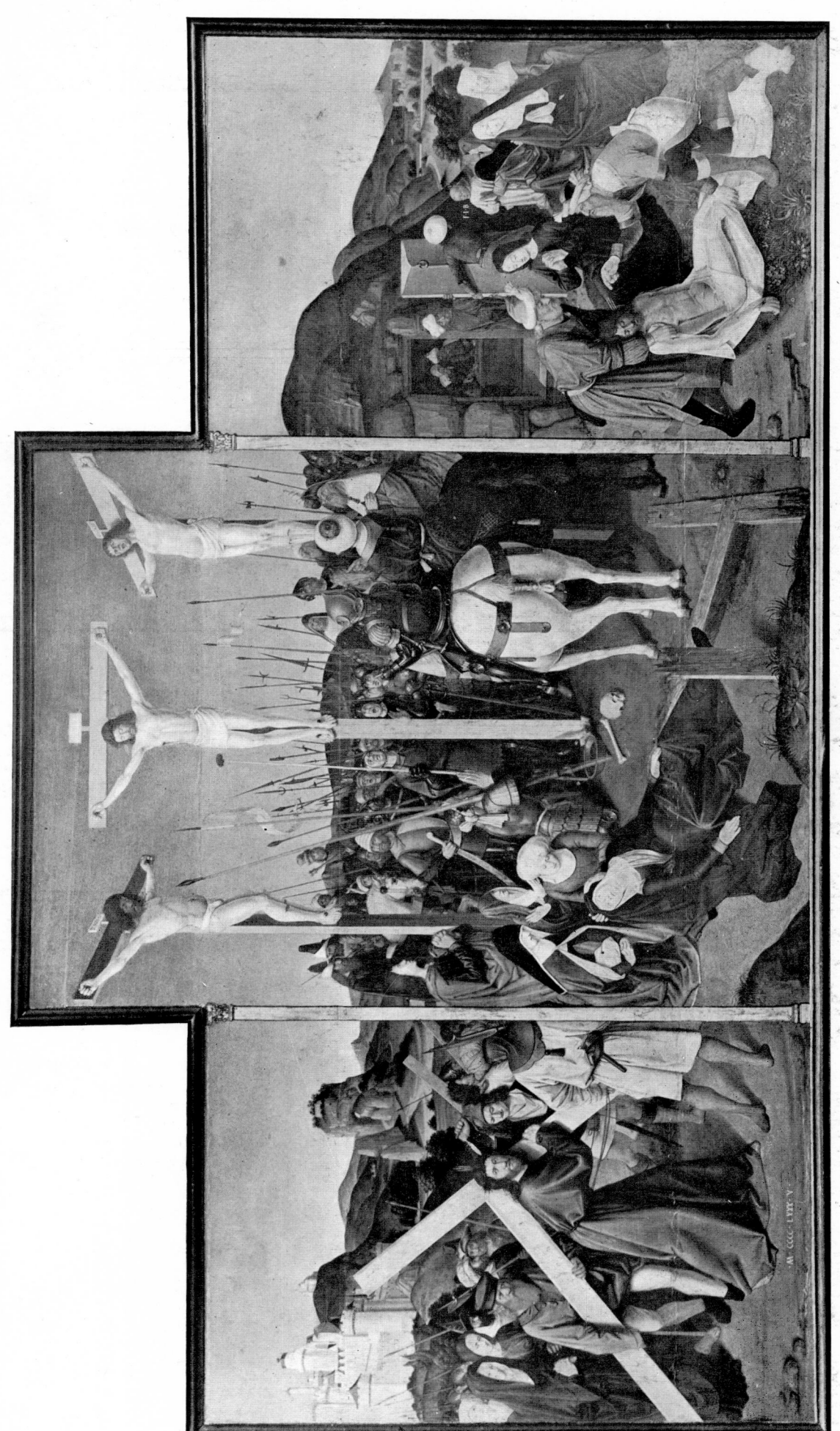

95. SCHOOL OR STUDIO OF FOUQUET, 1485: TRIPTYCH, KNOWN AS THE » TRIPTYQUE DE LOCHES «.
CHRIST CARRYING THE CROSS, CRUCIFIXION, ENTOMBMENT.
LOCHES, ÉGLISE S. ANTOINE
⟨ Cat. No. 147 ⟩

96. FRANCO-FLEMISH SCHOOL, ABOUT 1480: A COUPLE OF LOVERS AND DEATH.

SHIELD OF PARADE. LONDON, BRITISH MUSEUM

⟨ Cat. No. 202 ⟩

97. SCHOOL OF AMIENS, 1437: » LE SACERDOCE DE LA VIERGE «.

PARIS, MUSÉE DU LOUVRE

〈 Cat. No. 158 〉

98. SIMON MARMION: ST. JEROME AND A DONOR.

PHILADELPHIA, JOHN G. JOHNSON COLLECTION

⟨ Cat. No. 181 ⟩

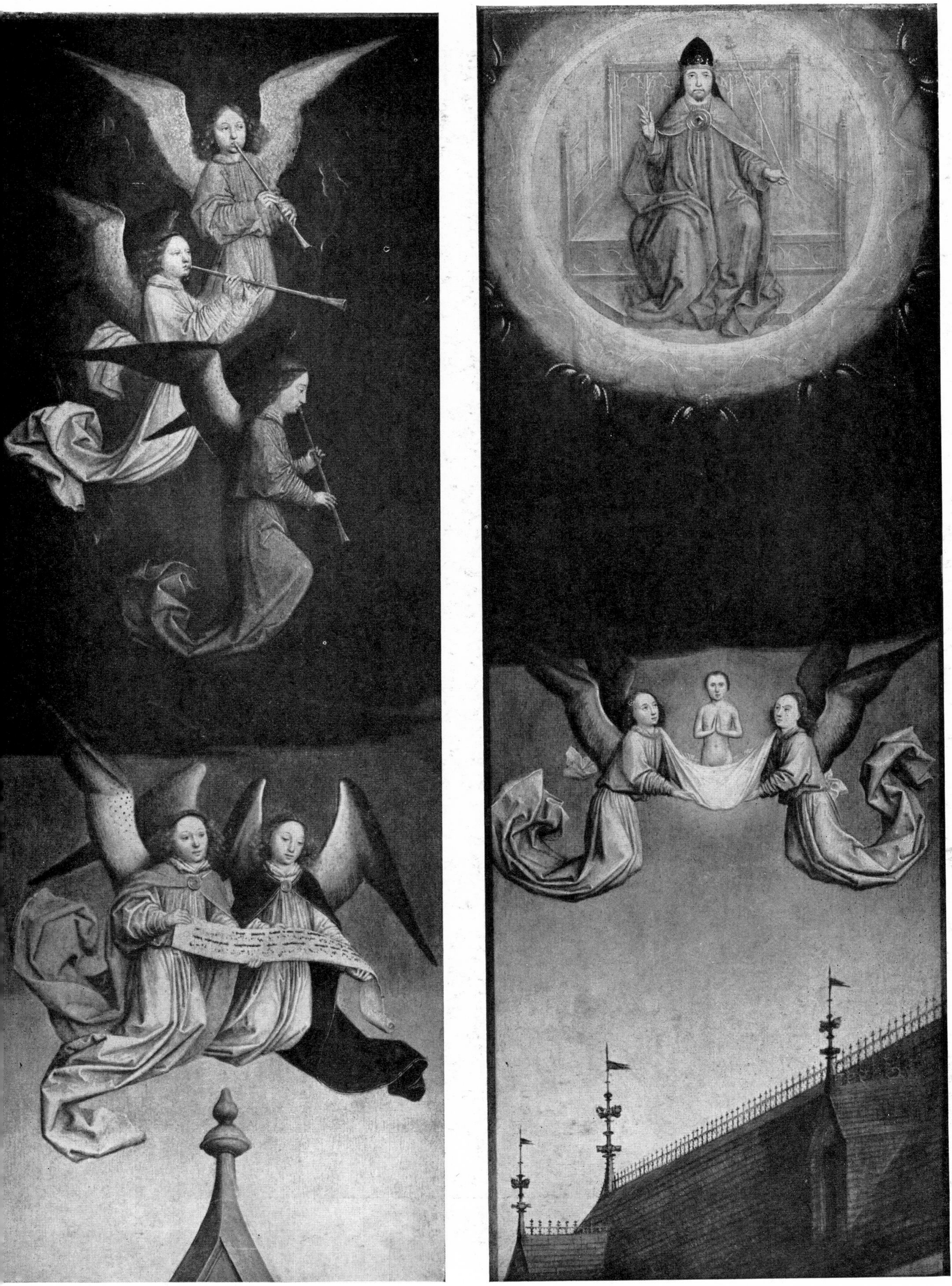

99–100. SIMON MARMION, 1459: A CHOIR OF ANGELS. THE SOUL OF ST. BERTIN CARRIED UP TO GOD.

TWO FRAGMENTS FROM THE ALTARPIECE OF ST. OMER.

LONDON, NATIONAL GALLERY

⟨ Cat. No. 171 ⟩

102. SIMON MARMION: ST. JEROME.

MINIATURE FROM A BOOK OF HOURS.

LONDON, BRITISH MUSEUM

⟨ Cat. No. 174 ⟩

101. SIMON MARMION: THE TEMPTATION OF ST. ANTHONY.

MINIATURE FROM A BOOK OF HOURS.

LONDON, BRITISH MUSEUM

⟨ Cat. No. 174 ⟩

103: SIMON MARMION, 1459: THE LIFE OF ST. BERTIN.

LEFT SHUTTER OF THE ALTARPIECE OF ST. OMER.

BERLIN, DEUTSCHES MUSEUM

⟨ Cat. No. 170 ⟩

104. SIMON MARMION: THE DONOR GUILLAUME FILLASTRE.
DETAIL FROM THE LEFT SHUTTER OF THE ALTARPIECE OF ST. OMER (PL. 103)

105–106. SCHOOL OF PICARDIE, ABOUT 1470–80:
ST. HONORIUS, BISHOP OF AMIENS. THE VIRGIN AND CHILD.

TWO PANELS FROM THE ALTARPIECE OF THUISON.

CHICAGO, ART INSTITUTE

⟨ Cat. No. 169 ⟩

107. SCHOOL OF AVIGNON, ABOUT 1460: THE ALTARPIECE OF BOULBON. PARIS, MUSÉE DU LOUVRE ⟨ Cat. No. 205 ⟩

108. SCHOOL OF AVIGNON, ABOUT 1460: PIETÀ, KNOWN AS THE » PIETÀ DE VILLENEUVE «. PARIS, MUSÉE DU LOUVRE (Cat. No. 206)

109. SCHOOL OF AVIGNON, ABOUT 1460: HEAD OF ST. JOHN.

DETAIL FROM THE » PIETÀ DE VILLENEUVE « (PL. 108)

110. SCHOOL OF AVIGNON, ABOUT 1460: HEAD OF CHRIST.

DETAIL FROM THE » PIETÀ DE VILLENEUVE « (PL. 108)

III. SCHOOL OF AVIGNON, ABOUT 1460: HEAD OF A DONOR.
DETAIL FROM THE ALTARPIECE OF BOULBON (PL. 107)

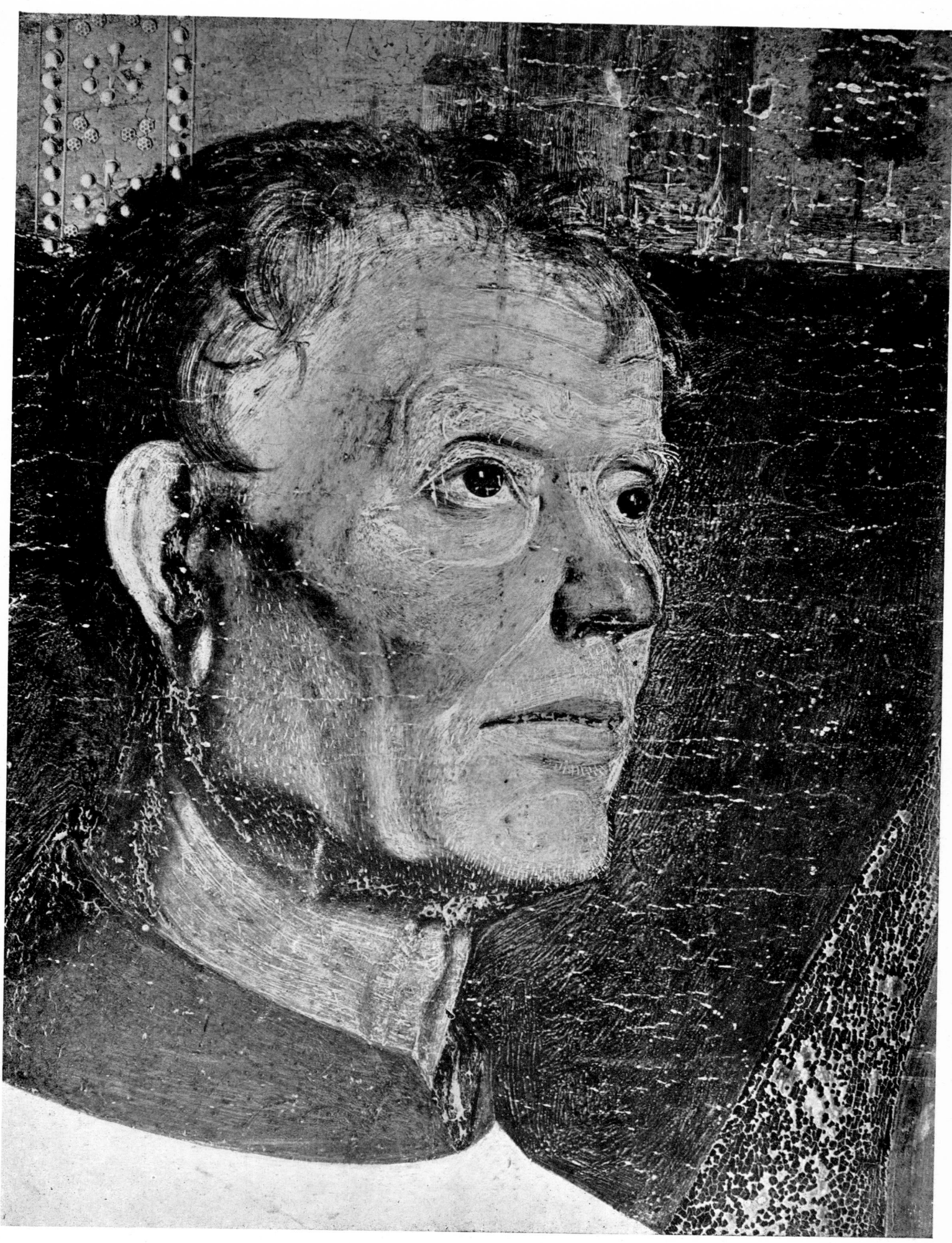

112. SCHOOL OF AVIGNON, ABOUT 1460: HEAD OF A DONOR.

DETAIL FROM THE » PIETÀ DE VILLENEUVE « (PL. 108)

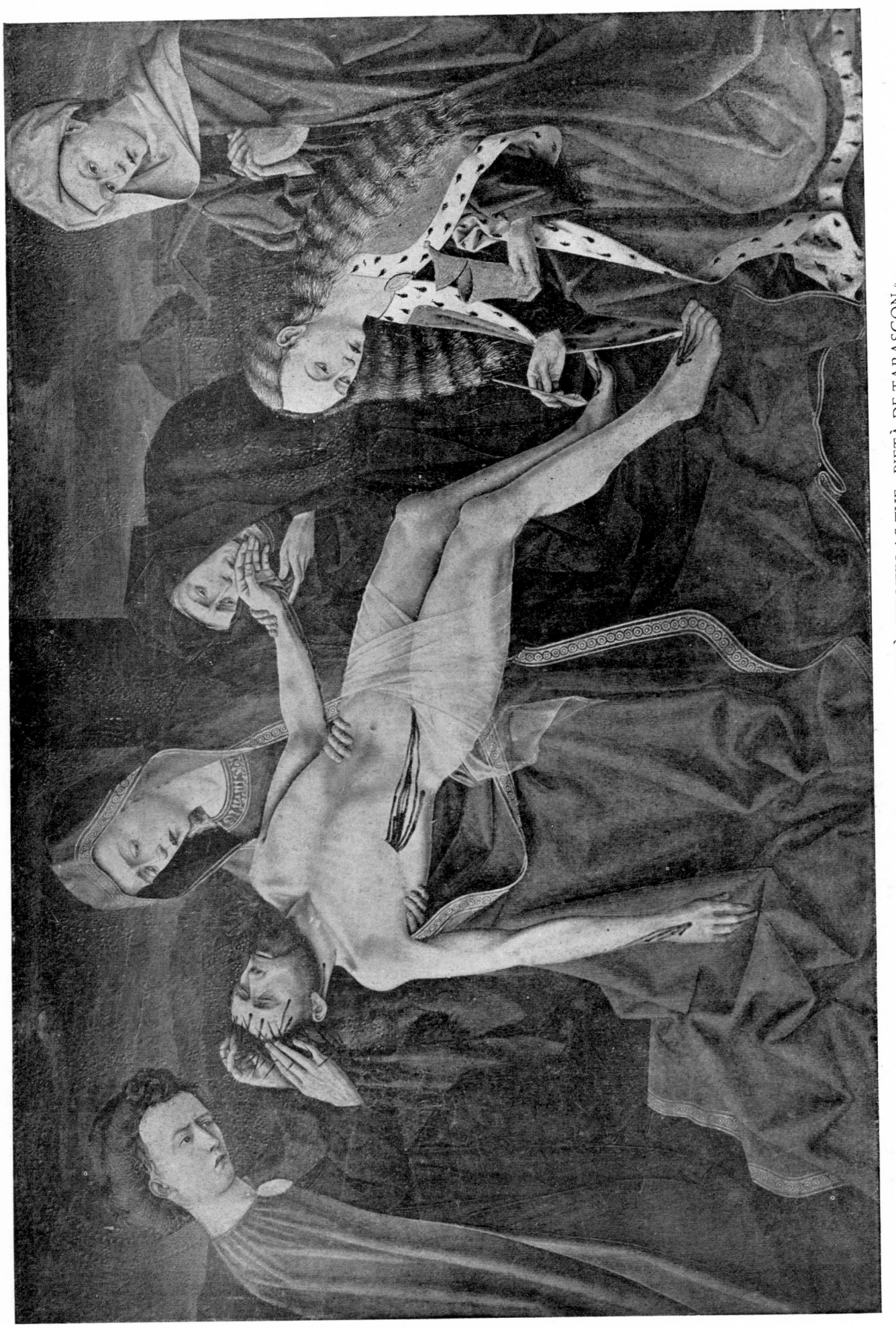

113. SCHOOL OF PROVENCE, ABOUT 1460: PIETÀ, KNOWN AS THE » PIETÀ DE TARASCON «.

PARIS, MUSÉE DE CLUNY

⟨ Cat. No. 209 ⟩

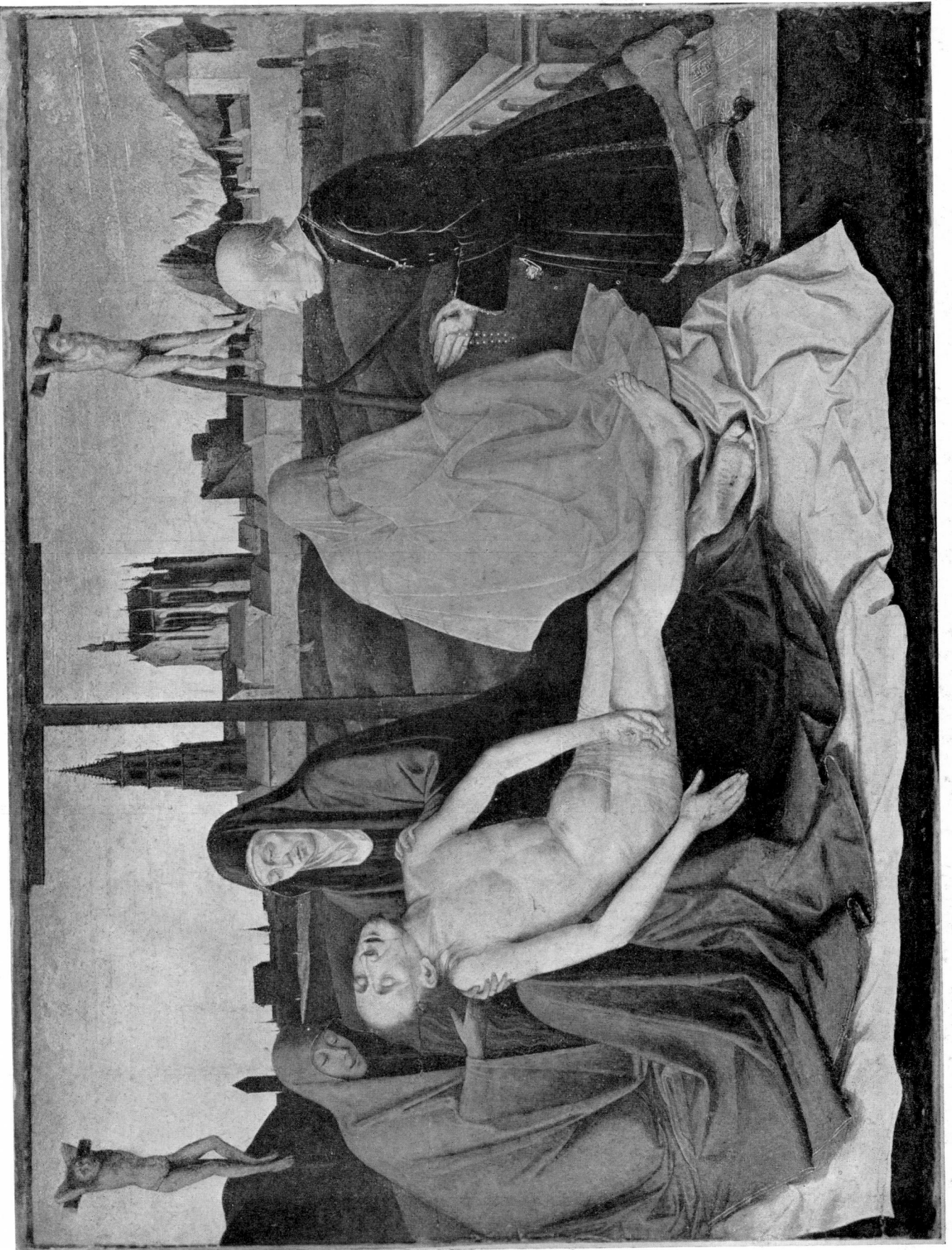

114. SCHOOL OF PROVENCE, ABOUT 1470: PIETÀ WITH A DONOR.

NEW YORK, FRICK COLLECTION

⟨ Cat. No. 210 ⟩

115. SCHOOL OF PROVENCE, ABOUT 1460: ST. GEORGE ON HORSEBACK.
CAROMB, PARISH CHURCH 〈 Cat. No. 213 〉

116. SCHOOL OF PROVENCE, ABOUT 1460: ST. GEORGE.

DETAIL FROM PL. 115

117. NICOLAS FROMENT: THE TRANSFIGURATION.

DRAWING. BERLIN, KUPFERSTICHKABINETT

⟨ Cat. No. 215 ⟩

118. NICOLAS FROMENT, 1461: THE RAISING OF LAZARUS.

CENTRE PANEL OF THE UFFIZI TRIPTYCH.

FLORENCE, GALLERIA DEGLI UFFIZI

⟨ Cat. No. 214 ⟩

119–120. NICOLAS FROMENT, 1461: MARTHA ANNOUNCING THE DEATH OF LAZARUS TO CHRIST.
MARY MAGDALEN ANOINTING CHRIST'S FEET.

SHUTTERS OF THE UFFIZI TRIPTYCH (OBVERSE).

⟨ Cat. No. 214 ⟩

121-122. NICOLAS FROMENT, 1461: VIRGIN AND CHILD. A DONOR, AN ATTENDANT AND A YOUNG MAN.

SHUTTERS OF THE UFFIZI TRIPTYCH (REVERSE)

⟨ Cat. No. 214 ⟩

123. NICOLAS FROMENT: LANDSCAPE WITH TWO LOVERS PLAYING CHESS.

DETAIL FROM PL. 120

124. NICOLAS FROMENT: HEAD OF THE » ATTENDANT «.

DETAIL FROM PL. 122

125. SCHOOL OF NICOLAS FROMENT: THE LEGEND OF SAINT MITRE.
AIX-EN-PROVENCE, SAINT-SAUVEUR CATHEDRAL
⟨ Cat. No. 223 ⟩

126. NICOLAS FROMENT, 1476: THE VIRGIN IN THE BURNING BUSH. (THE VISION OF MOSES.)

CENTRE PANEL OF THE TRIPTYCH OF THE BURNING BUSH.

AIX-EN-PROVENCE, SAINT-SAUVEUR CATHEDRAL

⟨ Cat. No. 216 ⟩

127–128. NICOLAS FROMENT, 1476: THE ANNUNCIATION.

GRISAILLE. SHUTTERS (REVERSE) OF THE TRIPTYCH OF THE BURNING BUSH

⟨ Cat. No. 216 ⟩

129–130. NICOLAS FROMENT, 1476:
KING RENÉ OF ANJOU PRESENTED BY STS. MARY MAGDALEN, ANTHONY AND MAURICE.
QUEEN JEANNE DE LAVAL PRESENTED BY STS. JOHN THE EVANGELIST, CATHERINE AND NICOLAS.
SHUTTERS (OBVERSE) OF THE TRIPTYCH OF THE BURNING BUSH ⟨ Cat. No. 216 ⟩

131. MASTER OF SAINT JEAN DE LUZ, ABOUT 1475:
PORTRAIT OF HUGUES DE RABUTIN.

NEW YORK, JOHN ROCKEFELLER JUN. COLLECTION

⟨ Cat. No. 235 ⟩

132. MASTER OF SAINT JEAN DE LUZ, ABOUT 1475:
PORTRAIT OF JEANNE DE MONTAIGU, WIFE OF HUGUES DE RABUTIN.

NEW YORK, JOHN ROCKEFELLER JUN. COLLECTION

⟨ Cat. No. 235 ⟩

137. MASTER OF ST. GILES: THE BETRAYAL OF CHRIST.

BRUSSELS, MUSÉES ROYAUX DES BEAUX-ARTS

⟨ Cat. No. 243 ⟩

138. MASTER OF ST. GILES: PORTRAITS OF A MAN AND HIS WIFE.

CHANTILLY, MUSÉE CONDÉ

⟨ Cat. No. 247 ⟩

139. MASTER OF THE ALTARPIECE OF THE LIFE OF THE VIRGIN: THE PRESENTATION OF THE VIRGIN.

PARIS, PRIVATE COLLECTION

⟨ Cat. No. 269 ⟩

140. MASTER OF THE ALTARPIECE OF THE LIFE OF THE VIRGIN: THE MARRIAGE OF THE VIRGIN.

MARSEILLE, COLLECTION COMTE DEMANDOLX-DEDONS

⟨ Cat. No. 267 ⟩

141. MASTER OF THE ALTARPIECE OF THE LIFE OF THE VIRGIN: THE ADORATION OF THE MAGI.

ZURICH, PRIVATE COLLECTION

⟨ Cat. No. 268 ⟩

142. MASTER OF THE ALTARPIECE OF THE LIFE OF THE VIRGIN: THE CRUCIFIXION.

ROME, PRIVATE COLLECTION

⟨ Cat. No. 270 ⟩

143. MASTER OF ST. SEBASTIAN: THE ANNUNCIATION.

AVIGNON, MUSÉE CALVET

⟨ Cat. No. 262 ⟩

144. MASTER OF ST. SEBASTIAN: THE MARRIAGE OF THE VIRGIN.
BRUSSELS, MUSÉES ROYAUX DES BEAUX-ARTS
⟨ Cat. No. 263 ⟩

145. MASTER OF ST. SEBASTIAN: ST. MICHAEL SLAYING THE DRAGON.

AVIGNON, MUSÉE CALVET

⟨ Cat. No. 262 ⟩

146. MASTER OF ST. SEBASTIAN: ST. SEBASTIAN DESTROYING THE IDOLS.
PANEL FROM THE ALTARPIECE OF ST. SEBASTIAN.
PHILADELPHIA, JOHNSON COLLECTION
⟨ Cat. No. 258 ⟩

147. MASTER OF ST. SEBASTIAN: ST. SEBASTIAN INTERCEDING FOR THE PLAGUE-STRICKEN.

PANEL FROM THE ALTARPIECE OF ST. SEBASTIAN.

BALTIMORE, WALTERS ART GALLERY

⟨ Cat. No. 259 ⟩

148. MASTER OF ST. SEBASTIAN: ST. IRENE NURSES ST. SEBASTIAN.

PANEL FROM THE ALTARPIECE OF ST. SEBASTIAN.

PHILADELPHIA, JOHNSON COLLECTION

⟨ Cat. No. 258 ⟩

149. LOUIS BRÉA, 1475: ALTARPIECE OF THE PIETÀ, WITH STS. MARTIN AND CATHERINE.

NICE-CIMIEZ, CHURCH ⟨ Cat. No. 283 ⟩

150. SCHOOL OF AVIGNON, ABOUT 1490–1500: THE ADORATION OF THE CHILD.

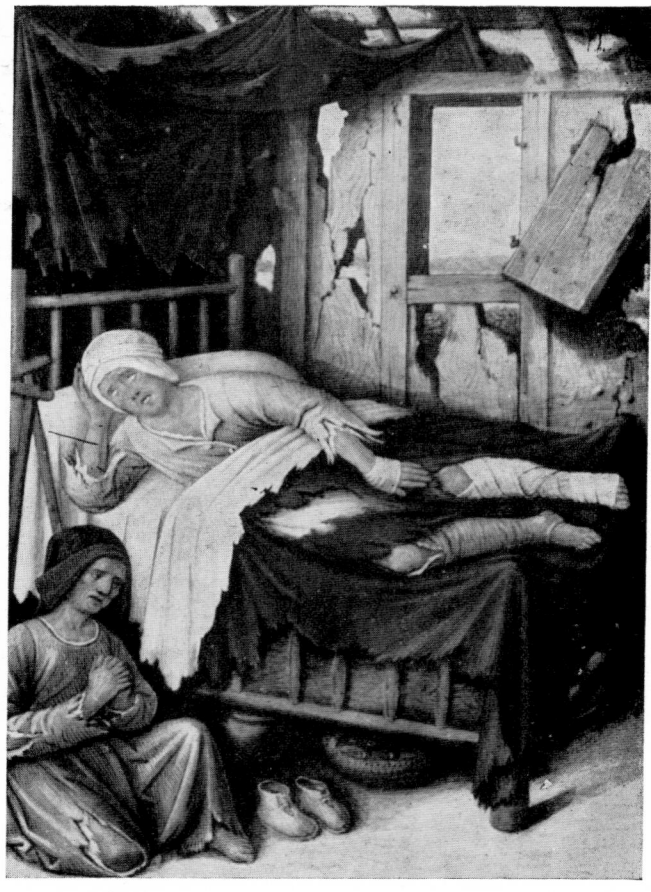

151–154. JEAN BOURDICHON: THE FOUR STAGES OF SOCIETY.

MINIATURES. FORMERLY COLLECTION J. MASSON, AMIENS

⟨ Cat. No. 321A ⟩

155. JEAN BOURDICHON: ST. MICHAEL AND ST. GEORGE.
UPPER PART OF THE SHUTTERS OF THE TRIPTYCH OF NAPLES.
NAPLES, MUSEO NAZIONALE
⟨ Cat. No. 319 ⟩

156. MASTER OF MOULINS, ABOUT 1494:
ST. MICHAEL APPEARS TO CHARLES VIII.
MINIATURE. TITLE PAGE OF THE STATUTES OF THE ORDER OF ST. MICHAEL.
PARIS, BIBLIOTHÈQUE NATIONALE
⟨ Cat. No. 304 ⟩

157. MASTER OF MOULINS, ABOUT 1480: THE NATIVITY, WITH CARDINAL JEAN ROLIN. AUTUN, MUSEUM ⟨ Cat. No. 292 ⟩

158. MASTER OF MOULINS: THE HEAD OF THE VIRGIN AND THE SHEPHERDS. DETAIL FROM THE » NATIVITY OF AUTUN « (PL. 157)

159–160. MASTER OF MOULINS: THE ANNUNCIATION.
GRISAILLE. SHUTTERS (REVERSE) OF THE MOULINS TRIPTYCH.
MOULINS, CATHEDRAL
⟨ Cat. No. 293 ⟩

161. MASTER OF MOULINS: VIRGIN AND CHILD SURROUNDED BY ANGELS.

CENTRE PANEL OF THE MOULINS TRIPTYCH.

MOULINS, CATHEDRAL

⟨ Cat. No. 293 ⟩

162–163. MASTER OF MOULINS: PIERRE II, DUKE OF BOURBON, PRESENTED BY ST. PETER.
ANNE OF FRANCE, DUCHESS OF BOURBON, PRESENTED BY ST. ANNE.

SHUTTERS (OBVERSE) OF THE MOULINS TRIPTYCH.

⟨ Cat. No. 293 ⟩

164. MASTER OF MOULINS: ST. MARY MAGDALEN AND A FEMALE DONOR.

PARIS, MUSÉE DU LOUVRE

⟨ Cat. No. 300 ⟩

165. MASTER OF MOULINS: THE ANNUNCIATION.

CHICAGO, ART INSTITUTE

⟨ Cat. No. 297 ⟩

166. MASTER OF MOULINS: CHARLEMAGNE AND THE MEETING AT THE GOLDEN GATE.

LONDON, NATIONAL GALLERY

⟨ Cat. No. 298 ⟩

167. MASTER OF MOULINS: VIRGIN AND CHILD SURROUNDED BY FOUR ANGELS.

BRUSSELS, MUSÉES ROYAUX DES BEAUX-ARTS

⟨ Cat. No. 299 ⟩

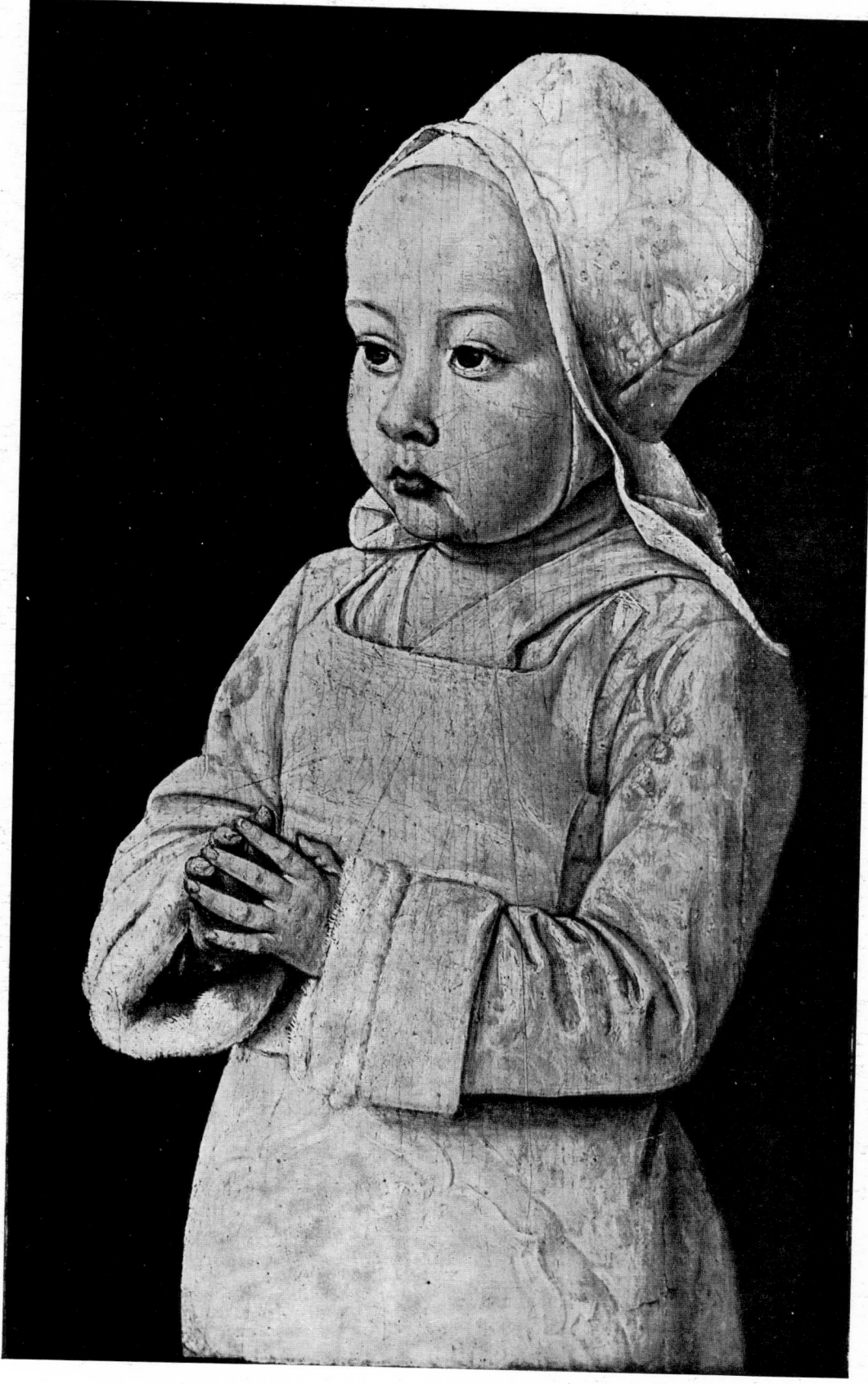

168. ATTRIBUTED TO THE MASTER OF MOULINS, ABOUT 1495:
PORTRAIT OF A PRAYING CHILD.

PARIS, MUSÉE DU LOUVRE

⟨ Cat. No. 307 ⟩

169. MASTER OF MOULINS: PORTRAIT OF A YOUNG PRINCESS.

NEW YORK, COLLECTION ROBERT LEHMANN

⟨ Cat. No. 303 ⟩

170. MASTER OF MOULINS, ABOUT 1485: PORTRAIT OF CARDINAL CHARLES II OF BOURBON.

⟨ Cat. No. 302 ⟩

171. FRENCH SCHOOL, ABOUT 1500: THE LADY WITH THE PANSIES.

PARIS, MUSÉE DU LOUVRE

⟨ Cat. No. 330 ⟩

172. FRENCH SCHOOL, END OF THE FIFTEENTH CENTURY:
» RHETORICA « ACCOMPANIED BY CICERO.

PART OF THE FRESCOES REPRESENTING THE LIBERAL ARTS.

LE PUY-EN-VELAY, CATHEDRAL

⟨ Cat. No. 313 ⟩

173. ATTRIBUTED TO JEAN PERRÉAL: PORTRAIT OF LOUIS XII OF FRANCE.
WINDSOR CASTLE, H.M. THE KING ⟨ Cat. No. 332 ⟩
Reproduced by gracious permission of H.M. The King

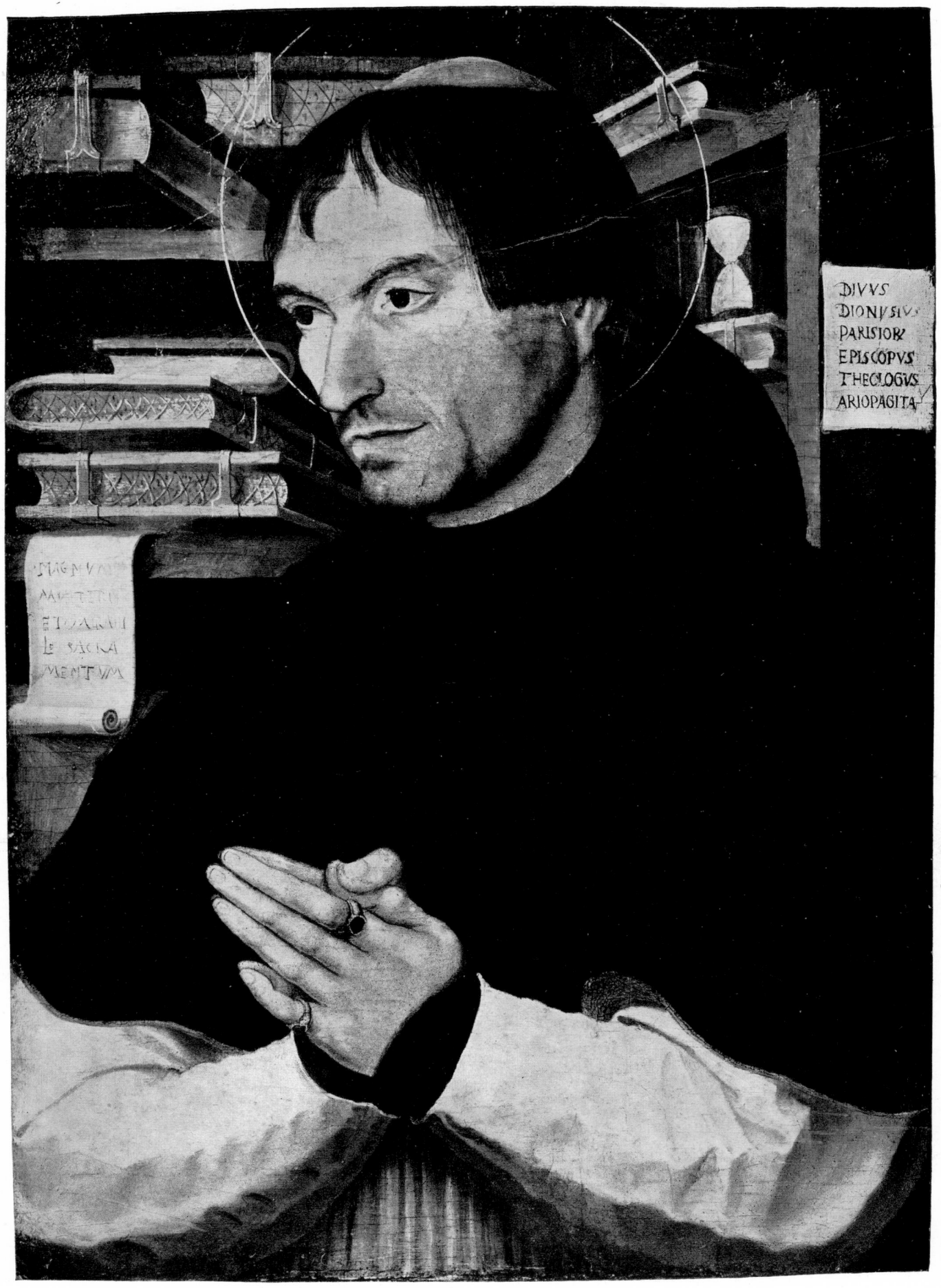

DIVVS
DIONYSIV
PARISIOR
EPISCOPVS
THEOLOGVS
ARIOPAGITA

MAGNVM
MISTERIV
ET DIVINV
ES SACRA
MENTVM

174. SCHOOL OF AVIGNON, ABOUT 1500–1510: ST. DIONYSIUS THE AREOPAGITE.

AMSTERDAM, RIJKSMUSEUM

⟨ Cat. No. 275 ⟩

175. FRENCH SCHOOL, ABOUT 1390:
THE THREE NAILS OF THE CRUCIFIXION IN A CROWN OF THORNS.
REVERSE OF THE » SMALL CIRCULAR PIETÀ « IN THE LOUVRE (PL. 4)
⟨ Cat. No. 8 ⟩

THE CATALOGUE

ABBREVIATIONS OF LITERATURE

BARNES — Albert C. Barnes and Violette de Mazia, *The French Primitives and their Forms*. Merion, Pa., 1931.

BAZIN — Germain Bazin, *La Peinture française des Origines au XVIe siècle*. Paris, Ed. Braun, 1937.

COX — Trenchard Cox, *Jehan Foucquet, Native of Tours*. London, 1931.

DAVIES 1945 — National Gallery Catalogues: *Early Netherlandish School*, by Martin Davies. London, 1945.

DAVIES 1946 — National Gallery Catalogues: *French School*, by Martin Davies. London 1946.

DIMIER 1911 — Louis Dimier, *Les Primitifs français*. Paris 1911.

DIMIER 1925 — Louis Dimier, *Histoire de la Peinture française des Origines au retour de Vouet, 1300 à 1627*. Paris/Bruxelles 1925.

DUPONT — Jacques Dupont, *Les Primitifs français (1350–1500)*. Paris 1937.

DURRIEU/MICHEL — *Histoire de l'Art*, published by André Michel:
Vol. III, 1, 1907: Paul Durrieu, *La Peinture en France de Jean le Bon à la mort de Charles V. Le Règne de Charles VI*.
Vol. IV, 2, 1922: Paul Durrieu, *La Peinture en France depuis l'avènement de Charles VII jusqu' à la fin des Valois*.

FIERENS-GEVAERT — *Histoire de la Peinture flamande des Origines à la fin du XVe siècle*. Bruxelles 1927 (Vol. I).

FOCILLON, OCCIDENT — Henri Focillon, *L'Art d'Occident: Le Moyen-âge roman et gothique*. Paris 1938.

FOCILLON, FORMS — Henri Focillon, *The Life of Forms in Art*. New Haven 1942.

FRIEDLAENDER, I–XIV — Max J. Friedlaender, *Altniederländische Malerei*, Vol. I–XI, Berlin 1924–1933; Vol. XII–XIV, Leiden 1935–1937.

GILLET — Louis Gillet, *Les Primitifs français*. Marseille 1941.

GUIFFREY MARCEL — Jean Guiffrey et Pierre Marcel, *La Peinture française : Les Primitifs*. Paris 1910–1912.

GUIFFREY MARCEL TERRASSE — Jean Guiffrey, Pierre Marcel et Charles Terrasse, *Les Primitifs*. Deuxième série, Paris 1926–1932.

HEIMANN — Adelheid Heimann, *Der Meister der 'Grandes Heures de Rohan' und seine Werkstatt*, Staedel Jahrbuch, Frankfurt a.M. VII/VIII, 1932, p. 1 ff.

HULIN, CAT. CRIT. — Georges Hulin de Loo, *Catalogue critique de l'Exposition de Bruges*. Gand 1902.

HULIN, VAN EYCK — Georges Hulin de Loo, *L'Exposition des Primitifs français au point de vue de l'influence des frères van Eyck sur la peinture française et provençale*. Société d'Art et d'Archéologie de Gand, Mai 1904.

HULIN, NOTES 1932 — Georges Hulin de Loo, *L'Exposition d'Art français à Londres en 1932: Notes sur quelques tableaux du XVe siècle*. Extrait du Bulletin de la Classe des Beaux-Arts de l'Académie Royale de Belgique, Bruxelles 1932.

JACQUES — Charles Jacques (Sterling), *Les Peintres du moyen-âge : La Peinture française*. Paris 1941. With Catalogue (Répertoire des tableaux français du moyen-âge).

(Rep. A 14th cent.) — XIVe siècle, Répertoire A ⎫
(Rep. A 15th cent.) — XVe siècle, Répertoire A ⎬ : pictures which according to Jacques can be regarded as French.

(Rep. B 14th cent.) — XIVe siècle, Répertoire B ⎫
(Rep. B 15th cent.) — XVe siècle, Répertoire B ⎬ : pictures whose French origin Jacques contests or considers doubtful.

JEDLICKA — Gotthard Jedlicka, *Französische Malerei, Ausgewählte Meisterwerke aus 5 Jahrhunderten*. Zürich 1938.

LABANDE — L. H. Labande, *Les Primitifs français: Peintres et Peintres-Verriers de la Provence Occidentale*. Marseille 1932.

LAVALLÉE — Pierre Lavallée, *Le Dessin français du XIIIe au XVIe siècle*. Paris 1930

LEMOISNE — Paul-André Lemoisne, *La Peinture française à l'époque gothique, XIVe et XVe siècle*. Ed. Pantheon 1931.

LEMOISNE, LOUVRE — *La Peinture au Musée du Louvre* (publié sous la direction de J. Guiffrey): Paul-André Lemoisne, *École française XIVe, XVe et XVIe siècles*. Paris 1925.

MÂLE — Émile Mâle, *L'Art religieux de la Fin de Moyen-Âge en France*, Paris, 1925.

NAT. GALL. ILL. — *National Gallery Illustrations*, Continental Schools, London, 1937.

PERLS (FOUQUET) — K. G. Perls, *Jean Fouquet*, Hyperion Press, 1940.

RÉAU — Louis Réau, *La Peinture française du XIVe au XVIe siècle*. Hyperion Press, 1939.

SCHNEIDER-COHEN — René Schneider et Gustave Cohen, *La Formation du génie moderne dans l'art de l'occident*. Paris 1936.

STERLING — Charles Sterling, *La Peinture française : Les Primitifs*. Paris 1938.

TH. B. — U. Thieme und F. Becker, *Allgemeines Lexikon der bildenden Künste*, Vol. I—. . . , starting 1901, still in progress.

TRÉSORS — *Les Trésors de la Peinture française*. Ed. Skira, Genève.

U.M. — *Unknown Masterpieces*, published by W. R. Valentiner. London/New York 1930.

VAN MARLE — Raimond van Marle, *The Development of the Italian Schools of Painting*. Vol. I–XIX, 1923–1938.

VENTURI — Adolfo Venturi, *Storia dell'Arte Italiana*. Milano 1901—. . . ; still in progress.

WESCHER (FOUQUET) — Paul Wescher, *Jean Fouquet und seine Zeit*. Basel 1945.

ABBREVIATIONS OF PERIODICALS

Burl. Mag. — *Burlington Magazine*.

OMD — *Old Master Drawings* (A Quarterly Magazine, 1926–1940).

Warb. Journ. — *Journal of the Warburg Institute*; since 1939 *Journal of the Warburg and Courtauld Institutes*.

Art Bull. — *The Art Bulletin* (A Quarterly, published by the College Art Association of America).

GBA — *Gazette des Beaux-Arts* (Paris; since 1942 New York).

RdA — *Revue de l'Art Ancien et Moderne*.

RAC — *Revue de l'Art Chrétien*.

AdA — *L'Amour de l'Art*.

Mon. Piot — *Monuments et Mémoires*, Fondation Eugène Piot. Paris. Académie des Inscriptions et Belles Lettres.

Pr. Jhb. — *Jahrbuch der preussischen Kunstsammlungen*, Berlin.

Mus. Ber. — *Berliner Museen, Berichte aus den preussischen Kunstsamm-lungen* (Beiblatt zum *Jahrbuch der preussischen Kunst-sammlungen*).

ZfbK — *Zeitschrift für bildende Kunst*, Leipzig.

Rep. f. Kw. — *Repertorium für Kunstwissenschaft*.

Monatsh. f. Kw. — *Monatshefte für Kunstwissenschaft* (Leipzig 1908–1922).

Jhb. f. Kw. — *Jahrbuch für Kunstwissenschaft* (1923–1930; continuation of *Monatshefte für Kunstwissenschaft*).

ZfK — *Zeitschrift für Kunstgeschichte* (since 1932; continuation of *Repertorium für Kunstwissenschaft*, *Zeitschrift für bildende Kunst* and *Jahrbuch für Kunstwissenschaft*).

Vienna Jhb. — *Jahrbuch der kunsthistorischen Sammlungen des Allerhöchsten Kaiserhauses* (since 1919: *Jahrbuch der kunsthistorischen Sammlungen in Wien*).

Vienna Zentralkomm. — *Jahrbuch des kunsthistorischen Instituts der Zentralkommission für Denkmalpflege*, Wien.

ABBREVIATIONS OF EXHIBITIONS

BRUGES 1902   *Exposition des Primitifs flamands*, Bruges 1902 (Catalogue by W. H. James Weale).

PARIS 1904   *Exposition des Primitifs français au Pavillon de Marsan et à la Bibliothèque Nationale*, Paris 1904.

(BOUCHOT 1904)   H. Bouchot, *L'Exposition des Primitifs français, La Peinture en France sous les Valois* (Commemorative publication with 100 plates, Paris 1904).

DÜSSELDORF 1904   *Kunsthistorische Ausstellung*, Düsseldorf 1904 (Commemorative Catalogue by P. Clemen and E. Firmenich-Richartz).

BRUGES 1907   *Exposition de la Toison d'Or à Bruges*, 1907.

PARIS 1926   *Exposition du Moyen-âge*, Paris, Bibliothèque Nationale 1926 (Commemorative publication by C. Couderc, Les Enluminures des Manuscrits du Moyen-âge de la Bibliothèque Nationale, Paris 1927).

NEW YORK 1927   *Loan Exhibition of French Primitives*, New York, Kleinberger Galleries, 1927 (Cat. with preface by L. Réau).

LONDON 1927   *Exhibition of Flemish and Belgian Art, 1200–1900*, London, Burlington House, 1927.

DETROIT 1928   *A Loan Exhibition of French Gothic Art*, Detroit, Art Institute, 1928 (Catalogue by W. R. Valentiner).

LONDON 1930   *Exhibition of Italian Art, 1200–1900*, London, Burlington House, 1930.

LONDON 1932   *Exhibition of French Art, 1200–1900*, London, Burlington House, 1932.

(COMMEM. CAT.)   Commemorative Catalogue of the Exhibition of French Art, held in London, January–March, 1932, London 1933.

CHICAGO 1933/1934   *A Century of Progress*, Chicago, Art Institute. Exhibitions held in 1933 and in 1934.

PARIS, PASSION 1934   *Exposition de la Passion du Christ*, Musée du Trocadéro et Sainte Chapelle, Paris 1934.

BRUSSELS, 1935   *Exposition Universelle et Internationale de Bruxelles, 1935*, Cinq Siécles d'Art, Tome V du Catalogue, Section française, organisée par Paul Jamot et J. Dupont.

CLEVELAND 1936   *The Twentieth Anniversary Exhibition*, Art Exhibit of the Great Lakes Exhibition, Cleveland, Museum of Art, 1936.

PARIS 1937   *Chefs d'Œuvre de l'Art français*, Palais National des Arts, Paris 1937 (Catalogue with introduction by Henri Focillon).

(COMMEM. PUBL.)   Commemorative publication: Germain Bazin, Chefs d'Œuvre de l'Art français du Moyen-âge au XXe siécle, 1937.

PARIS MS. 1937   *Les plus beaux Manuscrits français du VIIIe au XVIe siècle*, Paris, Bibliothèque Nationale 1937.
(Commemorative publication: Les plus beaux manuscrits français à peintures du moyen-âge de la Bibliothèque Nationale, Arts et métiers graphiques, 1937.)

WORCESTER/PHILADELPHIA 1939   *The Worcester Philadelphia Exhibition of Flemish Painting*, Worcester, Art Museum and John G. Johnson Collection at the Philadelphia Museum of Art 1939.

TURIN 1939   *Gotico e Rinascimento in Piemonte*, Seconda Mostra d'arte a Palazzo Carignano, Torino (Catalogue by Vittorio Viale).

FLORENCE 1945   *Exhibition of French Painting in Florence* (Catalogue with introduction by B. Berenson), Florence, Palazzo Pitti, 1945.

THE HAGUE 1945   *Nederlandsche Kunst van de XVde en XVI de Eeuw, Den Haag, Mauritshuis*, September/October 1945.

ROME 1946   *Tableaux Français en Italie*, Rome, Palazzo Venezia, 1946

PARIS 1946   *Chefs d'Œuvre de la Peinture française du Louvre*, Paris, Petit Palais 1946 (Catalogue with introduction by A. Chamson).

LOUIS XII   ANNE DE BRETAGNE

Medals, executed in Lyon, in 1499, by Nicolas Leclerc and Jehan de Saint-Priest, sculptors, and Jehan Le Pére, goldsmiths, after the designs by Jean Perréal.

FIG. 24.

CATALOGUE

1. SCHOOL OF PARIS, ABOUT 1360
PORTRAIT OF KING JEAN LE BON OF FRANCE. Paris, Louvre   FIG. 11
Canvas pasted on wood and covered by gilded plaster; tempera, 66 : 44 cm. (26 : 17¼ in.)
In profile; inscribed *jehan Roy de France*.
Jean II, 1319–1364, king since 1350, here seems to be about 40 years old.
In spite of several holes the preservation can be called satisfactory. The portrait gives the impression of an excellent likeness.
There is a tradition, not entirely reliable, to the effect that the picture was painted during the King's captivity in England (1356–1359) by his court painter Girard d'Orléans who shared this captivity. The picture has tentatively been identified with a recorded portrait of Jean le Bon in the apartments of Charles V at the Hotel St. Pol, forming a polyptych together with three other portraits which represented Edward III of England, the Emperor Charles IV of Germany and the Dauphin (later Charles V of France).
The picture belonged to the Gaignières Collection at the end of the 17th century and passed to King Louis XV for the Bibliothèque Royale in 1717.
Exhibited: *Paris 1904, No. 1 (Bouchot 1904, pl. I); London 1932, No. 29 (Commem. Cat. pl. 2); Paris 1946, No. 35.*

2. SCHOOL OF PARIS, ABOUT 1375
'LE PAREMENT DE NARBONNE'. Paris, Louvre   FIG. 26
Brush drawing in grisaille on white silk (samit). 78 × 286 cm.
In the centre, the Crucifixion; above, the Church and the Synagogue, each presented by a prophet. Below, King Charles V (1337–1380) and Queen Jeanne de Bourbon (1338–1378), praying. From left to right the following scenes of the Passion: the Betrayal, the Flagellation, the Carrying of the Cross, the Entombment, the Descent to the Limbo, the Apparition to St. Mary Magdalen. Each scene is set in gothic arcades. In the borders the letter *K*, pointing to Charles as the donor. The portraits of the royal couple date the painting between 1373 and 1378, the year of the Queen's death.
The 'Parement' is the most significant specimen of the purely Parisian style. *Bouchot (GBA, janv. 1904)* proposes Jean d'Orléans as its author.
According to *Hulin de Loo (Heures de Milan, 1911, p. 11 ff.)*, the 'Master of the Parement de Narbonne' has illuminated part of the 'Heures de Milan' (fol. 87 r., Hulin, pl. V: The Trinity adored by the Duke of Berri; cf. No. 45).
The 'Parement' is said to have been found at Narbonne, in the beginning of the 19th century, by the painter Jules Boilly.
Exhibited: *Paris 1904, No. 3 (Bouchot 1904, pl. IV–VI); London 1932, No. 34; Paris 1946, No. 1.*
Reproduced: *Guiffrey Marcel Terrasse, II, pl. 53–56.*

3. SCHOOL OF PARIS, ABOUT 1360–70
A BISHOP'S MITRE. Paris, Musée de Cluny (Inv. 12924)
Drawing in grisaille on white silk (samit)
Representations of the Entombment, the Resurrection, the Apostles, etc.
Technique and Style connect the 'Mitre' with the 'Parement de Narbonne'. Both pieces replace embroidery by drawing and both serve the same purpose: to adorn a 'chapelle quotidienne', particularly during Lent.
Found in the 'Archives Nationales'.
Reproduced: *Guiffrey Marcel Terrasse, II, pl. 39; 'Entombment', reprod. Lemoisne, pl. 16.*
Exhibited: *Paris 1904, No. 2.*

4. ATTRIBUTED TO JEAN D'ARBOIS, SCHOOL OF PARIS, ABOUT 1370–80
FOUR PANELS OF A RETABLE, THE SO-CALLED RETABLE DE BESANÇON. Besançon, Musée. 142 × 72 cm. each
The Nailing to the Cross, the Crucifixion, the Entombment, the Resurrection.
These panels are so completely ruined by restoration, which began as early as the 17th century, that I have never been able to detect a trace of genuine colour on them—perhaps with the exception of the 'Nailing to the Cross', which shows a few unspoilt spots. In any case the retable cannot be considered a reliable document of early French art.
Published by *F. Mercier, RdA, 1935, I, p. 141.* He dates the pictures between 1373 and 1375, attributing them to Jean d'Arbois, a painter of the Franche-Comté.
Reproduced: *'Le Pays Comtois', Revue régionaliste, 20 juin 1935, p. 406/407; Réau, pl. 39 (The Entombment).*

5. JEAN DE BANDOL AND NICOLAS BATAILLE
THE APOCALYPSE OF ST. JOHN THE EVANGELIST. Angers, Museum of Tapestries   FIG. 3
Tapestry, wool. The entire work was originally approximately 144 m. (470 ft.) long and 5 m. (16 ft.) high. It consisted of seven pieces showing 90 pictures, of which 69 are preserved. The tapestries have undergone various extensive restorations.
Each of the seven pieces starts with the large figure of a bearded man, sitting under an architectural canopy, reading the Apocalypse or meditating on it. These men represent (according to *L. E. Lefèvre, GBA, 1925, I, p. 206–225*) the bishops or guardians of the seven churches of Asia. On the right hand of each of these *évêques* the composition is divided into two zones, showing scenes of the Apocalypse on alternately red and blue ground.
In view of the fact that the mural paintings of the period have been nearly totally destroyed and that no contemporary easel panels of a decorative character have been left, the 'Apocalypse d'Angers' is of major importance for the understanding of early French painting.
The tapestries were woven at the end of the 14th century. They were commissioned by Louis I, Duke of Anjou, about 1375 and were probably finished before 1384, the year of the Duke's death; the fourth piece in any case was finished before that date as it bears the Duke's cypher.
The artist who made the cartoons was Jean Bandol (called Hennequin de Bruges), a painter of Charles V. He took his ideas largely from illuminated manuscripts, particularly from an 'Apocalypse', now in the library at Cambrai (Ms. 422, exhibited Paris 1937, No. 756), also from a manuscript now at the Bibliothèque Nationale in Paris, lent by Charles V to his brother of Anjou. The weaving was executed by Nicolas Bataille, a Parisian 'tapissier' of renown.
The tapestries decorated at first the state rooms of the Castle of Angers and the Chapel in which was preserved the True Cross from the monastery of La Boissière. After Louis I's death they passed by heritage to his son Louis II, to Louis II's widow Yolande of Aragon and to their son, King René. René bequeathed them to the Cathedral of Angers, where they have been since 1480. Put up for public sale in 1782, the tapestries found no bidder. They were sold in the 19th century and bought back by the Bishop of Angers for 300 francs.
L. de Farcy, Histoire et Description des Tapisseries de la Cathédrale d'Angers; J. Guiffrey, Nicolas Bataille, Tapissier Parisien du XIVe siècle (Mémoires de la Société de l'Histoire de Paris et de l'Île de France, XI, 1884); Delisle, Mémoire sur les figures de l'Apocalypse, Le Puy, 1901; Ch. Urseau, Le Musée des Tapisseries d'Angerss Paris 1930; cf. Marquet de Vasselot, Bibliographie de la Tapisserie en France, Paris, 1935, p. 123–127.
Exhibited: *Paris 1904, No. 259; London 1932, No. 22; Paris 1937, No. 1267; Paris, Musée d'Art moderne, 1946, No. 1–15; Amsterdam, Rijksmuseum 1946, No. 1–3; London, Victoria and Albert Museum, 1947, No. 1–10.*

6. SCHOOL OF PARIS, ABOUT 1390
DIPTYCH, COMPOSED OF TWO GOTHIC SHUTTERS, CALLED 'THE LARGE BARGELLO DIPTYCH'. Florence, Museo Nazionale, Palazzo del Bargello (formerly Coll. Carrand)   FIG. 24, PLATES 1–3
90 : 63 cm. (35½ : 24¾ in.), each shutter 90 : 29 cm. (35½ : 11⅜ in.)
On the left Madonna and Child among Saints, on the right the Crucifixion. The two representations, embedded in a richly sculptured framework, take up less than half of the entire space. In the arcades above prophets and angels. Gold ground.

The cleaning which has just started reveals a faultless state.

The impression of the whole work is that of an architecture on a minute scale, emulating the portal of a Cathedral—it is a reminder that until the end of the 14th century architecture and sculpture were the only leading arts in France. In order to judge the 'Diptych' fairly, one should accordingly apply the standard of an 'objet d'art' rather than that of an easel painting proper. In view of this 'craftsmanlike' character, the question whether to place the 'Diptych' in the School of Paris or in that of Avignon does not seem of primary importance.
Winkler, Mus. Ber. XLIX, 1928, p. 7.

Exhibited: *Paris 1904, No. 339, suppl. (Bouchot 1904, pl. II); London 1932, No. 31 (Commem. Cat. No. 4, pl. 3); Florence 1945, No. 1; Rome 1946, No. 1.*

7. FRENCH SCHOOL, ABOUT 1400

DIPTYCH. Berlin, Deutsches Museum (No. 1620)   PLATE 19

Each shutter 34 : 26,5 cm. (13⅜ : 10½ in.).

On the left: Christ on the Cross between the Virgin and St. John. On the right: 'Le Christ de Pitié' (the Man of Sorrows) adored by a Cistercian (Augustine ?) monk, who is presented by the Virgin. Ornamented gold ground in relievo.

Winkler, (Mus. Ber. 1928, p. 7) connects the picture with the Large Bargello Diptych (No. 6) and attributes both works to the same master, whom he locates in the South of France. I think that Sienese features are even more predominant in the Berlin than in the Bargello panels and that the connection is not striking.

The picture is reported to come from Southern French possession.

Exhibited: *London 1932, No. 20 (Commem. Cat. No. 7, pl. 1); Paris, 1937, No. 5.*

8. FRENCH SCHOOL, ABOUT 1390

PIETÀ; THE SO-CALLED 'SMALL CIRCULAR PIETÀ'. Paris, Louvre (No. 3158)   PLATES 4, 175

Total diameter 22,7 cm. (9 in.); painted part 16,7 cm. (6⅝ in.) Ornamented gold ground.

On the reverse, on red: THE THREE NAILS OF THE CRUCIFIXION in a crown of thorns

The colours are brilliant and variegated, like a bunch of flowers. Blue and gold prevail, besides a light red, a light olive green and a light purple. The preservation is excellent.

This picture as well as the small rectangular 'Entombment' (No. 9) and several other paintings about 1390/1400 have mostly been attributed of late to the School of Dijon, thus constituting a definite 'Franco-Flemish' sphere as opposed to the purely Parisian one of the Parement de Narbonne. Since all these works, however, show in the first place the influence of Parisian miniature painting, I think that one should not make too subtle distinctions—the ensemble of these little panels anyhow forms the 'École de Paris'.

Formerly Coll. C. Benoit; in the Louvre since 1918.

Introduced by *P. Durrieu, Une Pitié de Notre Seigneur, Mon. Piot, t. XXIII, 1918; G. Brière, Un nouveau Primitif Français au Musée du Louvre, G.B.A., 1919.*

Exhibited: *Paris 1946, No. 5.*

9. FRENCH SCHOOL, ABOUT 1380–90

THE ENTOMBMENT. Paris, Louvre (No. 997)   PLATE 5

32 : 24 cm. (12⅝ : 9½ in.) On ornamented gold ground.

This panel, which has rightly been linked with the 'Small circular Pietà' (No. 8) is also usually listed as 'School of Dijon'. It was formerly attributed—without apparent reason—to Jean d'Orléans. The colours are remarkably less brilliant than those of the Small circular Pietà.

Exhibited: *Paris 1904, No. 4 (Bouchot 1904, pl. VIII); Paris 1946, No. 6.*

10. FRENCH SCHOOL, ABOUT 1400

'PIETÀ' WITH A PRAYING MONK. Formerly Berlin, Private Collection

18,5 : 21,5 cm. On ornamented gold ground.   FIG. 25

This rather overrated picture, which I happened to know before its restoration, shows in its composition certain similarities to the 'Petite Pitié ronde' (No. 8), but its original quality is poorer and it cannot be compared with the established masterpieces of this group.

The picture came from Spain to the German art market about 1920; it was first in the Weiler Coll. (there mentioned by *Winkler, Altniederländische Malerei, 1924, p. 29*), later in the Berstl Collection.

Reproduced: *Sterling fig. 50, p 52; Jacques (Rep. A 14th cent. 27, pl. 30)*

Fig. 25 (Before Cleaning)   ⟨ Cat. No. 10 ⟩

11. SCHOOL OF PARIS, ABOUT 1390–1400

DEATH, ASSUMPTION AND CORONATION OF THE VIRGIN. Paris, Louvre   PLATE 8

Drawing, pen and ink wash on vellum, 65 : 32,7 cm. (25⅝ : 12⅞ in.)

This large and most impressive sheet, which at first sight may look Italian, is certainly a work of the School of Paris. It is in all probability the model for a stained glass window.

In the 17th century the drawing was the property of Filippo Baldinucci, the Florentine art historian, whose collection was acquired by the Louvre in 1806. Attributed to Beauneveu by *Durrieu (Un dessin du Musée du Louvre, Mon. Piot t. I, 1894, pp. 179–202, pl. XXV/XXVI); R. de Lasteyrie, Mon. Piot, t. III, 1896, pp. 71–80; Lavallée, p. 60, No. 14, pl. VII.*

Exhibited: *Paris 1904, No. 18; London 1927 No. 513; London 1932, No. 625; Paris 1937, No. 427.*

12. FRENCH SCHOOL, ABOUT 1390–1400

FOUR APOSTLES (STS. PETER, THOMAS, JAMES AND BARTHOLOMEW) Paris, Louvre (Inv. 09833)

Drawings, ink and water colour (yellow, light blue and light green) on vellum, 19 : 13 cm.

Some critics maintain the Italian origin of these drawings and place them in the neighbourhood of Michelino da Besozzo.

From the Baldinucci Collection.

Reproduced: *L. Dimier, G.B.A. 1936, p. 228/229, Figs. 13–16 ; St. Peter reprod. K. T. Parker, North Italian Drawings of the Quattrocento, 1927, pl. 3.*

Exhibited: *Paris 1904, No. 340/341.*

13. FRENCH SCHOOL, END OF 14TH CENTURY

STATUE OF THE VIRGIN. Coll. Mrs. Gutekunst, London

The base is supported by a bracket formed of a crouching angel.

Drawing, pen and ink, outlines with ink wash, 13,6 : 4,5 cm.

A companion drawing is in Rotterdam (No. 14).

From the Collections Storck (Milan, 1800), Prayer, von Lanna (Prague).

Reproduced: *Vasari Society, 2nd series, vol. IX, 1928, p. 13.*

Exhibited: *London 1932, No. 632 (Commem. Cat., No. 531).*

14. FRENCH SCHOOL, END OF 14TH CENTURY

STATUE OF A YOUTHFUL KING. Rotterdam, Boymans Museum (formerly Koenigs Coll.)

The base is supported by a bracket formed of a crouching angel.

Drawing, pen and ink, outlines with ink wash, 13,5 : 4,5 cm.

Companion piece to No. 13. From the Storck, Prayer and Lanna Collections.

Vasari Society (see No. 13).

Exhibited: *Rotterdam, Boymans Museum 1934/1935, No. 2; Paris 1937, No. 436.*

15. SCHOOL OF PARIS, ABOUT 1390

DIPTYCH: THE SO-CALLED 'SMALL BARGELLO DIPTYCH'. Florence, Museo Nazionale, Palazzo del Bargello (No. 33)   FIG. 27, PLATE 16

Each shutter 50 : 31 cm. (19¾ : 12¼ in.) Gold ground.

Left shutter: Adoration of the Magi. Right Shutter: Crucifixion with St. John the Baptist and St. Catherine. On the lower part of the Virgin's throne and on the reverse are unidentified coats-of-arms.

The painting, which is in an extraordinarily good state—even the gold seems perfect—shines in the cheerful colours of the Parisian 'enlumineurs'. Typical illuminator's shades are the very light rose of St. Catherine's mantle and the equally light green of St. John's wrapping. Christ's shroud is light blue, not the habitual white, the Virgin is in blue. A colour which might seem far too 'advanced' for early painting but which is usual for illumination is the 'change-ant' violet of St. Joseph's dress (left shutter).

The Diptych has been rightly compared to the 'Parement de Narbonne', thus setting it within the Parisian entourage.

Coloured reproduction: *Jacques, pl. VII (detail pl. 9).*

Exhibited: *Paris 1937, No. 3; Florence 1945, No. I bis; Rome 1946, No. 2.*

16. SCHOOL OF PARIS, ABOUT 1390

ANNUNCIATION. Santa Barbara, Cal., Coll. Arthur Sachs   PLATE 17

34,5 : 25,4 cm. (13⅝ : 10 in.) Gold ground

The Virgin is sitting on a canopied throne; on her left the angel with large peacock's wings. The infant Christ emanates from God the Father in a ray of light. On the reverse a coat-of-arms, with four lions rampant towards the left, recalling the lions of the house of Plantagenet. The reverse is also gilded and richly decorated with punch work.

This jewel-like little panel is in a perfect state; even the frame—with a delicate sculptured tendril in the moulding—is unspoilt.

When I first saw the picture—in 1925 in a private room of the Castle of Dessau—it never was in the Collections of the 'Gotisches Haus, Woerlitz'—it had the name of 'Duccio' affixed to it, but in spite of the grand name it had not found any notice. *Winkler (Belvedere XI, 1927, p. 6)* introduced it into literature, linking it convincingly with the 'Small Bargello Diptych' (No. 15). He even suggested that this Annunciation and the Bargello shutters may have belonged to the same altarpiece, although the sizes are different. As the Diptych has been definitely placed in the School of Paris, the 'Sachs Annunciation' should also be assigned to the Paris school and not to that of Avignon, as suggested by several critics.

U.M., p. 70.

Exhibited: *New York 1927, No. 4; Detroit 1928, No. 1; London 1932, No. 10 (Commem. Cat. No. 6, pl. 4)*

17. SCHOOL OF PARIS, ABOUT 1400

THREE REPRESENTATIONS OF THE VIRGIN AND CHILD. Basle, Print Room of the Öffentliche Kunstsammlung   PLATE 15

Drawing on greenish white vellum, 11,5 : 20,9 cm. (4½ : 8¼ in.)

Fig. 26   ⟨ Cat. No. 2 ⟩   FIG. 27   ⟨ Cat. No. 15 ⟩

First introduced by *Daniel Burckhardt* (*Pr. Jhb.* 1906, *p.* 184) as 'French-Basle Master about 1405'. *Wescher* (*OMD* 1937, *pl.* 18) points to the similarity of the Virgin on the right-hand side with Broederlam's Virgin in the 'Flight into Egypt' (No. 18).

I should like to draw attention to a likeness which seems to me more striking: that with the 'Adoration of the Magi', left shutter of the 'Small Bargello Diptych' (No. 15). The connection with this work would locate the Basle drawing also rather in the Paris than in the Dijon school.

⟨18.⟩ *MELCHIOR BROEDERLAM*
Four Scenes from the Life of the Virgin Mary. Dijon, Musée
On two panels. 1,62 : 1,30 m. each.

Each shutter is divided into two compartments. Left shutter: Annunciation and Visitation. Right shutter: Presentation in the Temple and Flight into Egypt.

On each panel the left side shows architectural interiors, the right side open landscapes.

The shutters belong to an altarpiece, the centre part of which was a sculptured retable. The altarpiece was commissioned by Duke Philippe the Bold of Burgundy and executed by two artists: Jacques de Baërze, who carved the sculptural centre in gilded wood, and Melchior Broederlam, who painted the shutters. It was destined for the Chartreuse de Champmol, Philippe's foundation. The work was done between 1394 and 1399 in Ypres.

As the 'Retable de Champmol' has luckily remained in Dijon ever since its installation, it has never suffered the unstable fate of most works of the period, and the preservation on the whole is excellent.

The entire work was executed not only by Flemish born artists—a fact we do not regard as decisive—but on territory that had always been and remained 'Flemish' in the stricter sense of the word. Moreover, the character of the paintings points rather to the purely Flemish than to the Franco-Flemish section. The general aspect is more naturalistic, the figures more ample, the landscape more spatial as compared to the 'School of Paris', although it is known that Broederlam was in Paris, between 1390 and 1393, where he certainly experienced the influence of Parisian court art.

C. Monget, '*La Chartreuse de Dijon*', 3 vol. 1898–1905. Reproduced: *Fierens-Gevaert, pl. XVI; Dupont, p. 16/17;* '*Le Musée de Dijon*' (*Mercier*), 1929 (with reproductions of the painted and the sculptured parts); *Réau, pl. 35/36*.

⟨19.⟩ *Formerly attributed to MELCHIOR BROEDERLAM*
Three Scenes: Nativity, Resurrection and, on the reverse, St. Christopher. Antwerp, Musée Mayer van den Bergh (No. 374)
33 : 21 cm. each. Fonds 'gaufrés' in gold.

These panels are part of a polyptych (Tabernacle? Châsse?), further parts of which are in the Walters Art Gallery, Baltimore (No. 20).

The connection with the 'Retable de Champmol' (No. 18) is not sufficiently obvious to secure the former attribution to Broederlam—it was mainly based on the tradition that these panels also come from the Chartreuse de Champmol. The style, although nearer to the Paris School than in the case of the 'Retable', is again more Flemish than Franco-Flemish and the considerations which led us to keep the shutters of the 'Retable' out of the purely French material should be equally applied here.

Formerly Chartreuse de Champmol, Dijon; Coll. Micheli, Paris.

Jacques (*Rep. A. 14th cent.* 26) thinks of a painter of the Hainault. *E. Michel, G.B.A.,* 1924, II, *p.* 41 *and* 58.

Reproduced: *Cat. de la Coll. Mayer van den Bergh* 1904, *No.* 1; *Fierens-Gevaert, p.* 32, *pl. XX; Dupont, p.* 18; *Réau, pl.* 5.

Exhibited: *Antwerp* 1930, *No.* 31; *London* 1932, *No.* 17 (*Commem. Cat. No.* 14, *pl.* 5); *Paris* 1937, *No.* 6.

⟨20.⟩ *Formerly attributed to MELCHIOR BROEDERLAM*
Three Scenes: Annunciation, Crucifixion and, on the reverse, Baptism of Christ. Baltimore, Walters Art Gallery
33 : 21 cm. each. Fonds 'gaufrés' in gold.

These panels belong to the same altarpiece as No. 19.

Formerly Chartreuse de Champmol, Dijon; Coll. Cuvillier, Niort.

Reproduced: *Bouchot* 1904, *pl. XX; Sterling, p.* 38, *fig.* 26–28.

⟨21.⟩ *Attributed to the FRANCO-FLEMISH SCHOOL, late* 14th *century*
Small Tabernacle, with Shutters, representing Nativity, Adoration of the Magi, Presentation in the Temple, Massacre of the Innocents, Flight into Egypt. Antwerp, Musée Mayer van den Bergh (No. 359)

Each shutter 57 : 17 cm. Gold ground. In the centre a niche destined for a sculptured statue.

Usually attributed to the School of Broederlam, but still more distant from the French circuit than the Retable de Champmol (No. 18) and of an earlier date (before 1400). The paintings have been rightly compared to the so-called 'Cardon Polyptych' (No. 22).

According to tradition formerly in the Chartreuse de Champmol.

Reproduced: *Catalogue de la Coll. Mayer van den Bergh* 1904; *Barnes, p.* 366 (*text p.* 361).

⟨22.⟩ *Formerly attributed to the SCHOOL OF PARIS or to the FRANCO-FLEMISH SCHOOL, about* 1400
Polyptych, the so-called 'Cardon Polyptych'. Paris, Louvre (No. 3157)
46 : 21 cm.

Scenes from the life of the Virgin and the Childhood of Christ, on shutters belonging to a little altar with a statuette of the Virgin.

These paintings have similarities with works of the School of Paris only in so far as they belong to the 'style international'. They are not purely French but rather 'Franco-Rhenish'. Some details—stylistic as well as iconographic—point to the region of the Middle Rhine.

Reproduced: *Lemoisne, pl.* 25 (*text p.* 59); *Fierens-Gevaert pl. XXI/XXII.*

Exhibited: *Bruges* 1902, *No.* 3; *Paris* 1904, *No.* 17 (*Bouchot* 1904, *pl. XI*), then in the Cardon Collection.

⟨23.⟩ *Attributed to the FRANCO-RHENISH SCHOOL, about* 1410
Presentation in the Temple. Merion, Pa., Barnes Foundation (No. 797)
38,1 : 19,7 cm. (15 : 7¾ in.) Gold ground.

The picture is in a perfect state. It has been rightly compared to the 'Cardon Polyptych' (No. 22). Its colouring and the use of gold are, however, nearer to French treatment than in the case of the 'Polyptych'.

Formerly Private Collection, Genova.

Reproduced: *Barnes, p.* 161 (*text p.* 156).

⟨24.⟩ *Formerly attributed to the SCHOOL OF PARIS, about* 1390
Madonna enthroned, adored by a kneeling Bishop, the so-called 'Madone aux Églantines' (Virgin with the Wild Roses). Paris, Louvre (Jnv. 2563)
35 : 21 cm. Ornamented gold ground.

The attribution to the School of Paris is not convincing. On the whole, the types seem nearer to the Bohemian than to the French School. The Bishop has a marked resemblance to Tommaso da Modena (cf. paintings in Treviso, San Niccolò). As Tommaso worked in Karlstein, this would lead again in the direction of Bohemia.

Reproduced: *Jacques, pl.* 11 (*Rep. A. 14th cent.* 11).

⟨25.⟩ *Formerly attributed to the SOUTHERN FRENCH SCHOOL, about* 1400
Two Panels: Adoration of the Magi; Death of the Virgin. New York, Pierpont Morgan Library
29 : 18,5 cm. each. Gold ground.

These pictures, formerly generally located in the South of France, are now mostly believed to belong rather to the Bohemian School.

Formerly Coll. F. Lippmann, Berlin.

Roger Fry, Burl. Mag., June 1903, *p.* 90; *Lemoisne, p.* 61 (*ill. pl.* 22); *Bazin, No.* 26 (*detail*); *Labande, pl. XVII–XVIII.*

Exhibited: *Paris* 1904, *No.* 5 *and* 6 (*Bouchot* 1904, *pl. XV*).

⟨26.⟩ *Formerly attributed to the FRENCH SCHOOL, late* 14th *century*
Madonna and Child. Boston, Museum of Fine Arts
8,5 : 6 cm. Gold ground.

This charming tiny Madonna has been called 'Burgundian' or 'Provençal'. It is strongly influenced by Italian art (Matteo da Viterbo, etc.). Friedlaender connects the picture convincingly with the panels in the Morgan Collection (No. 25) and I am accordingly inclined to regard both the Boston Madonna and the Morgan panels as Bohemian.

Bulletin of the Museum of Fine Arts, Boston, June 1935; Reproduced: *Bazin, No.* 27.

Exhibited: *London* 1932, *No.* 1 (*Commem. Cat. No.* 2, *pl.* 4).

⟨27.⟩ *Formerly attributed to the FRENCH SCHOOL, about* 1400
The Virgin with the Writing Desk. Paris, Louvre (No. 3156)
48 : 29 cm.

The character of this painting is obviously not French. Among the various

suggestions that have been made in regard to its origin—Cologne, Spain, Bohemia —the last, put forward by *Jacques (Rep. B. 14th cent.* 10) seems the most plausible (perhaps rather 'Austro-Bohemian').
Reproduced: *Guiffrey Marcel, I, pl. III; Lemoisne, pl.* 28 (*text p.* 62); *Barnes, p.* 368.

⟨28.⟩ *Formerly attributed to the FRANCO-BURGUNDIAN SCHOOL, about* 1400
The Holy Trinity with Angels. London, National Gallery (No. 3662)
116 : 115 cm. Gold ground.
Neither Burgundian nor Rhenish, as has been suggested lately, but certainly Austrian and belonging to a painter in the entourage of the 'Master of St. Lambert'.
Formerly in a Collection in Florence.
Reproduced: *Nat. Gall. Ill., p.* 128; *Beiträge zur Geschichte der deutschen Kunst,* I, 1924, *p.* 22 (*Hugelshofer*).

⟨29.⟩ *Formerly attributed to the FRENCH SCHOOL, about* 1390
Triptych in Quatrefoil Form: The Trinity; on the Wings the Four Evangelists. Berlin, Deutsches Museum (No. 1688)
Centre, 36 : 32 cm. Wings, 36 : 16 cm. each.
In the later editions of the Berlin Catalogue ascribed to the Netherlandish School. Certainly not French, not even Burgundian; perhaps German.
From the Collection of Consul Weber, Hamburg; according to tradition originally in the Chartreuse de Champmol.
Reproduced: *Berlin, Ill. Cat.* 1929, *p.* 223.
Exhibited: *Bruges* 1902, *No.* 2; *Paris* 1904, *No.* 8 (*Bouchot* 1904, *pl. VII*).

⟨30.⟩ *Formerly attributed to the FRANCO-BURGUNDIAN SCHOOL*
The Childhood of Christ. Berlin, Deutsches Museum
31 : 25 cm. (including old frame).
The picture has been connected with the Broederlam retable (No. 18). It is, however, neither French nor Burgundian but German, about 1405.
Formerly Figdor Collection, Vienna (3rd Figdor Sale, Berlin 1930, No. 34, with reprod. in Cat.)
B. Kurth, ZfbK XXXIII, 1922, *p.* 20, *ill.* 8; *F. Winkler, Altdeutsche Tafelmalerei* 1941, *p.* 49: 'Oberdeutscher (?) Meister'.
Exhibited: *London* 1932, *No.* 9.

⟨31.⟩ *Formerly attributed to the PARISIAN SCHOOL, about* 1400
The Wilton Diptych. London, National Gallery (No. 4451)
Two panels, 47 : 30 cm. each.
Left panel: Richard II (1367–1400, King of England since 1377) with the patron Saints Edmund, Edward the Confessor and John the Baptist. On the reverse: a shield with the arms of Edward the Confessor impaled with those of the Kingdom.
Right panel: The Virgin stands holding the Child, attended by eleven angels wearing wreaths of roses, collars of broomcods and badges of crouching harts. On the reverse: A white hart, the badge of Richard II, probably derived from his mother, the 'Fair Maid of Kent'.
The preservation is excellent, only the left reverse picture has suffered. The colours are bright and brilliant—the right obverse particularly conspicuous, being confined to blue, gold and white. The gold ground shows different patterns on each panel.
The diptych was usually dated about 1377, the year of the King's coronation, but *Miss M. V. Clarke (Burl. Mag. LVIII,* 1931, *p.* 283 *ff.*) has proved conclusively by heraldic evidence that the date cannot be previous to 1395/1399 and that the painting is connected with a Crusading Order of the Passion (the Child's halo is ornamented with symbols of the Passion). The later date seems stylistically correct. There still remains the old doubt regarding the diptych's country of origin. The attribution to the French School, which had been taken for granted of late, is not really satisfactory as the analogies that have been quoted—Beauneveu's 'prophets' or Jacquemart de Hesdin's pages in the 'Très belles Heures' (No. 46)—demonstrate nothing more than the usual similarities within the 'style international'. On the other hand, the English King, the English Saints and arms betray an obviously thorough knowledge of English concerns. Moreover, the types of the angels look decidedly English, nearly Pre-Raphaelite, quite apart from a general trend towards the purely ornamental, which is alien to the finer examples of the School of Paris. In confronting the diptych with the French specimens that have been set down for comparison one

realizes the fundamental difference between the plasticity of the French works and the plane, linear treatment of the diptych. The authorship of an English artist must be seriously reconsidered. I am glad to find a new supporter for the diptych's English origin in *Professor Th. Bodkin (Gallery Books No.* 16, 1947) who bases his argumentation convincingly on stylistic as well as on heraldic and hagiologic arguments.
The diptych has been engraved by Wenzel Hollar in 1639, when it was in the Collection of Charles I. It is first mentioned in the possession of the Earls of Pembroke, Wilton House, in 1724 and remained in the Wilton House Collection until it was purchased for the National Gallery in 1929.
Reproduced: *Bouchot* 1904, *pl. XIX; Nat. Gall. Ill.* 1937, *p.* 126–128.
For all literature and further references to reproductions see Davies 1946, *p.* 46–49.

⟨32.⟩ *ENGLISH ARTIST, about* 1390; *formerly attributed to ANDRÉ BEAUNEVEU*
Portrait of King Richard II (1367–1400). London, Westminster Abbey
214 : 110 cm.
He wears an ermine cape over a red robe, and a blue under-robe powdered with crowned 'R's. The gold background is not original. The picture has been frequently repainted and restored.
Possibly painted to commemorate the King's visit to Westminster Abbey in 1390.
S. C. Cockerell has attributed the picture to André Beauneveu (*Burl. Mag. vol. X, Nov.* 1906, *reprod. p.* 130). The remark which was supposed to support the attribution, made by Froissart (Chroniques, 1390) that 'maistre André Beauneveu' left 'tant de bons ouvraiges', some of which have remained 'au royaume d'Angleterre', is rather vague, and English authorship seems to be more probable than French. In its present state the picture is rather a heraldic relic than a reliable document of 14th-century painting.
Engraved 1718 by Vertue, 1786 by Carter.
Reproduced: *Michel III,* 1, *p.* 315, *fig.* 170.
Exhibited: *London* 1866 (*National Portrait Exhibition*); *London* 1909, *Burlington Fine Arts Club (Early English Portraiture); London* 1923, *Royal Academy (Exhibition of British Primitive Painting, No.* 30); *London* 1930, *Victoria and Albert Mus. (English Mediaeval Art, No.* 403); *London* 1932, *No.* 30.

33. SCHOOL OF AVIGNON, ABOUT 1390
CHRIST CARRYING THE CROSS, WITH TWO DONORS. Paris, Louvre
Tempera on vellum, 38,5 : 28,5 cm. (15⅛ : 11¼ in.).   PLATE 9
Although the colours have lost something of their original brilliance, the impression of the colour harmony, in which blue and white prevail, is remarkable. The composition recalls the little panel of the same subject by Simone Martini, also in the Louvre.
Acquired from the London trade in 1930 (P. M. Turner).
Reproduced in colours: *Jacques, pl. XLII; L'École Provençale, Trésors,* 1944 (*text by Bazin*).
Exhibited: *Paris* 1946, *No.* 4.

34. SCHOOL OF AVIGNON, END OF 14TH CENTURY
THE 'RETABLE DE THOUZON'. Paris, Louvre
Two panels. 126 : 113 cm. each. Gold ground.
1. Right wing: St. Andreas, at the request of the inhabitants of the town of Nicea, expels seven demons, who escape in the form of seven wolves. On the right St. Sebastian dressed as a knight. The gate of Nicea, before which the miracle takes place, is supposed to be the gate of the Fort S. André at Villeneuve-lès-Avignon, flanked by two towers.
2. Left wing: St. Andreas, praying, under the porch of a burning house. On the left a female Saint, standing—perhaps S. Claire.
The pictures are not in a perfect state.
Under the influence of Sienese painting, but rather provincialized and certainly Southern French, not Italian (to be compared with the earlier frescoes in Villeneuve, Chartreuse du Val de Bénédiction).
Formerly Castle of Thouzon, Thor near Avignon; Coll. Comte de Demandolx-Dedons, Marseilles.
A. Pérate, Le Retable de Thouzon, GBA 1924. Reproduced: *Guiffrey Marcel, I, pl.* 11/12; *Guiffrey Marcel Terrasse, II, pl.* 13/14; *Labande, pl. XIV–XVI; Réau, pl.* 13, *etc.* Reproduced in colours: *L'École Provençale, Trésors,* 1944.
Exhibited: *Paris* 1946, *No.* 2/3.

35. SCHOOL OF PROVENCE, ABOUT 1400

'LE BIENHEUREUX PIERRE DE LUXEMBOURG', PRESENTING A DONOR
TO THE VIRGIN. Worcester, U.S.A., Art Museum   PLATE 10
54 : 42 cm. (21¼ : 16¼ in.).

On the right the Virgin enthroned, on the left the Saint and the small-sized donor,
both in strict profile. Above the Saint is his coat-of-arms.

Pierre de Luxembourg, Cardinal at the age of 15, died in 1387, only 18 years old.
He was not beatified until 1527, but the official request for his canonization was
made in 1389 which would make possible his representation as a Saint on a
picture of the early 15th century.

The style is particularly near to Sienese art and happens to be even nearer to the
Quattrocento of Siena (Giovanni di Paolo, etc.) than to the great early period.
The possibility of an altogether later date for the picture should therefore not be
ruled out.

Bulletin of the Worcester Art Museum XIV, April 1923, p. 22-25.
Exhibited: *Chicago 1933, No. 4; Paris 1937, No. 7.*

36. THE MASTER OF THE 'HEURES DU MARÉCHAL DE BOUCICAUT'

'LES HEURES DU MARÉCHAL DE BOUCICAUT'. Paris, Musée Jacquemart-André

Jean II le Meingre, Maréchal de Boucicaut (1365-1421), commissioned the
manuscript, which was probably executed after 1409 when Boucicaut returned
from the Middle-East.

The Master has been convincingly identified with Jacques Coëne, who is known
to have specialized in architectural drawing. This seems a particularly good argument in favour of the identification, considering the interest in architecture that
becomes evident in the present *Hours*.

According to tradition, the manuscript was at one time in the possession of
Diane de Poitiers.

*P. Durrieu, 'Le Maître des Heures du Maréchal de Boucicaut', RdA 1906, t. XIX,
p. 401-415; t. XX, p. 21-35; Durrieu, GBA 1912, II, p. 84-96; RAC, t. LXIII,
1913, p. 151; t. LXIV, 1914, p. 31.*
Exhibited: *Paris 1904, Ms. No. 86; Paris 1937, No. 771.*

37. THE MASTER OF THE 'HEURES DU MARÉCHAL DE BOUCICAUT' OR HIS STUDIO

THE PARABLE OF THE RICH MAN AND THE POOR LAZARUS. Formerly
Coll. Engel-Gros, Château de Ripaille, Lac Léman   PLATE 7
39 : 31 cm. (15⅜ : 12¼ in.).

The little panel has been attributed to the master—or his studio—by *Grete Ring*
(GBA mars 1938, p. 156 ff., fig. 5/6) who compared it with the miniatures of the
'Houres' (No. 36) and other manuscripts of the same workshop. It seems in
keeping with the character of the master, who is of primary importance for the
development of French illumination, that he should also have adopted the progressive medium of easel painting, and it would not be surprising if more material
in this manner should come to light.

Catalogue of the Engel-Gros Collection (text by P. Ganz), 1925, vol. II, pl. 68.

38. THE MASTER OF THE 'HEURES DU MARÉCHAL DE BOUCICAUT', ABOUT 1412.

DEDICATION MINIATURE WITH A PORTRAIT OF JEAN SANS PEUR,
DUKE OF BURGUNDY, Paris, Bibl. Nat. (Ms. franç. 2810).   FIG. 9.
The Duke is being presented with a manuscript by J. Hayton.
Page inserted in the *Livre des Merveilles du Monde*

Dvořak, 'Das Rätsel der Brüder van Eyck', Vienna Jhb. XXIV, 1904, p. 306.
Exhibited: *Paris 1904, Ms. No. 63 (Bouchot 1904, pl. XXVII).*

⟨39.⟩ *Wrongly attributed to the Master of the Heures du Maréchal de Boucicaut,*
RHENISH SCHOOL, about 1400

*Triptych: Glorification of St. Mary; on the Wings St. Jerome and St. Augustin
(reverse, St. Paul and John the Evangelist).* Bonn, Provincial Museum
Wings 88 : 37 cm. each.

The figures of standing Saints on the wings have been ascribed to the master by
Durrieu (Les Arts Anciens de Flandre II, p. 20, with ill.). They are, however, not
French but German (Rhenish).
Exhibited: *Düsseldorf 1904 (Commem. Cat., p. 3/4).*

40. FRENCH SCHOOL, ABOUT 1400-1410

A LADY WITH A DOG AND A FALCON. Paris, Louvre (No. 20692;
Cat. Reiset, Collections étrangères 635)   PLATE 12
Pen and water-colour on vellum, 17,5 : 13,2 cm. (6⅞ : 5⅛ in.)

This drawing is a typical example of the 'style international', which makes it
difficult to place. As it corresponds, however, closely to French tapestries, it
seems reasonable to include it in the French school.

The figure of the lady recurs on the tapestry 'The Offering of the Heart' (No. 41).
The same subject is treated in a drawing in the Albertina, Vienna—there attributed—with reserve—to Pisanello (*Degenhart, Pisanello, 32-A, 'Studi'*). The
Vienna drawing is certainly Italian, derived from French drawings in the manner
of the Louvre example.

Reproduced: *Popham, Drawings of the early Flemish School, 1926, No. 1 (Franco-
Flemish School about 1410/20).*

41. SCHOOL OF ARRAS, ABOUT 1410

THE OFFERING OF THE HEART. Paris, Louvre, Duvillier Bequest (1883)
Tapestry.   PLATE 11
A lady sitting with a falcon on her hand calls a dog which bounds towards her.
A young courtier presents her with a heart, which he balances between two
fingers of his right hand. (Compare No. 40).
Woven in the North, probably in Arras.
Exhibited: *London 1947, Victoria and Albert Museum, No. 11.*

42. ANDRÉ BEAUNEVEU

PSALTER. Paris, Bibl. Nat. (Ms. fr. 13091)   PLATE 13-14
Illuminated for the Duc de Berri, before 1402.
24 Grisailles, representing the Evangelists, Apostles and Prophets.
The figures, clad in white, are set before coloured backgrounds, some of them
on pure red.

The authorship of Beauneveu, the sculptor-illuminator, is attested by a note in
the Inventory of the Duke's Manuscripts, of 1402: 'Psautier, escript en latin et
françois, très richement enluminé, où il y a plusieurs ystoires au commencement
de la main de maistre André Beaunepveu'. The 24 pages have a sculptural, almost
monumental aspect, in spite of their small size and delicate execution, and it
seems reasonable to regard them as works of an artist also employed in carving
statues.

Further miniatures of the manuscript show the style of Jacquemart de Hesdin. The
secretary of the Duke, Jean Flamel, has made an entry on a loose sheet of the
manuscript: 'Ce psautier qui est en Latin et en François est à Jehan filz du roy de
France Duc de Berri . . . Flamel.'

*Waagen, Kunstwerke und Künstler in Paris, III, 1839, p. 335; P. Durrieu, 'Les minia-
tures d'André Beauneveu', Le Manuscrit 1894, I, p. 51-56, 83-95; De Lasteyrie, 'Les
miniatures d'André Beauneveu et Jacquemart de Hesdin', Mon. Piot 1896, t. III.*
Exhibited: *Paris 1904, Ms. No. 67; Paris 1926, No. 74; Paris 1937, Ms. No. 101.*

43. JACQUEMART DE HESDIN

LES GRANDES HEURES DU DUC DE BERRI. Paris, Bibl. Nationale
(Ms. lat. 919)

This manuscript was completed in 1409, according to a note by Jean Flamel,
secretary of the Duc Jean de Berri. It is described in an Inventory of the Duke's,
of 1413 as follows: 'Une très grans moult belles et riches Heures très notablement
enluminées et historiées de grans histoires de la main de Jacquemart de Hesdin et
autres ouvriers de Monseigneur.' Another Inventory indicates 'Les Belles Grandes
Heures de Monseigneur qu' on appelle les Très Riches Heures'.

The manuscript has suffered, the first pages are damaged by water and the 'grans
histoires' mentioned in the Inventory have disappeared, probably as early as
towards the end of the 15th century. Nevertheless we can safely assume that
Jacquemart also collaborated on a number of the smaller miniatures, and the
manuscript thus keeps its significance as containing documented works by the
master. Other miniatures of the book are by the Master of the Maréchal de Boucicaut (cf. No. 36).

*Waagen, Kunstwerke und Künstler in Paris III, 1839, p. 338; Delisle, Bibliothèque de
l'École des Chartes LVII, 1896, p. 263; V. Leroquais, Les Livres d'Heures de la
Bibliothèque Nationale I, 1927, p. 9 ff.*
Exhibited: *Paris 1904, Ms. No. 68; Paris 1926, No. 48; Paris 1937, Ms. No. 102.*

44. JACQUEMART DE HESDIN

'LES PETITES HEURES DU DUC DE BERRI'. Paris, Bibl. Nat. (Ms. lat. 18014)

Attributed to the master by comparison with the 'Grandes Heures' (No. 43). The manuscript was probably executed earlier than the 'Grandes Heures', about 1390. The pages of the Calendar follow the model of the 'Bréviaire de Belleville' by Jean Pucelle (School of Paris, previous to 1343).

Leroquais, Les Livres d'Heures de la Bibliothèque Nationale II, p. 175–187.
Exhibited: Paris 1904, Ms. No. 69; Paris 1926, No. 42; Paris 1937, Ms. No. 103.

45. JACQUEMART DE HESDIN AND CO-OPERATORS

'LES TRÈS BELLES HEURES DE NOTRE-DAME' DU DUC DE BERRI. Paris, Baron Maurice de Rothschild (formerly Adolphe de Rothschild)

The so-called 'Paris fragment' of the Hours, the other parts of which are famous under the names of the 'Heures de Turin' and 'Heures de Milan'. The Paris fragment shows mostly pages by Jacquemart de Hesdin and his co-operators and followers. It was published by Durrieu (Société franç. de reprod. de Manuscrits à peinture, 1922). The 'Heures de Turin' (Durrieu, 1902) and the 'Heuresde Milan' (Hulin, 1911) show among others miniatures attributed to the van Eycks.

46. JACQUEMART DE HESDIN

TWO PAGES FROM THE 'TRÈS BELLES HEURES DU DUC DE BERRI'. Brussels, Bibliothèque Royale (Ms. 11060, fol. 10/11)   PLATES 21–22

On the left (fol. 10) Jean de Berri as donor, kneeling in adoration, presented by Sts. John and Andrew. On the right (fol. 11) the Madonna enthroned.

The pages are grisailles, emulating sculpture. On the left page the figures are set before a blue fonds with tendril ornaments; the floor shows a pattern of red and yellow squares. The faces are delicately modelled in various shades of grey, the hair is coloured. On the right page the face of the Virgin has a tinge of pink, her eyes are blue, her hair light blonde; a red golden brocade is spread over the stone-grey throne. The floor shows the same red and yellow squares but the background is different: terracotta-red with a pattern of angels.

Executed about or shortly before 1402, according to an entry in the Duc de Berri's Inventory of this date: 'Très belles Heures très richement enluminées et ystoriées de la main de Jacquemart de Odin (Hesdin)'.

The citation has been interpreted in different ways. Since the present, the first and principal illuminated pages are certainly by another hand than the rest of the manuscript, Jacquemart de Hesdin has been made responsible either for them or for the 18 less important subsequent pages. I should like to follow Durrieu and Winkler, who give these first pages to Jacquemart, assigning the rest to the 'Maître du Maréchal de Boucicaut' or his studio. Winkler sees in Jacquemart the foremost personality of French miniature painting before the Brothers de Limbourg, who were his successors in the service of the Duke. Other critics, like Delisle and Fierens-Gevaert, claim the first miniatures for André Beauneveu, the rest for Jacquemart.

Complete publication of the Ms. in 'Musée des Enluminures' I, 1905 (text by Pol de Mont). Further literature: L. Delisle, Les Livres d'Heures du Duc de Berri, GBA 1884, I, p. 400, No. 11; R. de Lasteyrie, Mon. Piot, t. III, p. 86 ff.; Winkler, Altniederl. Malerei, 1924, p. 23, and article on Hesdin in Th. B.; Fierens-Gevaert, 'Les très belles Heures du Duc de Berri', Brux. 1924.

47. FRANCO-BURGUNDIAN SCHOOL, ABOUT 1400, FORMERLY ATTRIBUTED TO JACQUEMART DE HESDIN OR TO ANDRÉ BEAUNEVEU

SKETCH BOOK. New York, Pierpont Morgan Library

Six panels of boxwood, about 13 : 7 cm. The boxwood has been treated with a thin wash of gouache in order to take the impression of the silver point.

Different representations, among them a Madonna with Child, a tourney, a 'bal masqué', etc.

There exist a number of similar books, destined to provide medieval artists with a choice of 'models' for their paintings (cf. No. 75). They seem to have been compiled by itinerant artists on their journeys. Whereas most of these books, as far as they are preserved, show a German or Austrian character, the Morgan book is obviously French or Franco-Burgundian. It has been attributed to André Beauneveu (Roger Fry, 'On a fourteenth century sketch book', Burl. Mag., October 1906, p. 31 ff.) and to Jacquemart de Hesdin (Lavallée) because of its alleged similarities to the two large miniatures in the 'Très belles Heures' (No. 46), which have also been called Beauneveu or Jacquemart alternatively. Fry dates the book between 1380 and 1393.

Before Mr. Pierpont Morgan acquired the book, it belonged to a private collection in Rome.

Reproduced: Lavallée, No. 15–19; Art News Annual, 1939.

(Referring to the precarious state of the book, the authorities of the Morgan Library have, to our regret, refused to send us photographs. It would have been a pleasure to reproduce some of these drawings, which are among the most delightful specimens of early draughtsmanship.)

⟨48.⟩ SCHOOL OF LOMBARDY, about 1400, formerly attributed to ANDRÉ BEAUNEVEU

Scenes of Court Life: A Lady and a Courtier playing Chess; An Archer; Lovers with a Dog, etc. Oxford, Ashmolean Museum

Brush and ink on vellum, 6 : 13,9 cm.

The drawing has been attributed to André Beauneveu by Roger Fry, who stresses the connection to the Morgan Sketch Book, and to a miniaturist in the neighbourhood of the so-called 'Maître aux Boquetaux' by Lavallée (No. 20). Recently its Italian—Milanese—character has been recognized by most critics.

R. Fry, 'A drawing by André Beauneveu', Burl. Mag., April 1910.
Exhibited: London 1932, No. 619 (reproduced Commem. Cat. pl. 145, No. 532).

49. FRENCH SCHOOL, ABOUT 1400/1410

CORONATION OF THE VIRGIN. Berlin, Deutsches Museum (No. 1648)

Circular panel, diameter 20,5 cm. (8½ in.) Gold ground.   PLATE 6

Christ places the crown on the Virgin's head while inquisitive angels watch the scene. Typical example of the later courtly art, which may equally well belong to the sphere of the Paris as to that of the Dijon court.

P. Durrieu, Mon. Piot XXIII, 1918/19, p. 80 ff.

Formerly attributed to Michelino da Besozzo, cf. Venturi VII, 1, fig. 157.
Exhibited: Paris 1937, No. 8.

50. FRENCH SCHOOL, BEGINNING OF THE 15TH CENTURY

CRUCIFIXION WITH A CARTHUSIAN MONK. Paris, Coll. Henri Chalandon

68 : 45 cm.

Introduced by L. Demonts, Une Collection française de Primitifs, RdA, janvier 1937, p. 247 ff., as a work by Malouel.

This interesting picture, which is not known to me in the original, is not easy to judge. As far as one can see from the reproductions it is not in a good state.

Reproduced: Jacques, pl. 37 (Rep. A., 14th cent., 34).

51. FRANCO-FLEMISH SCHOOL, ABOUT 1400/1410

MADONNA AND CHILD. Paris, Louvre   PLATE 25

21 : 14 cm. (8¼ : 5½ in.). Gold ground.

This lovely picture, delicately conceived and executed, belongs to the group of early panels which have been assigned to the School of Dijon. It has accordingly first been connected with the 'Pietà' (No. 53) and attributed to Malouel. More recently, a likeness with the Madonna on the 'Flight into Egypt', from the Retable de Champmol (No. 18) has been stressed and the name of Broederlam has been mentioned as the possible author's (Dupont, p. 1; Lemoisne, p. 60, etc.). In my opinion, the picture is far more French than Broederlam, decidedly Franco-Flemish, and the similarity not conclusive.

Formerly Coll. E. Aynard, Lyon, and Coll. C. de Beistegui, Biarritz. Given to the Louvre with the Beistegui Collection in August 1945 (see 'Arts', août 1945).

Exhibited: Paris 1904, No. 13 (Bouchot 1904, pl. X).

52. SCHOOL OF DIJON, ABOUT 1400/1410, ATTRIBUTED TO JEAN MALOUEL OR TO HENRI BELLECHOSE

PIETÀ: THE DEAD CHRIST SUPPORTED BY THE VIRGIN, ST. JOHN AND TWO ANGELS. Troyes (Aube), Museum   FIG. 28

39 : 26 cm. Engraved gold ground.

The picture, which is rather close in style to the St. Dionysius (No. 54) has suffered grave damage, the colour has completely gone off in some parts, leaving large holes. On the other hand, it has not been spoiled by repair and therefore shows the style distinctly in the well-preserved parts.

Exhibited: Paris 1904, No. 14 (Bouchot 1904, pl. XIV).

FIG. 28   ⟨ Cat. No. 52 ⟩

53. ATTRIBUTED TO JEAN MALOUEL OR TO HENRI BELLECHOSE, ABOUT 1400/1410

PIETÀ, THE SO-CALLED 'LARGE CIRCULAR PIETÀ'. Paris, Louvre (No. 996)   PLATE 18

Diameter 64 cm. (25¼ in.). Gold ground.

The dead Christ, supported by God the Father and the Virgin Mary, with St. John and angels. On the reverse the coat-of-arms of the Dukes of Burgundy.

For the iconography see *E. Panofsky, Imago Pietatis, Friedlaender-Festschrift, 1927, p. 276 ff. and p. 299, ann. 42.* Panofsky connects this type of the 'Pietà' with the 'Trinity' and the 'Gnadenstuhl' (Throne of Grace).

Among the bright and flowery colours light blue prevails, often set against gold and light red. Everything is grouped around the pale grey of the corpse. This picture, perhaps the most popular specimen of French art about 1400, is connected with Burgundy by the coat-of-arms, just as the 'St. Dionysius' (No. 54) is 'Burgundian' by the provenance from the Chartreuse de Champmol. These two works are in fact the most accomplished syntheses of the 'Ateliers de Dijon' and the 'École de Paris'; they are definitely akin—although the Pietà is more Parisian—and I should like to assign both pictures to one workshop if not to the same master's hand. According as the St. Dionysius is given either to Bellechose or to Malouel, the 'Grande Pitié ronde' should be claimed for one or the other painter.

From the Collections of the Dukes of Burgundy and of Napoleon III.
Exhibited: *Paris 1904, No. 15; Paris 1946, No. 9.*

54. ATTRIBUTED TO HENRI BELLECHOSE, 1416

THE HOLY COMMUNION AND THE MARTYRDOM OF ST. DIONYSIUS (S. DENIS). IN THE CENTRE: CHRIST ON THE CROSS. ABOVE: GOD THE FATHER. Paris, Louvre (No. 995)   PLATE 20

161 : 210 cm. (63 : 82 in.). Transferred from wood on canvas in 1852. Gold ground.

In spite of the transferring—which is noticeable—the state is in general satisfactory, including the gold ground. St. Dionysius is clad in blue and gold; besides these leading colours one notices some red, and a yellowish green on the jacket of the executioner on the right. On the whole the colouring is clear and brilliant, producing the effect of a book page enlarged and transposed into an easel painting.

Since the picture comes according to tradition from the Chartreuse de Champmol, it has been identified with one of five altarpieces Jean Malouel was ordered to execute for the Chartreuse in 1398. Another document, which sounds less vague, reports that in 1416 the painter Henri Bellechose bought 'chez Jean Lescot, espicier de Dijon, les couleurs de paintrerie nécessaires pour parfaire ung tableau de la Vie de S. Denis', destined for the Chartreuse de Champmol *(published by B. Prost)*. The two documents have been tentatively combined by a suggestion that Bellechose completed the picture, which had been left unfinished by Malouel. In any case the later date agrees better with the style of the painting, and since the impression of the picture is rather homogeneous, it seems best, at the present state of research, to attribute it entirely to Bellechose. The picture formed part of the collection of Napoléon III.

Exhibited: *Paris 1904, No. 16; Paris 1946, No. 10.*

⟨55.⟩ SPANISH SCHOOL, *first half of the 15th century. Wrongly attributed to* HENRI BELLECHOSE

Crucifixion and Scenes from the Life of St. George. On the left: St. George slaying the Dragon; on the right: The Martyrdom of St. George. Paris, Louvre (No. 998)

Transferred from wood on canvas. 160 : 210 cm.
The Crucifixus is adored by a Carthusian donor.

The picture has formerly been connected with the 'St. Dionysius' (No. 54). It is also reported to come from the Chartreuse de Champmol, the composition is arranged in a similar manner (with Christ on the Cross in the centre) and the dimensions are the same. The quality, however, distinguishes the two pictures decisively: the 'St. George' is rough and coarse, far from the courtly distinction of the Dionysius. The differences appear so fundamental in types, colour and technique that one can hardly believe the two panels to have come from the same country. It seems preferable to assign the St. George to the Spanish school and to date it about a generation later.

Reproduced: *Lemoisne, Louvre, pl. 11; Lemoisne, pl. 38.*

⟨56.⟩ *Attributed to the* SCHOOL OF SOUTHERN FRANCE, *about* 1410/20
Louis de Toulouse, the Saint Bishop, enthroned, adored by a small kneeling Donor. Cleveland, Museum of Art

173 : 107 cm.

This impressive painting, which had been placed in the South of France by most critics, was assigned to the Spanish School by *C. R. Post (History of Spanish Painting, 1930, vol. III, p. 55, fig. 267)*. More recently Post has made a still more determined move by proposing as the author the Valencian painter Lorenzo Zaragoza *(Spanish Painting, vol. VI, 2, p. 579)*. It is not quite easy to judge the picture as the Saint's head seems to have been repainted.

From the Collection Comte de Chastinet d'Esterre, near Toulouse.

American Magazine of Art, August 1927, p. 443 (with reprod.); W. M. Milliken, Art News, April 14, 1928; H. Tietze, Meisterwerke europäischer Malerei in Amerika, 1935, p. 243; Bazin, fig. 28; 'Paintings in the Cleveland Museum of Art' Picture Book I, p. 27.

Exhibited: *Cleveland 1936, No. 127 (Cat. pl. XLI).*

⟨57.⟩ SPANISH SCHOOL, *beginning of the 15th century. Formerly attributed to the* FRENCH SCHOOL

The Martyrdom of St. George. Paris, Louvre

Four panels, 103 : 50 cm. each.

Attributed in the older literature to Bellechose; *Dvořák (Vienna Jhb. XXIV, 1904, pl. XXIV/V)* assigns the panels to a French Master in the entourage of the Duc de Berri.

The panels are now generally regarded as Spanish and not French. They are however closely dependent on French painting about 1400; one can note an affinity with the frescoes in the Crypt of the Church of S. Bonnet-le Château (Loire), reprod. *Bazin* 36.

Exhibited: *Paris 1904*, No. 33–36 (then Coll. Th. Belin, Paris).

⟨58.⟩ *MASTER OF HEILIGENKREUZ*, ABOUT 1410
Two Wings: The Annunciation with Sts. Paul and James. On the reverse: St. Dorothy.
The Marriage of St. Catherine, with Sts. Dorothy and Barbara. On the reverse: Virgin and Child. Vienna, Kunsthistorisches Museum (No. 1781/1782)
72 : 43,5 cm.

These panels have been given alternately to the French and the Austrian School, the designation 'French' being mostly pronounced by Austrian critics while French critics are inclined to assume an Austrian origin.
I myself have ventured to connect the pictures with the Master of Rohan—a daring attempt, which has met with rather unanimous disapproval and which I am quite prepared to revise (*GBA, mars 1938*). Even in case of a purely Austrian origin the close affinity to Parisian miniature painting cannot be overlooked and one has to imagine the master in any case as an itinerant artist who worked in France as well as in Austria.
From the Convent of Heiligenkreuz, Lower Austria.
B. Kurth, ZfbK 1922, p. 14 ff.; E. Buchner, Beiträge zur Geschichte der deutschen Kunst, Munich I, 1924, p. 1; L. Baldass, Cicerone 1929, p. 65 ff. and p. 127 ff.; K. Oettingen, Vienna Jhb. N.F.X., 1936, p. 59; Réau, pl. 41/42.
Exhibited: *Vienna 1934 (Österreichische Tafelmalerei der Spätgotik), No. 1.*

⟨59.⟩ *MASTER OF HEILIGENKREUZ*, ABOUT 1410
Two Panels: Death of the Virgin; Death of a Saint (perhaps St. Agnes of Montepulciano). Cleveland, Museum of Art, and Munich Collection
66,5 : 54 cm.

These two panels, both formerly in a Munich Collection, have been ascribed to the Master by *Buchner (Beitr. z. Gesch. d. deutschen Kunst, I, p. 1 ff.).*
They are less French in type than the Vienna panels (No. 58), but the connection between the four paintings is undeniable.
The 'Death of the Virgin' was exhibited in *Cleveland 1936* (No. 198, ill. pl. XL of the Catalogue) and was subsequently acquired by the Cleveland Museum of Art (*Art News, 5 December, 1936; Panofsky, The Art Bulletin, Vol. XVII*). Another panel, the 'Marriage of St. Catherine', formerly Coll. Delmar, Budapest, also less French than the Vienna pictures, has been rightly attributed to the Master by *Baldass (Belvedere-Forum, 1936, p. 133).*

⟨60.⟩ *AUSTRIAN (SOUTH GERMAN?) SCHOOL*, ABOUT 1410; *formerly attributed to the FRENCH SCHOOL*
Three Young Ladies: the one on the left, with a Crown, plays with a Dog, the Central Figure has a Falcon sitting on her Wrist (she has sometimes been taken to be a Young Courtier), the Third plays with Apples. Paris, Louvre (Inv. R. F. 3811)
Pen and water-colour, on vellum, 10,4 : 18,6 cm.

This drawing has mostly been attributed to the French School. It belongs to the 'style international', but with a distinctly 'Northern' touch, placing it near the early Austrian examples. Winkler's suggestion to connect it with the 'Altarpiece of Seligenstadt' (Darmstadt), a work from the region of the Middle Rhine, is also worth considering.
Formerly Coll. Posonyi, Vienna; von Lanna, Prague (Sale May 1910).
Reproduced: *Lavallée, No. 21, pl. IX; Société de reproductions de dessins de maîtres, 1910; 'Bildnis und Gestalt der Frau', Basel, 1946, No. 16.*
Exhibited: *London 1932*, No. 618 (Commem. Cat. No. 534, pl. 145); *Paris 1937*, No. 429 (Cat. Seymour de Ricci 'Œuvre française').

⟨61.⟩ *Formerly attributed to the SCHOOL OF PROVENCE*, ABOUT 1400
Madonna and Saints. New York, late Coll. Mortimer Schiff
28 : 18 cm. Arched top. Gold ground.

Madonna enthroned, her dark mantle sprinkled with golden dots. She extends her right hand towards a kneeling Benedictine monk, on her left stands St. John the Evangelist. In the lower half of the panel, St. Louis of Toulouse, St. Ambrose and St. Mary Magdalen.
Rather purely Italian than Provençal. *Jacques (Rep. B 14th cent. 16)* sees a

connection with the Frick Madonna (No. 62). *R. Longhi* attributes the picture to Arcangelo di Cola da Camerino (*Critica D'Arte XXV–XXVI 1940, Tav. 141*).
Formerly Coll. Aynard, Lyon; Coll. G. Schwarz, Berlin. Sold with the Mortimer Schiff Collection in 1938 (Christies, June 24, 1938, lot 81).
Exhibited: *Paris 1904, No. 23; New York 1927, No. 7* (reprod. in Cat.)

62. SCHOOL OF AVIGNON, ABOUT 1415
MADONNA AND CHILD. New York, Frick Collection
On gold ground with tendril ornaments.
Of strongly Italian character, but possibly Southern French.
Reproduced: *Jacques, pl. 41 (Rep. A 14th cent. 45).*

63. FRENCH SCHOOL, ABOUT 1412/1415
PORTRAIT OF LOUIS II, DUKE OF ANJOU. Paris, Bibl. Nat., Cabinet des Estampes   PLATE 26
Pen and water-colour on paper. Originally 22:17 cm. (8½ × 6¾ in.), (has been enlarged to 30,7 : 21,5 cm.)

The inscription 'Louis d'Anjou R. de Naples et Sicile' is on the part which has been added, but is certainly based on an earlier authentic inscription.
This portrait is the original model for the Duke's portrait in the 'Heures des Ducs d'Anjou' (Rohan Master, No. 87). It has also been used as the model for the Duke's likeness on a miniature by Fouquet (Grandes Chroniques, No. 130).
Louis II Duc d'Anjou (born at Toulon in 1377, died at Angers in 1417) was the father of King René.
Formerly Coll. J. Ballesdens (Ballesdens was the competitor of Corneille at the 'Académie'); Coll. R. de Gaignières (17th century).
There is an enlarged version in the Gaignières Collection (Paris, Bibl. Nat.)
Henri Bouchot, 'Le Portrait de Louis II d'Anjou à la Bibliothèque Nationale', Gazette Archéologique, 1886, t. XI, p. 64–67, p. 128–131. Degenhart in his recent book on *Pisanello* quotes the picture as one of the instances of French profile portraiture which have influenced Pisanello.
Exhibited: *Paris 1904, No. 26; London 1932, No. 617 (Commem. Cat. No. 533, pl. 149); Paris 1937, No. 431.*

64. FRENCH SCHOOL, ABOUT 1410/1415
PORTRAIT OF A LADY IN PROFILE. Washington, National Gallery (No. 23)   PLATE 27
52 : 37 cm. (20½ : 14½ in.)
She wears French court dress. The deep blue velvet of her gown is embroidered with gold and draped with a double strand of gold filigree beads. Dark background.

The picture was formerly—while in the Collections Villeroy, Paris, Clarence H. Mackay and A. Mellon—mostly given to Pisanello; *G. M. Richter (Burl. Mag., 1929), Hill* and lately *B. Degenhart (Pisanello, ill. 5)* have suggested French origin.
B. Berenson, who formerly voted for Pisanello, has taken up the question again of late (*Maandblaad voor Beeldende Kunsten, Mai, 1947*, congratulatory letter addressed to M. J. Friedlaender). While stating that there is nothing visible on the panel that points to another school he exclaims: 'And yet, and yet . . .', hinting at the possibility of French origin. 'The tight lips, the prominent nose, and the assertive chin might have belonged to the mother of Louis XI.'
As far as one is allowed to judge from photographs without knowing the original, this fascinating and controversial picture seems to fit best into our present conception of early French art. This classification would mean that the picture served as a model for Italian Quattrocento profile portraiture, in the first line to Pisanello. The nearest analogy in France seems to be the portrait of Louis d'Anjou (No. 63), which incidentally is not an easel painting.
U.M.9 (Text by Valentiner).

65. PAUL DE LIMBOURG AND HIS BROTHERS
'LES TRÈS RICHES HEURES DU DUC DE BERRI'. Chantilly, Musée Condé   PLATES 27-29, 31-32—FIG. 2
These Hours, the most glorious achievement among the manuscripts commissioned by the Duke of Berri, are secured as the work of the brothers de Limbourg by an entry in the Duke's posthumous Inventory of 1416: 'Item en une layette plusieurs cayers d'une très riches Heures que faisoient Pol et ses frères très richement hystoriez et enluminez' (*Guiffrey, Inventaires du Duc de Berri, 1894, t. II, p. 280, No. 1164*).

'Pol' is identified with good reasons with Paul de Limbourg, 'Valet de Chambre' to the Duke; his brothers are Hennequin and Hermant; their surname is probably Malouel (Malwel).

The miniatures of the first series of this manuscript, containing the famous 'Calendar' and a number of other pages were executed for Jean de France, Duc de Berri (born in 1340 in Vincennes). The Duke died on 15th June 1416 and it is supposed that the work was interrupted by his death. These miniatures should accordingly be placed in or shortly before 1416.

The unfinished manuscript passed probably by inheritance from the Duke's daughter Bonne, Comtesse d'Armagnac, to Charles I, Duke of Savoy, and his Duchess, Blanche de Montferrat, who ordered it to be finished, probably between 1485 (the date of their marriage) and 1489 (the date of the Duke's death). The miniatures of the second series are due to the illuminator Jean Colombe of Bourges.

In the following text we shall only deal with the first series and we have only chosen illustrations from that part. For the second series see *Wescher, Fouquet* (ill. 53–55).

The manuscript is in perfect condition and of an unheard-of freshness. The colouring is gay, light, blonde, luminous. The favourite shade is a pure and intense azure, besides a clear light green and red, but there are also more delicate nuances in pale violet and greyish mauve. Gold is used lavishly in the ornaments of the dresses, in the fonds (golden clouds), etc. In the landscape backgrounds there are exact renderings of buildings (Castles of the Duc de Berri, views of Paris, the 'Mont St. Michel', the Louvre, the Ste. Chapelle, etc.).

It can be assumed that the Manuscript was in the possession of Margaret of Austria, the Governess of the Netherlands, and that it there served as a model for later 16th century Flemish Livres d'Heures (Breviarium Grimani, etc.). It further went to the Spinola and Serra families in Genova. In 1855 it was acquired by the Duc d'Aumale, then resident as a refugee in England. Notwithstanding his exile, the Duc d'Aumale left his art treasures, including the present manuscript, to the French nation.

Of the abundant literature I mention: *L. Delisle, 'Les Livres d'Heures du Duc de Berri,' GBA, 1884, t, I p. 401; Hulin de Loo, 'Les très riches Heures du Duc de Berri', Bulletin de la Société d'Histoire et d'Archéologie de Gand, 1903 p. 181 ff.* The standard publication is: *P. Durrieu, 'Les très riches Heures de Jean de France Duc de Berri', 1904.* For interpretation and historical position of the miniatures, their relations to Italy, etc., see: *Jacques Mesnil, L'Art au Nord et au Sud des Alpes . . . Études comparatives, Bruxelles 1911, I; M. Dvořak, 'Das Rätsel der Brüder van Eyck', Vienna Jhb. XXIV, 1904; Focillon, GBA, Janvier 1936, p. 19 ff.*
Catalogue Paris 1904, Ms. No. 72.

THE MONTH OF JANUARY   PLATE 28
The method of representing in 'calendars' the occupations peculiar to the various months, in association with the signs of the zodiac, is not a new feature of this manuscript, but it is here elaborated in a unique manner.
'January' shows the Duc de Berri—his head in profile, obviously true to life—during a meal. His famous 'little dogs' are allowed to run about freely on the table. Behind him tapestries; above a canopy with his coat-of-arms and emblems (swans and small bears). On the right a large salt pan, 'La Salière du Pavillon', described in the Duke's Inventories (*Bulletin de la Société des Antiquaires de France*, 1902, p. 354).

THE MONTH OF APRIL   PLATE 32
Young girls picking flowers; in the background the Castle of Dourdan.

TEMPORAL PARADISE   PLATE 31
Full-size page, placed before the 'Heures de la Vierge'. One of the most ingenious conceptions of the manuscript; extremely advanced in the rendering of the nudes. *Schlosser (Vienna Jhb., 1897)* finds a connection between the kneeling 'Adam' and a statue of the school of Pergamon in the Museum of Aix.

THE MEETING OF THE THREE HOLY MAGI   PLATE 29
Abundant use of oriental types and costumes.

THE PRESENTATION OF THE VIRGIN   FIG. 2

66. PAUL DE LIMBOURG AND HIS BROTHERS
'LES BELLES HEURES DU DUC DE BERRI', THE SO-CALLED 'HEURES D'AILLY'. Paris, Coll. Baron Maurice de Rothschild (formerly Edmond de Rothschild)
L. Delisle (Mélanges de Paléographie et de Bibliographie, 1880, p. 282–293) has first identified these Hours with the manuscript referred to in two Inventories of the

Duc de Berri's library, one drawn up in 1413 and the other—posthumously—in 1416: 'belles Heures très bien et richement historiées . . . lesquelles Monseigneur a fait faire par ses ouvriers'. Since the 'belles Heures' are not yet mentioned in the Inventory of 1402, they must have been executed between 1402 and 1413.
Paul Durrieu, who has published the 'Belles Heures' (*GBA, April 1906, p. 265 ff.*), characterizes them as 'more homogeneous and intimate' by comparison with the more grandiose Chantilly Hours. In another article (*RdA, 1912, II, p. 175*) Durrieu points to the fact that one of the pages of the 'Heures d'Ailly'—the 'Triumph of the Virgin'—has served as the model for the same subject in the 'Heures de Rohan' (No. 86). Taking up this clue, *J. Porcher (Warburg Journ., Vol. VIII, 1945, p. 1 ff.*) finds a number of similarities between the 'Belles Heures' and the 'Heures de Rohan' and suggests a direct connection between the two manuscripts.
According to a note added to the Berri Inventory of 1416, the 'Belles Heures' were acquired after the Duc de Berri's death by Yolande of Aragon, wife of Louis II of Anjou. At the time of Delisle's publication they belonged to the d'Ailly family, which has given them their temporary name.

67. PAUL DE LIMBOURG AND HIS BROTHERS
ST. JEROME IN HIS STUDY. Paris, Bibliothèque Nationale (Ms. Fr. 166)
Pen drawing, 25 : 22 cm.   FIG. 13
Inserted in an unfinished manuscript of the 'Bible Moralisée', frontispiece.
The affinity to the Hours of Chantilly has been recognized early and the attribution to the Limbourgs still holds good.
A complicated architectural framework of a similar type, with sculptural ornaments is to be found in several other manuscripts of this neighbourhood. The small figures of prophets and apostles may be compared to those on the 'Annunciation' in the 'Heures d'Ailly' (No. 66); the whole canopy recalls the 'Standing Madonna' in the Cambridge Hours (No. 88). St. Jerome's pulpit occurs nearly identically on the 'Annunciation' of the Aix Altar (No. 91).
A preparatory drawing is in the Boymans Museum, Rotterdam (No. 68).
De Champeaux et Gauchery, Les Travaux d'Art exécutés pour le Duc de Berri, p. 138; Durrieu, Le Manuscrit, t. II, p. 120; Durrieu, GBA, 1906, I, p. 265; R. Fry, 'On two miniatures by de Limbourg', Burl. Mag., 1905, p. 435; F. Winkler, 'Paul de Limbourg in Florence', Burl. Mag., 1930, p. 95.
Exhibited: *Paris 1904, Ms. No. 88 (Bouchot 1904, pl. XVIII); Paris 1937, Ms. No. 132.*

68. PAUL DE LIMBOURG AND HIS BROTHERS
ARCHITECTURAL FRAMEWORK. Rotterdam, Boymans Museum (formerly Coll. F. Koenigs.)
Drawing, silver point on parchment, 24,9 : 16,5 cm.
The drawing is an original preparation for the 'St. Jerome' in the Bibliothèque Nationale (No. 67). *P. Wescher,* who published the drawing in *Phoebus, Vol. I, No. 1, 1946, p. 33 ff.,* points to its affinity to the art of Lombardy.

69. ATTRIBUTED TO PAUL DE LIMBOURG
THE BETRAYAL OF CHRIST. London, Print Room of the British Museum   PLATE 35
Drawing, silver point on light green ground, heightened with white, 11,7 : 13 cm. (4⅝ : 5⅛ in.)
A. E. Popham (Drawings of the Early Flemish School, 1926, No. 2: 'Franco-Flemish about 1410') calls the Betrayal, 'a miniaturist's drawing, near in style to the brothers van Limbourg'. *Winkler (Th. B., Vol. XIII)* votes cautiously for Paul de Limbourg himself. *Beenken (OMD, September 1932)* thinks of Hubert van Eyck, *de Tolnai (Le Maître de Flémalle et Les Frères van Eyck, 1939)* of Ouwater. The drawing is very near to the earlier miniatures ascribed to the Limbourgs and one should leave it—with some caution—within the Limbourg œuvre. It certainly fits better into the French than into the Flemish or Dutch context.

70. FRANCO-BURGUNDIAN SCHOOL, ABOUT 1420
THE PLANET VENUS; FROM A SERIES OF PLANETS. Dresden, Print Room   PLATE 30
One of three sheets, each showing a drawing on the obverse and reverse.
25,1 : 15,3 cm. (10 : 6 in.).
The drawings represent planets under the guise of antique divinities corresponding at the same time to the days of the week.

First sheet: The Planet Jupiter, crowned, with the flashes of lightning in his right hand. Inscriptions: Jovis signum, Stagnum (pewter, the metal pertaining to Jupiter), Joidy (Thursday). On the reverse: the Planet Venus.

The drawings show a certain influence of the Limbourg 'Hours of Chantilly' (No. 65) and must accordingly be dated later than 1416. They are thus one of the latest products of the courtly 'Berri Master' style.

Published: *L. Demonts*, 'Dessins Français des Cabinets d'Allemagne', *Bulletin de la Société de l'Art Français*, 1909, p. 259 ff. Reproduced: *K. Woermann, Zeichnungen aus dem Dresdener Kupferstichkab.*, Lieferung I, pl. X/XI; *Lavallée*, pl. XII–XV, Nos. 24–27.

70A. FRANCO-BURGUNDIAN SCHOOL, ABOUT 1415.
AN AQUATIC TOURNAMENT. Dresden, Print Room

Pen and ink, with watercolour washes, 39,9 : 16,8 cm.
Fragment of a once considerably larger drawing, probably the design for a tapestry. Analogies to the 'Heures' of Chantilly (No. 65).
Reproduced: *J. Dupont, OMD, IX, 1934/35, pl. 51.*

⟨70B⟩. *SCHOOL OF THE LOWER RHINE*, 1415, *formerly attributed to the FRANCO-FLEMISH SCHOOL*
Group of Courtiers and Ladies. Upsala, Library.

Silver point drawing, 17, 5 : 22,2 cm.
One of the most charming specimens of the 'style international' which has been connected with the Limbourg 'Hours'. It is however a German work whose artist was influenced by the miniaturists of the Paris Court. The closest connections are with the miniature of 'The Virgin in the Flower Garden' (manuscript cod. germ., 4° 42, Berlin, Staatsbibliothek, exhibited Düsseldorf 1904, No. 562a, written for Mary, Duchess of Guelders, in 1415, in the dialect of the Lower Rhine).
Reproduced: *Vasari Society 1935, 2nd series, part 16 No. 8 (C. Dodgson); Die Graphischen Kuenste II, 1937, Heft I (Benesch:* Master of the Utrecht Life of the Virgin); *Stange, Deutsche Malerei der Gotik III, 1938, ill. 151.*

⟨71⟩. *BURGUNDIAN SCHOOL, beginning of the 15th century; formerly ascribed to CLAUS SLUTER*
Study for a 'Pleurant': A Mourning Monk, wearing a Long Cloak and a Hood pulled over his Face. Paris, Louvre

Drawing, ink, pen and brush heightened with gouache, on grey paper, 17 : 9 cm.
This drawing is of particular interest by its subject, otherwise reserved to sculpture. *Huizinga* (p. 235) speaks beautifully of the figures of the 'plourants', the most profound expression of mourning known in art, 'a funeral march in stone'.
The drawing had first been attributed to Claus Sluter (certainly a too optimistic choice) or to Claus de Werve. Later on the still less acceptable name of Jacques de Gérines has been put forward. It is best called 'Burgundian' but there is a certain affinity to South German art (cf. the grisaille paintings by the Bavarian 'Master of the Passion of Tegernsee').
Formerly Coll. Walter Gay.
Reproduced: *Société de reproductions des dessins de Maîtres, tome I, 1910; Lavallée, No. 35; AdA, février, 1938, p. 26 (G. Bazin).*
Exhibited: *Paris 1904, No. 12; London 1932, No. 633 (Commem. Cat. pl. 148); Paris 1937, No. 430.*

⟨72.⟩ *Attributed to the FRENCH SCHOOL, beginning of the 15th century*
Rider on a Rearing Horse. Reverse: Embalming of a corpse. London, formerly Coll. Henry Oppenheimer

Drawing, pen and ink, 25,5 : 18 cm.
Attributed to the 'Master of the Playing Cards' (German) or to the circle of Pisanello. Recently *B. Degenhart (Handzeichnungen aus 5 Jahrhunderten)* gives it to the French School. In my opinion rather North Italian, influenced by French art.
Reproduced: *K. T. Parker, North Italian Drawings, 1927, p. 24, pl. 8; Sale Catalogue of the Oppenheimer Collection,* Christies, 10–14 July 1936, lot 146, Plate 36.
Exhibited: *London 1930, No. 612.*

⟨73.⟩ *Ascribed to the BURGUNDIAN SCHOOL, beginning of the 15th century*
St. Christopher. Dessau, Museum (Dept. of Drawings)

Drawing, pen washed with bluish water colour, 20 : 15 cm.
Published by *Wescher (OMD, Sept. 1937)* as a Burgundian drawing belonging

to the environment of the Limbourgs, but of a slightly more developed style, beginning to approximate the early works of Eyckian character.
In my opinion rather Flemish than Franco-Burgundian.

74. FRENCH SCHOOL, 15TH CENTURY
VIEW OF A GOTHIC CATHEDRAL. Erlangen, Universitäts-Bibliothek (B. 28)

Pen and ink drawing, 21,3 : 28,5 cm.
Cathedral with two frontal towers; above to the right sketch of a statue of St. Michael. On the reverse: Sketches of St. John and a female Saint.
E. Bock, Die Zeichnungen in der Universitäts-Bibliothek in Erlangen, 1928, I, p. 13, No. 28; II, pl. 18 (reprod.)
Exhibited: *London 1932, No. 622 (Commem. Cat., pl. 144, No. 535); Paris 1937, No. 428*

75. JACQUES DALIWE (D'ALIVE?)
SKETCH BOOK. Berlin, Staatliche Bibl. (Cod. pict. 74)   PLATE 23–24

Twenty-two silverpoint drawings on twelve small boxtree panels, ten of them prepared on both sides.
8 : 12 cm. (3¼ : 4¾ in.) each.
The name of the otherwise unknown painter appears on the first page of this little volume, which was evidently the model book of an itinerant artist.
Like all these model books, the present example contains various types of holy and profane figures, animals, etc., seen in the most varied positions, portrait studies, etc.
The style places the book in the Franco-Flemish context, in the beginning of the 15th century. All the drawings show the hand of the same artist.
Published in 1830 in lithographs by *Fr. Wilken, Entwürfe und Studien eines niederländischen Malers aus dem 15 Jahrhundert.* I have been informed that the sketchbook is fully treated in a doctor thesis by *Maria Th. Hasselberg (Königsberger Dissertation, 1936)* but I was unable to trace this paper.
Meder, Die Handzeichnung, 1919, p. 196; Dvořak, Vienna Jhb. XXIV, 1904, p. 296, Fig. 52; cf. J. v. Schlosser, Zur künstlerischen Überlieferung im späten Mittelalter, Vienna Jhb., XXIII, 1902, p. 315 ff., who treats the subject of medieval model books in general.

WOMAN RIDING ON A 'HIPPOGRYPH'   PLATE 23
HEADS; one in profile recalling Pisanello   PLATE 24

76. MASTER OF THE DUKE OF BEDFORD OR HIS STUDIO, ABOUT 1422/1423
THE LAST JUDGEMENT. Paris, Musée des Arts Decoratifs

110 : 65 cm. Transferred from wood on canvas.
In a very bad state; the upper part has been totally repainted and the rest has suffered whilst being transferred.
This picture is certainly a work of the School of Paris, executed in the workshop of the master who owes his name to his great client, John of Lancaster, Duke of Bedford. It is the first easel painting that can be connected with the master, who is otherwise only known as a miniaturist. It is also one of the rare instances, if not the only one, where the connection of a panel with an illuminator is supported by 'objective' evidence in addition to style criticism: the identical composition appears on a miniature of the 'Last Judgement' in a Book of Hours, belonging to H.M. the King (No. 79). The panel, notwithstanding its poor state of preservation, is not inferior to the miniature and must be regarded as an original, not as a copy after the manuscript.
Published and reproduced by *Gr. Ring, GBA, mars 1938, p. 151 and 155, fig. 1 and 4. Wallraf Richartz Jahrbuch, 1939, p. 162, ill. 119, No. 83. Charles de Tolnai (Münchener Jhb. N. F., IX, 1932)* has ascribed the picture to the Dutch School, linking it with the 'Last Judgement' of Diest (Brussels), which incidentally is neither Dutch nor in any way connected with the present painting.

77. MASTER OF THE DUKE OF BEDFORD
'LE BRÉVIAIRE DE SALISBURY' OR THE BREVIARY OF THE DUKE OF BEDFORD. Paris, Bibl. Nat. (Ms. lat. 17294)

Written for John Duke of Bedford, Regent of France during the English occupation 1422–1435. Executed between 1424 and 1435 and left unfinished at the time of the Duke's death.
Leroquais, Les Bréviaires Ms. des Bibl. publ. de France, pl. LIV–LXV; vol. III, 1934, p. 271; Blum et Laur, La miniature française, pl. 4 and 5.
Exhibited: *Paris 1904, Ms. No. 106.*

78. MASTER OF THE DUKE OF BEDFORD   FIG. 10
'THE BEDFORD HOURS'. London, British Museum (Add. mss. 18850)
Executed for the Duke of Bedford, on the occasion of his marriage to Anne, sister of Duke Philippe of Burgundy, in 1423.
Published: *British Museum, Reproductions from Illuminated Manuscripts, Series III, 1925, pl. 32–34; Société franç. de reprod. de ms. à peinture, 17e année 1933.*

79. MASTER OF THE DUKE OF BEDFORD AND HIS STUDIO
BOOK OF HOURS OF THE DUKE OF BEDFORD. Windsor Castle, H.M. The King
Probably commissioned by the Duke as a wedding present to his sister-in-law Margaret, another sister of Duke Philippe of Burgundy, on the occasion of her marriage, in 1423, to Arthur of Richmond. One of the miniatures—the Last Judgement—corresponds to the picture No. 76.
Exhibited: *London 1908, Exhibition of Illuminated Manuscripts, Burlington Fine Arts Club, No. 209 (reprod. Commem. Catalogue, pl. 134).*

80. SCHOOL OF PARIS, ABOUT 1410/20
'LA VIERGE PROTECTRICE'. Le Puy-en-Velay, Musée Crozatier
Tempera on canvas, 145 : 190 cm. Probably used originally as a banner in a procession.
The Virgin wears a red dress sprinkled with golden 'fleurons'; her wide ermine mantle is held by two holy women in nun's costumes. Beneath her mantle, on the left, dignitaries of the Church, Pope, Cardinal, etc., on the right, devout laymen, among whom Bouchot recognizes Charles VI ('the King'), Isabeau de Bavière ('the Queen'). The three persons on the extreme right seem to be the donors: a wealthy bourgeois between two women.
Notwithstanding its large size, the picture shows the manner of the Parisian miniaturists. It can in this respect be compared with the 'Last Judgement' (No. 76), but the style is not that of the Bedford Master—it rather recalls the illuminators in the circuit of Jacquemart de Hesdin (cf. the group of kneeling worshippers on 'le Saint Esprit et les Fidèles', Paris fragment of the 'Très belles Heures de Notre-Dame' [No. 45]; *Soc. franç. de Ms. à peinture, 1922, pl. XV*).
From the 'Couvent des Carmes du Puy'.
Reproduced: *Jacques, pl. 23; P. Perdrizet, La 'Mater Omnium' du Musée du Puy, Congrès Archéologique de France, 1905.*
Exhibited: *Paris 1904, No. 28 (there called 'École de l'Auvergne'; Bouchot 1904, pl. XXII).*

81. FRENCH SCHOOL, ABOUT 1420
VOTIVE PICTURE OF YOLANDE BELLE. Ypres, Hôtel de Ville
62 : 117 cm.
The Virgin is adored by Yolande Belle (daughter of Jean Sr. de Boesinghe) and her husband Josse Bride, who donated the picture in her memory. She is accompanied by their three daughters and presented by St. Catherine; he is accompanied by their four sons and presented by St. George in full armour. Two angels carry the coat-of-arms, two others are holding the curtain.
The arrangement recalls the so-called 'pierres de Tournai', the votive reliefs in and near Tournai (*Gr. Ring, Belgische Kunstdenkmäler I, 1923, p. 269*). The picture is of a heraldic-decorative character, a type of votive picture later on taken up by works like the group portrait of the 'des Ursins' (No. 112).
Formerly in the Hospice Belle at Ypres.
Reproduced: *Fierens-Gevaert, pl. XXXIII.*
Exhibited: *Bruges 1902, No. 1.*

82. FRENCH SCHOOL, ABOUT 1410/20
VIRGIN AND DONORS PRESENTED BY ST. JOHN THE BAPTIST. Saint-Floret (Puy-de-Dôme), Église du Chastel
Fresco.
The attitudes and costumes of the donors have a certain similarity to those on the votive picture of Yolande Belle (No. 81), but the types are different; they seem to point to central France.
Bazin 38 (Detail, after a 'relevé'.)

83. JACQUES IVERNY, ABOUT 1420/1425
TRIPTYCH: MADONNA AND CHILD, BEFORE A CURTAIN HELD BY TWO ANGELS. Turin, Galleria Sabauda
161 : 191 cm.
On the left St. Stephen, on the right St. Lucia. Predella: Christ in his coffin between Sts. Peter and Paul. Coat-of-arms of the Marquesses of Ceva (on the left the arms of the elder branch of the family, on the right those of the younger branch).
The historical value of this painting is by far superior to its artistic quality. Though looking exactly like an Italian work, it is secured for French painting by the signature: *Jacobus Iverni de (Av)inione pinxsit*.
Formerly in a chapel of the territory of the 'Ferrazzi', near Ceva, a small town in Piedmont and capital of the Marquisate of Ceva.
Lionello Venturi, Renaissance, 1919 (May), p. 230 f. Reproduced: Dupont, p. 24 (Madonna only); Sterling, ill. 102; Réau, pl. 31 (text p. 18); Labande, p. 92; Jacques, pl. 43.
Exhibited: *Paris 1937, No. 17; Turin, 1939 (Cat. Tav. 23, Text p. 50.)*

84. JACQUES IVERNY, ABOUT 1420/30
FRESCOES: NINE HEROES AND NINE HEROINES OF ANTIQUITY; THE FOUNTAIN OF YOUTH AND ITS MIRACULOUS EFFECTS. Castello della Manta, Piedmont   PLATES 33–34
These representations are commented on by French verses, connected with the poem 'Chevalier errant' by Thomas III, Marquis of Saluzzo. (Cf. P. d'Ancona, 'Gli affreschi del Castello di Manta', L'Arte, 1905, VIII, p. 94–106 and 184–195, with complete illustration.)
Lionello Venturi (Renaissance, May 1919, p. 230 f.) notices points of contact with the triptych No. 83, allowing for the differences between the picturesque fancy costumes of the legendary figures in Manta and the traditional apparel of the holy figures in Turin. I agree with Venturi's statement that the Manta murals can be derived from the School of Avignon and ascribed to Iverny. As far as I see they are even nearer to French art than the triptych. They are a striking example of the practice of the noblemen in the entourage of the princes of Savoy to introduce into their domain French fashions and French artists.
Venturi, VII, 1, p. 141 (fig. 78–80); Lemoisne, pl. 44/45 (text, p. 82); Dupont, p. 23; van Marle, vol. VII, p. 191 ff. (fig. 123–125). Cf. B. Kurth, Vienna Zentralkomm. I, 1911, p. 9 ff.

85. FRENCH SCHOOL, FIRST THIRD OF THE 15TH CENTURY
FRESCOES: NINETEEN FIGURES OF SAINTS, ETC. Fénis (Piedmont), Val d'Aosta, Chapel of the Castle
These frescoes recall the style of the Manta frescoes, but in a more provincial variety. They were also in all probability painted by an artist of French origin. Aosta is situated on the road from France to Lombardy and the work may have been executed by an itinerant painter taking this road.
Reproduced: *Dimier, 1925, pl. XIII; Lemoisne, pl. 24 (text p. 58); van Marle VII, p. 192, fig. 126.*

86. MASTER OF THE HEURES DE ROHAN
'LES GRANDES HEURES DE ROHAN'. Paris, Bibliothèque Nationale (Ms. lat. 9471)   COLOUR PLATE, P. 17, PLATES 37–40
This volume, which has been recognized more and more as one of the most outstanding achievements of French art of all times, is already impressive by its size, 29 : 20,8 cm. (11½ × 8⅛ in.), and by the abundance of its illustrations: 65 large miniatures, among them 11 full-page ones.
The preservation is on the whole excellent; only a few sheets have suffered. The favourite colour scheme is a pale red set against a pale green on a strong blue fonds. The fonds often shows golden ornaments in line drawing; a special feature are stylized golden clouds.
The 'Grandes Heures de Rohan' owe their name to the coat-of-arms of the Rohan family on folio 26 (verso). A. de Laborde (*La Bible moralisée, V, 1927, p. 118 ff.*) has already noted that these arms are not original, and the latest research by J. Porcher (*Warb. Journ., vol. VIII, 1945, p. 1 ff.*) emphasizes that it was certainly not for the Rohan family that the manuscript was executed in the first place, but rather for the house of Anjou. We retain the old name, sanctioned by custom

Among the manuscripts assigned to the 'Rohan' studio, the 'Grandes Heures, show by far the greatest number of pages by the *chef d'atelier* himself, and it was therefore with good reasons that this manuscript has been selected to provide a temporary name for the as yet anonymous great master.

In spite of the ever-growing amount of learned literature on the 'Grandes Heures', the problem of their style, date, place of origin, etc., is still far from being solved. According to A. *Heimann's* careful and penetrating paper, which laid the foundation for the present knowledge about the matter, the studio which produced the 'Grandes Heures' and the contiguous manuscripts should be located in Paris (apart from stylistic evidence, the manuscripts that Heimann mentions are arranged 'à l'usage de Paris', with two exceptions only) and the date of the execution of the 'Grandes Heures' should be fixed between 1420 and 1425. The 'Grandes Heures' are obviously influenced by Paul de Limbourg; the connection with the Limbourg 'Belles Heures' (No. 66) has been treated in detail by *Porcher* (this is in fact the main support for his thesis that the 'Rohan Hours' were in reality 'Anjou Hours': the 'Belles Heures' belonged to Yolande d'Aragon, widow of Louis II d'Anjou, and can therefore have served as a direct model for the younger artist at the court of Anjou). But the connection with the 'Chantilly Hours' (No. 65) is also evident; this dates the 'Grandes Heures de Rohan' in any case *after* 1416. They can, however, not be as late as *Durrieu* proposes ('Le Maître des Grandes Heures de Rohan et les Lescuier d'Angers', RdA, XXXII, 1912, p. 81–98, 161–183) He places the production of the master between 1430 and 1470, wishing to identify him with a painter Adenot Lescuier, 'enlumineur de la Reine de Sicile' (i.e. Jeanne de Laval), who worked up to about 1471. Durrieu locates the master in Angers—a hypothesis which would agree with Porcher's idea of an Angevin origin. Porcher draws renewed attention to another model for the 'Grandes Heures', a 'Bible historiée' (Paris, Bibl. Nat. Ms. fr. 9561), an Italian work of the 14th century which was a model in a purely iconographical sense. Porcher supposes the 'Bible' also to have then been in the House of Anjou.

A connection which is at least as close as that with the Limbourg workshop can be detected between the Rohan master and the 'Maître des Heures du Maréchal de Boucicaut' (now mostly identified with Jacques Coëne). This connection, already noticed by Heimann, has been made more probable by a recent find: a Book of Hours (from the Collection of Major J. C. Balfour, sold at Sotheby's, 18th December 1946, lot 567, not yet published) shows the Rohan style in its calendar and the hand of the Boucicaut Master in the other illuminations. The co-operation seems the more noticeable as there is no artistic congeniality between the mild and balanced temper of the elder master and the wild pathos of the younger—there is only the concrete evidence of the facts, which seem to point to a direct association between the two studios and would support the thesis of the Parisian origin of the 'Rohan' manuscripts.

The distribution of the illuminations of the 'Grandes Heures' among the *chef d'atelier* and his collaborators is another controversial point. Durrieu ascribed the 11 whole pages to the great master, A. Heimann tends to make many subtle distinctions, establishing a number of various 'hands'. Be that as it may: the spirit of one great personality, the *chef*, and his unique imagination pervades the whole work so strongly that one should perhaps not be over-cautious, although it is a fact that the quality of execution varies considerably. We have tried to illustrate only such examples as can be assigned to the chief master himself entirely or in great part.

After having possibly been commissioned by a member of the house of Anjou, the manuscript was in the possession of the Rohan family. It was later on the property of the 'maison professe des Jésuites' and of the Duc de la Vallière and finally entered the 'Bibliothèque du Roi'.

Literature (besides the articles mentioned): E. Mâle, 'La miniature à l'Exposition des Primitifs Français', GBA, 1904, II, p. 52/53; Mâle, p. 33 ff.; Leroquais, Les Livres d'Heures de la Bibl. Nat., Paris 1927, t. I, p. 281–290 and Pl. XXXVIII–XLII; Les plus beaux Manuscrits Français à peintures du Moyen-Age, Paris 1937 (text by L. Gillet, p. 47); Les Grandes Heures de Rohan, Trésors, 1943, colour plates (text by Porcher).

Exhibited: Paris 1904, Ms. No. 89; Paris 1926, No. 56 (Couderc, Commem. Cat. p. 44); Paris 1937, Ms. No. 139.

THE LAST JUDGEMENT.   PLATE 37
Heimann, ill. 18.)

Christ, the supreme Judge, represented as an old man with a white beard, wrapped in a pale pink coat. Very near to the chief master, if not entirely executed by him.

G

PIETÀ.   PLATE 38
(*Heimann, ill. 16.*)

The Virgin is clad in gold, her coat pale pink lined with whitish green. Fonds strong blue with a pattern of angels and stars in gold. This miniature is of the highest quality and entirely by the great master himself.

MAN BEFORE HIS JUDGE.   PLATE 39
(*Heimann, ill. 17.*)

Iconographically most unusual: the lying corpse is not Christ, but 'the Dead Man'. Christ is to be detected under the figure of God the Father in the upper right corner; he has a white beard and carries sword and globe; the halo bears the inscription: 'Jhesus nazarenus—rex judeorum', a proof that the Son is here represented as well as the Father. The soul of the Dead has just escaped his body —in the guise of a naked child—and St. Michael is contesting for it with the devil who had got hold of it.

The corpse is greenish, God is clad in pale red lined with green: the fonds is dark blue with golden angels. The most important miniature of the manuscript. The authorship of the chief master is evident.

THE ANNUNCIATION.   PLATE 40
(*Heimann, ill. 19*)

The scene is placed in a kind of enclosure under a canopy with small figures of angels, very much like the setting of the 'Standing Madonna' in the 'Cambridge Heures' (No. 88, folio 141v).

Angel in pale pink lined with green, Virgin in blue. Execution in great part, if not entirely, by the chief master.

THE ANNUNCIATION TO THE SHEPHERDS.   COLOUR PLATE P. 17
(*Heimann, ill. 21.*)

The figure of the dancing shepherd is certainly conceived by the chief master— an ingenuous invention, foreshadowing Bruegel.

87. MASTER OF THE HEURES DE ROHAN
'LES HEURES DES DUCS D'ANJOU'. Paris, Bibliothèque Nationale (Ms. Lat. 1156 A)   FIG. 5

On the whole of secondary quality as compared to the other principal manuscripts from the Rohan studio. Not only less careful in execution, but also less original in invention—several compositions are directly borrowed from the Boucicaut Master (*Heimann, p. 13 ff.*). Durrieu (Rd A, 1912) claims 5 miniatures for the *chef d'atelier*, Heimann only recognizes one of them ('Christ en douleur' folio 82; *Heimann, ill. 10*).

The most striking feature of the manuscript is the portrait on folio 81 verso. It represents King René d'Anjou, dressed after the Italian fashion and with Italian haircut and beard. According to Durrieu, the portrait and hence the whole manuscript is to be dated shortly after René's return from Italian captivity (1431–1437). The matter becomes complicated by the presence of another Anjou portrait—the profile of Louis II, René's father (on folio 61) after the original in the Bibliothèque Nationale (No. 63). This has led to various misunderstandings with regard to the chronology of the 'Anjou Hours' and of the entire œuvre of the Rohan Master. The best explanation seems to be that René commissioned the manuscript and ordered his father's likeness to be inserted. According to Heimann, folio 61 originally also showed a portrait of René, which—after his accession to the throne—he ordered to be overpainted by the portrait of his father, while he arranged his 'Italian' portrait to be executed in larger size on a spare page.

Literature: see No. 86. The Anjou Hours have been treated in detail by Leroquais, Les Livres d'Heures de la Bibl. Nat., Paris, 1927, t. I, p. 64–67, etc.; P. Durrieu, 'Les armoiries du Bon Roi René', Comptes-rendus des Séances de l'Académie des Inscriptions et Belles Lettres, 1908, p. 102–114.

Exhibited: Paris 1926, No. 82.

88. MASTER OF THE HEURES DE ROHAN
BOOK OF HOURS, CALLED THE 'CAMBRIDGE HOURS'. Cambridge Fitzwilliam Museum (No. 62, Founder's Bequest 1816)

Apart from the 'Grandes Heures', these Hours are probably the most attractive and the most richly decorated product of the Rohan workshop. They have so far not been treated in a separate publication.

The 'Cambridge Hours' should be placed rather early (*Heimann, p. 5 ff.*), certainly not later than 1420. The largest and most elaborate illumination, the 'Standing Madonna' (folio 141 v., *Heimann, ill. 8*) has a close affinity to the drawing of St. Jerome (No. 67), which is usually attributed to Paul de Limbourg. *Roger Fry*, noticing the connection, has accordingly claimed the 'Standing Madonna' for the same master (*Burl. Mag., VII, 1905, p. 435*). In our opinion, the 'Madonna' shows already the 'Rohan' style. The miniature, however, in which the *chef d'atelier* is most clearly discernible is the 'Christ en douleur' (folio 199, *Heimann, ill. 9*). This beautiful page is equal in rank to the best illuminations of the 'Grandes Heures'.

On account of the portrait on folio 20—which represents Isabelle, the daughter of James I of Scotland and wife of Francis II of Brittany—the Cambridge Hours have been called 'Les Heures d'Isabelle Stuart' (*RdA, 1912*). This princess was certainly at one time the owner of the manuscript, but she was not the original donor, as her portrait and coat-of-arms appear to be later additions (cf. *R. Fry* and *Heimann, p. 10*). Francis II's first wife was Yolande of Anjou, the youngest sister of King René, and after her death these 'Hours' may have been taken over by Isabelle. That would again lead us to the Anjou family and form another link between the 'Rohan Master' and René's entourage.

89. MASTER OF THE HEURES DE ROHAN OR HIS STUDIO

APOSTLES AND PROPHETS. ON THE REVERSE: THE ANGEL OF THE ANNUNCIATION. Laon, Museum   PLATES 41-42
95 : 103,5 cm. (37½ : 40¾ in.).
Standing figures of Apostles; below in niches four heads of prophets and one Evangelist's symbol (the bull of St. Luke). Golden haloes, and rests of ornamented gold ground. The Angel of the Annunciation approaches in a bluish-white tunic; his wings are half of gold. Behind him a female Saint, clad in grey, presents a kneeling donor in a coat of oriental (sassanidean) pattern. The fonds is vermilion. Right wing of a diptych (or part of a polyptych) of the Annunciation.
The figures of the Apostles recall the 'Apôtres de Durfé' in the Hours of the Collection Martin Le Roy (*Durrieu, 'Les Heures à l'Usage d'Angers de la Collection Martin Le Roy', Société Française de Reproductions de Ms. à Peinture, 1912*). The profile of the Angel, his coiffure and his costume correspond very closely to the Angel of the Annunciation in the 'Grandes Heures' (folio 45, No. 86).
This fascinating and until now entirely unnoticed panel is the first instance of an easel picture which can be connected with the 'Maître des Heures de Rohan'. I am indebted to Paul Wescher for having drawn my attention to it, and to M. Jacques Dupont for having kindly provided the photographs and having arranged for me to study the picture in the original.
Although the panel has suffered considerably, its importance is still fully evident and I have no doubt that after the restoration which is planned it will take its fitting place in the corpus of early French paintings of distinction. The question whether it should be assigned to the chief 'Rohan Master' or to his studio can only be decided after cleaning.

90. MASTER OF THE HEURES DE ROHAN

THE POOL OF BETHESDA. Brunswick, Herzog Anton Ulrich Museum
     PLATE 36
Drawing on vellum, ink heightened with white, 15 : 22 cm. (6 : 8¾ in.)
The drawing, which represents sufferers who have come to try the miraculous healing waters of the pool of Bethesda (St. John, V, 2–4) has been most convincingly attributed to the Master by *Millard Meiss* ('*Un dessin par le Maître des Grandes Heures de Rohan', GBA, February 1935, p. 864*). Besides the general similarity of style, Meiss points to the exact conformity of a figure in the drawing (the lame man trying to get up) with a figure on the 'Last Judgement' of the 'Grandes Heures'. According to Meiss, the drawing is earlier than the 'Grandes Heures', before 1425.

91. MASTER OF THE ANNUNCIATION OF AIX

THE ANNUNCIATION. Aix-en-Provence, Église des Prêcheurs ('Église de la Madeleine')   PLATES 43-46 FIG. 14
155 : 176 cm. (61 : 67 in.)
The very blonde Madonna wears a mantle of gold brocade ('brocart de Tours'), the Angel a purplish dalmatic with a broad gold-embroidered border. The colourful figures are set before grey stone architecture. The scene is placed in the vestibule of a Gothic Cathedral, the interior of which appears in perspective in the background (Hulin points to the symbolic significance of this arrangement, the 'Annunciation', as the introduction to Christendom, not yet having its place in the Church proper. Cf. *Panofsky, Art Bull., Dec. 1935*). Above, God the Father and in the rays of light proceeding from Him, the Infant Christ

gliding down towards the Virgin. At the end of the aisle, on the right, small figures are attending mass.
On one of the stained glass windows the coat-of-arms of the Maillé family. The Madonna kneels before a pulpit which is nearly identical with the pulpit of the St. Jerome drawing (No. 67). The capitals of the church resemble those of the cloisters of S. Sauveur of Aix. The small figures of prophets decorating the architecture of the vestibule recall the prophets of Sluter's 'Fountain of Moses'. An Annunciation with a similar Church interior seen in perspective is to be found on a miniature of the 'Heures de Louis de Savoie' (No. 99, folio 17).
The Aix Annunciation is the centre piece of an altar executed in accordance with the last will of the draper Pierre Corpici, dictated 9th December 1442 for his burial place in the Choir of the Cathedral S. Sauveur of Aix. The wings which were separated from the centre probably as early as the 17th century, are now in the Museums of Brussels and Amsterdam and in the van Beuningen Coll., Vierhouten (Nos. 92–94).
A photomontage of the ensemble has been made by *Dupont (p. 26/27)*.
The date of the Corpici testament corresponds to the style of the altar, which had already been placed between 1440 and 1445 before the document had been found by *Labande*.
Unsuccessful attempts have been made to identify the painter with Barthélemy de Clerc, one of the painters of King René of Anjou, or with Colantonio of Naples. *Hulin* believes him to be a pure Fleming who had come in touch with Conrat Witz between 1430 and 1440 and who afterwards worked in the South of France (*Hulin, Van Eyck*). Many years later, *Aenne Liebreich* came back to the Flemish thesis (*GBA, February 1938, p. 63 ff.*), deriving the master from Sluter and van Eyck. *Tolnai* (*Le Maître de Flémalle et les Frères van Eyck*), also stressing the Flemish component, follows the wrong track, trying to trace the style back to the 'Maître de Flémalle'.
On the other hand, the affinity of the master to Italian art, particularly to Antonello da Messina has been amply commented on (*Lionello Venturi, L'Arte, X, 1908*). A specially close connection has been established between the Aix Altar and the 'St. Jerome' (No. 97), a documental work by Colantonio, Antonello's teacher. *Demonts* (*RdA, May 1928 and Mélanges Hulin de Loo, 1931*) attributes both works to the anonymous Master of Aix, in whom he sees a Fleming. Meanwhile the famous letter of Pietro Summonte to Marcantonio Michiel of March 3, 1524, had been correctly published (*F. Nicolini, Napoli Nobilissima, 1922/1923*—a publication not yet known to Demonts), establishing Colantonio's authorship of the 'Jerome' beyond doubt. Subsequently, *Carlo Aru* (*Dedalo, X September 1931*) chose the other alternative and ascribed the Aix Altarpiece together with the 'Jerome' to Colantonio, thus declaring the 'Maître d'Aix' to be a Neapolitan (cf. No. 97, Fig. 29).
The London Exhibition of 1932 gave the opportunity of comparing the two works. The confrontation showed fundamental divergences in style and particularly in quality, and the 'Jerome' fell definitely out of the corpus of French art, whereas the Annunciation seemed to fit the more firmly within the French context. For once disagreeing with Hulin, I do not believe in a Flemish or even a Burgundian origin of the painter. I believe him to be a Frenchman working in the South of France, and, as already mentioned, I can best imagine him in the entourage of the painters of King René.
Lately a new suggestion to identify the master has been put forward by *Jean Boyer* ('*Arts*', *19 mars 1948*), based on documents left by the late Abbé Requin. According to the new thesis, the 'Maître d'Aix' was Jean Chapus, a native of Avignon resident in Aix, the son of a citizen of Chambéry who—according to entries in the archives already published by *Labande*—worked among others for King René. The suggestion has much to recommend it. It corroborates the connection with René, and the reference to Chambéry seems a good explanation for the Aix Master's relations to Burgundy as well as to Conrat Witz.—Incidentally one of the documents left by Requin gives the exact date of the completion of the altarpiece: July 1445.
Large details in colour: *L'École Provençale, Trésors, 1944 (Text by Bazin)*.
Exhibited: *Paris 1904, No. 37; Paris, Art Belge, 1923, No. 6; Paris, Louvre November-December, 1929; London 1932, No. 77a; Paris 1937, No. 19*.

92. MASTER OF THE ANNUNCIATION OF AIX

THE PROPHET JEREMIAH. RIGHT WING OF THE ALTARPIECE OF THE ANNUNCIATION. Brussels, Musées Royaux des Beaux-Arts (No. 95c)
152 : 86 cm. (59¾ : 34 in.)   PLATES 51-52, 4
He stands on a pedestal, within a niche. Grey stone, red robe lined with green, red cap. In his hand a blue book. Above, still life of books, papers, pots, etc. On the pedestal the inscription JEREMAS PHTA.

FIG. 29

⟨ Cat. No. 97 ⟩

REVERSE: NOLI ME TANGERE

Aenne Liebreich (GBA, February 1938) derives the prophets Jeremiah and Isaiah (No. 93) from the 'pleurants' on the tombs of the Dukes of Burgundy in Dijon. She points to a likeness of Jeremiah with the portrait of René d'Anjou on Froment's 'Burning Bush' (No. 216).

Several critics see a dissimilarity of quality and even of style between the obverse and the reverse paintings of the Aix wings. *Jacques (Rep. A* 15th cent. 43) observes a difference of technique and thinks of a Provençal studio assistant; Liebreich even thinks of a Spanish (Catalan) co-operator. I do not see any reason to make distinctions of the kind; the differences are in no case greater than those usual between obverse and reverse, the reverse being habitually of a less elaborate execution.

In the Brussels Museum since 1923 (Vente Normand).

Exhibited: *Paris, Art Belge,* 1923, No. 8; *Paris, Louvre, November–December* 1929; *London* 1932, No. 77b; *Paris* 1937, No. 20.

93. MASTER OF THE ANNUNCIATION OF AIX

THE PROPHET ISAIAH. LEFT WING OF THE ALTARPIECE OF THE ANNUNCIATION, LOWER PART. Vierhouten, Coll. van Beuningen

101 : 69 cm. (39¾ : 27¼ in.)

PLATES 49, 47

He wears a green robe lined with red.

REVERSE: ST. MARY MAGDALEN KNEELING.

The picture has become famous and has been widely discussed comparatively early, whilst in the Cook Collection in Richmond, Surrey. It was first called 'Spanish under the influence of van Eyck' (*Cat. of the Burlington Fine Arts Club,*

1907, No. 14). *Suida* published it as '*A newly discovered picture by Conrat Witz*' (*Burl. Mag.* XV, 1909, p. 107).

Exhibited: *Paris, Art Belge,* 1923; *Paris, Louvre, November–December* 1929; *London* 1932, No. 77c; *The Hague, September/October* 1945, No. 14.

94. MASTER OF THE ANNUNCIATION OF AIX

STILL LIFE. LEFT WING OF THE ALTARPIECE OF THE ANNUNCIATION, UPPER PART. Amsterdam, Rijksmuseum

25 : 56 cm. (9⅞ : 22¼ in.)   PLATE 50 and COLOUR PLATE P. 29

Books, papers, etc., are piled on a wooden shelf, within a niche.

Acquired for the Rijksmuseum in 1909 (Sale Fred. Muller, 30 Nov. 1909 No. 23).

F. Schmidt-Degener, Verslagen van's Rijksverzamelingen van Geschiedenis en Kunst, 46, 1923, p. 19; *Jamot, RdA,* 1927, II, p. 155.

Exhibited: *Paris, Louvre,* 1927–1929; *London* 1932, No. 77d; *Paris* 1937, No. 21; *The Hague* 1945, No. 15.

95. ATTRIBUTED TO THE MASTER OF THE ANNUNCIATION OF AIX

STANDING MAN, PRAYING. Rotterdam, Boymans Museum (formerly Koenigs Collection)   PLATE 53

Pen and wash on greyish-white paper, 28 : 12,5 cm. (11 : 5 in.)

The attribution has not been generally accepted. *Dupont (RdA,* 1936, I, p. 261) misses the 'ampleur bourguignonne', which is for him the chief characteristic of the Master. *Jacques (Rep. A* 15th cent. 44, note) connects the drawing with the portrait ascribed to Colantonio (No. 98).

Although the quality is perhaps not of the highest standard of the masterpiece of Aix, the close relation to the prophets on the shutters is undeniable.
Exhibited: *Rotterdam, Boymans Museum, 1934, No. 1; Paris 1937, No. 435.*

⟨96.⟩ *Attributed to the MASTER OF THE ANNUNCIATION OF AIX*
Head of an Old Man. Copenhagen, Museum (Cat. of 1922, No. 68)
Vellum, 13 : 11,3 cm.
Dupont introduces the picture as '*Un portrait du Maître de l'Annonciation d'Aix au Musée de Copenhague*', *RdA*, 1936, I, p. 261. He connects the head with the 'Jeremiah' of the Brussels shutter (No. 92).
The picture always seemed to me closer to the style of Jan van Eyck—to whom it had been traditionally attributed—than to anything French or even Franco-Flemish, but I have not seen the picture after the cleaning to which Dupont refers.

⟨97.⟩ *COLANTONIO (sometimes identified with the MASTER OF THE ANNUNCIATION OF AIX)*
St. Jerome in his Study. Naples, Museo Nazionale. 125 : 150 cm.   FIG. 29
The Saint, in Cardinal's dress, is seated at his desk, surrounded by books. He is extracting a thorn from the Lion's foot.
This picture, which was formerly attributed to van Eyck, Marmion and others, is secured for Colantonio, the teacher of Antonello da Messina, by the letter of Pietro Summonte to Marcantonio Michiel, of March 1524, who cites as a work by Colantonio, in San Lorenzo, 'la figura di San Jeronimo che sede in uno studio dove son molti libri e si vari di forma, con certe cartucce fixe nel muro con cera, dalle quali alcuna parte sta separata dal loco come si stessa in aere. Opera assai celebrata fra nostri pittori, etc.' (*F. Nicolini, L'arte Napoletana del Rinascimento e la lettera di Pietro Summonte . . . Napoli, 1925*). For detailed literature see No. 91.
Although the identification of Colantonio and the Master of the Annunciation, as proposed by some critics, must be strictly rejected, there certainly is a resemblance between the still-lifes of books, etc., in St. Jerome's study and on the Aix wings. The common model may again have been a work by Jan van Eyck, who has repeatedly represented St. Jerome in his study (Cf. *F. Winkler, Festschrift für M. J. Friedländer, 1927, p. 94*).
Exhibited: *London 1932, No. 83*, together with the complete Altarpiece of Aix.
The other work which can be given to Colantonio on the strength of Summonte's letter, the Polyptych of San Vincent Ferrier in San Pietro Martire, Naples, has never yet been exhibited in this connection. The whole 'Colantonio' question should therefore be postponed until the three works—the St. Jerome, the Polyptych and the Aix Altar—can be compared in the originals.
Formerly Cappella di San Girolamo, Napoli (1502); San Lorenzo Maggiore, Napoli (1808).

⟨98.⟩ *COLANTONIO (sometimes identified with the MASTER OF THE ANNUNCIATION OF AIX)*
Portrait of a Man. Cleveland (Ohio), Museum of Arts (Don. Holden)
60,6 : 44,8 cm. (23⅝ : 17⅞ in.)   FIG. 33
This picture, which was traditionally given to Ghirlandaio and which Berenson had called J. van Ghent, has been attributed to Colantonio by *Lionello Venturi* (*L'Arte, XXXIII, May 1930, p. 291/292*), by comparison with the St. Jerome of Naples and because of its affinities to Jan van Eyck on the one hand and to Antonello da Messina on the other. *Demonts* (*Mélanges Hulin de Loo, 1931, p. 123 ff., pl. XVI*) sees in the picture the corroboration of his thesis, which identifies Colantonio with the Master of Aix.
The picture—which is not known to me in the original—seems well placed in the œuvre of 'Colantonio', as far as we can visualize the figure of this artist. I would not like to include it in the context of French painting. It is perhaps not to be regarded as a pure portrait, but rather as the representation of a prophet.
Illustrated: *L. Venturi, Pitture Italiane in America, 1931, pl. CCLXXIX; H. Tietze, Meisterwerke Europäischer Malerei in Amerika, 1935, p. 50.*
Exhibited: *Boston, Foreign Art Exhibition, 1883–1884, No. 15; New York, Metrop. Museum, 1912; Cleveland 1936, No. 82* (as 'Colantonio del Fiore', *ill. pl. XII*).

99. MASTER OF THE HOURS OF SALUCES
HOURS OF LOUIS DE SAVOIE. Paris, Bibliothèque Nationale (Ms. lat. 9473)

FIG. 30   ⟨ Cat. No. 212 ⟩

In these 'Hours', which were executed after 1458 by the minor of the two 'Saluces' Masters, one finds several miniatures which may be records of lost panel paintings. Some of these paintings seem to be connected with Conrat Witz and with the Master of the Aix Annunciation. (The 'Hours of Saluces' which have provided the temporary name are in the British Museum.)
Folio 17 (reprod. *Leroquais, Les Livres d'Heures de la Bibl. Nat., 1927, pl. LVII*) shows a marked resemblance with the Annunciation of Aix (No. 91).

⟨100.⟩ *Attributed to the SCHOOL OF SOUTHERN FRANCE, about 1450*
St. Jerome and his Disciples translating the Gospels. Dublin, National Gallery of Ireland. 140 : 80 cm.
The book shelves may recall similar arrangements in the works of Colantonio and the Aix Master, but the style in its entirety points rather to the so-called Catalan School.
Formerly Coll. Lambert, Oudenarde; Otto H. Kahn, New York.
Published '*Cicerone' 1928, p. 67; reprod. U.M., 71 (text by Winkler); Sterling, p. 110, fig. 130.*

101. MINIATURIST OF KING RENÉ, ABOUT 1436
BOOK OF HOURS. London, British Museum (Egerton Ms. 1070)

FIG. 8 and P.

In these Hours, which contain mostly illuminations in the usual 'Berri Master' style, about 1400–1420 (Maître du Maréchal de Boucicaut, etc.), five large whole page miniatures have been inserted, one of them showing the arms of King René of Anjou. These miniatures are the works of a highly gifted artist who can be regarded as a predecessor of the René Master ('Maître du Cuer d'Amours Espris').
Fol. 4 verso: Coat-of-arms of King René; treated in detail by *Durrieu* ('*Les armoiries du Bon Roi René', Académie des inscriptions et belles lettres, Comptes rendus 1908, p. 102 ff.*). It is the type of royal arms which the King used between 14.. and 1453.
Fol. 5: View of the Holy Tomb in Jerusalem and the mosque of Omar. Published by *Durrieu* ('*Florilegium' dedicated to M. de Vogüé, Paris 1909, p. 196–207, with i.*

who dates the miniature exactly between 1435 and 1436. He recalls that René had the title of King of Jerusalem.

Fol. 55: 'Le Roi mort'. *Wescher (Fouquet, p. 62, Text ill. XI)* recalls that René had his tomb executed about 1450 according to his own design, and above this tomb, on the vault of his burial chapel in Saint-Maurice in Angers, a fresco by Coppin Delf, showing him also as 'Le Roi Mort'.

Fol. 110: 'Dieu de Pitié'.

Fol. 139: Three strong men bringing water from the cistern of Bethlehem to King David.

The manuscript, which is reported as being in England since the 15th century, was perhaps brought over by René's daughter Marguerite, the wife of Henry VI of England.

102. THE RENÉ MASTER (THE MASTER OF THE CUER D'AMOURS ESPRIS)

'LE CUER D'AMOURS ESPRIS'. Vienna, Staatsbibliothek (Cod. 2597)

29 : 201 cm.   PLATES 54–58

The allegorical novel of the 'heart seized with love', written by King René d'Anjou, was finished in 1457. It is a late revival of knightly poetry, moulded on the 'Roman de la Rose'. The knight 'Cuer', accompanied by 'Désir', tries to liberate and win the lady 'Doulce Mercy' by gallant deeds.

The Vienna manuscript was probably the private copy of King René, who commissioned the miniatures, supervised their execution, corrected the text, etc. The manuscript is dedicated to René's 'Cousin et nepveu Jehan Duc de Bourbon et d'Auvergne' (Jehan II de Bourbon, died in 1488, married to Jeanne de France, niece of René).

The miniatures, the outstanding achievement of French book illumination in the second half of the 15th century—beside Fouquet—should be dated about 1460–1470. Several attempts have been made to identify the master with one or another of the painters of King René, known from written records, especially with Barthélémy de Clerc, but the attempts have remained unsuccessful.

The book is in perfect condition. Although the miniatures have so often been carefully reproduced—in black and white as well as in colours—the impression of the originals is rather unexpected and slightly disconcerting. The original colours are very clear and distinct, the whole effect is far less romantic, the clair-obscur less mysterious than one should expect from the reproductions.

King René, the author of the text, was born at Angers in 1409 as the second son of Louis II d'Anjou. At the time when he was writing the 'Cuer' novel he was married to Jeanne de Laval and lived a retired life, dedicating himself to his literary and artistic pursuits. After René's death, the manuscript went most probably to his nephew Charles of Anjou. It was later on owned by Prince Eugene of Savoy and in 1737, during the reign of Emperor Charles VI, it entered the Vienna 'Hofbibliothek' with the entire Eugenian library.

E. Chmelarz, Vienna Jhb. II, 1890, p. 116 ff.; Durrieu, Notes sur quelques manuscrits français, in Bibliothèque de l'École des Chartes, Paris 1892, Vol. LIII, p. 138 ff.; O. Smital and Emil Winkler, Herzog René von Anjou, Livre du cuer d'amours espris, Wien 1926 (the fundamental publication); E. Trenkler in Bulletin de la Société Franç. de reproductions de manuscrits à peinture, Paris 1938, p. 33 ff.; Trenkler, Das Livre du cuer d'amours espris des Herzogs René von Anjou, Wien 1946.

Another copy of the 'Cuer' novel, with illustrations of considerably lower quality, is in Paris (Bibl. Nat., Ms. franç. 24399).

Exhibited: *Zurich, Kunstgewerbemuseum 1947, No. 79; Paris, Petit Palais 1947, No. 192.*

PLATE 54: 'AMOUR', THE GOD OF LOVE, comes to the bed of the love-sick King and takes his heart ('Cuer') away, giving it to 'Désir'. Night scene, clair-obscur. (*Trenkler, pl. 2/3*).

PLATE 58: CUER AND DÉSIR MEET THE UGLY DWARF 'JALOUSIE', who refuses them the entrance to her hermitage. (*Trenkler, pl. 5.*)

PLATE 57: CUER NEAR THE MAGIC WELL. He reads on a black memorial the inscription which is to explain to him the happenings of his last adventurous night. Désir is resting near his horse. Sunrise. (*Trenkler, pl. 7.*)

PLATE 55: CUER AND DÉSIR, LED BY THE OLD WOMAN 'MÉLANCHOLIE', come to the bridge 'Pas-Périlleux', which is guarded by the knight 'Soulcy'. (*Trenkler, pl. 9.*)

PLATE 56: CUER AND DÉSIR, ACCOMPANIED BY THE KNIGHT LARGESSE, embark for the island of the 'Ospital d'Amours'. In the boat, two friendly girls, in court dress, with 'hénins' on their heads, are waiting for them. (*Trenkler, pl. 20.*)

103. THE RENÉ MASTER

THE LEGEND OF THESEUS. Vienna, Staatsbibliothek (Cod. 2617)

French translation of the epic poem by Boccaccio, commissioned by King Réne. The poem deals with the tragic love of two princes of Thebes for Emilia, sister of King Theseus.

Dedicated in 1468 to 'Jehanne fille et sœur des Roys de France' (i.e. daughter of Charles VII).

The book has been illuminated by the Master of the 'Cuer d'Amours espris' and by a minor artist, author of the 'Angel's book' in Geneva; cf. *F. Winkler, Reisefrüchte, Z f b K, 55, p. 206.*

Although stylistic details point to the identity of the chief illuminator with the 'René Master', the unique sparkle of genius which distinguishes the 'Cuer d'Amours' miniatures is never attained in the 'Théséide'.

In 1524 the manuscript was in the possession of the Archduchess Margaret of Austria, sister of Maximilian I.

E. Chmelarz, Eine französische Bilderhandschrift von Boccaccios Theseide, Vienna Jhb. XIV, 1893, p. 318 ff.; reproductions in Wescher, Fouquet, ill. 44, 50 and in J. van der Elst, The last Flowering of the Middle Ages, 1944, pl. 6.

104. THE RENÉ MASTER

'LE LIVRE DES TOURNOIS DU ROI RENÉ'. Paris, Bibliothèque Nationale (Ms. fr. 2692, 2693, 2695)

Illuminated in part by the Master of the 'Cuer d'Amours espris', about 1460. The text is a later romantic evocation of a tournament held in Bruges in 1392.

The Bibliothèque Nationale owns three copies of the 'Traité de la Forme et Devis d'un Tournoi'. Two of them (Mss. 2692–2693) were executed for Louis de Bruges, Sire de la Gruthuyse, who offered the first copy to the king and kept the second.

According to the recent publication by *E. Pognon, Le Livre des Tournois du Roi René (Verve, Vol. IV, No. 16, 1946)*, the Manuscript 2695 preserves the original sketches for the two other copies. These sketches—water-colour drawings on paper ('dessins aquarellés')—in a very free and loose manner, seem to show the hand of the René Master himself.

Reproduced: *Durrieu Michel IV, 2, p. 713, fig. 475; Lavallée, pl. XX, No. 32; Wescher, Fouquet, ill. 43.*

Exhibited: *Paris 1904, Ms. Nos. 162–164; Paris 1937, Ms. No. 126.*

105. THE RENÉ MASTER OR HIS STUDIO

'LE MORTIFIEMENT DE LA VAINE PLAISANCE'. Berlin, Print Room (78 C 5)

Allegorical poem by King René, in which he demonstrates the futility of temporal vanity. Finished in 1455, illuminated by the 'René Master' or his studio. There exist two copies of this manuscript, one in the Library of Metz, the other in Berlin, executed for Jeanne de Laval (*Wescher, Fouquet, p. 69–70*).

106. SCHOOL OF AVIGNON, ABOUT 1450

THE 'BIENHEUREUX PIERRE DE LUXEMBOURG' IN ECSTASY.

Avignon, Musée Calvet (No. 3)   PLATE 59

78 : 58 cm. Ornamented gold ground (brocade). On the pulpit the Saint's arms. He wears Cardinal's robes, lined with white. The picture is in good state; of a rather simplified summary execution. (For the Saint: cf. No. 35).

The Saint died in 1387, in his 18th year, having become a Cardinal soon after his 15th year. His veneration was mostly confined to Avignon, where he lies buried. The dates of the Saint's life do not give a clue to the date of the picture which is clearly a posthumous, hardly individualized portrait of archaizing character. All dates between 1387 and 1470 have accordingly been suggested; we should like to compromise, the more as the folds of the Cardinal's cassock correspond best to the folds in, say, Enguerrand Charonton's 'Madone de la Miséricorde' of 1452 (No. 117).

Huizinga (p. 167) comments on Pierre de Luxembourg: 'Another ascetic sprung from court circles. This scion of the house of Luxembourg is a striking representative of the type of "under-witted" Saint—a narrow mind which can only live in the sphere of devotion ... Ascetic, horribly dirty and covered with vermin, amidst the unbridled luxury of the courts of Berry and Burgundy'.

Formerly in the Convent of the Célestins de Gentilly (Avignon), where it was hanging above the tomb of the 'Bienheureux'.

Exhibited: *Paris 1904, No. 70; Paris 1937, No. 27.*

107. SCHOOL OF AVIGNON, ABOUT 1450/60

STS. CATHERINE AND LAZARUS. Avignon, Musée Calvet (No. 4)

68 : 49 cm. Gold ground.

Part of an altarpiece, another part of which is in Poitiers (No. 108). Without doubt a work of the Provençal school and for this reason of a certain interest, but a work by a small and retardatory artist. The figures are in good state, the gold has suffered.

Reproduced: *Bouchot, 1904, pl. LVII; Labande, pl. XXXIV; Guiffrey Marcel, I, pl. XLV; Barnes, p. 406 (text, p. 401).*

Exhibited: *Paris 1904, No. 368 (supplement).*

108. SCHOOL OF AVIGNON, ABOUT 1450/60

TWO SAINTS AND A CARDINAL IN ADORATION. Poitiers, Musée

68 : 58 cm. Gold ground.

Published by *Dupont*, as belonging to the same altarpiece as No. 107, in '*Un primitif Avignonnais au Musée de Poitiers*', GBA, 1934, I, p. 378 (School of Avignon about 1450/1470).

109. SCHOOL OF PROVENCE(?), ABOUT 1450

ST. JEROME IN HIS STUDY. Van Beuningen Collection, Vierhouten (Holland)

24 : 18 cm. Gold ground (punched).

The style recalls vaguely the 'Bienheureux Pierre' (No. 106).

Sale Catalogue of the Figdor Collection, Berlin, 1930, No. 36, pl. XXII.

110. SCHOOL OF PROVENCE, ABOUT 1450

CRUCIFIXION WITH TWO DONORS AND THEIR PATRON-SAINTS, SEBAS-TIAN AND GILES. Aix-en-Provence, Musée Paul Arbaud   PLATE 61

62 : 207 cm. (24½ : 81½ in.)

In the extensive landscape, rendered with topographic accuracy, a town with minarets representing Jerusalem. Gold ground.

The picture is in perfect state and has luckily remained untouched by restorations. The animals in the foreground—partridges, a bear, a camel—recall North Italian drawings. The donor, presented by St. Sebastian, is seen in sharp profile, also after the North Italian manner, but his face is not Italian in expression; it is more ascetic, more austere, connecting the picture rather with the type of Southern French paintings fringing the Spanish borderline.

Hulin (Van Eyck) has grouped the picture together with the Pietà de Villeneuve (No. 206) This is convincing as far as the region is concerned, but—quite apart from the obvious difference of quality—the Crucifixion is earlier, more 'primitive'.

The arms of the donors have been interpreted by *Gustave Bayle*, in a monograph on the picture (*Étude historique sur un tableau flamand du 15e siècle, Avignon 1894*) as those of the famous Rolin family, a hypothesis which has been energetically rejected by *Bouchot (Cat. 1904).*

Formerly owned by the family d'Albertas; said to have been acquired in Villeneuve-lès-Avignon.

Exhibited: *Paris 1904, No. 73; Marseille, Exposition d'Art Provençal à l'Exposition Coloniale, 1906.*

111. SCHOOL OF AVIGNON, ABOUT 1450/60

HEAD OF THE VIRGIN; ON THE REVERSE: 'SANTA FACIES'. Paris, Coll. Comtesse Durrieu

43 : 32 cm. Gold ground, ornaments in 'relievo'.

Characteristic example of the italianizing trend of Southern French painting, near to Sienese Quattrocento types.

According to *Bouchot (Cat. 1904)* this is one of the few 'tableaux portatifs' which have survived.

Reproduced: *Jacques, pl. 73.*

Exhibited: *Paris, 1904, No. 55.*

112. FRANCO-FLEMISH SCHOOL, ABOUT 1450

PORTRAITS OF THE FAMILY OF JEAN JUVÉNAL DES URSINS, BARON DE TRAINEL. Paris, Louvre (No. 999)

161 : 345 cm.

This votive picture, conspicuous by its size, is one of the very rare examples of Parisian panel painting about the middle of the 15th century (executed between 1445 and 1449). It is a rather poor and uninspired specimen, of mainly historical and period dress interest.

Perls ('*Le tableau de la famille des Juvénal des Ursins, le Maître du Duc de Bedford et Haincelin de Haguenau*', RdA, Dec. 1935, p. 173 ff.) points to analogies with the 'Hours of the Neville Family' (Bibl. Nat. Ms. lat. 1158) and other manuscripts illuminated in the workshop of the so-called Master of Bedford, whom Perls identifies with Haincelin de Haguenau. Thence the most haphazard attribution of the votive picture to Haincelin.

For the des Ursins family see Fouquet, 'Guillaume Jouvenel' (No. 126); for 'Haincelin' see Portrait of Dunois (No. 141).

From the Chapel of the Cathedral of Notre-Dame, Paris.

Reproduced: *Barnes, p. 500.*

113. FRANCO-BURGUNDIAN SCHOOL, ABOUT 1440, OR LATER.

THE PRESENTATION IN THE TEMPLE, WITH DONORS. Paris, Louvre

86 : 52 cm.

The scene is set in a gothic church, perhaps the 'Sainte Chapelle de Dijon' (now destroyed). The donatrix has been identified (after the drawing fol. 99 in the 'Recueil d'Arras') as the mistress of Philippe le Bon, Jeanne de Presles, the mother of the 'Grand Bâtard' Antoine de Bourgogne. The donor is her husband, Hennequin de Fretin, and it is likely that the picture was executed shortly after their marriage in 1432.

The style is a mixture of French and Flemish elements. It seems to point to the neighbourhood of the School of Tournai, particularly around the Maître de Flémalle, but it is far inferior to that great master. The early date, supported by the identity of the donors, is somewhat disconcerting; the possibility that this is only a later record of a lost original from the period of the Maître de Flémalle cannot be entirely excluded.

According to tradition originally in the Chartreuse de Champmol (recorded as being there in 1793); later Collections Vivant Denon and Pelletier.

S. Reinach, Burl. Mag., May 1927; Ed. Michel, Bulletin des Musées de France, Janvier 1931; J. Dupont, RdA, Juillet 1935, p. 87 (with reproduction).

Exhibited: *Bruxelles 1935, No. 904.*

114. FRENCH SCHOOL, ABOUT 1450

'LES ANGES DE BOURGES'. Bourges, Hôtel Jacques Cœur   FIG. 4

Mural paintings on the vault of the Chapel of the Hôtel Jacques Cœur.

Twenty angels holding scrolls, in white robes, on blue ground bespangled with golden stars. The paintings must have been executed before 1453, the year when Jacques Cœur incurred the King's displeasure. On the other hand they are 'post-eyckian', and hence to be dated about 1450. Flemish influence is noticeable, but if the painter was of Flemish origin he has been thoroughly frenchified. *Hulin (Van Eyck, p. 23)* sees in the master a forerunner of the Maître de Moulins, whose angels would have been inspired by the 'Anges de Bourges'.

The first connoisseur who noticed these murals and immediately recognized their extraordinary quality was *Prosper Mérimée (Notes d'un Voyage en Auvergne, 1838, p. 24)*: 'Fresques d'une admirable exécution ... à un dessin toujours correct, souvent d'une pureté singulière, l'artiste a su joindre une si grande variété de types et d'expressions qu'on serait tenté de prendre cette multitude de têtes pour autant de beaux enfants.'

Published in *Éditions de la Caisse Nationale des Monuments Historiques (Huisman-Vitry), 1938. Reproduced: Lemoisne, pl. 51.*

115. FRENCH SCHOOL, ABOUT 1450

THE DANCE OF DEATH. La Chaise-Dieu (Haute-Loire, near Le Puy), Church   FIG. 20-21

Mural paintings, done in a kind of 'sgraffito' technique, drawings rather than paintings, on red ground.

The dancing skeleton which we see coming forward again and again to lead away the living is rather a corpse than death itself—the living man such as he will presently be. According to *Huizinga (p. 130)* these murals should be specially noticed as they may give an idea of the most celebrated painted version of a 'Dance of Death', on the walls of the cloister of the Churchyard of the 'Innocents', Paris, of 1424, which is not preserved.

The unfinished and as it were improvised character of the 'Chaise-Dieu' murals enhances the spectral effect.

Reproduced: *Lemoisne, pl. 56; Bazin, fig. 44 (detail); Gillet, pl. 33.*

116. ENGUERRAND CHARONTON (QUARTON), 1454

THE CORONATION OF THE VIRGIN. Villeneuve-lès-Avignon, Hospice (No. 36)   PLATES 63–68

183 : 220 cm. (72 : 86½ in.)

The composition is divided into various compartments, in each of which separate scales are used. Above, in Heaven, in large size, the Virgin crowned by the Holy Trinity—God the Father and God the Son being of identical type and age. On the right and the left the Beatific Vision—rows of medium-sized Angels, Saints and beatified Souls, in adoration, among them representatives of all ranks and classes, beginning with King, Pope, Emperor. Below, in small size, the Earth—on the right Jerusalem, on the left Rome, where one recognizes buildings from Villeneuve-lès-Avignon; the Mass of St. Gregory and the Burning Bush. In the centre the Crucifixus, adored by the kneeling donor. Still further down Purgatory and Hell, richly populated by innumerable tiny figures. The work has its origin in a commission which the painter followed literally in every detail. By rare good luck the document which reveals both the donor and the artist has been preserved; it was traced by the *Abbé Requin* (*Réunion des Sociétés des Beaux-Arts des Départements, 1889, Documents inédits, pp. 132–135, 176–183; see also Abbé Requin, Un tableau du Roi René . . . Paris 1890*). The document is a contract, registered by Jean Morelli in 1453: 'Pactum de Pingendo unum Retabulum pro Domino Johanne Montanhacci Presbytero: Die XXIIII aprilis (1453) magister Enguerandus Quarton, diocesis Laudunensis, pictor habitator Avinionis pactum fecit'. Then follows the order for the retable which 'Messire Jean de Montagnac fait faire par maistre Enguerrant paintre pour mettre en l'Église des Chartreux de Villeneufve-lez-Avignon en lautier de la sainte trinité'. As the order states that the retable was to be placed on the altar of the 'Ste. Trinité' of the Église des Chartreux de Villeneuve for the festival of St. Michael in the following year, the work must have been completed by September 1454.

I had the opportunity of examining the picture closely before the cleaning when the surface was beautifully dry and the state, in my opinion, most satisfactory. I then saw it in 1938 just after the cleaning, which had been done carefully and tactfully. The preservation is in fact extraordinary, even the gold ground is in good order. The holes, as for instance in the blue, have been filled in without attempts of disguise. (On the cleaning see: *Bulletin des Monuments Historiques de France, 1939, fasc. 2, p. 52–56.*)

The Virgin is clad in red and gold brocade, God the Father and the Son in purple, the angels behind this group in a lighter red tinged with yellow. Otherwise the whole picture shows an abundant use of blue. The carnation of the faces varies: St. Mary and God the Father and Son are very pale, nearly without modelling, the male faces in the 'Paradise' part are dark with strong shadows. The execution in the upper and in the lower regions is noticeably different: the main group carefully finished, the figures below more sketchy. The landscape, uniformly light green, shows views of Provence.

The supreme importance of the picture has first been noticed by *Prosper Mérimée* (*Notes d'un voyage dans le Midi de la France, 1835, p. 161 ff.*), who had it removed from the Église des Chartreux to the Hospice de Villeneuve.

An extensive monograph on the picture has been published by *Ch. Sterling, 'Chefs d'Œuvre des Primitifs Français', Le Couronnement de la Vierge par E. Quarton, Paris, 1939. All references to literature see there.*

Exhibited: *Paris 1900 (Petit Palais, Exposition rétrospective de l'Art Français), No. 4542; Paris 1904, No. 71; Paris 1937, No. 11.*

117. ENGUERRAND CHARONTON AND PIERRE VILLATTE

THE VIRGIN OF MERCY. Chantilly, Musée Condé (No. 111) PLATE 62,

66 : 187 cm. (26 : 73½ in.)   FIG. 16

Transferred from wood on canvas. Gold ground.

The Virgin of Mercy, adored by Jean Cadard—on the left—presented by St. John the Baptist, and his wife Jeanne—on the right—presented by St. John the Evangelist.

The Virgin, in a dress of gold brocade, has a wide blue mantle lined with white. John the Baptist is in wine red, the Evangelist in blue with a red coat. The state is satisfactory in spite of the transfer on canvas, only the gold has suffered.

The picture was commissioned in 1452 by Jean Cadard's son Pierre, as a votive picture of the Cadard family. According to the contract, it was to be executed by E. Charonton and P. Villatte, associated for this work. Jean Cadard, Seigneur du Thor, native of Picardie, was professor of medicine at the University of Paris (1412–1415). He was physician to the children of Charles VI, the doctor in charge

of the young Charles VII. Dismissed and exiled for political reasons, he went to Provence.

Painted for the Chapel of S. Pierre de Luxembourg, Église des Célestins, Avignon.

The authentication of the picture is due to the combined efforts of *Abbé Requin* (see No. 116), *Bouchot* (*GBA, June 1904*) and *Durrieu* (*GBA, July 1904*).

Reproduced in litho (1823) by G. Renès.

⟨118.⟩ *Attributed to ENGUERRAND CHARONTON*

Mater Dolorosa. Paris, Musée Jacquemart-André

36 : 33 cm.

According to *Labande*, by a painter of the Rhône valley, not too distant from Froment; *Demonts* attributes this picture as well as a praying Madonna in the Coll. E. Wanieck, Vienna, to Charonton. In my opinion neither the Paris nor the Vienna Madonna is by Charonton. The Paris picture is the replica of a well-known type invented by Rogier van der Weyden and frequently repeated in the Bouts studio. It may—or may not—be of French origin, in any case the Flemish archetype prevails.

Labande, 'Notes sur quelques Primitifs de Provence', GBA, févr. 1933. p. 102; L. Demonts, 'Uune Sainte Vierge en oraison d'Enguerrand Charonton', RdA, Janv. 1927, and 1935, I, p. 41.

Reproduced: *Labande, pl. LX.*

119. SCHOOL OF PROVENCE, ABOUT 1470

TRIPTYCH. CENTRE PANEL: THE CORONATION OF THE VIRGIN. LEFT WING: THE ABBOT ST. SIFFREIN EXORCIZING AN EVIL SPIRIT. RIGHT WING: ST. MICHAEL. Carpentras, Cathédrale Saint-Siffrein

150 : 227 cm. (with the old frame). Not a proper triptych, but one large panel consisting of three parts separated by small painted bands.

On the frame the arms of the 'de la Plane', a family of Carpentras. Above in the mouldings the symbols of the Evangelists and the Agnus Dei.

The colours are light and mild, the faces flat, nearly without modelling. The Virgin, in full frontal view, wears a blue coat over red gold brocade. God the Father and the Son (here distinctly characterized as old and young) are uniformly clad in light pink over white. Gold ground.

The preservation is not too good, the execution more summary than careful, the whole aspect sober and bare. Everything is reduced to a few rigid, nearly geometrical forms. It is a kind of simplified, somewhat rustic reduction of the great 'Coronation' of Villeneuve (No. 116) and seems therefore better placed in the orbit of Charonton than in the School of Froment, which had been suggested.

Reproduced: *Lemoisne, pl. 82; Labande, pl. LXXXVIII; Barnes, p. 357; Doré, 'Art en Provence', 425.*

120. JEAN FOUQUET

PORTRAIT OF CHARLES VII, KING OF FRANCE. Paris, Louvre (No. 289)   PLATE 69

Panel, 86 : 72 cm. (33⅞ : 28⅜ in.)

The king is portrayed life-size, looking out through light green curtains from a green niche (perhaps his box in the Ste. Chapelle at Bourges). He wears a dark-blue hat, with a V-shaped golden braid and a dark wine-red velvet doublet, bordered with fur. Complexion coppery-brown with strong highlights. On the old black frame the inscription: 'Le très Victorieux Roy de France Charles Septiesme de ce nom'.

Charles VII, born in 1403 (died in 1461) succeeded to the throne in 1422. It has usually been assumed that the King's designation as 'le très Victorieux' dates the picture with certainty not prior to 1450 (battle of Formigny) or 1451 (reconquest of the Guyenne), that would mean, after Fouquet's return from Italy. *Sterling* (*Art Bulletin, June 1946, p. 127*), following *Lemoisne* (*Louvre*) points to the Truce of Arras (1444) and demonstrates with good reasons that contemporary France considered this event the turning-point in the war against England. The portrait could thus have been painted about 1444/5, before Fouquet's journey to Italy. Such a date would account for the absence of any Italian or Renaissance traits and for the general 'primitivism' of the picture.

The King seems to look slightly younger than on Fouquet's miniature of the 'Adoration of the Magi' in the Heures de Chantilly (Pl. 70), executed shortly after 1450.

The Louvre picture is probably identical with a portrait of the King which is reported to have been hanging at the Sainte Chapelle de Bourges, before it entered the 'Cabinet des tableaux du Louvre' in 1757. Removed during the revolution, it was bought in 1838 by Louis Philippe for the Museum of Versailles.

The picture had probably a pendant, the portrait of Marie d'Anjou, lost in the original, but recorded by a drawing in the 'Recueil Gaignières' (Paris, Bibl. Nat., Est. Oa. 14, folio 15, Photo Giraudon 1929, No. 29184).

Wescher (*Fouquet, p. 26*) recalls that Piero della Francesca represented in his frescoes (1453/1454) in the room which was later called 'Stanza d'Eliodoro' among other well-known personages King Charles VII, and he suggests that Piero might have used the Fouquet portrait as a model. There exist a number of sixteenth- and seventeenth-century portraits of Charles VII, derived from the present picture; a copy is in the Gaignières Collection.

Exhibited: *Paris 1904, No. 38; London 1932, No. 74.*

121. JEAN FOUQUET
PORTRAIT OF POPE EUGENE IV. (Lost)

He is represented with two persons of his entourage, probably two prelates.

Executed before 1447. Lost in the original, but recorded by various documents.

Filarete (*Trattato dell'Architettura, 1460–1464*) states that 'Giachetto ('Grachetto') Francioso' painted the Pope 'e due altri de' suoi appresso di lui che veramente parevano vivi proprio' ('truly as if they were alive').

The identification of this 'Giachetto' with Jean Fouquet has not always been accepted. *Jacob Burckhardt, Beiträge zur Kunstgeschichte von Italien, Basel 1898, p. 315 (annotation)*, rather suggests Jaquet of Arras ('Giachetto di Benedetto d'Arras'). *Milanesi* (*Vasari II, p. 461, Firenze 1878*) makes a distinction between two painters who portrayed the Pope: 'Giacchetto', the author of the 'lifelike' effigy described by Filarete, and 'Giovanni Fochetta', i.e., Fouquet, mentioned by Vasari, whose portrait is not specifically defined. *Francesco Florio*, in a letter addressed to a friend in Italy about 1477, speaks again of the Pope's portrait, on the whole corroborating Filarete (*Mémoires de la Société Archéologique de Touraine, 1855, p. 82*).

A print in the Collection of Onuphrius Panvinius (1568), reproduced: *F. Gregorovius, Geschichte der Stadt Rom im Mittelalter, II, 1926 (Ed. by F. Schillmann)*, is supposed to preserve the Pope's likeness after Fouquet's portrait.

Cf. *A. de Montaiglon, Jean Fouquet et son portrait du Pape Eugène IV, in Curmer's 'Fouquet', 1866, p. 35.*

122. JEAN FOUQUET
ÉTIENNE CHEVALIER, PRESENTED BY ST. STEPHEN. LEFT PART OF THE 'DIPTYCH OF MELUN'. Berlin, Deutsches Museum (No. 1617)

93 : 85 cm. (36½ : 33½ in.)   PLATE 73

The donor is dressed in a carmine-red 'houppelande', the same garment that we know from his tombstone (cf. the drawing in the Gaignières Collection). He has dark hair and a dark reddish complexion. The Saint's skin is of a lighter shade, standing out against the shining white of the collar. His dress is of a dark grey-blue. Background marble and gold. On a stripe in the background the name (*Cheval*)IER ESTIEN(*ne*) recurs repeatedly.

In a very good state; the picture has not been cleaned since it entered the Berlin Collections in 1896.

Executed shortly before or about 1450: after this date the particular cut of the donor's sleeves went out of fashion (*Hulin, Van Eyck, p. 26*).

Étienne Chevalier was born in Melun; his grandfather Pierre Chevalier was Valet de Chambre of Charles V, his father Jean, secretary of Charles VII, Étienne himself was ambassador to England (1445), *trésorier* of France (1451) and afterwards Secretary of State.

The picture and its companion piece (No. 123) are known under the name of 'Diptyque de Melun': both were hung in Notre-Dame de Melun from 1461 to 1775. A detailed testimony of *Denys Godefroy* (*Remarques sur l'histoire de Charles VII, Paris 1661, p. 886*), correctly cited by *Ch. Sterling* (*Art Bulletin, June, 1946, p. 128*), describes the pictures as 'se fermant l'un dans l'autre' (closing one into another). This should dispose of the conjecture, presented by *Bouchot* as early as in 1890 (*GBA; cf. RdA, XIII, 1903, p. 122*) and lately taken up again by *Wescher* (*Fouquet, p. 50*) that the two panels were rather parts of a triptych, whose third, lost, part represented the donor's wife Cathérine Budé with her patron St. Catherine. The composition of the 'Chevalier' wing seems to corroborate the 'Diptych' conception; it asks for a supplement on the right.

Godefroy also remarked on the frame of the pictures, of blue velvet, with 'E's, done in pearls, linked by love-knots of gold and silver thread (*Huizinga, p. 143*). The frame was further adorned by medals of gilded silver, two of which have

been tentatively identified with an enamel in the Louvre (No. 124) and one in the Berlin Schlossmuseum (No. 125).

The attribution of the picture to Jean Fouquet has first been proposed by *Waagen*, who was also the first (in 1837) to connect the 'Chevalier Hours' (No. 130) with the authenticated 'Antiquités Judaïques' (No. 129).

After 1775, the picture left Melun and was separated from its companion piece. It turned up in Munich under the first Empire and was acquired by M. Brentano-Laroche of Frankfort-on-Main, who also owned the 'Hours', now in Chantilly (No. 130). *M. J. Friedländer, 'Die Votivtafel des Étienne Chevalier von Fouquet', Pr. Jhb., 1896, p. 206 ff.*

Exhibited: *Paris 1904, No. 41; London 1932, No. 69; Paris 1937, No. 13.*

123. JEAN FOUQUET
VIRGIN AND CHILD SURROUNDED BY ANGELS. RIGHT PART OF THE 'DIPTYCH OF MELUN'. Antwerp, Museum (No. 132)   PLATE 74

93 : 85 cm. (36½ : 33½ in.)

The Virgin, in a steel-grey-blue dress and red mantle, is set before the flaming onyx plaques, the gold and the sparkling jewels of the throne. Her face and her bust, with one breast uncovered, as well as the Child are greyish-white, nearly colourless, in the manner of a grisaille; the shades are pale greyish. The angels in the background, cherubim and seraphim, are of a vivid unbroken red and blue.

The picture has been rather thoroughly cleaned, but the condition is on the whole good. When I last saw the picture (in 1937) I noticed rather coarse cracks in the blue, while the rest of the surface showed an uninterrupted net of fine regular craquelure.

According to a tradition transmitted by various historiographers, among them Denys Godefroy, the Madonna has the features of Agnes Sorel, the Mistress of Charles VII (see her biography by *Pierre Champion, La Dame de Beauté, Agnès Sorel, 1931*). Agnes died in 1450. Her tombstone, with her effigy, is preserved in the Castle of Loches. A drawing of her head is in the Bibliothèque Nationale (Est. Rés. Na. 21, T. I, fol. 15, reprod. *Perls, Fouquet, 43*). Another drawing is in the 'Album Médicis' (*Champion, frontispiece*); a picture is at the Château de Monchy (with uncovered breast, but without a child). All these portraits show a good likeness to the Fouquet picture and seem to confirm the tradition that this is in fact 'La Belle Agnès'.

An inscription on the back of the panel, of 1775, states that the Melun Diptych was a vow—'un vœu'—of Étienne Chevalier, made at the death of Agnes Sorel. The date of the painting would thus be about 1450.

Owing to an alleged discrepancy between the colour scheme and the style of the two pictures, different dates of origin have been suggested. *Durrieu* (*Michel, IV, 2, p. 731*) has gone so far as to suggest another painter for the 'Madonna', while sustaining that it formed part of the 'Melun Diptych'. He bases his thesis, as may be expected, on a document: a painter Piètre André, working in Tours about 1455–1495, is reported to have painted 'une vierge avec des vêtements de couleur claire, ayant derrière elle des anges, peints les uns entièrement en bleu, les autres entièrement en rouge'. The representation of holy figures before a background of seraphim and cherubim is in no way unusual in French art—it appears repeatedly on miniatures of the 'Berri masters'. The documentary 'evidence' is certainly not sufficient to break the well-established correlation of the Fouquet 'œuvre': the panels of the Melun Diptych correspond to the introductory pages in the 'Hours of Étienne Chevalier' (No. 130, Plates 75/76); these Hours again are without any doubt illuminated by the same hand as the 'Antiquités Judaïques' (No. 129), which in their turn are secured for Fouquet by documents. Thus the whole chain holds together—quite apart from the stylistic 'evidence', which links the panels of the Melun Diptych unsolubly to one another. In regard to certain incongruities of the surfaces of the two pictures I have to point once more to the differences in their condition.

The picture has been analysed and interpreted in an enlightening way by *Huizinga, p. 142 f.*

After having been separated from its companion piece in 1775, the picture entered the Coll. van Ertborn, Antwerp, and with this Collection the Antwerp Museum.

Exhibited: *Paris 1904, No. 40; London 1932, No. 70; Paris 1937, No. 12.*

124. JEAN FOUQUET
SELF-PORTRAIT. Paris, Louvre (Cat. Marquet de Vasselot No. 465)

PLATE 89

Enamel in camayeu d'or on black ground, circular, diameter ca. 7,5 cm. (3 in.)

Inscribed in Capitals on either side of the head: IOH͠ES FOVQVET.

The copper plate is covered on one side with black enamel without 'contre-émail', on which the bust is painted in gold with a brush. Some of the features, the eyes and the mouth, have been scratched out with the point of a needle. It is supposed that Fouquet had learned this technique in Rome from Filarete, who executed a small copy of an equestrian statue of Marc Aurel and decorated it with enamels of this kind (*Cox*, p. 57). Fouquet can, however, have learned the new technique at a Flemish goldsmith's workshop in Tours (cf. *O. Goetz*, 'Holbeins Bildnis des Simon George of Quecoute, Ein Beitrag zur Geschichte desRundbildes', *Städel-Jahrbuch*, VII/VIII, 1932, p. 133). Generally speaking, the technique is a variation of North Italian enamels and a predecessor of the enamel paintings of Limoges. The 'rehaussement' in gold corresponds exactly to the use of gold on Fouquet's miniatures.

This is the earliest known self-portrait by a French painter and the first instance of an independent portrait in circular shape. It can thus be regarded as the direct forerunner of Holbein's circular portraits (*Goetz*).

The self-portrait and its companion piece (No. 125) are usually considered to have belonged to the frame of the Melun Diptych. Denys Godefroy describes this frame—in blue velvet—as being decorated with 'des médailles d'argent doré'. In order to believe in the reconstruction, one would therefore have to suppose that Godefroy mistook enamels, richly painted with gold, for medals of gilded silver *Sterling*, (*Art Bulletin*, June 1946). Furthermore, Godefroy does not mention a self-portrait—a queer omission in view of the rarity of the subject.

In my opinion the connection of the two enamels with the Diptych is not conclusive. Apart from Godefroy's text, it does not seem proper for a 15th-century painter, however famous, to plant his own undisguised likeness so near to the official portrait of an important client, not to mention the royal mistress.

The probable date of the portrait is about 1450, after Fouquet's return from Italy. Cf. *Molinier*, L'Émaillerie, 1891, p. 252 (reprod.); *P. Leprieur*, 'Note sur le cadre du diptyque de Melun', *Bulletin de la Société des Antiquaires de France*, 1897, p. 315; *Marquet de Vasselot*, 'Deux Émaux de Jean Fouquet', *GBA* 1904, II, p. 140; ibid. 'Portrait en émail de Jean Fouquet', *Bulletin de la Société des Antiquaires de France*, 1904.

Description of the portrait by *Focillon*, GBA, Janvier 1936, p. 17.

Exhibited: *Paris 1904, Émaux, No. 237; London 1932, No. 580 m.*

125. JEAN FOUQUET

BELIEVERS AND UNBELIEVERS (THE EFFUSION OF THE HOLY SPIRIT ON THE FAITHFUL AND THE INFIDELS). Formerly Berlin, Schlossmuseum   PLATE 90

Enamel in camayeu d'or on black, circular, diameter 7,5 cm. (3 in.)

Companion piece to Fouquet's Self-Portrait (No. 124)

The figures on the left, bearded and in robes and mantles, are making gestures of negation and astonishment, those on the right, beardless and wearing long tunics, stand with folded hands looking upwards in an attitude of serenity. The rays from above illuminate only the figures on the right.

This piece is supposed to have belonged to the frame of the Melun Diptych (No. 122/123) which according to the 17th century description was decorated with gilded silver medals (see No. 124) 'de moyenne grandeur, représentant quelque histoire saincte dont les personnages sont peints admirablement bien'. This would correspond quite well to the present piece. But apart from the already-mentioned disparity of technique, the subject does not seem to fit. Next to Étienne Chevalier and the Virgin one would rather expect scenes from the legend of St. Stephen and from the Life of St. Mary.

First attributed to Fouquet by *Marquet de Vasselot*, GBA, 1904, II.

Exhibited: *London 1932, No. 580 n* (Souvenir of the Exhib., pl. 4; Commem. Cat., pl. 244, No. 1064).

The former director of the 'Schlossmuseum', Dr. Robert Schmidt, to whom I am indebted for the photograph, kindly informed me of the sad fact that the enamel has been destroyed in 1945.

126. JEAN FOUQUET

PORTRAIT OF GUILLAUME JOUVENEL DES URSINS. Paris, Louvre (No. 288)   PLATE 72

Panel, 92 : 74 cm. (36 : 29 in.)

He wears a red velvet coat; a large 'escarcelle' (money bag) hangs at his belt. Background of rich Renaissance architecture: gilded panelling with marble fillings. Coat-of-arms of the Orsini family. The perfect and elaborate execution brings the panel very near to Fouquet's finest miniatures.

Guillaume Jouvenel (Juvénal) des Ursins, Baron de Traynel, born in 1400, died in 1472. He was the younger brother of the famous historiographer Jean

Jouvenel, Archbishop of Rheims. Their father was prefect of the Chamber of Commerce of Paris. Guillaume held office as Chancellor of France under Charles VII (1445–1461) and Louis XI (1465–1472).

On this portrait he seems to be 50 to 60 years old. Since the haircut with the shaved nape of the neck was no longer in use after 1460, the picture should be dated before that time, about 1455.

The coat-of-arms of the noble family of the Orsini of Rome had been taken over by the 'Ursins', originally bourgeois immigrants from Italy.

Perls (Fouquet, p. 11) suggests that Fouquet had met the Chancellor in the studio of 'Haincelin de Haguenau', identified by Perls with the 'Maître du Duc de Bedford', to whom Perls ascribes the group portrait of members of the 'Ursins' family in the Louvre (No. 112). According to Perls, Fouquet's contact with the court of Charles VII possibly resulted from this meeting (*Fouquet*, p. 20). All this is pure guesswork. Neither the authorship of the legendary 'Haincelin' for the group portrait, nor his identification with the Bedford master, nor Fouquet's direct connection with this master are in any way established.

A preparatory study for the head is in Berlin (No. 127).

From the Gaignières Collection. Bought in 1835 for the Musée de Versailles; Collection of Louis-Philippe.

Exhibited: *Paris 1904, No. 45; Paris 1946, No. 29.*

127. JEAN FOUQUET

HEAD OF GUILLAUME JOUVENEL DES URSINS. Berlin, Kupferstich-kabinett   PLATE 71

Black and coloured chalk on grey paper, 26,7 : 19,5 cm. (10½ : 7⅞ in.)

Recognized as a work by Fouquet and as the preparatory drawing for the picture of Guillaume Jouvenel (No. 126) by *M. J. Friedländer*, Eine Bildnisstudie Jean Fouquet's, Pr. Jhb., XXXI, 1910, p. 227.

The drawing seems to be the earliest known instance of the use of crayons in delicate colours and can be regarded as an incunabulum of pastel technique.

From the Rumohr Collection (Sale of Carl Friedrich von Rumohr, Dresden, 19 Oct. 1846, No. 3388a).

Exhibited: *London 1932, No. 620; Paris 1937, No. 438.*

128. JEAN FOUQUET

HEAD OF A MAN. Leningrad, Hermitage (No. 209)

Black chalk on grey paper with additions in 'encre de chine' and water colour, 27 : 20 cm.

He wears a domed hat with a rim over a skull cap.

The attribution, which is perfectly convincing, has been nearly generally accepted. The date may be the same as that of the 'Jouvenel' picture and drawing (Nos. 126, 127), about 1455.

Introduced into literature by *J. Guiffrey*, 'Un Portrait Français du XVe siècle au Musée de l'Ermitage', Les Arts, Sept., 1906.

Illustrated: *Lavallée*, pl. XVII, No. 29; *Perls, Fouquet*, p. 88, ill. 53; *Jacques*, pl. 58 (In his text *Rep. A 15th cent.* 11, *Jacques* attributes the drawing to the artist who painted the little portrait in the Heugel Coll., No. 142).

129. JEAN FOUQUET

'LES ANTIQUITÉS JUDAÏQUES'. Paris, Bibliothèque Nationale (Ms. fr. 247)   PLATES 79, 83

French translation of the work by Flavius Josephus 'De Antiquitatibus Iudaeorum'. Two volumes.

The first three miniatures of volume I are by one of the Berri miniaturists, the following miniatures (eleven) by Jean Fouquet. This corresponds to the note by François Robertet, secretary and librarian of Pierre II de Bourbon: 'En ce livre à douze ystoires les troys premières de l'enlumineur du Duc Jehan de Berri et les neuf de la main du bon peintre et enlumineur du roy Loys XIe, Jehan Foucquet, natif de Tours'. Although the number of the Fouquet miniatures is not correctly quoted, the note must be regarded as perfectly reliable, since Robertet was a contemporary of Fouquet and moved in the same circle as the painter.

The two volumes belonged originally to Jean Duc de Berri; later they became the property of his great-grandson Jacques d'Armagnac, Duc de Nemours, also a passionate bibliophile, who commissioned Fouquet to complete the illustrations. Jacques d'Armagnac had a tragic destiny: four years after his succession to the Dukedom of Nemours (in 1461) he joined the 'Ligue du Bien Public', was consequently confined to the Bastille and executed in 1477. The miniatures must therefore have been finished before 1476 and cannot have started earlier than 1455, when Jacques d'Armagnac adopted the coat-of-arms found in vol. I. The date is thereby approximately fixed; according to their style, the miniatures should be placed rather late, between 1470 and 1476.

The second volume of the manuscript was believed to be lost, until in 1903 Mr. Yates Thompson discovered it in London, but several of the miniatures had been removed and were missing. In 1905 Sir G. F. Warner found these in an album in Windsor Castle, given to Queen Victoria. Mr. Yates Thompson offered his volume to Edward VII, who had the missing miniatures replaced and in 1906 presented the whole volume, thus reconstituted, generously to the President of the French Republic for the Bibliothèque Nationale.

In this second volume only one miniature—the Entrance of Herod into Jerusalem —is by Fouquet's own hand, the others (ten miniatures of smaller size) are works of his school.

The 'Antiquités Judaïques' are the only manuscript secured for Fouquet by contemporary evidence; all our notions about the master's style as an illuminator, and consequently as an easel painter, are based on their authority.

Waagen, Kunstwerke und Künstler in Paris, 1839, p. 371; Durrieu, Les Antiquités Judaïques et le peintre Jean Fouquet, Paris 1908; Cox, p. 94 ff. (with details regarding the history of the manuscript), pl. XXXVI–XLIX; Perls, Fouquet, ill. 239–249, pl. XIV.

Exhibited: *Paris 1904, Ms. No. 128/129; Paris 1926, No. 61; London 1932, No. 747e.*

130. JEAN FOUQUET

'LES HEURES D'ÉTIENNE CHEVALIER'. Chantilly, Musée Condé; Paris, Louvre; etc. PLATES 70, 75, 76, 77, 78, 82, COLOUR PLATE P. 213
On vellum, the Chantilly sheets mounted on wood.

The most famous manuscript by Fouquet, executed for Étienne Chevalier between 1452 and 1460 (see his portrait, No. 122).

The attribution to Fouquet rests on the analogy with the documented 'Antiquités Judaïques' (No. 129). The manuscript must be dated after the master's Italian journey, owing to various Italian reminiscences such as the introduction of Roman architecture on several miniatures and—a point which has been particularly stressed—the application of a perspective construction of space after the instructions of Leone Battista Alberti's 'Treatise'. The 'Chevalier Hours' seem to testify to Fouquet's stay in Florence as well as in Rome.

The volume has been dispersed, probably in the late 18th century. It had remained in the possession of the Chevalier family until the death of Nicolas Chevalier, Baron de Crissé, in 1630. Gaignières (who died in 1715) still saw the volume intact. Afterwards all trace of it was lost until 1805, when George Brentano-Laroche (half brother of the romantic poet Clemens Brentano) of Francfort-on-Main acquired 40 of the miniatures. They were bought from Brentano's son Louis in 1891 by the Duc d'Aumale, who bequeathed them to the Nation (Institut de France).

Two of the miniatures have entered the Louvre: 'St. Martin cutting off his coat' and 'St. Margaret and St. Olybrius'. They were identified by *Durrieu (Bulletin des Musées Nationaux, Nov. 1891)*, exhibited *Paris 1904, No. 50/50 A; London 1932. Nos. 747 b and c; Paris 1946, No. 7.* One miniature, 'St. Anne with the three Marys', is in the Bibliothèque Nationale (Nouv. acq. lat. 1416), exhibited *Paris 1904, Ms. No. 131.*

One miniature, 'David praying', is in the British Museum (Add. 37421). It was discovered by Passavant in the Collection of the poet Samuel Rogers and acquired for the British Museum in 1886. Another miniature, 'St. Michael slaying the dragon', is in the Collection of Viscount Bearsted. Exhibited *London, Burl. Fine Arts Club, Winter, 1923/1924, No. 116; London 1932, No. 747f. (Commem. Cat. No. 955).*

In 1946 two further sheets turned up in the Collection of M. Louis Fenoulhet, of Shoreham, Sussex: 'Vespers of the Holy Spirit', with the west front of the Cathedral of Notre-Dame and the city of Paris in the background; 'Memorial of St. Veranus, Bishop of Cavaillon', with the interior of Notre-Dame. They were sold at Sotheby's, 18th December 1946, lots 568/569 (*Cat. pl. XIII/XVI*). Now in the Collections of Mr. Robert Lehman, New York and of M. Georges Wildenstein, New York. *J. Porcher, Deux feuillets retrouvés du Livre d'Heures d'Étienne Chevalier, comm. à la Société Nationale des Antiquaires de France, 19 févr. 1947.* Exhibited: *Paris 1947, Les Grandes Heures de Notre-Dame de Paris, No. 28/29.*

The number of recovered sheets is now 47, and it is estimated that at least 11 more are missing, besides the calendar.

M. Gruyer, Chantilly, 'Notices des peintures', Les Quarante Fouquet (1900); Henry Martin, Les Fouquet de Chantilly, 1926; Gustave Cohen, The Influence of the Mysteries on Art in the Middle Ages, GBA, Dec. 1943, p. 339. (Cohen treats in

detail the miniature of the Martyrdom of St. Apolline, which reflects a scene from a mystery play of the Saint, with spectators in stalls and boxes.)

THE ADORATION OF THE MAGI	PLATE 70

THE MADONNA ADORED BY ÉTIENNE CHEVALIER who is presented by his patron Saint Stephen. Angels in the background. Probably frontispiece miniatures of the manuscript. PLATES 75–76

THE CORONATION OF THE VIRGIN	PLATE 77
THE TRINITY IN GLORY (LA TOUSSAINT)	PLATE 78
ST. MARGARET AS A SHEPHERDESS	PLATE 82

131. JEAN FOUQUET AND COLLABORATORS

BOCCACCIO, 'DES CAS DES NOBLES HOMMES ET FEMMES'. Munich, Staatsbibliothek (Ms. fr. 6, Cod. Gall. 369)   PLATE 81
The copy of the French text was finished on 24th November 1458 by Pierre Faure, vicar of Aubervilliers near St. Denis.

Miniatures by Fouquet and collaborators. The attribution to the master rests on a comparison with the Chevalier Hours, but on the whole the present miniatures are of lower quality. Only the large frontispiece is outstanding, the trial of the Duke Jean of Alençon, called the 'Lit de justice', held under Charles VII at Vendôme in 1458, in which sentence of death was passed upon the Duke. Among the assistants at the trial one can identify Jean Jouvenel des Ursins (brother of the chancellor), le sr. de la Tour d'Auvergne, Jean Bureau, Tristan l'Hermite, Étienne Chevalier and others.

The donor has been found by Durrieu to be Laurens Gyrard, Controlleur de la recette générale des finances, who belonged to the circle of Charles VII's advisers.
P. Durrieu, Le Boccace de Munich, 1909; Perls, Fouquet, ill. 104–193, Cox, p. 84 ff.— O. Paecht, Warb. Journ., vol. IV, 1940/41, p. 92, treats the 'Lit de Justice' in detail, pointing to the lozenge shape of the composition which he calls Fouquet's favourite pattern of design. Cf. Abbé Delaunoy, Jehan Fouquet, Paris 1865/66. Catalogue Paris 1904, Ms. No. 131 bis.

132. JEAN FOUQUET

FOUR MINIATURES FROM A MANUSCRIPT 'HISTOIRE ANCIENNE JUSQU'À CÉSAR ET FAITS DES ROMAINS'. Paris, Louvre
On vellum, each 45 : 33, 5 cm.

1. The Coronation of Alexander. Exhibited: *Paris 1904, No. 354; London 1932, No. 747g.*
2. The Battle of Cannae. Exhibited: *Paris 1904, No. 354; London 1908, Burlington Fine Arts Club, 'Illuminated Manuscripts', No. 119; London 1932, No. 747a.*
3. Julius Caesar about to cross the Rubicon. Exhibited: *Paris 1904, No. 354; Paris 1946, No. 8.*
4. Pompey escaping after his defeat at Pharsalia. Exhibited: *Paris 1904, No. 354; Paris 1946, No. 8.*

The four miniatures can be ascribed to Fouquet with certainty. They show his later style, and are very close to the 'Antiquités Judaïques'; they may be dated between 1461 and 1476.

All of them belonged to the H. Yates-Thompson Collection, London—the numbers 3 and 4 have entered the Louvre in 1945, as a bequest by Mr. and Mrs. Yates-Thompson.
Reproduced: *Perls, Fouquet, ill. 263–265.*

133. JEAN FOUQUET

FRONTISPIECE OF THE STATUTES OF THE ORDER OF ST. MICHAEL: KING LOUIS XI PRESIDING OVER A 'CHAPITRE DE L'ORDRE DE SAINT MICHEL'. Paris, Bibliothèque Nationale (Ms. fr. 19819)   PLATE 84
The King is attended by the Knights of the Order, Duc Charles de Guyenne (the King's brother), Duc Jean II de Bourbon, Louis, Bâtard de Bourbon, Comte de Roussillon, etc. In the background the steward Jean Robertet.

The order was founded by King Louis in 1469 and the miniature is accordingly to be dated about 1469–1470.

The assembly room in which the 'Chapitre' is held is decorated with a picture representing St. Michael fighting the dragon. This picture may be the record of a lost work by Fouquet. It is, in any case, probable that it existed as an independent panel, which served as model to various representations of St. Michael. The figure of the Saint recurs in a similar attitude on a miniature of the later 'Statutes of the Order of St. Michael' (No. 304) executed by one of Fouquet's minor

FIG. 31. JEAN FOUQUET: ST. ANNE AND THE THREE MARYS. Miniature from the » Hours of Étienne Chevalier «
⟨ Cat. No. 130 ⟩

followers, in the manner of Colombe. Another example is the 'St. Michael' on the banner of the tapestry 'Les Cerfs volants' (Rouen, Musée des Antiquités), which has also been connected with the foundation of the 'Ordre de St. Michel'.
Durrieu, Gazette Archéologique, 1890; Perls, Fouquet, Colour pl. XI.
Exhibited: *Paris 1904, Ms. No. 132.*

134. JEAN FOUQUET AND OTHERS
'LES GRANDES CHRONIQUES DE FRANCE'. Paris, Bibliothèque Nationale (Ms. fr. 6465)   PLATE 80
Only some of the miniatures can be attributed to Fouquet. Probably executed in the first half of Louis XI's reign.
H. Omont, Les Grandes Chroniques de France, Paris 1906; Perls, Fouquet, ill. 54–103.
Durrieu, in *Mélanges G. B. de Rossi* (de l'École Française de Rome), 1892, treats separately one page of the manuscript which is of special topographical interest: the 'Coronation of Charlemagne' with an interior view of St. Peter's in Rome, as it was during Fouquet's sojourn in this city.
Exhibited: *Paris 1904, Ms. No. 130.*

135. JEAN FOUQUET AND OTHERS
'LES HEURES DE LA DAME DE BAUDRICOURT, ANNE DE BEAUJEU'.
Paris, Coll. Comtesse Durrieu
The principal page shows Anne de Beaujeu, kneeling, accompanied by ladies of

the court, in prayer before the Virgin (reprod. *Durrieu, Michel*, IV, 2, *p.* 727, and *Perls, Fouquet, ill.* 236). The donatrix on this page may be compared with the 'Lady with a hénin' (No. 153).
The 'Half-figure of Christ' (reprod. *Perls, ill. 238*)—which is certainly not by Fouquet himself—recalls in some details (arrangement of the hands on the parapet) the portraits sometimes attributed to the so-called 'Master of 1456' (Nos. 143/144).

136. JEAN FOUQUET
THE DESCENT FROM THE CROSS, KNOWN AS THE 'PIETÀ DE NOUANS'.
Nouans (Indre et Loire), Parish Church   PLATES 85–88
147 : 236 cm. (58 : 93 in.)
On the left, Joseph of Arimathia wearing a violet and green robe with white drapery, and Nicodemus in a yellow tunique and green cap. St. John is in red, the Virgin in blue with a white cloak. In the centre four (holy?) women, three of them dressed as nuns in grey and white. On the right the donor, kneeling, accompanied by St. James in pilgrim's dress.
The composition is essentially complete, although the panel is slightly cut at its upper part; the background is repainted. On the whole, the execution is perhaps not quite of the same perfection as the invention of this grandiose work. Nevertheless the caution of some critics who call the 'Pietà' 'School of Fouquet' seems to me excessive. In my opinion it should be considered a work entirely by the

master himself. The fact that the colouring is less brilliant than on Fouquet's other paintings has been partly explained by *Hulin* (*Notes*, 1932): he believes that in view of the large size of the panel less expensive material has been used, since colours like lapislazuli and cinnabar would have raised the price unduly. Hulin points, however, also to the use of similar 'neutral' colours in Fouquet's latest miniatures.

The Pietà has been introduced into literature by *P. Vitry* (*Communication faite à la Société des Antiquaires de France*, *Déc.* 1931, and *GBA*, 1932, I, *p.* 254 *ff.*) who supposes that the picture was originally intended not for Nouans but more probably for the nearby Abbaye de Villeloin or for the Chartreuse du Liget. He further suggests that the picture had some connection with the decorations which Fouquet was commissioned to design for Louis XI's entry into Tours in 1461.

The picture belongs to Fouquet's late period and should be dated about 1470–1475 (after 1475 such costumes came out of fashion).

Abbé Yves de Raulin (*GBA, June 1936*) wants to identify the donor with Archbishop Jean de Bernard, who in 1463 commissioned 'une image de la B. V. Marie' for the Cathedral of Tours. This identification is not convincing: the 'Pietà' can hardly be called a 'picture of the Virgin', and a donor, introduced by St. James, would not be called John.

Hulin's suggestion (*Notes*, 1932) has more to recommend itself: he sees in the donor the 'directeur' of a congregation of pious women, three of whom are shown under the cross in nun's costumes.

Exhibited: *London 1932, No. 46; Paris 1937, No. 15.*

137. JEAN FOUQUET
PORTRAIT OF A (HOLY?) MONK. Marseille, Coll. Comte Demandolx-Dedons

34,3 : 27,3 cm.

Fragment from a large composition. The background shows on the left architecture, on the right the sky.

The picture should be regarded as an original by Fouquet in his mature manner. Although largely repainted, it is therefore a document of great interest.

Introduced into literature by *L. Dimier, GBA*, 1935, I, *p.* 76–79 (with illustration); *Dupont* (*p. 50*) thinks it may be a part of a composition similar to the 'Pietà de Nouans', but earlier, about 1455.

Acquired from a collector in Nazelles near Amboise.

Reproduced: *Réau, pl. 64; Perls (Fouquet), ill. 250; Gillet, Colour Plate VIII.*
Exhibited: *Paris 1937, No. 14.*

⟨*138.*⟩ *Attributed to JEAN FOUQUET*
Man in a Turban. Santa Barbara, Cal., Coll. Arthur Sachs (On loan to the Museum of Sta. Barbara, Cal., in 1946.)

Circular; diameter 24 cm. (9½ in.)

He is seen on red background, holding a flower.

On the (old) frame a French inscription and, four times recurrent, the letter 'S'.

The attribution to Fouquet has been put forward repeatedly; recently—with a question mark—by *Wescher* (*Fouquet, p. 55 and 101, ill. 41*). Wescher finds a connection between this portrait and the heads on Fouquet's miniatures of the last decade, about 1470.

I do not see Fouquet in this very expressive portrait, and it seems to me nearer to Flemish than to French portraiture. The possibility of a French origin should, however, not be totally excluded.

Reproduced: *Pantheon, I, 1928, p. 51.*
Exhibited: *New York 1927, No. 13; Cambridge (U.S.A.), Fogg Art Museum 1927; Detroit 1928.*

139. ATTRIBUTED TO JEAN FOUQUET, ABOUT 1470
PORTRAIT OF A PAPAL LEGATE. New York, Coll. of the late Lord Duveen   PLATE 92

Silver point on cream-coloured paper, 19,5 : 13 cm. (7¾ : 5⅛ in.)

He wears a hat and a scarf knotted round his neck. Inscribed near the right upper corner: 'ung Roumain légat de nostre St-Père en France.'

It has been suggested that the sitter might be Teodoro Lelli, Bishop of Trevise, who, as papal legate in 1464, aged 40, accompanied the Bishop of Ostia on a mission to Louis XI (*Bouchot 1904, pl. XXXVIII*).

A copy of the drawing, in red chalk, is in the Royal Library at Windsor.

The attribution to Fouquet has first been proposed by *Hulin,* who dates the drawing rather late, in the period of the 'Statutes of the Order of St. Michael'

FIG. 32   ⟨ Cat. No. 140 ⟩

(No. 133). Although the quality of this celebrated and impressive drawing is certainly worthy of a great master, I have never seen conclusive reasons for attributing it just to Fouquet.

Formerly Collections P. H. Lanckrink, J. P. Heseltine, Henry Oppenheimer (*Sale July 1936, Catalogue by K. T. Parker, lot 428*).
Exhibited: *Paris 1904, No. 44; London, Grafton Galleries, 1909–1910, p. 175 No. 119; London 1932, No. 626; Paris 1937, No. 437.*

140. ATTRIBUTED TO JEAN FOUQUET
FIGURE OF A YOUNG MAN. Vaduz, Fürst of Liechtenstein   FIG. 32
Drawing, pen and bistre, heightened with white, on orange coloured paper. 21,5 : 14, 7 cm.

He stands leaning on a stick, on his left two little dogs. On the upper part of the sheet two initials which have not yet been explained, and traces of more initials.

Attributed to Fouquet by *Meder* (*Albertina Publication 643*); cf. *Lavallée*, pl. XVIII No. 30.

The drawing, which I had the opportunity of examining carefully in the original, is certainly French but hardly by Fouquet. It shows an earlier, more 'Gothic' style.

141. ATTRIBUTED TO JEAN FOUQUET
PORTRAIT OF DUNOIS, BASTARD OF ORLÉANS. New York, Coll. William Goldman

43,8 : 27 cm.

He wears a close-fitting dark cap; his coat is bordered with fur.

Jean, Comte de Dunois et de Longueville, was the illegitimate son of Louis of Orléans. He has become famous as commander-in-chief of the French forces and powerful supporter of Jeanne d'Arc. Here he is represented as an old man, shortly before his death in 1468.

A portrait of the *Bâtard* is recorded to have been in the Gaignières Collection and before in the collection of the Duchesse de Longueville-Estouteville, a descendant of the Dunois family. It is the question whether the New York picture is identical with the Gaignières portrait or an old copy after it.

P. Vitry introduces the picture as the Gaignières original, painted by a great master, perhaps by Fouquet (*RdA*, 1903, XIII, *p.* 255 and *La Renaissance*, 1926, *p.* 299). *Winkler* (*U.M.*, 73) publishes it as by Fouquet himself, *Jacques* (*Rep. A 15th cent.* 13) thinks of a free imitation after Fouquet. *Perls* (*Fouquet, ill.* 280, *p.* 250) proposes 'Haincelin de Haguenau' without any apparent reason, since the resemblance with the portraits of the des Ursins family (No. 112), which are also given arbitrarily to 'Haincelin', is not evident.

The picture has been cut and is altogether not in a satisfactory state of preservation. It should therefore better be left out of the corpus of Fouquet originals. I must, however, state that I have not seen the picture after its recent cleaning to which Jacques refers.

Formerly Coll. Gabeau d'Amboise.
Exhibited: *Paris 1904, No.* 52.

142. SCHOOL OF TOURAINE, ABOUT 1460; FORMERLY ASCRIBED TO FOUQUET

PORTRAIT OF A MAN (FRAGMENT). Paris, Coll. Heugel   PLATE 93
Panel, 30 : 25 cm. (12 : 9⅞ in.)
This neat and lively portrait is by an independent master, a contemporary of Fouquet. It is also to be placed in Touraine.
Jacques, Rep. A 15th cent. 10, *pl.* 57.
Exhibited: *Paris 1904, No.* 352 (*suppl.*)

143. SCHOOL OF SOUTHERN FRANCE, 1456; FORMERLY ASCRIBED TO FOUQUET

PORTRAIT OF A YOUNG MAN, DATED 1456. Vaduz, Fürst of Liechtenstein   PLATE 91
Vellum on panel, 51 : 41, 8. cm. (20⅛ : 16½ in.)
Brown doublet, ochre-coloured background, date in creamish white. The light falls on the fore-shortened side of the face, forming rather strong contrasts of light and shade.

The recent cleaning in 1938 has resulted in several alterations. The cap and the buckle at the collar disappear. The background which had been reddish brown turns ochre yellow. The greenish tinge of the doublet comes off. The colour of the face, formerly a uniform yellow becomes more vivid. The cleaning has corroborated an observation I ventured to make some time ago: that the picture is painted on vellum. The state is on the whole satisfactory; the surface shows a number of tiny dark spots—a peculiarity of parchment paintings. Published after the cleaning by *E. v. Strohmer, Pantheon XVI, Heft* II, *Febr.* 1943, *p.* 25 (X-Ray record, ill. 81).

Acquired in 1677 by Karl Eusebius, Prince of Liechtenstein, from the Imperial court painter Johann Spillenberger. Old descriptions give evidence that the repaints existed already in 1780. It can be assumed that they were done in Spillenberger's time.

Many authors have been proposed for this superb picture. Prince Karl Eusebius bought it as a 'Mantegna'. The 18th-century catalogue of the Liechtenstein Collection quotes it as a self-portrait by Burgkmair. *W. von Bode* (*Die graphischen Künste*, 1895), *Friedlaender* (*Pr. Jhb.*, 1896, *p.* 213, and *ZfbK*, 1912) and *Bouchot* (*Paris* 1904) vote for Fouquet; *Durrieu* (*Michel*, IV, 2, *p.* 730) for Colin d'Amiens; *S. Reinach* for Nuño Gonçalvez (*Revue Archéologique*, 1910, II, p. 236). *Hulin* (*van Eyck*) gives it to a master of Netherlandish origin influenced by van Eyck, who painted in Burgundy or in Provence; *Dupont* (p. 52) to a master of Tours who was trained in Flanders. *Wescher* (*Fouquet, p.* 57) is reminded of the great miniaturist, the 'Maître du Roi René'.

Nearly all critics connect the picture closely with the 'Man with a glass of wine' in the Louvre (No. 144). A 'Master of 1456' has been constructed and has been credited with other works, none of which seem to go well together.

In my opinion, the connection of the Liechtenstein and the Louvre pictures should no longer be taken for granted. The similarity of the left hands on both pictures, lying in the same manner on a parapet, is no irrefutable argument: the same hand in exactly the same position is to be seen on a miniature—half-figure of Christ—in the 'Hours of Anne de Beaujeu' (No. 135, *Perls, Fouquet, ill.* 238), which is otherwise not specially associated with the two portraits. After the cleaning, the French origin of the Liechtenstein picture has become evident

beyond any doubt, but the painter is not Fouquet (Dr. Friedlaender has also recently abandoned this attribution). I should like, following Wescher, to connect the picture—with due caution—with the illuminator of the 'Cuer d'Amours espris', and with the Aix Annunciation. In any case I see in the artist a great master of the South of France.

If the style is different from that of Fouquet, the resemblance of the sitter to Fouquet's Self-Portrait (No. 124) remains remarkable. In particular the wide open eyes, without eyelashes, one of them slightly squinting, reveal a likeness. The enigma of the 'Portrait of 1456' still awaits its final solution.

Exhibited: *Paris 1904, No.* 51 (*Bouchot 1904, pl. XXXV*); *Lucerne, Kunstmuseum 1948, No.* 102.

⟨144.⟩ PORTUGUESE(?) *follower of JAN VAN EYCK; formerly ascribed to FOUQUET or to the so-called MASTER OF 1456*

Portrait of a Man with a Glass of Wine. Paris, Louvre (No. 1000)
63 : 44 cm.   FIG. 36 (cf. FIGS. 33–35)
Olive yellowish background. The light falls in from the left.
This picture has mostly been connected with the Portrait of a Man, dated 1456, (No. 143). The recent cleaning of the latter painting has enhanced the differences between the two pictures. If the Liechtenstein painting must now be regarded as certainly belonging to the French school, the 'Man with a glass of wine' seems to move farther and farther away from the French context. The still-life and the whole genre-like set-up are definitely not French. They are rather to be found on Flemish portraits, and a certain affinity between this portrait and the 'Man with the carnation' by Jan van Eyck in the Berlin Museum has been noted. The 'Man with a glass of wine' is, however, not purely Flemish. He belongs to another world and to a more Southern one. The attribution to the entourage of Gonçalvez and the Portuguese school, not at all convincing in the case of the Liechtenstein portrait, must here be seriously considered.

The picture is in a good state. An examination in the laboratory of the Louvre has led to the discovery (made by J. Dupont) that traces of large letters, in the manner of the date on the Liechtenstein picture, can be observed in the background. (This is, by the way, not an unusual feature in 15th century portraits, cf. Rogier's 'Froimont' in Brussels.)

Formerly in the Collections of Archduke Leopold in Brussels (17th century) and of Count Wilczek, Vienna.

S. Reinach, 'L'Homme au verre de vin', Revue Archéologique, 1910, *p.* 236. For further literature see No. 143.

Exhibited: *Paris 1904, No.* 43 (*Bouchot 1904, pl. XXXVI*); *Brussels* 1935, *No.* 905; *Paris 1946, No.* 33.

⟨145.⟩ PORTUGUESE(?) *MASTER; sometimes attributed to the so-called MASTER OF 1456*

Woman with a Fruit Still-life. Amsterdam, Coll. Proehl   FIG. 35
82 : 50 cm.
This impressive and enigmatic picture has not yet been satisfactorily explained. It is probably not a pure portrait but may rather represent a figure from ancient history or mythology, perhaps a Sibyl (there again none of the Sibyls has a plate of fruit as her attribute). The costume is in any case more archaic than the style of the painting, which points to the last quarter of the 15th century; it is a kind of fancy costume. The gesture of one hand lying on the breast seems to have a symbolic meaning.

Ludwig Goldscheider suggests that this might be a representation of Pomona, a wood nymph 'who was supposed to preside over gardens and to be goddess of all sorts of fruit-trees' (*Lemprière's Classical Dictionary, 1804*).

Wescher (*Pantheon, Jan.* 1938) ascribes the picture resolutely to the so-called 'Master of 1456'. It has some affinity to the elderly woman on the 'Wing of the Infante' by Nuño Gonçalvez (Polyptych of St. Vincent, reprod. *Reynaldo dos Santos, L'Art Portugais, Plate* XVI) and it may on the whole fit better into the Portuguese than into the French context.

Another connection which seems to present itself is with the Polyptych of San Vincenzo Ferrier, Naples, San Pietro Martire, probably a work of Colantonio (cf. No. 97). One may remember that the Head of an elderly Man attributed to Colantonio (No. 98) should also be regarded as the representation of a prophet rather than as a portrait proper.

Formerly Collection Hainauer, Berlin.

Exhibited: *Rotterdam, Boymans Museum, 'Meesterwerken uit Vier Eeuwen'* 1938, *No.* 4 (*cat. ill.* 21).

⟨146.⟩ *PORTUGUESE MINIATURIST, sometimes attributed to the so-called MASTER OF 1456*

Portrait of Prince Henri le Navigateur (born 1394). Paris, Bibliothèque Nationale (Ms. port. 41)

K. Perls ('Une œuvre nouvelle du Maître de 1456', AdA, Nov. 1935, p. 313) connects this rather poor miniature with the portraits which have been united under the heading of the 'Maître de 1456'. The whole construction does not hold together, and it is not even necessary to see in this miniature a copy after a lost work either by the painter of the Portrait of 1456 (No. 143) or by the painter of the 'Man with a glass of wine' (No. 144).

A portrait of the 'Navigateur' appears on the 'Wing of the Infante', Polyptych of St. Vincent, by Nuño Gonçalvez, (cf. No. 145). This great Portuguese artist is, however, so far superior to the author of the present miniature that the latter can at best be regarded as belonging to his very distant entourage.

147. SCHOOL OR STUDIO OF JEAN FOUQUET

TRIPTYCH OF THE PASSION OF CHRIST, DATED 1485. Loches, Église S. Antoine   PLATE 95

143 : 283 cm. (56½ : 111½ in.)

The three scenes—Bearing of the Cross, Crucifixion and Entombment—are reunited on one large panel, separated by thin columns painted in gold.

The colours are remarkably bright and vivid, the sky a shiny blue, the landscape green-blue and clearly visible up to the farthest distance. The faces of the women are very pale, those of the men brownish. Frequent use of brilliant highlights. The Virgin, in greenish-blue, is surrounded in each scene by holy women, two of them in nun's costumes and the third in red with a large white cap. On each of the two lateral parts one man is clad in strikingly bright yellow.

When I had the opportunity of studying the picture at leisure, in 1934, it looked as if it had just been energetically cleaned and restored. It had been given a brilliance which suits an 'objet de dévotion' in a dark church better than a distinguished work of art in a gallery. A restoration had probably been necessary since at the time of the Exhibition of Tours in 1890 the picture was reported to be 'en piteux état' (GBA, 1901, II, p. 92 ff.).

The Triptych shows the date 1485 on the left part, and the initials F.I.B. near the clerical donor who kneels on the right part. These letters have been interpreted in different ways: they have been declared to be a signature 'Fecit Jean Bourdichon' or to refer to the donor 'Frère Jean Bourgeois'. Both explanations are not satisfactory. The style does not support the attribution to Bourdichon, which has been taken up again by Wescher (Fouquet, p. 84 ff.), and the donor cannot be 'Frère Bourgeois', the Father-Confessor of Charles VII, since the portrait of this priest in his 'Book of Hours', illuminated by Bourdichon, shows another likeness (Innsbruck, Universitäts-Bibliothek, Cod. 281, published by H. J. Hermann, 'Beiträge zur Kunstgeschichte, F. Wickhoff gewidmet', 1903, p. 46-63, pl. I, ill. p. 59). The similarity of the painting with the miniatures of the 'Livre d'Heures de Marguerite de Rohan, Comtesse d'Angoulême', mostly ascribed to Bourdichon, is also not cogent (formerly Coll. M. Thévenin, published in 1903; later Coll. McGibbon, London; two of the miniatures reprod. Bouchot, 1904, pl. LXXI).

The Triptych of Loches is the only surviving large altarpiece painted in the near entourage of Fouquet, beside the Pietà de Nouans. Although the date points to the time after Fouquet's death, we should like to imagine it as being, at least partly, conceived by him and executed in his studio, perhaps, as has been suggested, by one of his sons. Durrieu (RdA, 1904, XV, p. 420) attributes the triptych tentatively to Jean Poyet, a painter of Touraine, known from the archives only. Originally painted for the Chartreuse du Liget, near Loches. The donor may have been one of the monks of the Chartreuse.

Exhibited: *Tours 1890; Paris 1904, No. 69; Paris, Passion 1934, No. 124*

148. SCHOOL OF TOURAINE, ABOUT 1480

TRIPTYCH: BEARING OF THE CROSS, CRUCIFIXION, ENTOMBMENT OF CHRIST. Moulins, Musée (No. 11)   PLATE 94

The three pictures are reunited by the original old frame to one large piece, the measurements of which are roughly 59,7 : 165 cm. (23½ : 65 in.), or about 56 : 51 cm. (22 : 20 in.) each picture.

On all three representations the Virgin wears a light-blue mantle lined with purple, St. John a red coat over violet-brown. The faces of the women are colourless, those of the men deep brown, with the exception of the perfectly pale Christ. The colour scheme is clear and simple without subtle nuances.

The state is not good but not too unpleasant: there are a number of holes, but the preserved parts are neither rubbed nor repainted and show the original brush work clearly—this was at least the case when I last saw the pictures, in 1938.

As far as I know, the Triptych has not yet been mentioned in literature. It is in style and types near to the Triptych of Loches (No. 147) and it even shows affinities to the Pietà de Nouans, although, of course, in a very simplified manner, on a modest scale. In view of the small number of altarpieces from the School of Touraine, the pictures should be worth some attention.

149. SCHOOL OF TOURAINE, ABOUT 1460/1470

THE VIRGIN AND CHILD WITH ST. BENEDICT; THE ADORATION OF THE MAGI; THE DESCENT FROM THE CROSS; THE MARTYRDOM OF ST. HIPPOLYTUS. Le Mans, Musée Hôtel de Tessé (No. 1 bis-4)

Four panels. About 112 : 115 cm. each; originally two panels painted on both sides.

The colour scheme is rather unusual and select, particularly in the first picture. The Virgin wears a white coat over a light-grey dress, the throne on which she sits is lined with dark red. The Child on her knees is dressed in a long wine-red shirt, and the same wine-red appears in the cushion under her feet, contrasting with the dark red of the throne. The preservation of the panels is on the whole good, only the 'Descent from the Cross' has suffered, and the composition of the 'Martyrdom of St. Hippolytus' looks strangely fragmentary.

The influence of Fouquet is noticeable, although his dignity has turned into stiffness, his sculpturesque quality has become wooden. In spite of these deficiencies, the panels have a provincial charm of their own, and they certainly deserve more attention than has hitherto been paid to them.

I find similarities between these panels and a manuscript of the Bibliothèque Nationale (Ms. lat. 1160), particularly a 'Madonna between Angels' (folio 20, reprod. *Leroquais, Les Livres d'Heures de la Bibl. Nat., Paris 1927, pl. LXXXVIII*). The reference given by Jacques (Rep. A 15th cent. 12) to possible relations between the Le Mans panels and Dutch painters like the 'Master of the Virgo inter Virgines' and 'Jan de Cock', reveals a regrettable misconception of early Dutch art.

From the Priory of S. Hippolyte de Vivoin (Sarthe), where the panels were hanging on the vault of the church. Offered to the Museum of Le Mans in 1848 by the Abbé Tournesac.

Detailed description of the panels in the *Catalogue of the Museum of Le Mans, edited by Arsène le Feuvre and Arsène Alexandre, in 1932*, with illustrations.

Reproduced: *Sterling, fig. 90* (The 'Madonna' only).

150. SCHOOL OF TOURAINE

THE LAMENTATION OVER CHRIST. London, Private Collection

68,6 : 77,5 cm.

This rather crude but impressive picture can still be derived from the later School of Fouquet. It shows some affinity to the 'Entombment of Christ' in Moulins (No. 148), particularly in details (the sarcophagus with the iron rings), and to the panels of Le Mans (No. 149); but on the whole the types are nearer to the enamels of the period than to easel paintings, and it may be the work of a painter otherwise working as an enameller. The picture has, as far as I know, not yet been mentioned in literature.

Formerly Coll. Arnot, London.

A 'Descent from the Cross' with St. Sebastian and St. Roch, dated 1515, by the same hand, is in a Collection in Paris.

151. SCHOOL OF TOURAINE, ABOUT 1490/1500

MADONNA AND CHILD. New York, Metropolitan Museum (Coll. G. Blumenthal.)

The Child Christ, dressed in a long shirt and looking remarkably grown up, gives benediction.

This stately and statuesque picture is not in a perfect state. The background, now yellow, may have been gilded.

By a late follower of Fouquet; perhaps the work of an archaizing painter in the beginning of the 16th century.

Reproduced: *Jacques, pl. 63.*

152. ATTRIBUTED TO THE SCHOOL OF TOURAINE, ABOUT 1480/1490

THE LEGEND OF A SAINT. Formerly Coll. J. H. Percy, Guy's Cliff, Warwick   FIG. 41

105 : 70 cm. (41½ : 27½ in.)

The young Saint, dressed in a white coat with golden pomegranate pattern stands

FIG. 33   ⟨ Cat. No. 98 ⟩ (cf. Cat. No. 145)

FIG. 34   (cf. Cat. No. 144)

FIG. 35   ⟨ Cat. No. 145 ⟩

FIG. 36   ⟨ Cat. No. 144 ⟩

in full frontal view. He seems to take leave from his worldly friends—on the right—and turns to the left, giving benediction to three more humble worshippers kneeling before him. In the background the Saint appears again leaning over the railings of a bridge. He throws an object into the water, which splashes high up. Probably part of a retable showing a series of scenes from the Life of the not yet identified Saint.

The composition, the types and particularly the background buildings and landscape seem to point to Touraine.

The picture has not yet been mentioned in literature.

153. FRENCH SCHOOL, ABOUT 1460
PORTRAIT OF A YOUNG LADY. New York, Coll. Robert Lehmann
57 : 40 cm.
She wears a 'hénin', her head is turned in three-quarter profile to the right.
The picture has been cleaned rather thoroughly.
Attributed (with a question mark) to Petrus Christus by *Friedländer* (I, p. 158). The clear decorative outline seems rather to point to France, apart from the conformity in costume and type to the ladies on a miniature—sometimes attributed to Fouquet—'Anne de Beaujeu in prayer' (Heures de la Dame de Baudricourt, No. 135).
Formerly Coll. Cardon, Brussels.
Reproduced: *Pantheon*, 1930, p. 115; *Friedländer, I*, pl. LXX; *Pantheon 1941, Vol. XXVIII*, p. 200 (*Wescher*: 'Portrait of Mary of Burgundy').
Exhibited: *Bruges, 1907, No. 191*.

⟨154.⟩ *Wrongly attributed to the FRENCH SCHOOL*
Portrait of a Lady. New York, Coll. Robert Lehmann
She wears a 'hénin'; her head is seen in strict profile to the left.
This picture is certainly not French but German (Friedländer suggests convincingly B. Strigl as the possible author). The execution is considerably later than the costume would lead us to suppose, not before the beginning of the 16th century.
Reproduced: *Pantheon*, 1930, p. 116 (as 'Northern French').

155. NORTHERN FRENCH MASTER OF 1451
ALTARPIECE: THE CRUCIFIXION OF ST. PETER WITH A KNEELING DONOR; ST. ANTHONY IN PRAYER WITH A KNEELING DONATRIX; THE ANGEL AND THE MADONNA OF THE ANNUNCIATION. New York, Metropolitan Museum
Four panels, 120 : 78 cm. each. Formerly two panels, the Annunciation originally forming the outside wings.
The panels have been split, but their condition has remained satisfactory. On the picture representing the 'Angel of the Annunciation' the date '1451'. The Annunciation is set on a vivid red.
The figures of the donors show an affinity to the School of Rogier van der Weyden. The composition of the 'Annunciation' recurs in South German art (cf. the Hofer-Altar by Schuechlin, the altarpieces of Sterzing and Tiefenbronn). The figures of the spectators on the 'Crucifixion of St. Peter' seem also akin to the types of South German followers of Rogier (Pleydenwurff, etc.). The colour scheme, the landscape and a certain simplicity in the arrangement, a reticence of gesture, persuade us, however, to leave the panels within the French context, though not as a very characteristic French specimen.
Sterling (*Metropolitan Museum Bulletin, Oct. 1945, vol. IV, No. 2*) notes particularly that the outside wings ('Annunciation') are not grisailles, as stated in the previous literature.
Reproduced: *Guiffrey Marcel Terrasse, II, pl. XXXII–XXXVIII* ('ancienne Collection Levesque'); *Gillet, pl. 58*.
Exhibited: *New York 1927, Nos. 15–17*.

156. NORTHERN (?) FRENCH MASTER, ABOUT 1470
CHRIST APPEARING TO ST. MARY MAGDALEN; THE INCREDULITY OF ST. THOMAS. ON THE REVERSE: ST. ANTHONY AND ST. SEBASTIAN
Marseille, Coll. Comte Demandolx-Dedons
Two panels from an altarpiece, painted on both sides. 73 : 35 cm. each.
These panels, which have been attributed to the School of Nicolas Froment, seem rather to belong to the North of France. They show certain similarities to the 'Retable of 1451' (No. 155), but they are painted a generation later, about 1470.
Reproduced: *Labande, pl. LXXI/LXXII; Gillet, pl. 47 and colour plate V*.

⟨157.⟩ *FLEMISH PAINTER working in Paris, about 1460*
'Le Retable du Parlement de Paris'. Paris, Louvre (No. 998 A.)
210 : 269 cm.
Crucifixion, on the left Sts. Louis and John the Baptist, on the right Sts. Denis and Charlemagne. In the background views of Paris: on the left the Tour de Nesle, the Seine and the Louvre with the 'Petit Bourbon'; on the right the Palais. As far as I know this is the first time that Parisian views, which had already appeared in miniatures, were introduced into easel painting.
Although it must be considered certain that the picture was executed in Paris, the style shows no trace of French character and we may imagine the author as a Flemish artist who completed this one commission and left Paris again directly afterwards. No other picture could as yet be assigned to him.
Before the revolution, the 'retable' was placed in the 'grande chambre dorée' of the Parliament of Paris (it is reproduced as being there on an engraving by Poilly, after a drawing by Delamonce, representing a 'lit de justice' held in 1715). During the revolution it passed to the Musée des Monuments Français; afterwards in the Palais de Justice, Paris.
J. Guiffrey, 'Le Retable du Parlement de Paris', Les Arts, November 1904; F. Mély, 'Le Retable du Parlement', RdA, July 1914. Reproduced: *Guiffrey Marcel, Terrasse, pl. 20/21; Lemoisne Louvre, pl. 27 and 28; Lemoisne, pl. 68–69 A and B; Réau, pl. 7.*
Exhibited: *Paris 1904, No. 355 (Bouchot 1904, pl. LXVII–LXVIII bis).*

158. SCHOOL OF AMIENS, 1437
'LE SACERDOCE DE LA VIERGE'. Paris, Louvre   PLATE 97
100 : 60 cm., arched top.
In the nave of a gothic church (the Cathedral of Amiens), in front of an altar, stands a female figure clad in the robes of a High Priest, extending her left hand to a child. Both have haloes. On the right a kneeling donor carrying a scroll with the legend: 'Digne vesture au prestre souverain'. On the upper left-hand corner, under a coat-of-arms, the date 1462, which does not correspond to the style of the picture and seems to be due to a later modification.
This is a symbolical representation of the Virgin as a priest (Virgo Sacerdos) officiating the first mass. The Child is Christ.
J. Dupont (GBA, Dec. 1932, p. 265–274) ingeniously connects the picture with the 'Puy d'Amiens'. He cites an entry in the annals of the 'Confrérie du Puy' which states that in 1437 Jean du Bos, then Master of the Brotherhood, commissioned a picture 'vesture'. The identification seems obvious. Style criticism can accept the attribution to Northern France as well as the early date. It is the date of Jan van Eyck's 'St. Barbara' in Antwerp, and the 'Sacerdoce'—which shows in its composition similarities to Jan's 'Madonna in the Church' (Berlin) —can be imagined as a contemporary of the earlier van Eyck period. Details and types incidentally have no connection with the van Eyck sphere; the type of the donor seems to point rather to the neighbourhood of the Maître de Flémalle.
The 'Confrérie du Puy d'Amiens' was a literary society dedicating itself specially to the worship of the Virgin Mary. It was the custom of this brotherhood that each year its appointed 'Master' presented a picture, the device of which was given by a refrain ('palinod') fixed in the year's poetical contest. The Master is habitually represented in adoration before the Virgin.
Most of these 'Puy' pictures have been destroyed, but 47 of them are recorded by copies in a manuscript (of 1517/1518; Ms. of Louise de Savoy, Bibl. Nat., Ms. franç. 145; exhibited: *Paris 1904, Ms. No. 199*; cf. *G. Durand, Chants royaux et Tableaux de la Confrérie du Puy d'Amiens, 1911, p. I–VII).*
Originally in the Béguinage in Malines (Mechlin).
F. Peeters, Revue Belge d'Arch. et d'Histoire de l'Art, t. I, fasc. II. Août, 1931, p. 121.
Exhibited: *Antwerp 1930, No. 345* (then in the Coll. Clemens-Ulens, Antwerp); *Bruxelles 1935, No. 902; Paris 1946, No. 13.*

159. SCHOOL OF AMIENS, 1499
'PUY D'AMIENS' WITH THE DEVICE 'ARBRE PORTAIT FRUIT D'ÉTERNELLE VIE'. Amiens, Musée de Picardie (Salon Notre-Dame du Puy, No. 8)
Presented to the 'Confrérie du Puy' in 1499 by the Master of that year, Firmin Crequerel, conseiller au Baillage d'Amiens.
This picture is of importance as one of the very few surviving 15th-century examples of the 'Puy'. It has suffered considerably; whole parts of the painting are destroyed, but the preserved parts show the style clearly, in particular in the many dry but characteristic portraits. On the whole, portraiture is the most noticeable trait in the entire Amiens production.
Literature on the 'Puy d'Amiens' see No. 158.

160. SCHOOL OF AMIENS

CHRIST BLESSING, WITH ST. JOHN THE BAPTIST, ST. BARBARA AND DONORS. Amiens, Musée de Picardie (Salon Notre-Dame du Puy, No. 9)

Christ, in full frontal view, stands before a canopy held by flying angels who recall the angels in Marmion's St. Bertin fragment (No. 171). Among the donors again a number of remarkable portrait heads.

P. Dubois, La Picardie et l'Exposition des Primitifs Français, 1904, Bulletin de la Société des Antiquaires de Picardie, XXII.

161. SCHOOL OF AMIENS, ABOUT 1500

DIPTYCH: THE CORONATION OF KING DAVID; THE CORONATION OF A KING OF FRANCE. ON THE REVERSE: VIERGE DE PITIÉ. Paris, Musée de Cluny. 195 : 110 cm.

The King of France is Louis XII; he was consecrated at Rheims in 1498.
On a canopy the legend Ung Dieu, ung roy, une foi. It has been supposed with good reasons that this is a picture by one of the 'Puy d'Amiens' artists.
Dupont, Bulletin des Musées de France, Janvier 1933, p. 6–9.
Exhibited: Paris 1904, No. 366 (Bouchot 1904, pl. C).

162. SCHOOL OF AMIENS, BEGINNING OF THE 16TH CENTURY

MADONNA STANDING IN A GOTHIC CHURCH. Paris, Musée de Cluny (No. 1681)

120 : 61 cm.
A 'Puy d'Amiens' picture. The device 'Église où Dieu a fait sa résidence' on a scroll held by the ecclesiastical donor kneeling on the right.
Exhibited: Paris 1904, No. 369

163. SCHOOL OF PICARDIE, ABOUT 1500/1510 (PROBABLY SCHOOL OF ABBEVILLE)

THE MADONNA OF THE WHEAT ('LA VIERGE AU FROMENT'). Paris, Musée de Cluny (No. 1680)

112 : 73 cm. Arched top.
The picture belongs to the 'Puy d'Amiens' type. The Madonna stands before a field of wheat; above God the Father and the Dove; below a grain of wheat (the symbol of the conception) in a circle of rays. Many donors and worshippers. The portraits—with the very pale flesh colour—are characteristic for the School of Picardie.
Dehaisnes (RAC 1890, p. 183–190) believes the picture to be executed rather for the Confrérie of Abbeville than for that of Notre-Dame du Puy proper.
André Pigler, GBA, August/September 1932, p. 129 (with reprod.); Dupont, Bulletin des Musées de France, Janv. 1933, p. 8.
Exhibited: Brussels 1935, No. 901.

164. SCHOOL OF AMIENS, ABOUT 1479/1480

THE ANGEL OF THE ANNUNCIATION WITH GOD THE FATHER. Amiens, Musée de Picardie

180 : 58 cm.
The Angel in a white tunique on red ground.
This large fragment can be regarded as the starting point for the cognition of the style of 'Picardie'. It corresponds to the mural paintings in the Cathedral of Amiens which surround the tomb of the Bishop de Mailly (Angels, the twelve Apostles holding scrolls, etc.)
Durand, La Cathédrale d'Amiens, 1903, Vol. II; J. Dupont, GBA, Nov. 1931, p. 284 ff.
Exhibited: Paris 1904, No. 65.

165. SCHOOL OF AMIENS

FOUR WINGS WITH THE APOSTLES (THREE APOSTLES ON EACH WING); BELOW HALF-FIGURES OF PROPHETS (ALSO IN GROUPS OF THREE) WITH SCROLLS. Paris, Musée de Cluny
Gold ground.

166. ATTRIBUTED TO THE SCHOOL OF AMIENS, ABOUT 1500

TRIPTYCH: THE HOLY KINSHIP OF THE VIRGIN, WITH DONORS. ON THE REVERSE: PROPHETS, IN GRISAILLE. Cologne, Wallraf Richartz Museum (No. 426)

Centre: 156 : 106 cm.; shutters 108 : 70 cm. each.
The donors are kneeling in prayer before French Livres d'Heures. They are Baron de Mérode-Petersheim (died 1497) and his wife Marguerite de Melun (died 1532).
This triptych has been ascribed alternatively to the school of Cologne, to the neighbourhood of Froment or to a Franco-Flemish master. It is neither pure German nor Flemish and I should like to include it tentatively in the Amiens school, particularly on the evidence of the donor's portraits.
Michel, III, 1, p. 251, fig. 139.

167. SCHOOL OF AMIENS, ABOUT 1450/1460

THE MASS OF ST. GREGORY. Paris, Louvre (Bequest Paul Jamot, 1939)

60 : 40 cm.
On the left a kneeling ecclesiastic donor. Gay harmony of colours, among which red predominates.
Introduced as a work of the School of Amiens about 1440 by Jacques Dupont (GBA, Nov. 1931, p. 284 ff.). He points to the characteristic simplicity of the composition and to the particular form of Christ's halo.
The picture is certainly French and from the neighbourhood of Amiens in spite of its near relation to the School of Tournai. I should, however, like to date it later, not before 1450.
Reproduced: Jacques, Pl. CXXXIII.
Exhibited: Brussels 1935, No. 903; Paris 1946, No. 14.

168. SCHOOL OF AMIENS, END OF THE 15TH CENTURY

SCENES FROM THE LIFE OF STS. JOACHIM AND ANNE. Amiens, Musée de Picardie

57,1 : 41 cm.
Two wings. Modest examples of the ordinary provincial production of Picardie, only noticeable as certainly belonging to this region.
Reproduced: Barnes, p. 394 (text p. 399).

169. SCHOOL OF PICARDIE, ABOUT 1470/1480

'LE RETABLE DE THUISON'. Chicago, Art Institute (Ryerson Collection) PLATES 105–106

Seven panels, each 117 : 49 cm. (45 : 19¼ in.). On gold ground. Originally four panels painted on either side, representing: (1) The Last Supper; (2) The Assumption of Christ; (3) The Descent of the Holy Ghost; (4) Madonna and Child; (5) St. Hugh of Grenoble; (6) St. John the Baptist; (7) St. Honorius, Bishop of Amiens; (8) The Resurrection. No. (8) has been lost. The panels are said to have been split in 1860.
The pedigree of these paintings, which can be traced back to the Carthusian monastery of St. Honoré, at Thuison-lès-Abbeville, places them without any doubt in the School of Picardie, more precisely in the School of Amiens-Abbeville.
In the centre of the altar was a gilded sculpture of the Passion of Christ, since lost. During the revolution, in 1795, the whole retable was sold by auction and the paintings were purchased by the Abbé Cauchy, Curator of the Church of the Holy Sepulchre at Abbeville.
G. T. Hoogewerff (Noordnederlandsche Schilderkunst, II, 1937, p. 32) points to a connection between the 'Last Supper' of the Thuison Altar and an engraving by the 'Master I. M. Zwoll'. His further conclusions regarding a lost altarpiece donated by Philippe le Bon which might have provided the common model for the picture and the print seem rather far-fetched.
E. Delignières, Réunion des Sociétés des Beaux-Arts des Départements, 1898, p. 305 (detailed description); W. Heil, Pantheon, Febr. 1929, p. 76–78; Barnes, p. 378; Dupont, p. 36.
Exhibited: Bruges 1902, No. 319/320 (Hulin, Cat. Crit.); Paris 1904, No. 353 (suppl.); New York 1927, No. 25–31 (reprod.); Detroit 1928, No. 7; Chicago 1933, No. 3 a–g; Cleveland 1936, No. 183.

170. SIMON MARMION

THE LIFE OF ST. BERTIN. Berlin, Deutsches Museum (Nos. 1645–1645 A.) FIG 19, PLATES 101–102

Two shutters of the Altarpiece of St. Omer, finished about 1459.
Each shutter 56 : 147 cm. (22 : 58 in.).
Left shutter: (1) The Donor Guillaume Fillastre, abbot of St. Bertin; (2) The Birth of the Saint; (3) He is invested with the robes of the Benedictine order in

F

the Convent of Luxueil; (4) The Saint as a pilgrim is received in Thérouane; (5) Dedication and Building of a new monastery. Right shutter: (6) The Saint separates water and wine in a barrel; (7) The convert enters the monastery; (8) The vow of the four noblemen; (9) The Temptation, represented by a claw-footed female, is expelled by St. Martin of Tours; (10) The Death of the Saint. On the reverse of both panels figures of Prophets and Evangelists, the Virgin and the Angel of the Annunciation, all in grisaille, imitating sculptures standing in niches.

The panels are in a very good state. The colours have the enamel-like surface and finish characteristic for the miniature painter.

The pictures, together with the small top parts in London (No. 171), formed the shutters of a sculptured retable of gilded silver which has been destroyed. According to the archivist of the Abbey of St. Bertin, Dom Charles de Witte (1746–1790), the altarpiece was ordered by the abbot Guillaume Fillastre (bishop of Toul) to be placed on the High Altar of the Abbey Church in 1459. It disappeared from St. Omer in 1789. The shutters are first mentioned by Dom Martène and Dom Durand (*Voyage littéraire de deux Bénédictins*, 1703); they report that Rubens had volunteered to cover the panels with ducats if he could buy them. Brought to England in 1822 by the romantic painter Louis Francia, the shutters were acquired by C. J. Nieuwenhuys, who after having apparently cut off the top pieces sold the main parts to King William I of Holland. In 1850 they appear at King William II's auction but were bought in by the royal family; they then passed by inheritance to the Princess of Wied, Neuwied.

The identification of the master of the altarpiece of St. Omer with Simon Marmion was first put forward convincingly by *Mgr. Dehaisnes* (*Recherches sur le Retable de Saint-Bertin et sur Simon Marmion*, 1892). The altar was—as has been mentioned—finished in 1459, in Valenciennes, and Marmion is reported as being resident there since 1458. He is praised as 'Prince d'enluminure' in Lemaire's 'Couronne Margaritique', which agrees with the fact that a great number of illuminated manuscripts show the style of the St. Omer shutters. Furthermore one of these manuscripts (Les Grandes Chroniques de St. Denis, No. 172) was also commissioned by Guillaume Fillastre.

Maurice Hénault, 'Les Marmion', *Revue archéologique*, 1907, t. IX, p. 119 *ff*., 282 *ff*., 410 *ff*.; t. X, p. 108 *ff*; *L. de Fourcaud*, 'Simon Marmion d'Amiens et la Vie de S. Bertin', *RdA*, 1907, t. XXII, p. 321 *ff*.; 417 *ff*; *B. Klemm*, 'Der Bertin Altar im Kaiser Friedrich Museum zu Berlin', 1914, *Beiträge zur Kunstgeschichte*, N. F. XLI (review by *Grete Ring*, *Monatsh. f. Kw.*, 1914).
On Marmion as a panel painter: *M. J. Friedländer, Einige Tafelbilder Simon Marmions*, *Jhb. f. Kw.*, 1923, p. 167; *F. Winkler, Die nordfranzösische Malerei des 15. Jahrhunderts und ihr Verhältnis zur altniederländischen Malerei*, *Belg. Kunstdenkmäler*, I, 1923, p. 247.
Reproduced: *Guiffrey Marcel*, I, pl. XXVII–XXXIII; *Jedlicka*, *pl. 22–25*.
Exhibited: *Düsseldorf 1904*, *Nos. 242–243*.

171. SIMON MARMION

THE SOUL OF ST. BERTIN CARRIED UP TO GOD; A CHOIR OF ANGELS. ON THE REVERSE OF EACH PICTURE A SPIRE-LIKE GOTHIC CONSTRUCTION IN GRISAILLE. London, National Gallery (Nos. 1302 and 1303)   PLATES 99–100

Two panels: 57,5 : 20,5 cm. (22½ : 8 in.) each.
These panels are fragments, being the top parts to the shutters of the St. Bertin Altarpiece (No. 170). The 'Soul of St. Bertin' belonged to the 'Death of the Saint', the 'Choir of Angels' to the 'Donor Guillaume Fillastre'.
Both pieces are in good condition and of the finest quality of the master.
Crowe and Cavalcaselle (*Early Flemish Painters*, 1857, p. 267) state that it was C. J. Nieuwenhuys who separated these top pieces from the main panels and sold them to Edmond Baucousin in Paris between 1824 and 1833.
For further literature see Davies 1945.
Reproduced: *Nat. Gall. Ill. p. 206; reprod. of the reverse of No. 1302: Martin Davies, 'Paintings and Drawings on the Backs of National Gallery Pictures', 1947, pl. 26.*

172. SIMON MARMION

'LES GRANDES CHRONIQUES DE SAINT DENIS'. Leningrad, Library
Illuminated about 1449–1460, commissioned by the abbot Guillaume Fillastre of St. Omer, the donor of the St. Bertin retable, to be presented to Duke Philippe le Bon of Burgundy.
S. *Reinach* (*Un manuscrit de Philippe le Bon à la Bibliothèque de St. Petersbourg, GBA*, 1903, p. 265 *ff*.; *Mon. Piot*, 1904; both papers amply illustrated) was

the first to connect this manuscript with the St. Bertin shutters and has thereby provided the strongest support to the identification of the 'St. Bertin Master' with Simon Marmion.
The frontispiece, showing Fillastre presenting the manuscript to Duke Philippe is particularly characteristic for Marmion (reprod. *GBA*, *p. 270*). Reinach recognizes among the entourage of the Duke his sons, the Comte de Charolais (later Charles le Téméraire), and Antoine, the 'Grand Bâtard'; the Chancellor Rolin and others.
F. Winkler, *Pr. Jhb.*, XXXIV, 1913, *p. 251*; *Winkler, Die flämische Buchmalerei*, 1925, *p. 37–40*.

173. SIMON MARMION

PONTIFICALE OF SENS. Brussels, Bibliothèque Royale (No. 9215)
Executed before 1467. The chief miniature is the 'Crucifixion', ascribed with good reasons to Marmion by *Hulin* and *Winkler* (*Belg. Kunstdenkmäler*, I, 1923, *p. 253, ill. 270*).
Camille Gaspar, Le Pontificale de l'Église de Sens, Bruxelles, 1925.

174. SIMON MARMION

BOOK OF HOURS, London British Museum (Add. Ms. 38126, Coll. Huth)   PLATES 101–102
Among the full-page miniatures some can be attributed to Marmion, e.g. St. Jerome and the Temptation of St. Anthony. Other pages are by Horebout, etc. A copy of the 'Temptation of St. Anthony' is in Sir John Soane's Museum, (Lincoln's Inn Field, London, Ms. 4). *Winkler*, in his article on Marmion in *Th.B.* (1930) brings forward the suggestion that this manuscript, which is not complete, may have been part of the 'Bréviaire' which Marmion is known to have executed for Duke Philippe Le Bon about 1467. The book seems to show the initials of Margaret of York, the Duke's daughter-in-law (cf. Margaret's portrait, No. 192, attributed to 'Marmion'—another argument for the identification).
Winkler, Fläm. Buchmalerei, p. 37, pl. 10; E. G. Millar, Les Manuscrits à Peinture des Bibliothèques de Londres, Paris 1914–1920.

175. SIMON MARMION

THE INVENTION OF THE TRUE CROSS BY ST. HELENA. Paris, Louvre (No. 1001 D.)
68 : 59 cm.
The attribution to Marmion, put forward by *C. Benoit* (*Mon. Piot*, 1903, *Vol. X, p. 268 ff*.) and adopted by *Winkler* (*Belg. Kunstdenkmäler* I, 1923, *p. 248 ff*.) and by Friedländer (*Jhb.f.Kw.*, 1923, *p. 167*) seems indisputable; the picture is very near to the St. Bertin Altarpiece (No. 170) in style as well as in quality and should accordingly be dated about 1460.
Formerly in the Collections J. van Huynettes, Ghent; Harst, Antwerp, and René de La Faille de Waerloos, Amsterdam (Sale 1903, No. 4).
Reproduced: *Lemoisne Louvre, pl. 31; Lemoisne, pl. 67 A; Réau, pl. 53.*
Exhibited: *Brussels, 1935, No. 957.*

176. SIMON MARMION

MADONNA AND CHILD. Formerly Amsterdam, Coll. Goudstikker
36 : 26 cm.
The Virgin, her hands folded in prayer, is shown in front of a piece of red and gold brocade. A landscape on both sides.
The picture is in a rather poor state, particularly the Child has suffered. A replica is in the Czartoryski Museum, Cracow.
Published: *E. Michel, GBA, 1927, II, p. 141–154.*
Exhibited: *London, 1927, No. 69; New York 1927, No. 18 (reprod. in cat.).*

177. SIMON MARMION

MADONNA AND CHILD. Zurich, Private Collection
43 × 29 cm. (with the old frame).
Arched top. On red background. The Virgin wears a blue coat; her blue dress is trimmed with grey fur.
Designation by M. J. Friedlaender. Characteristic painting by the master's own hand, not yet mentioned in literature.

178. SIMON MARMION

MADONNA AND CHILD. Blaricum, Coll. Kleiweg de Zwaan

26,5 : 17 cm.

A poor copy of the picture was sold in Brussels, 16th June 1916, No. 104.

Exhibited: *Rotterdam, Boymans Museum, Kersttentoonstelling 1930/1931, No. 13 (reprod. in cat.); Rotterdam 1938 (Meesterwerken uit vier Eeuwen), No. 12 (Ill. 20 in cat.); The Hague, Mauritshuis 1945, No. 65.*

179. SIMON MARMION

MADONNA AND CHILD. Paris, Louvre

Bought by the Louvre in 1930. Genuine but not very remarkable specimen.

180. SIMON MARMION

MADONNA AND CHILD. Stuttgart, Oberlenningen, Coll. Heinrich Scheufelen

34 : 26 cm.

Virgin and Child are set before a light red brocade; on the left a window with a view on a landscape. Reverse: Ecce Homo.

The obverse is not in a good state, the reverse is nearly totally destroyed.

Formerly in the De Boer Collection, Amsterdam.

Exhibited: *Wiesbaden 1938 (Text of the Catalogue by Hermann Voss).*

181. SIMON MARMION

ST. JEROME AND A DONOR. Philadelphia, John G. Johnson Collection (Inv. No. 1329)   PLATE 98

62,5 : 45 cm. (25⅝ : 19¼ in.)

Probably the left wing of a diptych.

The coat-of-arms of the donor has been interpreted as that of the Busleyden family by Weale, the letters *J.B.* standing in that case for Jerome Busleyden. The donor can, however, not be Canon Jerome Busleyden, the founder of the University of Louvain, since his dates (about 1470–1517) are too late to agree with the style of the picture. Bouchot has read the arms as belonging to the French family of Baradat.

The picture has been attributed to Marmion by M. J. Friedlaender and the attribution has been fairly generally accepted. It is in fact a major work by the master; the divergences from the St. Bertin Altarpiece (No. 170) being easily explained by the difference of size (the heads of Jerome and the Donor alone are about 15 cm. high). The landscape on the right is particularly characteristic of Marmion.

Friedlaender, Jhb.f.Kw., 1923, p. 169/170, ill. 7; Johnson Collection Catalogue of 1941, p. 31.

Exhibited: *Bruges 1902, No. 101; Paris 1904, No. 120 (then Coll. F. P. Morrell, Black Hall, Oxford); Worcester-Philadelphia 1939, No. 18.*

In the Worcester-Philadelphia Exhibition the picture first appeared in the present restored state (which is shown on our reproduction); the short beard of St. Jerome was found to have been repainted and lengthened, the donor's right hand has now regained its original shape, etc.

182. SIMON MARMION

PORTRAIT OF A DONOR PRESENTED BY THE POPE ST. CLEMENT. London, National Gallery (No. 2669)

49 : 37 cm.

The picture formed the left wing of a triptych, the two other parts of which are in the Rohoncz Collection (Nos. 183–184).

Painted about 1480. Rightly attributed to Marmion on the evidence of the flying angel and of the landscape, which correspond to the master's style, though the picture has not the quality of his finer works.

Davies (1945) characterizes the picture appropriately as being 'considerably softened by repairs'.

Nat. Gall. Ill. 1937, p. 130.

Exhibited: *Bruges 1902, No. 148 (then in the Coll. Somzée, Brussels); London, Royal Academy, 1904, No. 3; Paris 1904, No. 75 (Bouchot 1904, Pl. LVIII; then in the Salting Coll., London).*

183. SIMON MARMION

MADONNA IN A LANDSCAPE. Lugano, Coll. Rohoncz

50 : 37 cm.

Centre piece of a triptych, the other parts being Nos. 182 and 184.

Not in a good condition.

Exhibited: *Munich (Neue Pinakothek) 1930, 'Sammlung Schloss Rohoncz', No. 210.*

184. SIMON MARMION

PORTRAIT OF A FEMALE DONOR PRESENTED BY ST. ELIZABETH OF HUNGARY. Lugano, Coll. Rohoncz

50 : 37 cm.

Right wing of a triptych, the other parts being Nos. 182 and 183.

Not in a good condition.

Exhibited: *Munich (Neue Pinakothek) 1930, 'Sammlung Schloss Rohoncz', No. 211; reprod. Catalogue, pl. 114.*

185. SIMON MARMION

CRUCIFIXION. Philadelphia, John G. Johnson Collection

90 : 98 cm.

Important piece in excellent state. Painted about 1470.

The attribution, first suggested by *Hulin de Loo* and accepted by *Friedlaender* and *Winkler* (*Jhb.f.Kw., 1923, p. 168, ill. 2; Belg. Kunstdenkmäler, I, p. 251, ill. 269*) is supported by the provenance: the picture is said to come from St. Bertin, St. Omer. It was later in the Coll. Kums, Antwerp.

Winkler compares the picture convincingly to the 'Crucifixion' in a manuscript illuminated by Marmion: the 'Pontificale de Sens' (No. 173).

Valentiner, Johnson Catalogue, II, No. 318 (attributed to Justus van Ghent); Johnson Catalogue of 1941, p. 31 (Simon Marmion).

Exhibited: *Worcester-Philadelphia 1939, No. 19.*

186. SIMON MARMION

CRUCIFIXION. Rome, Galleria Corsini

68 : 57 cm.

Attribution by Friedlaender. The picture is in a very bad state.

Reproduced: *Duelberg, 'Frühholländer in Italien', pl. 22; Jhb.f.Kw., 1923, p. 170, ill. 10; Cat. Lafenestre-Richtenberger, Rome, No. 756.*

Exhibited: *Utrecht, Ausstellung frühholländischer Malerei und Plastik, 1913, No. 46 (detailed description in the Catalogue).*

187. SIMON MARMION

'MATER DOLOROSA' AND 'CHRIST CROWNED WITH THORNS'. Strasbourg, Museum (Nos. 51a–b)

43 : 29 cm. each.

Half-figures, on gold ground ornamented with dark dots.

In very good condition. The subjects have often been treated by the successors of Bouts. The style of the present paintings, however, in its ornamental elegance combined with delicate feeling, is clearly distinct from the Loewen workshop. These paintings are works by Marmion's own hand and of his finest quality.

Attribution by *Friedlaender, Jhb.f.Kw., 1923, p. 168, reprod. pl. 74, ill. 4 and 5.*

Replicas of both pictures in the Museum of Bruges and in the Dome of Caliari (reprod. *Pantheon, July 1939, p. 240*); replica of the Virgin formerly in the Coll. Aynard, Lyon (vente Paris, 1913).

188. SIMON MARMION

LAMENTATION FOR CHRIST. New York, Coll. Robert Lehmann

About 40 : 25 cm.

On the reverse the arms of Charles the Bold, Duke of Burgundy, and of his wife Margaret of York (cf. No. 192), also the initials 'C.M'. The picture must therefore be dated after the marriage of the ducal couple, i.e., after 1468.

Attributed to Marmion by *Friedlaender, Jhb.f.Kw., 1923, p. 168, ill. 6 and 11 (reverse).*

Marmion is known to have worked on a Book of Hours for Charles the Bold between 1467 and 1470. This confirms the stylistic evidence and supports once more the identification of the 'Master of the Bertin Altarpiece' with Marmion.

189. STUDIO OF SIMON MARMION

THE MARTYRDOM OF TWO SAINTS, PROBABLY ST. ADRIAN AND ST. QUENTIN. New York, Metropolitan Museum (No. M 34 S—1; Bequest Dreicer)

Wings of an altarpiece, 58,1 : 28,2 cm. each.

Attributed to Marmion by *Friedlaender (Jhb.f.Kw., 1923, p. 170, ill. 8 and 9)* who notices, however, uncharacteristic details in these panels.

Formerly Abbey of Eaucourt, Arras.

Bulletin of the Metropolitan Museum, 1920, p. 188; 1922, p. 101.

⟨190.⟩ *ATTRIBUTED TO SIMON MARMION*
Madonna and Child. Formerly Montpellier, Coll. D'Albénas

32 : 19 cm. On brocade background.

Connected with Marmion by *Winkler, Belg. Kunstdenkmäler I 1923, p. 254 f.* (*reprod. p. 255, ill. 272*). This picture has been copied faithfully—with a different background—on a miniature in the Berlin Print Room, which is certainly a work of Marmion or his nearest entourage. (Reprod. *Belg. Kunstdenkm. p. 254, ill. 271*). The 'Albénas Madonna' should, however, rather be left within the school of Dirk Bouts, where it had been located by *Friedlaender* (III, *No. 95*).

Exhibited: *Bruges 1902, No. 94.*

191. ATTRIBUTED TO SIMON MARMION OR TO PHILIPPE DE MAZEROLLES
THE VIRGIN AND CHILD WITH SIX SAINTS AND A YOUTHFUL DONOR. London, National Gallery (No. 1939)

27 : 20 cm.

The donor, wearing the collar of the Golden Fleece, kneels in the entrance to a small castle; above the window is carved the device of the Dukes of Burgundy, the flint and flames.

Popham (*Annuaire des Musées Royaux des Beaux-Arts de Belgique, I, Bruxelles 1938, p. 9 ff., fig. 1*) therefore believes that the donor may be Charles the Bold (born 1433). Popham explains the 'amateurishness' and 'technical ineptitude' of the picture by the fact that the author was not by profession an easel painter but a miniaturist. He proposes the name of Philippe de Mazerolles, who worked for the court of Burgundy, and dates the picture about 1465 or slightly earlier.

The forms of Virgin and Child are Flemish and derived from Rogier van der Weyden (cf. *Winkler, Der Meister von Flémalle und Rogier van der Weyden, 1913, p. 76/77*); the colours, light and delicate, seem to point to the North of France. The picture has, however, no connection either with the 'Master of St. Giles' (*Jacques, Rep. B 15th cent. 31*) or with the 'style of Marmion' (*Davies, 1945, p. 59/60*).

Reproduced: *Nat. Gall. Ill. p. 129.* The picture was seen by *Passavant* (*Kunstreise ... 1833, p. 96*) in the collection of the German merchant Karl Aders in 1831; Passavant then considered it an 'Antonello'.

Popham reproduces a drawing in the Brit. Mus., London, 'The Virgin appearing to St. George', the design for a stained glass window, which he gives to a follower of 'Mazerolles'. The drawing has in fact a marked resemblance to the picture, but it seems a Flemish, not a French work, whereas the picture should be left within the French school.

192. ATTRIBUTED TO SIMON MARMION
PORTRAIT OF MARGARET OF YORK. Paris, Louvre (Donation Walter Gay, 1937)

20 : 12 cm. She wears a red dress sprinkled with gold. On her head a high 'hénin' with broad black revers. Probably the right wing of a diptych: she folds her hands in adoration.

Margaret of York was married to Charles the Bold of Burgundy in 1468. *Hulin* ('*Tableaux perdus de Simon Marmion*', in '*Aan Max J. Friedlaender*', 1942, p. 11 ff.) identifies the princess by several indications: her necklace shows a pattern where the roses of York and Lancaster alternate; the initials C(harles) and M(argaret) adorn the necklace as a pendant. Another piece of jewellery in the form of a 'b' (Burgundy) is pinned on the 'hénin'; a small daisy (the flower 'marguerite') is pinned to the bodice.

The attribution to Marmion is due to Hulin. Although the stylistic evidence is not too striking, it is convincing enough to justify the incorporation of the picture in the master's orbit. A certain caution must, of course, always be observed when dealing with princely portraits, which follow certain conventions and usually exist in various replicas. The quality is not of the first rank.

A good support for the attribution is given by the reverse of another 'Marmion' painting, the 'Lamentation for Christ' (No. 188), which shows the same initials C and M together with the coat-of-arms of Charles of Burgundy and Margaret of York.

Reproduced: *Jacques, pl. 142; Colour Plate 'L'École Franco-Flamande', Trésors 1941 (text by Bazin).* cf. *Pantheon XXVIII, 1941, p. 195 and 272.*

Exhibited: *Paris 1946, No. 36.*

193. ATTRIBUTED TO SIMON MARMION
ST. BENEDICT IN HIS CELL; ST. BENEDICT RESCUES PLACIDUS FROM DROWNING. New York (formerly Berlin), Coll. E. Garbaty

Two scenes on one panel.

Ascribed to Marmion by *Winkler* (*Pantheon, 1934, I, p. 65, with illustration*). The attribution which is based particularly on the affinity with Marmion's dedication miniature in the 'Grandes Chroniques' (No. 172) has not been generally accepted.

194. ATTRIBUTED TO SIMON MARMION
PORTRAIT OF A YOUNG GENTLEMAN, SUPPOSED TO BE A MEMBER OF THE FAMILY OF BUSLEYDEN. England, Private Collection

23 : 15,5 cm. On gold background with dark brown dots.

He wears a purple suit and dark olive coat; on his long black hair a red cap.

Probably right wing of a diptych; the sitter is represented praying, with folded hands. Above his head the arms which have been interpreted as those of the Busleyden family. The elegant young nobleman can hardly be Jerome Busleyden, the founder of the 'Collegium Busleydanum' as has been suggested, since Jerome was a canon.

This serious and sensitive portrait seems to be a work from Northern France about 1480, but not by Marmion.

Reproduced (as Marmion): *Réau, pl. 55.*

195. SCHOOL OF SIMON MARMION
CHRIST BEFORE CAIPHAS. ON THE REVERSE: A SAINT BISHOP. Philadelphia, John G. Johnson Collection

51 : 30 cm.

A rather weak specimen of the school of Marmion, about 1480.

Valentiner, Johnson Catalogue III, No. 763; Cat. of 1941, p. 31.

196. ATTRIBUTED TO THE SCHOOL OF SIMON MARMION
ABRAHAM AND MELCHISEDEK. Formerly New York, J. Seligmann & Co.

32 : 30 cm.

This picture, which has been connected with the 'Invention of the Cross' in the Louvre (No. 175), is of a far less distinguished quality and could only be assigned to the more distant school of the master.

Reproduced: *Réau, pl. 54.*

197. SCHOOL OF SOUTHERN FRANCE, WRONGLY ATTRIBUTED TO SIMON MARMION
PIETÀ. Oxford, Ashmolean Museum

29 : 31 cm.

This charming picture has been placed in the neighbourhood of Marmion by *A. Michel, 'À propos de Simon Marmion', GBA, 1927, II, p. 141–154* (with reprod.). It is in my opinion undoubtedly a work of the French School, but neither by nor near Marmion. Moreover the recent cleaning has revealed a perfectly different colour scheme; particularly the cool pallid grey of Christ's body is alien to the glowing enamel of the painter miniaturist, and reminds one more of the South than of the North of France.

Bequest Mr. John D. Chambers, 1897.

198. SCHOOL OF SOUTHERN FRANCE, ABOUT 1470; WRONGLY ATTRIBUTED TO SIMON MARMION
ST. BERNARDIN'S VISION OF THE ANGEL; TWO DONORS IN ADORATION. Marseille, Musée Grobet-Labadié   PLATE 60

37 : 68 cm. (14½ : 26¾ in.)

The female donor wears a blue dress and red cap, the man a red doublet and high black cap. A brick-red band divides the left part of the picture—with the donors—from the Vision of the Saint on the right.

The picture has been tentatively ascribed to Marmion (*Le Musée Grobet-Labadié, 1930, with text by Gibert and Gonzalès, p. 30*). In my opinion, it should be placed in an entirely different context, rather in the region of the Rhône than in the North of France.

199. WRONGLY ATTRIBUTED TO SIMON MARMION

LA TRANSLATION DE LA CHÂSSE DE STE. PERPÉTUE. Chantilly, Musée Condé

Benoit (*GBA*, 1901, II, *p.* 98) has connected the picture with Marmion's 'Invention of the Cross' (No. 175). I rather agree with *Winkler*, who calls the picture 'probably Northern French', of the same period, but does not attribute it to Marmion (*Belg. Kunstdenkmäler*, I, 1923, *p.* 256, *ann.* 4).

200. WRONGLY ATTRIBUTED TO SIMON MARMION

ST. GEORGE ON HORSEBACK FIGHTING THE DRAGON. New York, late Coll. Otto H. Kahn

50 : 37 cm.

The Castle in the background has been believed to be the Castle of Tarascon.

The picture has been persistently associated with the name of Marmion. It is certainly not by Marmion but by an unknown painter, possibly also from the North of France, about 1480/1490.

Exhibited: *Paris 1904, No. 91* (then in the Coll. Haro, Paris; *Bouchot 1904, pl. XCIII*); *New York 1927, No. 20; London 1932, No. 38; (Commem. Cat. No. 31, pl. 12); Paris 1937, No. 18.*

201. NORTHERN FRENCH SCHOOL, ABOUT 1460

RESURRECTION OF CHRIST, WITH ST. CATHERINE PRESENTING THREE FEMALE DONORS. Montpellier, Musée Fabre (No. 811, Sabatier Bequest)

48 : 31 cm.

The flying angels and the landscape have some affinities to Marmion. The chief donatrix with her enormous white headdress is rather near in costume and bearing to the representation of 'Philosophy' on an illuminated page from the 'De Consolatione' of Boethius (London, Wallace Collection, M. 320) which has already been connected with the Marmion workshop. The Montpellier picture should accordingly be attributed to the School of Northern France, more exactly to that of Valenciennes.

Reproduced: *Cat. of the Musée Fabre* (A. Joubin), 1926, *pl. XXIX.*

202. FRANCO-FLEMISH SCHOOL, ABOUT 1480

SHIELD OF PARADE, WITH A PAIR OF LOVERS. London, British Museum (Burges Bequest)   PLATE 96

Wooden shield lined with leather, faced with canvas, over which a layer of gesso has been laid. Gold ground with reddish dots. The surfaces are finely curved, following the shape of the shield.

Left side: a young lady with a dress of gold brocade and a high 'hénin', standing. Right side: a young knight, kneeling before her. He wears gothic armour, his armet and poll axe lie on the ground. Behind him the figure of death. A script roll interprets his words: 'Vous ou la mort'.

The lady, in spite of her marked heraldic stiffness, may be compared with the temptress on Marmion's miniature of St. Anthony (No. 174). Her face seems to be repainted. The knight's face recalls the 'Young Man' on red ground, (No. 203). Although the brush work is here laid on an 'objet d'art' and not on an easel painting, the quality is high enough to justify the inclusion of this work in our material—overstepping for once the usual line of demarcation.

Reproduced: *J. Starkie Gardner, Foreign Armour in England, London 1898 (Frontispiece, Colour Plate); British Museum, Guide to Mediaeval Antiquities, 1924, p. 15, fig. 10.*

203. BURGUNDIAN SCHOOL, ABOUT 1480

PORTRAIT OF A YOUNG MAN HOLDING A PRAYER BOOK. Vierhouten (Holland), van Beuningen Collection

38 : 29 cm. On the original frame the inscription 'En L'age de XXVI ans', coat-of-arms and the initials 'A Y'.

The sitter recalls the young knight on the 'Shield of Parade' (No. 202).

Formerly Coll. Weyer, Cologne, No. 213; Coll. Prince of Hohenzollern-Sigmaringen; F. Koenigs Collection, Haarlem.

Reproduced: *Réau, pl. 47.*

Exhibited: *Frankfort-on-Main, Staedel Institute (Sigmaringen Collection), 1928, No. 4; Rotterdam, Boymans Museum, 1935, No. 6 (Cat. ill. VII); Utrecht, Centraal Museum, 'Herwonnen Kunstbezit', 1946, No. 16 (Cat. pl. 2).*

204. FRENCH SCHOOL, ABOUT 1460/1470

YOUNG MAN IN PRAYER BEFORE AN ALTAR. Rotterdam, Boymans Museum (formerly Coll. F. Koenigs)

Drawing, pen on vellum, 13,3 : 9,3 cm.

From the Rodrigues Collection.

Reproduced: *Lavallée, No. 39, pl. XXVI.*

Exhibited: *Rotterdam, Boymans Museum, 1934/1935, No. 3; Paris 1937, No. 434.*

205. SCHOOL OF AVIGNON, ABOUT 1460

THE ALTARPIECE OF BOULBON. Paris, Louvre (No. 1001 c)

168 : 223 cm. (66 : 88 in.)   PLATES 107, 111

Transferred from wood on canvas (in 1923).

Christ, standing in His tomb, in full frontal view, is surrounded by the instruments of the Passion. The head of God the Father, the Dove of the Holy Ghost, both near to Christ's head, seem to point to the theme of the Trinity. On the left a clerical donor, presented by St. Agricol, Bishop and Patron-Saint of Avignon.

Nearly a monochrome in grey and whitish on black; only St. Agricol is in red. It is difficult to judge this picture which was in a deplorable state before it entered the Louvre and which has since undergone extensive and visible restorations. The previous state, with holes, etc., is recorded in *GBA, XXXI*, 1904 (*ill. p.* 449) and in *Abbé Requin, L'École Avignonnaise de Peinture, p.* 15.

Only the composition of the picture can thus be duly estimated and some details like the landscape view on the left. I should like to cite from *Dr. Barnes's* excellent analysis (*p.* 446): 'Drama arises from contrasts of simple rhythms . . . ; the body of Christ is of a chalky ivory, tinged with peachblow and slightly toned with green, his face is still more chalky. . . . The face of the donor is modelled much like the one in the "Villeneuve Pietà", but not so sculptural, it is a little lighter in colour and has more dark blue shadows . . . By discounting the many restored parts, painted with banal academic literalism, one can perceive the simplicity, dignity, grandeur and majesty which this altarpiece shares in common with the "Villeneuve" Pietà'.

The connection of the picture with the Pietà de Villeneuve (No. 206) seems to me much stronger than that with the Aix Annonciation, which has mostly been stressed. The comparatively best preserved part, the donor's head, is nearest to the Villeneuve panel.

The coat-of-arms in the upper right-hand corner is that of Pope Jean XXII, founder of the 'Collégiale avignonnaise de Saint-Agricol', the crest of which is placed in the lower right-hand corner. These details support the supposition—which has been put forward—that the Retable, coming from Saint Marcellin of Boulbon, near Tarascon (Vaucluse), has been presented in honour of the incorporation of this church into the chapter of St. Agricol, in 1457.

Exhibited: *Paris 1946, No.* 15.

206. SCHOOL OF AVIGNON, ABOUT 1460

PIETÀ (LA PIETÀ DE VILLENEUVE-LÈS-AVIGNON). Paris, Louvre (No. 1001B)   FRONTISPIECE, PLATES 108–110, 112

162 : 218 cm. (64 : 86 in.)

Christ lies on the knees of St. Mary, who, without supporting His body, folds her hands in prayer. On the left, St. John and a kneeling donor; on the right, St. Mary Magdalen.

The Virgin, her face very pale, is wrapped in a blue coat with white lining. St. Magdalen wears a maroon-coloured robe and a garnet-red coat; the donor, an ecclesiastic, has a white pleated surplice. Gold ground. In the landscape on the left, a town with buildings of an oriental (African) type, with minarets, crescents, etc. The haloes, deeply engraved, show the names of the Virgin, St. John and Magdalen in Latin; from Christ's head rays in 'relievo' are emanating.

The picture is in a good but not in a perfect state. When I last saw it it was not cleaned. *Sanpere y Miquel (Los cuatrocentistas Catalanes*, 1906) has ascribed the picture to Bartolomeo Bermejo (Vermejo), connecting it with the great Catalan's Pietà of 1490 in the Cathedral of Barcelona. This certainly erroneous designation has already been disposed of by *C. de Mandach ('Un atelier provençal du XVe siècle', Mon. Piot, XVI, pp.* 147 *ff.*), who stresses the Provençal origin of the picture, suggesting Froment or perhaps Pierre Villatte, the otherwise unknown co-operator of Charenton's 'Vierge de Miséricorde' (No. 117), as possible authors.

More recently the picture has been treated in great detail, with full consideration of the general iconography of the 'Pietà' in France, by *James B. Ford and G. S. Vickers (Art Bulletin, March 1939, p.* 5-43). They propose Nuño Gonçalvez

FIG. 37   ⟨ cf. Cat. No. 210 ⟩

as the author, pointing out that 'there was no more vigorous nation in Europe in the 15th century than Portugal' which 'anticipated the tendencies culminating in Columbus' discovery of the new world'. Subsequently they grant the highest credit to Portuguese art. According to them, stylistic similarities between the 'Pietà' and the two triptychs of St. Vincent by Gonçalvez (cf. Nos. 145 and 146) are conspicuous—the triptychs are dated between 1458 and 1462—the 'Pietà'—always following Ford and Vickers—ought to be placed later, between 1470 and 1475; it might either have been painted in Avignon or painted in Portugal and sent to France.

In my opinion the picture is the work of a Provençal master who has not yet been identified, and to whom no other picture could be attributed until now. The Iberian touch is unquestionable, but I fail to see any similarities with Gonçalvez. The nearest affinity, as far as I see, is with the 'Retable de Boulbon' (No. 205).

The literary roots of the type are to be found in the 'Méditations' of the so-called Pseudo-Bonaventura (*Pinder, Die dichterische Wurzel der Pietà, Rep. f. Kw. 42, 1920*).

Large colour reproductions (with many details): '*La Pitié d'Avignon*', '*Trésors*' *1941* (*text by Bazin*).

Exhibited: *Paris 1904, No. 77* (then in the Hospice of Villeneuve-lès-Avignon).

207. SCHOOL OF AVIGNON, ABOUT 1460

ST. JEROME. Paris, Louvre (No. 1050)

54 : 41 cm. Excellent state of preservation.

The face, strongly stamped with an individual character, and the arrangement in half-figure with praying hands—most unusual for a representation of St. Jerome—seem to point to a portrait. Perhaps the donor was portrayed under the guise of the Saint.

The head has been compared to the heads of the donors on the 'Pietà de Ville-

neuve' and the 'Retable de Boulbon'. The 'Jerome' was certainly painted about the same time and probably in the same region, although he has a still stronger affinity to Iberian art. The light falls on the fore-shortened side of the face, in the same way as in the 'Man with a glass of wine' (No. 144).

Left to the Louvre by the painter Jean Gigoux.

Reproduced: *Barnes, p. 470 (detailed description on p. 471); Jacques, pl. 104*.

Exhibited: *Paris 1904, No. 367; Paris 1946, No. 16*.

208. SCHOOL OF SOUTHERN FRANCE, SECOND HALF OF 15TH CENTURY

HEAD OF A MAN. Vienna, Albertina (Inv. No. 4842)

Silver point drawing. 14,8 : 11,9 cm.

He wears a cap on his long hair. Strong modelling.

Published by *O. Benesch, Annuaire des Musées Royaux de Belgique, I, 1938, p. 44*, as a drawing by Nuño Gonçalvez. In my opinion rather French, recalling the portraits on paintings of the School of Provence.

209. SCHOOL OF PROVENCE, ABOUT 1460

PIETÀ ('LA PIETÀ DE TARASCON'). Paris, Musée de Cluny

85 : 132 cm. (33½ : 52 in.)   PLATE 113

The colours are clear and simple; the Virgin is clad in a uniform blue, the holy figure on the left has an olive-green coat over a deep-red dress, the elderly woman, who kisses Christ's hand, wears the same pure deep red. Only St. Mary Magdalen shows more complex shades: a light-green coat richly trimmed with hermine over a broken-reddish garment. In the landscape, classical italianizing buildings, which can, however, not be easily judged as the entire background is heavily repainted.

The composition has a certain likeness to the 'Pietà de Villeneuve', particularly in the position of Christ's body, with the fundamental difference that here the

Mother supports His body instead of praying. The aspect as a whole is much softer, less emotional, nearer to Italian than to Iberian examples, and the picture fits best in the 'Antonellesque' group of French painting.

The date about 1460, as proposed by *Jacques* (*Rep. A.* 15th cent. 46) seems convincing. He connects the picture, which comes from Tarascon (Hospice), tentatively with an Inventory notice of the Castle of Tarascon, drawn up in 1457, mentioning 'Un retable neuf, Notre-Seigneur dans les bras de Notre-Dame'. This would date the picture just about 1457 and would make it an exact contemporary of the 'Retable de Boulbon' (No. 205).

210. SCHOOL OF PROVENCE, ABOUT 1470/1480
PIETÀ WITH A DONOR. New York, Frick Collection   PLATE 114
42 : 57 cm. (16½ : 22½ in.)   FIG. 37

Christ lamented by the Virgin Mary and by two holy women, adored by a kneeling donor. In the background, alpine landscape with snow-covered mountains, a fortified town, a church, a belfry. The donor, bald and elderly, wears the costume of a knight.

The enigma of this fascinating picture is far from being solved. The problem has been complicated by the fact that about twenty years after its first public appearance (in 1902), a second version turned up, nearly identical but without the donor. In spite of an avalanche of literature no agreement has been reached as to which of the two versions should be granted priority in date and quality, nor has there been a decision in regard to the country of origin.

The original attribution of the version with donor to Antonello da Messina was already disposed of in 1902 by *Friedlaender* ('*Die Brügger Leihausstellung von 1902*', *Rep.f.Kw.*) and *Hulin* (*Cat. Crit.*), who both vote for France. Later on *Berenson* refuted the Antonello thesis in detail, coining the significant phrase that the picture was 'more Beethoven than Bach' and accordingly rather Northern than Italian (*Art in America*, III, 1915, p. 141; *Venetian Painting in America*, 1916, p. 31). When the second version (without donor) appeared, it was mostly supposed to be the earlier treatment of the theme, being grander, simpler, more 'primitive' in character. The close affinity of that version to Conrat Witz has been recognized, and it has been incorporated in the great Swiss master's œuvre by various scholars, among them Friedlaender. *Valentiner,* while leaving the 'Pietà without a donor' to Witz, reverses the roles and gives priority to the 'Pietà with donor', which he regards as a work by Conrat's mythical father Hans Witz, supposed to have worked in Burgundy (*Art in America* XII, 1924, p. 130).

In my opinion the 'Pietà with a donor', which, if less powerful, is more subtle, is French without any doubt. It is best connected with those works that show 'Antonellesque' traits, like the Aix Altarpiece and the—also enigmatic—Adoration (No. 212). The region of its origin seems to be the South of France, most probably the neighbourhood of Avignon.

As to the 'Pietà without a donor', which I consider the original earlier version, about 1450, I should also like to include it in the French context. This would broach the entire subject of the so-called 'small Witz panels', which might be worth a revision. The 'Crucifixion' (Berlin), the 'Holy Family in a Cathedral' (Naples), ascribed to Witz, certainly show connections with French art, the resemblance of the Naples picture with the Aix Annunciation (church interiors) has often been discussed. The daring theory has been put forward (by Otto Demus in a lecture given at the Courtauld Institute, London, some years ago) that the 'small Witz panels' should all be assigned to the French School, an annexation which I do not venture to adopt but which has something to recommend itself. The solution of the problem of the 'Two Pietàs' may lie in this direction. Without commentary I further want to note that the landscape and buildings on the version with donor show striking similarities to the background of one of the panels by 'Isenmann' in Colmar (The Resurrection of Christ).

Cf. *Guiffrey*, 'Note sur deux tableaux avignonnais,' in *Mélanges Hulin de Loo*, 1931, p. 204, pl. XXIV/XXV.

The 'Pietà with donor' came from the Collection of M. Renouvier, who is said to have found it in Catalonia, into the Coll. d'Albénas, Montpellier; it was later acquired by Roger Fry and went to the Frick Collection.

Exhibited: *Bruges 1902*, No. 32; *Paris 1904*, No. 84 (*Bouchot 1904*, pl. LXI).

The 'Pietà without a donor' which, in 1923, was with Durlacher Brs., London, is now in the Collection of Miss Helen Frick.

⟨210A.⟩ ITALO-PROVENÇAL SCHOOL (?), about 1480
Pietà. Vercelli, Museo Borgogna (Istituto di Belle Arti)
51 : 1,07 cm.

The dead Christ standing, supported by His mother, showing the wound in His side.

The picture has been tentatively ascribed to G. M. Spanzotti—certainly a wrong designation, as the similarities with the acknowledged 'Pietà' by Spanzotti in Castel S. Angelo, Rome, remain on the surface. I am inclined to connect the picture rather with the 'Frick Pietàs'; particularly the types of St. Mary seem to show a striking likeness.

Exhibited: *Turin 1939* (*Cat. p. 58, No. 2, pl. 44*).

⟨211.⟩ SCHOOL OF PROVENCE (?), about 1470/1480
Sts. Jerome, Augustine and Ambrose. Paris, Louvre
160 : 135 cm. each.

The fourth Father of the Church, St. Gregory, is missing.

Of a mild, not very distinct style, roughly corresponding to the Cologne 'Master of the Life of St. Mary', mostly influenced by Dirk Bouts. French origin is possible but not unquestionable.

Reproduced: *Labande, pl. LXVII* (then in the Coll. Comte Demandolx-Dedons, Marseille).

⟨212.⟩ FRENCH(?) SCHOOL, about 1475
Adoration of the Child. Glasgow, Art Gallery and Museum Kelvingrove
(No. 158)   FIG. 30
50 : 40 cm. (20 × 16 in.)

With St. Gregory the Pope, and St. Jerome, who presents a kneeling Cardinal, probably the donor.

The Virgin is dressed in steel-blue; St. Jerome's Cardinal's dress is exceptionally of the same colour, only his hat is red. St. Joseph is in red with a purple head-shawl, St. Gregory in blue brocade. The donor's ample coat shows a broken wine colour. On the left a woman, in olive-green, with the turban-shaped head-dress of late 15th-century French miniatures. Bright sky, wherein flies a tiny blue angel. The landscape, bounded by mountains with pointed peaks, is executed with precision up to the most remote distance, without attempts at 'aerial perspective'. The buildings in the background—a castle surrounded by water, etc.—are of a French character.

The picture has not yet been satisfactorily placed. It was traditionally called 'Antonello' (*Catalogue of the Corporation of Glasgow, 1935*); the name of Antonello's teacher Colantonio has been suggested of late. Other Italian schools have been proposed, like Verona and Piedmont. In my opinion, the blend of Northern and Italian elements—which had given rise to the denomination 'Antonello'—might once again point to France. I see the comparatively nearest analogy in the 'Pietà' of the Frick Collection (No. 210), both paintings corresponding to the conception of 'Alpine Art'.

From the McLellan Collection (gift in 1854).

van Marle, XV, 1934, cap. IX, p. 484/485; *Jan Lauts, review of van Marle, ZfK,* 1935, IV, p. 162; *Vienna Jhb.,* N.F. VII, p. 15 *ff.*—Lauts also thinks of a French, more precisely of a Burgundian master.

213. SCHOOL OF PROVENCE, 15TH CENTURY
ST. GEORGE ON HORSEBACK, FIGHTING THE DRAGON. Caromb
(near Carpentras), Parish Church   PLATES 115-116
135 : 65 cm. (53 : 25½ in.)

The panel of St. George is inserted in an altar as its centre, while four smaller pieces (one above the other on either side) are arranged to form the shutters. The measurements, however, do not fit, the centre piece being too high; the smaller pictures represent scenes from the legend of a warrior but not of St. George, and their style does not cogently connect them with the central part—although they should also be regarded as 'Provençal'. One may therefore consider the 'St. George' a part of an otherwise lost retable.

The Saint, about three-quarter life-size, wears steel armour, the metal quality of which is emphasized; he rides a greyish white horse, whose brown leather harness is adorned with large golden buttons. The Saint's head is modelled with sharply illuminated contours; everything is reduced to the simplest formulae of geometry.

A connection with the 'Master of the Aix Annonciation' seems to present itself, particularly with the italianizing—Antonellesque—trend of the master, but the 'St. George' seems still nearer to Antonello. The idea had therefore occurred to me to connect the panel with Colantonio (cf. Nos. 97/98), the more as an image of 'San Giorgio' by Colantonio is recorded in Summonte's letter of 1524 (*F. Nicolini, L'Arte Napolitana, 1925*). Summonte's detailed description unfortunately does not correspond to the Caromb 'St. George', but I should like to go on looking for its author within this circuit.

It is difficult to date the picture, which could be placed in any year between 1450 and 1475 (the development of this type of 'Saint on horseback' in Italy, as represented by Butinone's St. Martin in Treviglia, painted in the 1480's, looks so considerably later that one should imagine a rather long interval of years between the two representations; this would date the present picture nearer to 1450/1460). According to *Labande* (*Pl. LXXXVII*) the Caromb panel was painted for the Chapelle de S. Georges, founded by the Seigneur of Caromb, Bertrand de Budos (see *Pithon-Curt, t.* II, *p.* 98).

214. NICOLAS FROMENT

TRIPTYCH. Florence, Uffizi (No. 1065)   PLATES 118–124
Centre panel, 175 : 134 cm. (69 : 53 in.), shutters, 175 : 66 cm. (69 : 26 in.) each. Centre: The Raising of Lazarus; Right wing: St. Mary Magdalen anointing Christ's feet; Left wing: Martha, announcing the death of Lazarus to Christ. On the outside of one wing the Virgin and Child, on the outside of the other the Donor with an attendant and a young man standing.
Inscribed on the outside: NICOLAVS FRVMENTI ABSOLVIT HOC OPUS XV KL JVNII MCCCCLXI.
The head of a young man with a high cap on the upper left-hand corner of the central panel is supposed to be the self-portrait of the painter.
According to *Labande* (*Notes sur quelques Primitifs de Provence,* II, *GBA, Février* 1933, *p.* 85 *ff.*) the date 'XV Kalendas Junii' means that the picture was finished on May 18th, 1461.
The picture seems to have been destined originally for the 'Observatins' of Mugello, Convento del Bosco, near Florence. If it was executed in or near Florence, as Labande supposes, it would be the only testimony for Froment's stay in Italy. The style is not affected by Florentine art.
The tradition which wants to see in the picture a commission by Cosimo de' Medici, presented by him to the 'Observatins', must probably be relegated to the domain of fiction; the actual donor, portrayed on the reverse, is a canon. His arms have not yet been identified.
Hulin de Loo, Pr. Jhb., XXV, 1904, *p.* 72 *ff.*; *W. Burger, Zf.bK,* 1927/1928, *vol.* 61, *p.* 317.
Exhibited: *Paris 1889, Musée du Trocadéro 'Portraits Historiques'; London 1932, No. 50; Florence 1945, No. 2; Rome 1946, No. 3.*

215. NICOLAS FROMENT

THE TRANSFIGURATION OF CHRIST. Berlin, Kupferstichkabinett
Drawing.   PLATE 117
The drawing has been ascribed to Froment by *Friedlaender* (*Pr. Jhb.,* 1896, *p.* 207) because of its affinity to the centre panel of the Uffizi Triptych.

216. NICOLAS FROMENT

TRIPTYCH OF THE BURNING BUSH, completed in 1476. Aix-en-Provence, Cathédrale Saint Sauveur   PLATES 126–130
410 : 305 cm. (161 : 120 in.)
Centre: The Virgin Mary in the Burning Bush (Vision of Moses). Left wing: King René of Anjou with Sts. Mary Magdalen (the patron-Saint of Provence), Anthony (patron of the Anjou) and Maurice (patron of the 'ordre du croissant', founded by René). Right wing: Queen Jeanne (de Laval) with Sts. John, Catherine and Nicholas.
On the outside wings the Annunciation, in grisaille, the figures standing in niches. The triptych is on the whole in a very good state, the colours are deep and saturated, not bright and shiny. The principal colours are red and green, the red often going towards the purple. The whole aspect is soft and mellow, in marked contrast to the Triptych in Florence (No. 214).
In the centre Moses, in red, taking off his sandals. His slightly grimacing face, of a leathery brown, seems to be the only link with Froment's earlier style. He is confronted by an angel in the attitude of the Angel of the Annunciation. In the wide and sunny Southern landscape Moses' flock of sheep. Above, St. Mary, clad in a subdued blue, sits in a rose bush, a reminiscence of the theme of 'Maria im Rosenhag'. She holds the Child, Who is playing with a mirror.
The central panel is set in a painted golden frame emulating sculpture; above and below are inscriptions, which give indications as to the meaning of the scene. The inscription below begins with the words 'Rubrum quem viderat Moyses' and the picture is referred to accordingly in the payment, made by its donor, King René, in 1476: 'À maistre Nicholas qui a fait rubrum quem viderat Moyses, la somme de . . .'.

This is clearly an 'emblematic' picture, where every detail has a symbolical meaning. According to medieval typology, the bush which burned but was not consumed by the flames is a symbol of Mary, who remained a Virgin after her maternity. It is a peculiarity of the picture that it puts the Madonna in the place of God the Father who appeared to Moses in the Old Testament (Exodus III).
A convincing interpretation of the scene and its details has been given by *E. Harris* (*Warb. Journ.* I, 1938, *p.* 281 *ff.*). She points particularly to the symbolical connection of the 'Burning Bush' and the theme of the 'Annunciation'. The explanation of the picture as representing St. Joachim in the desert before the birth of the Virgin Mary—which had been put forward by several critics—is disproved by the inscriptions.
The triptych was destined by King René for the 'Église des Grands Carmes' in Aix; it stayed there until 1791 (*Nouvelles Archives de l'Art Français,* 1877, *p.* 399; *Abbé Arnaud d'Agnel, Comptes du Roi René,* No. 517, cf. *Labande, GBA, Févr.* 1933, *p.* 90).
Exhibited: *Paris 1904, No. 78; Paris 1937, No. 16.*

217. ATTRIBUTED TO NICOLAS FROMENT

DIPTYCH WITH THE PORTRAITS OF KING RENÉ AND JEANNE DE LAVAL, THE SO-CALLED 'DIPTYQUE DES MATHERON'. Paris, Louvre (No. 304 A)   FIG. 7
17,5 : 13,7 cm. each.
Usually dated about 1475, in analogy to the portraits of the royal couple in the 'Burning Bush'. The sitters are presented in the same position, but now in everyday dress; the King wears a dark fur-trimmed coat, and the order of St. Michael, the Queen a black velvet cap. *Labande* (*GBA, Février* 1933, *p.* 92, *Ill. p.* 87) assumes that the little panels were the studies 'd'après nature' which served as models for the great altarpiece.
Formerly belonging—according to tradition—to Jean de Matheron, one of the followers of King René and sometime his chancellor and ambassador. In the possession of the Matheron family until 1872, hence the designation.
In view of this perfect pedigree and the irrefutable connection with the 'Burning Bush' (No. 216) the diptych has universally been judged most favourably; it has even been accepted by Dimier. The quality is, however, rather poor and the pedigree can, after all, only guarantee the period, not the master himself. I should prefer to regard it as a specimen of princely portraiture from the Froment studio or school, and to date it slightly later than the 'Burning Bush'. There exist several replicas of about the same merit.
Reproduced: *Lemoisne, Louvre, pl. 29 and 30; Labande, pl. LVI.*
Exhibited: *Paris 1904, No. 79. (Bouchot 1904, pl. L).*

218. SOMETIMES ATTRIBUTED TO NICOLAS FROMENT

S. SIFFREIN. Avignon, Musée Calvet (No. 14)
207 : 66 cm. Gold ground. Arched top.
Fragment of an altarpiece. The Saint, Archbishop of Carpentras, stands in frontal view, his right hand giving benediction. Life-size figure.
In the lower left-hand corner a horse's bit—the emblem of the city of Carpentras. This impressive but provincial panel, painted about 1470–1475, is in my opinion not a work by Froment himself. It should rather be assigned to his school than to his studio.
The suggestion, put forward by *Sanpere y Miquel* (*Los cuatrocentistas Catalanes,* II, *p.* 85/86) to include the picture in the Catalan School is not convincing.
The picture comes from the Church of Mazan, where it is said to have served as the cover to a chest.
Reproduced: *Labande, pl. LXXXVI; Guiffrey Marcel Terrasse, II, p. XLI/XLII; Réau, pl. 28; Gillet, Colour Plate IV.*
Exhibited: *Paris 1904, No. 76 (Bouchot 1904, pl. XLVI); Paris 1937, No. 29.*

⟨219.⟩ FORMERLY ATTRIBUTED TO NICOLAS FROMENT

The Raising of Lazarus, in a Landscape. Paris, Louvre
76 : 140 cm.
The picture should no longer be included in the context of French art, although some actual resemblances with the Uffizi Triptych (No. 214) cannot be overlooked.
Hulin de Loo (*Die Auferweckung des Lazarus der Samml. v. Kaufmann und die niederländischen Maler des Koenigs René von Anjou, Pr. Jhb.,* XXV, 1904, *p.* 72 *ff.*) believes the author to be a Flemish painter in the entourage of King René. According to Hulin, the picture is earlier than the Uffizi Triptych—before 1460—

and Froment was influenced by it. *W. Burger, ZjbK, 1927/1928, p. 317*, thinks of a Dutch master.

Formerly Coll. Richard von Kaufmann, Berlin (Sale 1917, Cat. 119—there attributed to Froment).

Reproduced: *Labande, pl. LII.*

Exhibited: *Paris 1904, No. 81 (Bouchot 1904, pl. LI).*

220. ATTRIBUTED TO THE ENTOURAGE OF NICOLAS FROMENT, ABOUT 1475/1480

PORTRAIT OF A MAN. Philadelphia, John G. Johnson Collection (No. 404)

30 : 22 cm.

In *Valentiner's Catalogue of the Johnson Collection* as 'Flemish School about 1510'. The picture which I have not seen in the original seems rather to fit in the Froment entourage. It is most probably a work from the South of France; the calligraphical undulating outline recalls some of the heads of the Uffizi Triptych (No. 214).

221. SCHOOL OF PROVENCE, ABOUT 1475/80

'JACOB'S DREAM' AND 'GIDEON AND THE FLEECE'. Formerly London, Durlacher Bros.

129 : 103 cm. each.

The two pictures formed originally the two faces of one panel; they have been split, transferred from wood on canvas and have suffered by these operations.

Both pictures are in great part grisailles; in 'Jacob's Dream' only the faces and hands have some colouring.

It is known by documents that Froment has treated the history of Gideon among the decorations which he executed in Avignon for the 'Fête-Dieu' in 1477. This in itself does not necessarily connect Froment with the pictures, but as their style is certainly Provençal, Froment's decorations may have inspired their author.

The complete two-faced panel was found about 1926 near Avignon.

Labande, GBA, Févr. 1933, p. 100 ff.; Labande, pl. LXVIII/LXIX; Jacques, Rep. A 15th cent. 82, pl. 120.

Exhibited: *London 1932, Nos. 4 and 37 (Commem. Catalogue, No. 36, 37).*

222. SCHOOL OF NICOLAS FROMENT

RETABLE OF SAINT ROBERT. Aix, Private Collection

Three panels; centre 130 : 41 cm.; lateral panels, 130 : 37 cm. each.

On the central panel St. Robertus, in his bishop's robes, in full frontal view, giving benediction. On the left St. Peter with a donor, on the right St. Anthony with a donatrix. Two coats-of-arms and the mark of the donor 'P' and 'S'.

The derivation from Froment seems striking, particularly from the earlier Froment style of the Uffizi Triptych (No. 214). The figure of St. Robert can also be compared to another work of the Froment School, in the artist's late manner—the St. Siffrein (No. 218).

The retable of St. Robert represents the borderline type between Provençal and Spanish art, but it may be left on the French side of the border.

The retable is reported to have been found by M. de Bresc in the stable of a country house near Mille.

Reproduced: *Labande, pl. LXXXIV.*

223. SCHOOL OF NICOLAS FROMENT, ABOUT 1470

THE LEGEND OF ST. MITRE. Aix, Cathédrale Saint-Sauveur

160 : 157 cm. (63 : 61¾ in.)   PLATE 125

St. Mitre, who is represented carrying his head in his hands, is essentially a Saint of the city of Aix. Of Greek origin, he took his residence in 'Aquae Sextiae' at the end of the 5th century.

The family of the donor, kneeling in the foreground to the right and the left of the Saint, is supposed to be a later addition. I do not see the necessity of making a division of the kind. The figures of the donors fit perfectly in the composition, their costumes correspond to the time of the picture, everything suggesting a date between 1470 and 1480. If the donors are somehow provincial, so is the entire painting, which is inspired by Froment but hardly executed by him.

According to *Labande (GBA, Février 1933, p. 99, ill. p. 97, fig. 9)* the picture was commissioned about 1470 by a distinguished merchant of Aix, Mitre de la Roque, for his burial place in a Chapel of the Cathedral of Aix.

Exhibited: *Paris 1904, No. 80.*

224. ATTRIBUTED TO NICOLAS FROMENT

THE PÉRUSSIS ALTARPIECE, 1480. Amsterdam, Coll. Fred. Muller

162 : 210 cm.

Triptych. Centre: The Cross standing in the midst of a wide landscape with a view on Avignon, the Rhône and its bridge. Above two angels flying. Left wing: a member of the Pérussis family presented by St. John the Baptist. Right wing: a younger member of the same family presented by St. Francis.

The 'Pérussis' (originally called Peruzzi) were a family of rich Florentine refugees who settled down in Avignon and became citizens, consuls, etc., in this town during the 15th century (see *Pithon-Curt, Histoire de la noblesse du comté Venaissin d'Avignon, Paris, 1743*).

The picture has suffered and has been carefully restored.

A drawing of the 18th century reproduces the picture in its old frame, bearing the inscription 'Aloisius Rudolphi de Perussiis hanc tabellam fieri fecit Anno Domini MCCCCLXXX'. Another altarpiece, also donated by a Pérussis (Ludovicus) in 1480, but lost in the original, is recorded by a similar drawing. This second altarpiece was before the revolution in the Chapelle de la Passion des Célestins in Avignon (*Labande, GBA, Févr. 1933, p. 99 ff. ill. p. 92 f. See also M. Marignane, Nicolas Froment, 1936, p. 68 ff., ill. 11/12*).

The Pérussis altarpiece has been ascribed to the nearest entourage of Froment or even to the master himself. I fail to see the cogency of the connection, the present triptych being far closer to the Flemish school than any secured work by Froment. Without the sites in the background pointing to Provence and the inscription naming the donors, style criticism would rather place the picture in the Rogier school.

Formerly at the Chartreuse de Bonpas near Avignon. M. Marignane claims to have seen the painting in a Chapel of the Pénitents in the village Védène near Avignon.

Reproduced: *Dimier 1925, pl. XXI; Labande, pl. LXIII–LXVI; Jacques, pl. 102.*

225. SCHOOL OF PROVENCE, ABOUT 1480

VIRGIN AND CHILD WITH SAINTS AND DONORS. Paris, Private Collection

110 : 130 cm.

The picture, which is only known to me from the reproduction in *Jacques, pl. 103 (Rep. A. 15th cent., 67)*, seems to go well together with the 'Pérussis' Altarpiece (No. 224).

226. SCHOOL OF PROVENCE, ABOUT 1470/1480, SOMETIMES ATTRIBUTED TO NICOLAS FROMENT

'LE CHRIST DE PITIÉ'. Worcester, Mass., Art Museum

77 : 97 cm.

Christ sitting on the edge of His tomb, supported by two angels. Ornamented gold ground.

Attributed to the master and reproduced by *M. Marignane (Nicolas Froment, 1936, p. 51, pl. 3)*, who dates the picture about 1465–1468. The connection with Froment does in no way seem conclusive. According to *Jacques (Rep. A 15th cent. 42)* a recent cleaning has revealed that the lower part of the picture had been repainted. Jacques points rightly to the similarity of the composition with a panel in a private Collection in Paris (*Rep. A 15th cent. 40, pl. 76*), not known to me in the original.

⟨227.⟩ *Neapolitan School, sometimes attributed to NICOLAS FROMENT*

Wings to a (lost) Adoration of the Kings. Naples, Museo Nazionale (Nos. 313/314)

These panels, each representing a King with followers, are traditionally called 'King of Sicily' and 'Duke of Calabria'.

The attribution to Froment (put forward by *Gerspach, L'Art, t. IV, p. 264* and taken up by *Marignane, p. 64 ff.*) is certainly erroneous, the pictures belonging to the Neapolitan School, which at that time was strongly influenced by Flemish art; but the affinity of the types to Froment's Uffizi Triptych (No. 214) is striking enough to make the panels worth noticing.

Reproduced: *Venturi, VII, 4, fig. 82/83.*

228. ATTRIBUTED TO THE SCHOOL OF AVIGNON, 15TH CENTURY

CRUCIFIXION. Paris, formerly Coll. L. A. Gaboriaud

Transferred from wood on canvas, 112 : 106 cm.

FIG. 38   ⟨ Cat. No. 232 ⟩   FIG. 39   ⟨ Cat. No. 231 ⟩

The Virgin wears a red dress and a black mantle lined with orange; St. John wears a red cloak. In the background a town said to resemble Avignon.

The connection with the School of Avignon seems possible. According to *Post* (*Spanish Painting, VII, 2, fig. 196*), by Jaime Ferrer.

Published by *Roger Fry, Burl. Mag., August 1922, p. 53*, with reprod.

Exhibited: *London 1932, No. 7 (Commem. Cat. No. 10)*.

229. SCHOOL OF AVIGNON, ABOUT 1460 (OR LATER)

'FONS PIETATIS'. Avignon, Musée Calvet (No. 8)

89 : 164 cm.

Christ on the Cross, which rises from a pond of His blood, between St. Mary Magdalen and St. Maria Aegyptiaca. Vast landscape. Inscriptions, in French, explain the subject.

The picture is not easy to judge or to date, as it is a rather rustic example of Alpine art and could be the work of a later archaizing artist. It is not in a good state of preservation.

Reproduced: *Labande, pl. XCII; Guiffrey Marcel, I, pl. 48*. On the subject cf. *Mâle, p. 106–109*.

230. ATTRIBUTED TO THE SCHOOL OF SOUTH-EASTERN FRANCE, ABOUT 1460

ST. ROBERT DE MOLESMES, ABBOT OF CLUNY. Detroit, Coll. J. H. Haas.

61 : 32 cm.; gold ground. Right wing of an altarpiece.

Colour harmony of gold and white enhanced by the red of the book in the Saint's left hand.

The style is closely related to Italian art.

Reproduced: *U.M., 72 (Text by Valentiner)*.

Exhibited: *New York 1927, No. 14; Detroit 1928, No. 2*.

231. FRENCH SCHOOL, ABOUT 1470

PIETÀ, BEFORE A LANDSCAPE WITH ARCHITECTURE. Hartford, Conn., Wadsworth Atheneum.   FIG. 39

Gold ground.

The style of this painting is indistinct; it shows, as *Jacques* has already noticed (*Rep. A 15th cent. 78, pl. 97*), traits of the school of Touraine and of the Rhône school. The closest connection seems to be with the 'Pietà' in enamel, attributed to the 'Monvaerni' Studio (No. 232).

232. STUDIO OF THE SO-CALLED 'MONVAERNI'

PIETÀ WITH TWO DONORS. Paris, Musée de Cluny.   FIG. 38

Rectangular enamel plaque on black ground. Black 'contre-émail', stippled and clotted. The connection of this plaque with French Pietàs on panel has been rightly noticed—it could be compared with the Pietà by Louis Bréa (No. 283) and even with the famous 'Pietà de Villeneuve' (No. 206). The nearest affinity seems to be with the Pietà in Hartford, Conn. (No. 231): both compositions show the Virgin supporting Christ's body whereas in the Pietàs of Villeneuve and Cimiez His body lies unsupported while the Virgin prays.

Marquet de Vasselot, Les Émaux Limousins, 1921, No. 45, pl. XV.

233. ATTRIBUTED TO PIERRE SPICRE, ABOUT 1470/1471
THE RAISING OF LAZARUS; THE STONING OF ST. STEPHEN. Beaune (Côte d'Or), Chapelle Saint-Léger de Notre-Dame
Frescoes.

The Chapel of Saint-Léger was decorated in the 15th century by Cardinal Jean Rolin, Bishop of Autun (his portrait is on the 'Nativity' by the Maître de Moulins, No. 292). A document stating that 'Pierre Spicre' was commissioned in 1474 to draw the cartoons for a tapestry with scenes from the life of the Virgin for Notre-Dame de Beaune has been found in the 'Archives de la Côte d'Or' and this tapestry is preserved. J. Bacri (GBA, April 1935) interprets another document from the same Archives as recording a commission from Cardinal Rolin to 'Pierre Spicre' to execute mural paintings for the Chapel of Saint Léger between 1470 and 1471, and he accordingly attributes the murals which have been found in 1901 by M. Mathieu-Faivre in this chapel to the enigmatic 'Spicre'.
The mural paintings, which are described by F. Mathieu (with some ill.: Extraits des Mémoires de la Société d'Histoire et d'Archéologie de Beaune, 1901/1902) and in full detail by H. Chabeuf (R.A.C., 1904, p. 190–200, and Mémoires de la Commission des Antiquités du Département de la Côte d'Or, t. XIV, 1901–1905, p. 113–134, without ill.) are not in a good state; the 'Stoning of St. Stephen' particularly is in great part destroyed. Nevertheless the parts of the 'Lazarus' which are visible show no special affinity to the style of the documented tapestry and I do not think the construction of Pierre Spicre as the author of both works a very lucky guess. I should like to keep Lemoisne's designation as 'School of Dijon, middle 15th century'. (Lemoisne hints at the possibility that a master 'Guillaume Spicker' may be the painter of the murals).
Reproduced: Lemoisne, pl. 58; GBA, 1935, p. 5, fig. 3 and p. 6, fig. 4 (details).
Cf. Maurice Denis, 'Théories', 'Le peintre de Beaune', Bibliothèque d'Occident, 1912, p. 129–131.

234. ATTRIBUTED TO PIERRE SPICRE, AFTER 1473
REPRESENTATIONS OF THE FOUR GREAT PROPHETS, THE FOUR EVANGELISTS, THE FATHERS OF THE CHURCH. Autun, Cathedral, Chapelle Ferry de Clugny, known as 'Chapelle Dorée'
Frescoes.

Mostly in a poor state; the best preserved part is the 'Procession of St. Gregory during the plague in Rome'. Very colourful: the Cardinals in their wide red coats, the men with houppelandes in red and black with blue doublets, the women, wearing 'hénins', also in black and red trimmed with hermine. Many portrait heads.
Connected by J. Bacri (GBA April 1935) with the frescoes in Beaune (No. 233) and also attributed to 'Pierre Spicre'. The style which we are used to call Burgundian is much more marked in these frescoes than in the 'Raising of Lazarus'. The Beaune composition has italianizing traits, particularly in the background, some of its types could remind one of Ghirlandaio; the Autun picture has all the force and heaviness of the types which are characteristic of Burgundy.
The 'Chapelle Dorée' was founded by the Canon Ferry de Clugny in 1465; the decoration must have been executed after 1473, as an inscription calls the donor 'Bishop of Tournai', a title which he only acquired in that year.
Reproduced: Michel, IV, 2, p. 721, fig. 481; Lemoisne pl. 57; GBA, April 1935, p. 8 fig. 5, p. 10 fig. 6.

235. MASTER OF SAINT-JEAN-DE-LUZ, ABOUT 1475
PORTRAITS OF HUGUES DE RABUTIN, SEIGNEUR D'ÉPIRY AND HIS WIFE, JEANNE DE MONTAIGU. New York, Coll. John Rockefeller Jun.   PLATES 131–132
60 : 49 cm. (23½ : 19¼ in.) each.
Half-figures; both with folded hands in adoration before small sculptured stone figures: he before the Virgin, she before John the Evangelist. The stone figures, each about 5 in. high, stand on consoles beneath gothic canopies. Hugues wears a high black cap and red coat trimmed with brown fur, Jeanne a cardinal-red headdress of stiff material and a dark blue-green costume. Green background. Although the pictures may look as if cut out from a large altarpiece, they are, according to the scholars who have studied them closely, not fragments, but represent a special version of the theme 'Donor with patron-Saint'.
F. Mercier, who introduced these superb paintings into literature (RdA, 1930, I, p. 213 ff.) also identified the sitters: Hugues de Rabutin is mentioned in

documents between 1467 and 1487; he and his wife (an illegitimate granddaughter of Philippe le Bon) were allowed by Jean Rolin (see Nos. 233 and 292), in 1472, to celebrate divine service in one of the chapels they had donated. The pictures come directly from the residence of the portrayed, the Château d'Épiry at Saint-Émiland (near Beaune and Autun), formerly called Saint-Jean de-Luz. Mercier therefrom derived the temporary name of the master, which I preserve. No other paintings could so far be assigned to the same hand.
J. Bacri (GBA, April 1935) springs a surprise by attributing the pictures to 'Pierre Spicre'—a suggestion which seems to lack all foundation, quite apart from the fact that the entire figure of this painter still remains rather mythical in spite of Bacri's efforts and a number of more or less convincing documents.
Reproduced in colour: Jacques, pl. CXXIV/CXXV.

236. BURGUNDIAN SCHOOL, ABOUT 1470/1480

(a) PORTRAIT OF CLAUDE DE TOULONGEON, PRESENTED BY HIS PATRON-SAINT CLAUDE, BISHOP OF BESANÇON. Worcester (U.S.A.), Art Museum (Cat. of 1922, p. 25)   PLATE 133
On the back the remains of a grisaille: a bearded Saint, half-figure.
105 : 77 cm. (41½ : 30½ in.). Originally arched top. Gold ground with dark dots. Left wing of a diptych or a triptych, the right wing being the donor's wife (see below); the supposed centre piece is missing.
Claude de Toulongeon, Comte de la Baslie, the leading baron of the Franche-Comté, died between 1500 and 1505. The picture shows him between 1470, the year of his marriage, and 1481, when he was elected knight of the Golden Fleece. The identification of the sitter is due to A. van de Put ('Some Golden Fleece Portraits', Burl. Mag., June 1923, p. 297 ff.).
The painter was certainly connected with the Burgundian court; the style of the painting is Burgundian and not Flemish; the name of Jan Provost, that has been suggested of late, must be strongly refuted; Provost has a well-known, clearly defined style, which has no affinity to these portraits.
Formerly in the Hainauer Collection, Berlin (Cat. W. von Bode, 1897, No. 65 a). Worcester Art Museum Bulletin, IV, 1913, No. 2; H. Tietze, Meisterwerke Europ. Malerei in Amerika, 1935, No. 247.
Exhibited: Berlin, Kunstgeschichtliche Gesellschaft, 1898, No. 97 ('Le Grand Bâtard de Bourgogne'); Paris 1904, No. 350; Worcester/Philadelphia 1939, No. 73.

(b) PORTRAIT OF GUILLEMETTE DE VERGY, PRESENTED BY ST. ELIZABETH OF HUNGARY (OR BY ST. BRIDGET OF SWEDEN?) Worcester (U.S.A.), Art Museum   PLATE 134
On the back a grisaille: St. Martin of Tours, half-figure.
106 : 78 cm. (41½ : 30½ in.). Originally arched top. Gold ground with dark dots. Right wing of a diptych or triptych, see above.
Wife of Claude de Toulongeon, Heiress of Charles de Vergy, Sénéchal of Burgundy.
This panel has suffered considerably, the heads are repainted, and it may therefore seem to be of lower quality than the portrait of the husband; the dissimilarities are, however, only due to the different state of preservation.
The picture, formerly also in the Hainauer Collection (Cat. Bode, No. 65 b) was for a number of years in Providence, Rhode Island School of Design. It has since been luckily reunited with its companion piece.
Rhode Island School of Design Bulletin, XI, October 1923, p. 39 ff.
Exhibited: Berlin, Kunstgeschichtliche Gesellschaft, 1898, No. 98; Paris 1904, No. 351; Worcester/Philadelphia, 1939. No. 74.

237. BURGUNDIAN(?) SCHOOL, ABOUT 1500
PORTRAIT OF A MAN WEARING A CAP ON HIS LONG HAIR. The Hague, late Coll. A. W. Volz
36 : 28,5 cm. On gold ground ornamented with dark dots.
Some features of the picture, particularly the handling of the background, recall the portraits of Claude de Toulongeon and his wife (No. 236) and it may be placed in their neighbourhood.
From the Collection of Baron van Woelmont, Ammersrode (Sale Coll. Six and others, Amsterdam, 10 July 1923, No. 121).
Exhibited: Rotterdam, Christmas Exhibition, 1931/32, No. 1 (reprod. in Cat.); The Hague, Oude Kunst uit Haagsch Bezit, 1936/37, No. 142; The Hague, Nederlandsche Kunst van de XVde en XVIde eeuw, 1945, No. 10.

FIG. 40   ⟨ Cat. No. 240 *a* ⟩

238. BURGUNDIAN SCHOOL

CHRIST ON THE CROSS BETWEEN ST. MARY AND ST. JOHN. Dijon, Musée

This picture is in any case the record of a remarkable 'Burgundian' composition, showing the full amplitude and force of this school. The execution—as far as one can judge in the present state—is not of the period of the invention, which goes back to the middle of the 15th century. The painting is either totally re-painted or a late 16th-century copy. The most puzzling figure is St. John(?) dressed in a kind of dalmatic, a fact that causes the Dijon Catalogue to call him a 'donor'.

Reproduced : *Magnin, 'La Peinture au Musée de Dijon,' 1929, p. 118; Sterling, fig. 167.*

239. MASTER OF ST. GILES

TWO SCENES FROM THE LEGEND OF ST. GILES (AEGIDIUS). London, National Gallery (Nos. 1419 and 4681)

(*a*) ST. GILES AND THE HIND.   PLATE 135

On the reverse, in grisaille, a bishop in a niche (perhaps St. Remigius).

61,5 : 46,5 cm. (24¼ : 18¼ in.).

This picture and the 'Mass of St. Giles' (below) belonged in all probability, to-gether with two panels in New York (No. 240), to one rather large altarpiece, the London panels having been part of the left shutters, the New York panels part of the right shutters. The centre piece, which is lost, may have shown scenes from the legends of St. Denis and of the apostle St. Peter; its measurements should have been about 1,30 m. by 2 m. (with open shutters).

The hind takes refuge with St. Giles. The King and a bishop are kneeling before the Saint, asking his pardon for having hunted the animal, which was his friendly companion (see *Davies, 1945, p. 71*).

According to *Canon Nicholas (Une nouvelle Histoire de S. Gilles, 1912, p. 137)* the town in the background is Saint-Gilles du Gard, near Arles.

The painter, whose temporary name is derived from the London panels, was active at the end of the 15th century. He worked in Paris, as the present altar-

piece demonstrates, and is definitely distinct from the artists of the purely Flemish School.

Formerly Coll. Th. Baring; Coll. Lord Northbrook (*Northbrook Catalogue, 1889, No. 2*).

Friedlaender, Mus. Ber. XXXIV, 1912/1913, p. 185, and GBA, 1937, p. 223/4; reprod. of the reverse: *M. Davies, Paintings and drawings on the backs of Nat. Gall. pictures, pl. 27; GBA 1937, p. 226, Fig. 6.*

Exhibited: *London, Royal Academy, 1872, No. 224; London, Burlington Club, 1892, No. 35 (review of the exhibition by H. von Tschudi, Rep. f. Kw., XVI, 1893, p. 105); London, Royal Academy, 1894, No. 181.*

(*b*) THE MASS OF ST. GILES.   PLATE 136

On the reverse, in grisaille, St. Peter in a niche.

61,5 : 45,5 cm. (24¼ : 18 in.)

St. Giles elevates the Host. The King (Charles Martel; in some versions of the legend Charlemagne) kneels on the left. An angel flies towards the altar, carrying a paper with an inscription stating that, thanks to St. Giles's prayer, the sin of the King was forgiven, if he repented and confessed.

The miracle is placed in the Abbey of Saint-Denis, near Paris. Many of the objects represented, such as the retable of gold studded with gems on the high-altar, the cross above, the monument of St. Dagobert on the right, etc., are known from old accounts and inventories (*Doublet, Histoire de l'Abbaye de S. Denis, 1625; M. Conway, The Abbey of St. Denis and its ancient treasures, Oxford, Society of Antiquaries, 1913; Archaeologia, 1915, Vol.LXVI, p. 103; Davies, 1945, p. 72–74; Erwin Panofsky, Abbot Suger, Princeton 1946, p. 179*).

The picture, the pedigree of which can be traced back until 1756 (*Vente Duc de Tallard, Paris*), was seen by Passavant in 1831 in the Collection of the Earl of Dudley; by Waagen in 1835 (*Kunstwerke und Künstler in England, II, 1838, p. 205*).

Reproduction of the reverse: *M. Davies (see above), pl. 41; GBA 1937, p. 226, Fig. 6.*

Exhibited: *Manchester 1857; London, Royal Academy, 1871, No. 326; London, Royal Academy, 1892, No. 173; London, Burlington Club, 1892, No. 24 (then Coll. E. Steinkopff); London, Royal Academy, 1902, No. 9; London, Society of Antiquaries, 1915; London, 1927, No. 70 (Lord Seaforth).*

240. MASTER OF ST. GILES

TWO SCENES FROM THE LEGEND OF SAINT REMI (REMIGIUS). New York, M. Georges Wildenstein   COLOUR PLATE P. 25; FIG. 40

61 : 45 cm. each.

Belonging to the same altarpiece as No. 239 (*q.v.*).

(*a*) The Baptism of Clovis by S. Remi. The chapel in which the scene is set reproduces the 'Sainte-Chapelle' of Paris (Lower Chapel). The grisaille on the reverse is lost but known by an old photograph: it represented St. Giles.

(*b*) St. Remi, standing in front of Notre-Dame de Paris, gives benediction. In the background an evil spirit is exorcized, etc. The grisaille on the reverse is lost but known by a photograph: it represented St. Denis.

The localities have been identified by *Julius Held (Zwei Ansichten von Paris beim Meister des heiligen Aegidius, Pr. Jhb., LIII, 1932, p. 3 ff.).* When Held published his article, the pictures were only known from reproductions in the Catalogue of the Beurnonville Sale of 1883. The originals have since been found; they are published by *M. J. Friedlaender, GBA, 1937, p. 228–229, fig. 9 and 10 (text p. 223).*

Reproduction of the outside grisailles: *Friedlaender, GBA, 1937, p. 226, fig. 6.*

241. MASTER OF ST. GILES

ST. JEROME. Berlin, Deutsches Museum (No. 1704)

61 : 51 cm.

The Saint kneels before a crucifix in a landscape.

Winkler, Altniederländische Malerei, p. 190; Friedlaender, GBA, 1937, p. 222, reprod. p. 225, fig. 5.

242. MASTER OF ST. GILES

THE FLIGHT INTO EGYPT; THE PRESENTATION IN THE TEMPLE. Vierhouten, Coll. van Beuningen

Two panels, 28 : 16 cm. each.

The architecture on the 'Presentation' is derived from a print ascribed to Bramanate (*Pr. Jhb., VIII, 1887, p. 191*).

Formerly in the Collections Richard von Kaufmann, Berlin (*Sale Catalogue, Berlin, 1917, Nos. 120/121, with reproductions*) and Stephan von Auspitz, Vienna. *Friedlaender, GBA, 1937, p. 222.*

Exhibited: *Berlin, Kunstgeschichtliche Gesellschaft, 1898, No. 53; Rotterdam, Kersttentoonstelling, 1934/1935, No. 12/13; Maestricht, Oude Kunst, 1939, No. 6/7; The Hague, Sept./Oct., 1945, No. 23 a and b.*

243. MASTER OF ST. GILES

THE BETRAYAL OF CHRIST. Brussels, Musées Royaux des Beaux-Arts (No. 864)   PLATE 137

21 : 29 cm. (8½ : 11½ in.)

One of the early documents of clair-obscure. The only source of light is the lantern.

Formerly in the Coll. Cardon, Brussels (Sale 1921).

Friedlaender, GBA, 1937, p. 222, reprod. p. 224, fig. 4.

244. MASTER OF ST. GILES

ST. CHRISTOPHER AND A SAINT BISHOP. Zug (Switzerland), Coll. Abegg

48 : 16 cm. each.

Two wings; the centre piece was, according to Friedlaender, a 'Madonna with Angels' and not the 'St. Anne' (No. 249) as had been suggested (communication by letter).

Formerly Coll. Begarrière (Sale Lucerne, 7th July 1926).

Friedlaender GBA, 1937, p. 222/223, fig. 2 and 3.

245. MASTER OF ST. GILES

MADONNA AND CHILD. New York, Coll. Robert Lehmann

26, 7 : 18,4 cm.

Reproduced in the *Catalogue of the Philip Lehmann Coll.; Friedlaender, GBA, 1937, p. 230, fig. 11.*

246. MASTER OF ST. GILES

MADONNA AND CHILD. Paris, Louvre

21,5 : 13,5 cm. Gold ground.

Not of the first quality of the master. The composition is a free variation after Rogier van der Weyden.

Sold in Amsterdam, Coll. Mme. M., 13th July 1926.

Replicas in Bruges, Karmelklooster, and in Besançon (communication from M. Jacques Dupont).

Published by *J. Dupont, Une Vierge du Maître de S. Gilles, Bulletin des Musées de France, July 1936; mentioned by Friedlaender, GBA, 1937, p. 222.*

247. MASTER OF ST. GILES

PORTRAITS OF A MAN AND HIS WIFE. Chantilly, Musée Condé (No. 104)   PLATE 138

17 : 12 cm. each (6¾ : 4¾ in.)

On red background. Originally with arched tops; perhaps fragments, cut from a larger composition (Portraits of donors?).

Formerly Coll. Reiset (there called 'Jan van Eyck').

Friedlaender, Mus. Ber., 1912/1913, p. 187; Friedlaender, GBA, 1937, p. 221, fig. 1.

248. MASTER OF ST. GILES

PORTRAIT OF PHILIPPE LE BEAU. Winterthur, Coll. Dr. Oscar Reinhart

30,5 : 21,5 cm. Arched top.

On the original frame the device *En Imperiales*. On lacquer-red ground; he wears a dress of gold brocade with dark sleeves and brown fur; his hair is red with a golden tinge, his complexion pale, his lips bright red.

According to the age of the prince, who was born in 1478 and who here appears to be about 18 to 20 years old, the picture was painted in the last years of the 15th century. It is in excellent state; the quality is far superior to that of the average princely portrait.

Formerly Coll. Engel-Gros (*Catalogue of the Collection, compiled by P. Ganz, 1925, with reproduction*).

Friedlaender, GBA, 1937, p. 222, reprod. p. 231, fig. 12.

249. MASTER OF ST. GILES (SCHOOL)

ST. ANNE WITH THE VIRGIN AND CHILD, ST. JOSEPH AND ST. JOACHIM. Joigny (Yonne), Église Saint-Jean

47 : 31 cm.

One of the best-known pictures of the group, but rather a weak specimen, hardly worthy to be attributed to the master himself. The picture does not belong to the two wings of St. Christopher and a Saint Bishop (No. 244) as had been suggested.

Reproduced: *Réau, Les richesses de l'Art de la France, La Bourgogne, La Peinture, 1929, pl. 27; Friedlaender, GBA, 1937, p. 223 (without reprod.)*

Exhibited: *Paris 1904, No. 64 (Bouchot 1904, pl. XCIV).*

⟨250.⟩ *Wrongly attributed to the MASTER OF ST. GILES*
Portrait of a Man on Blue Background. Boston (Mass.), Museum of Fine Arts

17,8 : 15,2 cm.

Formerly attributed to the Master of Moulins, afterwards to the Master of St. Giles, but certainly not by either of them and rather a Flemish than a French work about 1480.

Reproduced: *Studio, September 1924; Wescher, Die französischen Bildnisse von Karl VII. bis Franz I., Pantheon, Jan. 1938, p. 1.*

Mentioned by *J. Held, Pr. Jhb., 1932, p. 3 ff.*

⟨251.⟩ *MASTER OF THE PIETÀ OF SAINT GERMAIN*, about 1490/1495
The Pietà with a view of Paris. Paris, Louvre (No. 998 c.)

100 : 204 cm.

Christ taken from the cross is lamented by the Virgin, St. John, three holy women and Sts. Nicodemus and Joseph of Arimathia.

In the background on the left the Abbey of Saint Germain-des-Prés and, on the 'rive droite' of the Seine, the Louvre and the 'butte Montmartre'.

The picture, which provides the temporary name for the master, has apparently never left Paris, where it was executed. It was originally in the Abbey of S. Germain-des-Prés (*Bouillart, Histoire de Saint Germain-des-Près, IV, p. 169*) and went from there to the Musée des Monuments Français and to the Abbey Church of Saint-Denis. This unbroken pedigree, together with the view in the background, should be the strongest evidence for a Parisian origin of the panel; it has accordingly been attributed to the School of Paris.

Once again, style criticism cannot agree. The style of the painting is not Parisian, it is not French at all, but nearer to the art of Western Germany.

Wescher (GBA, Janvier, 1937, p. 59–62), who has constituted an 'œuvre' of the master, attributing various other works to him or to his entourage, suggests with good reasons that he might have been a Cologne painter who worked for some time in France, possibly at the court of Louis XI.

Reproduced: *Lemoisne, Louvre, pl. 36 and 37; Barnes, p. 501.*

Exhibited: *Paris 1904, No. 92 (Bouchot 1904, Pl. XCIX); Paris 1946, No 19.*

⟨252.⟩ *MASTER OF THE PIETÀ OF SAINT GERMAIN*
The Bearing of the Cross. Lyon, Musée (No. 206)

Light and variegated colours. Christ in steel-blue; the warrior on the left in pink trousers, his doublet with yellow sleeves; the warrior on the right in pink doublet and light-blue stockings.

Wescher (GBA, Janv., 1937, p. 61, fig. 4) connects the picture convincingly with the 'Pietà' (No. 251). It is still more distant from Parisian art than the Louvre picture, its composition and colouring rather showing similarities with Dutch primitives.

⟨253.⟩ *MASTER OF THE PIETÀ OF SAINT GERMAIN*
The Resurrection. Lübeck, Museum

95 : 103 cm.

The type of the old warrior near Christ's tomb is very similar to the soldiers on the 'Bearing of the Cross' (No. 252). The attribution to the master, proposed by *Wescher (GBA, Janv. 1937, p. 61, fig. 3)*, is convincing.

Exhibited: *Berlin, Kaiser Friedrich Museums-Verein 1925, No. 286 (there called 'North German').*

⟨254.⟩ *MASTER OF THE PIETÀ OF SAINT GERMAIN*
The Bearing of the Cross, with Donors. Formerly Lucerne, Coll. Chillingworth. 60 × 85 cm.

The donors, inserted at a later period by different hands, give evidence of the connection of the artist with the School of Cologne. The male donors on the

left show the style of the 'Master of the Holy Kinship' (active in Cologne about 1500); the female donors on the right are in the manner of Barthel Bruyn (Cologne 1493-1557).
Chillingworth Sale, Lucerne, 3 Sept. 1922, *Cat. No. 62 (with reproduction)*.
Wescher, GBA, Janv. 1937, p. 61/62, fig. 5.

⟨255.⟩ *Attributed to the MASTER OF THE PIETÀ OF SAINT GERMAIN*
The Entombment of Christ. Chicago, Art Institute (No. 26, 570)
48,3 : 68,6 cm.
The picture has been connected with the Pietà (No. 251) by *W. Heil (Pantheon, 1929, p. 78)*.
Formerly Collections Rod. Kann, Paris; Lamponi, Florence.
Reproduced: *Barnes, p. 509; Gillet, pl. 13*.
Exhibited: *New York 1927, No. 9; Detroit 1928; Chicago 1933, No. 33*.

256. FRENCH SCHOOL, ABOUT 1490
SALOME PRESENTING THE HEAD OF ST. JOHN THE BAPTIST. Aix-en-Provence, Musée (No. 187)
35 : 25 cm.
The forms have a certain affinity to Rhenish-Dutch paintings, particularly to the School of Utrecht, but the colours are different and decidedly un-Dutch: they are firm and metal-like, never vague. Salome has a 'changeant' dress of violet-greyish blue, Herodias is in blue with yellow revers to her bonnet, Herod in red gold brocade with green sleeves, the page on the left in olive-green with red trousers.
The nearest analogy within our material seems to be with the 'Pietà of S. Germain' (No. 251), but the present picture is clearly French.
Reproduced: *Guiffrey Marcel Terrasse, II, pl. XI ('École Provençale'); Barnes, p. 193 (text, p. 189)*.

257. FRENCH SCHOOL, ABOUT 1490
CIRCUMCISION. Merion, Pa., Barnes Foundation (No. 869)
44 : 25 cm.
The types are very near to those of the 'Salome' (No. 256)—a likeness which has already been noticed by Barnes—but the colours are more pale and delicate. The colour scheme as well as some details are reminiscent of the Dutch master (distant follower of Geertgen tot Sint Jans) who painted the 'Entombment of Christ' in Budapest and the 'Bearing of the Cross' in the Claasen Coll., Rotterdam, but just as in No 256 the French character prevails in the present picture.
Reproduced: *Barnes, p. 196 (text, p. 198)*.

258. MASTER OF ST. SEBASTIAN
FOUR SCENES FROM THE LEGEND OF ST. SEBASTIAN. Philadelphia, John G. Johnson Collection (Nos. 765-768)   PLATES 146 and 148
(1) St. Sebastian destroys the idols. (2) The Martyrdom of St. Sebastian. (3) St. Irene nurses St. Sebastian. (4) The death of St. Sebastian.
Panels belonging to an altarpiece, 79 : 49 cm. (32½ : 21¾ in.) each.
The master's most important work, from which his temporary name is derived.
Ch. Sterling has tentatively identified the master with the painter 'Josse Lieferinxe'. The hypothesis is based mainly on the fact that 'Lieferinxe' and a Piedmontese associate of his, Bernardino Simondi, were commissioned in 1497 to paint an altar with 8 scenes from the life of St. Sebastian, the centre piece representing St. Sebastian between St. Anthony and St. Roch. After the associate's death in 1498, Lieferinxe finished the work alone. The divergence between the 8 scenes mentioned in the document and the four Johnson scenes is counterbalanced by the appearance of other panels belonging to the same series in Baltimore and in Rome (Nos. 259-260). Furthermore, Mr. B. Berenson wrote to Mr. Johnson in 1912 that he had found a 'Martyrdom of St. Sebastian' by the same artist in the Church of Brega Marittima, which might be yet another part of the same altarpiece.
The painter of the Johnson panels, whether we identify him with 'Lieferinxe' or leave him in anonymity, worked near the Rhône valley, as Hulin de Loo has already stated in 1913.
From an English Collection (formerly with Thos. Agnew's, London).
C. Benoit, GBA, 1901, II (with reproductions of scene 1 and 4); Valentiner, Johnson Catalogue, III (1914); Jacques, Rep. A 15th cent., 72, pl. 113-116; Johnson Catalogue, 1941, p. 48; Ch. Sterling, GBA, November 1942, p. 135-148.

259. MASTER OF ST. SEBASTIAN
ST. SEBASTIAN INTERCEDING FOR THE PLAGUE-STRICKEN.
Baltimore, Walters Art Gallery   PLATE 147
77 : 47 cm. (31¼ : 19½ in.)
The panel belongs to the same series as the scenes from the life of the Saint in the Johnson Collection (No. 258); it has practically the same dimensions, and is analogous in colour, technique and style.
Published by *Ch. Sterling, The Art Quarterly, Vol.. VIII, Summer 1945, No. 3, p. 216 ff., fig. 1*.
From English possession (formerly with Messrs. Koetser, London).

260. MASTER OF ST. SEBASTIAN
PILGRIMS WORSHIPPING THE RELICS OF A HEALING SAINT. Rome, Palazzo Venezia (Cat. of 1947, p. 39)
82,7 : 56,3 cm. Dark and subdued colours; brown prevails, faintly enlivened by some reddish and greenish tones.
First published by *G. Briganti, Critica d'Arte, III, June 1938, p. 104, pl. 65, fig. 2* (the author cites R. Longhi, who has attributed the picture to an unknown Provençal master). *Sterling (The Art Quarterly, 1945, p. 217, reprod. p. 223, Fig. 6)* suggests that the picture may be the last scene from the 'Sebastian' altarpiece.
Exhibited: *Rome, 1946, No. 8*.

261. MASTER OF ST. SEBASTIAN
PIETÀ. Antwerp, Museum (formerly Ghent, Coll. Georges Hulin de Loo)
88 : 101 cm.
Important and characteristic work by the master.
The late owner of the picture, Prof. Hulin, had immediately recognized the connection of his 'Pietà' with the Johnson panels (No. 258). His statement is deposited in a letter of March 1914, addressed to Mr. John G. Johnson, cited by *Jacques (Rep. A 15th cent. 71)*.
Reproduced: *Jacques, pl. III*.

262. MASTER OF ST. SEBASTIAN
ST. MICHAEL SLAYING THE DRAGON. ON THE REVERSE: THE ANNUNCIATION. Avignon, Musée Calvet (No. 10)   PLATES 145, 143
80 : 59 cm. (31½ : 23 in.)
The obverse on light olive-green background, ornamented with a darker green brocade pattern. The entire colour scheme is based on green and red, only the armour of St. Michael is of shining steel-blue metal and his coat is dark blue. The 'Annunciation' is set in an Italian renaissance chapel. Obverse and reverse are in a very good state.
Part of an altarpiece, another part of which is the 'Marriage of the Virgin' (No. 263). The connection has first been observed by *H. Voss (Monatsh. f. Kstw., 1911, p. 414/415, 'Werke eines Anonymus in den Museen von Avignon und Brüssel')*; measurements, types, details of the architecture, etc., agree perfectly; the marble columns have identical capitals.
The suggestion of *Sanpere ÿ Miquel (Los cuatrocentistas Catalanes, 1906, II, 98)* to ascribe the 'St. Michael' to Bermejo—on account of an alleged resemblance to Bermejo's 'St. Michael' in the Coll. of Lady Wernher—must be strongly refuted.
The *Paris Catalogue of 1904*, while calling the picture 'Suite de Nicolas Froment', draws attention to its relation to two panels in the Museum of Budapest (St. Barbara and St. Catherine, Nos. 693/4, dated 1520). The Budapest pictures are, however, not only far later but purely Flemish.
Jacques (Rep. A 15th cent., 68) combines the present panel, the one in Brussels (No. 263) and a fragment in the Louvre (No. 264) to one group, which he confronts with another group formed by the Johnson and Antwerp panels (Nos. 258-261). He believes both groups to be probably painted by the same master at different periods.
Exhibited: *Paris 1904, No. 87; London 1932, No. 60*.

263. MASTER OF ST. SEBASTIAN
THE MARRIAGE OF THE VIRGIN. Brussels, Musées Royaux des Beaux-Arts (No. 634)   PLATE 144
80 : 60 cm.
Belonging to the same altarpiece as No. 262.
The picture is painted on one side only. It is in a very good state.
Reproduced: *Jacques, pl. 109 and 112 (text: Rep. A 15th cent., 69)*.

264. MASTER OF ST. SEBASTIAN

THE ADORATION OF THE CHILD. ON THE REVERSE: THE LOWER PART OF THE FIGURE OF A SAINT BISHOP. Paris, Louvre (Inv. No. R. F. 966)

38 : 47 cm. Fragment.

It has been suggested that this picture is part of a wing belonging to the same altarpiece as Nos. 262 and 263.

The hands of the Virgin, which were destroyed, have been repainted. The picture is altogether not in a perfect state and inferior in quality to the other works attributed to the Master.

Formerly in the Musée de Cluny, Paris.

Reproduced: *Jacques, pl.* 107 *(Rep. A 15th cent.,* 70); reprod. in colours: *'L'École Provençale', Trésors,* 1944.

Exhibited: *Paris 1946, No.* 18.

265. FRENCH SCHOOL, ABOUT 1480: 'ÉCOLE DU RHÔNE'

THE DEATH OF THE VIRGIN; THE CORONATION OF THE VIRGIN. Lyon, Musée (Nos. 229/230)

135 : 75 cm. each.

Two panels of an altarpiece. Both are untouched and in perfect condition.

Deep and glowing colours, frequent use of red.

The clear disposition, the noble if somewhat vacant types lead to the neighbourhood of the more italianizing trend of French painting. The relatively nearest points of comparison can be found in the paintings attributed to the 'Master of St. Sebastian' (Nos. 258–264). The painter might therefore also be included in the 'École du Rhône'.

Reproduced: *Réau, pl.* 40 *(Coronation); Jacques, pl.* 129.

Exhibited: *Paris 1904, No.* 97/98 *(Bouchot 1904, pl. LXXXVIII and LXXXIX).*

266. SCHOOL OF PROVENCE, ABOUT 1490/1500; ATTRIBUTED TO NICOLAS DIPRE

THE MEETING OF ST. JOACHIM AND ST. ANNE AT THE GOLDEN GATE. Carpentras, Museum

38 : 45 cm. Fragment.

In view of the attested provenience from S. Siffrein, Carpentras, Sterling has identified the picture with one of four scenes from the life of St. Anne, painted in 1499 for the 'Confrérie de la Conception de la Vierge' in S. Siffrein by a local painter, Nicolas Dipre. The identification is based on a document published by *M. H. Chobaut, Mémoires de l'Académie de Vaucluse,* IV, *Avignon,* 1940, *p.* 101.

Reproduced: *Labande, pl. LXX; Ch. Sterling, Two XVth century Provençal Painters revived,* (1) *Nicolas Dipre, GBA, Oct.* 1942; *Jedlicka, pl. 4*

Exhibited: *Paris,* 1937, *No.* 30.

267. SCHOOL OF PROVENCE, ABOUT 1490/1500 (MASTER OF THE ALTARPIECE OF THE LIFE OF THE VIRGIN)

THE MARRIAGE OF THE VIRGIN. Marseille, Coll. Comte Demandolx-Dedons   PLATE 140

26 : 35 cm. (10¼ : 13¾ in.)

The picture has been grouped together with the fragment of Carpentras (No. 266.)

Three further panels which correspond perfectly to the present picture have turned up lately (Nos. 268–270), one of which—the 'Presentation'—may just as well belong to a series of the Life of St. Anne as to the Life of the Virgin, whereas the two others—'Adoration of the Magi' and 'Crucifixion'—can only belong to a Life of the Virgin. I believe that all four panels (No. 267–270) are parts of the same altarpiece, although the measurements do not perfectly coincide. The identification of the master with N. Dipre, based on 'Scenes from the Life of St. Anne', would thereby lose its main support.

Formerly Chapel of the Convent of the 'Trinitaires de Marseille' *(Dimier, GBA,* 1938, *p.* 231).

Sterling, GBA, Oct. 1942; *Gillet, pl. VI (in colour).*

268. SCHOOL OF PROVENCE, ABOUT 1490/1500 (MASTER OF THE ALTARPIECE OF THE LIFE OF THE VIRGIN)

THE ADORATION OF THE MAGI. Zurich, Private Collection PLATE 141

28 : 47,5 cm.

The picture is closely connected with the 'Marriage of the Virgin' (No. 267).

The figures have the same short proportions, some of the heads (head of St. Joseph) are practically identical.

So far the picture has not been mentioned in literature.

269. SCHOOL OF PROVENCE, ABOUT 1490/1500 (MASTER OF THE ALTARPIECE OF THE LIFE OF THE VIRGIN)

THE PRESENTATION OF THE VIRGIN. Paris, Private Collection

31,7 : 50 cm. (12½ : 19⅝ in.)   PLATE 139

St. Joachim is clad in red; St. Anne, whose left hand seems to give benediction, in olive-green on pure green, the little Virgin in blue.

The picture is of particularly good quality and in a faultless state.

I am indebted to Dr. Curt Benedict, of Paris, for having kindly drawn my attention to this picture and to the following No. 270. Both pictures have so far not been mentioned in literature.

270. SCHOOL OF PROVENCE, ABOUT 1490/1500 (MASTER OF THE ALTARPIECE OF THE LIFE OF THE VIRGIN)

CRUCIFIXION. Rome, Private Collection   PLATE 142

29,5 : 44,5 cm. (11⅝ : 17½ in.).

The Madonna is in blue, St. John in vermilion. In the landscape to the right and the left gothic Cathedrals—in the left upper corner the 'Palais des Papes' of Avignon. The picture comes from the collection of Marchese Durazzo, Genova.

271. SCHOOL OF PROVENCE, ABOUT 1460–1480

RETABLE OF THE FOUR SAINTS: ST. LAURENCE, ST. ANTHONY, ST. SEBASTIAN AND ST. THOMAS AQUINAS. Saint-Maximin, Église des Dominicains

Each panel, 180 : 80 cm.

The retable consists of several parts executed at different periods. The figures of the Saints—all repainted with the exception of St. Anthony—can be dated about 1460.

Described in *Abbé Albanès, Le Couvent Royal de Saint-Maximin, p.* 172–176.

Jacques (Rep. A 15th cent., 47) sees a connection between the figure of St. Anthony and that of St. Joachim in the Carpentras fragment (No. 266).

Reproduced: *Labande, pl. XLII (detail; text p.* 200).

272. SCHOOL OF PROVENCE, ABOUT 1470

ST. ANTHONY, PATRIARCH OF THE CENOBITES, WITH A BLACK BOAR. Carpentras, Museum (From S. Siffrein).

71 : 42 cm. Probably part of a retable, the other parts of which are lost.

The Saint is represented in strict frontal view, on gold ground. The style shows the utmost simplification and, as it were, petrification of the Southern French type. The nearest affinities seem to be with the (earlier) Retable of St. Robert (No. 222) and with the (later) panels of the Virgin with the Rosary and St. Laurence (No. 280). The picture has been repainted.

Reproduced: *Labande, pl. XCI; Guiffrey Marcel Terrasse, II, pl. LI.*

273. SCHOOL OF AVIGNON, ABOUT 1490/1500

THE ADORATION OF THE CHILD. Avignon, Musée Calvet (No. 9)

95 : 110 cm. (37½ : 43½ in.)   PLATE 150

The Child Jesus is adored by His mother and a knight, presented by a holy bishop (perhaps S. Louis de Toulouse). The arms behind the head of the bishop have been interpreted as those of the Baron of Languedoc.

The Virgin has a blue robe and red coat, the bishop a dalmatic of gold brocade; the knight, with very white hair, wears black armour over a blue tunic.

The picture is in a rather poor state. Large restored holes can be detected everywhere, particularly in the dress of St. Mary. The head of the Child has become quite indistinct—this is no 'sfumato' but just a rubbed surface.

The style shows the Italian infiltration in late Avignon art. The Virgin looks like a Milanese Madonna. On the other hand, the bishop lifts his mitre with the old gesture of St. Donatian in Jan van Eyck's 'Madonna van de Paele'.

Exhibited: *Paris 1904, No.* 85; *London 1932, No.* 58 *(Commem. Cat. No.* 38); *Paris 1937, No.* 33.

274. SCHOOL OF AVIGNON, ABOUT 1480/1490

'LE RETABLE DE VENASQUE'. Avignon, Musée Calvet (No. 7)

272 : 252 cm.

A holy Pope (St. Peter?) between Sts. Maurice and Marthe. On the reverse six half-length figures representing ancestors of the Virgin.

This is a typical example of the later school of Avignon and must be quoted in spite of its ruined condition. When I last saw it, in 1938, it had still remained unrestored and unvarnished, and offered a good opportunity of studying this style without embellishments.

From the Church of Venasque (Vaucluse).

Reproduced: *Labande, pl. LXXXVI (detail); Guiffrey Marcel Terrasse, II, pl. 49–52.*

275. SCHOOL OF AVIGNON, ABOUT 1500/1510

DIONYSIUS THE AREOPAGITE IN PRAYER. Amsterdam, Rijksmuseum

49 : 35 cm.   PLATE 174

On a parchment hanging on the left the inscription 'Magnum Mysterium et mirabile Sacramentum'; on the right another parchment, inscribed 'Divus Dionysius Parisior Episcopus Theologus Ariopagita'.

The books on shelves in the background recall the still-lifes of the Aix Master and of 'Colantonio'. The picture belongs in the same neighbourhood, only at a considerably later period.

When *Jacques (Rep. A 15th cent., 90)* comments on the fact that 'Saint Denis' is here represented not 'according to the usual tradition' as a bishop, carrying his head in his hands, but as a philosopher, he follows the venerable example of Hilduin, abbot of St. Denis in the 9th century, who first mixed up Saint Denis of Paris, the martyr, with Dionysius the Areopagite, and who attributed to him the celebrated writings of the Pseudo-Areopagite. The person portrayed on the present picture is in any case meant to be the theological writer and mystic exclusively, in spite of the controversial words 'Parisior Episcopus'.

Exhibited: *London 1932, No. 33 (Commem. Cat. No. 34).*

276. SCHOOL OF PROVENCE, ABOUT 1500

THE ANNUNCIATION WITH ST. STEPHEN AND DONORS. Paris, Coll. H. Chalandon

Strongly italianizing example of the Avignon type.

Published by *L. Demonts, RdA, Janv. 1937, p. 247 ff.*

277. SCHOOL OF PROVENCE, ABOUT 1500

ST. MICHAEL. Tarascon, Cathédrale Sainte Marthe

115 : 49 cm.

Fragment of the wing of a retable. The figure of the Archangel is cut at the knees; he presents a donor, whose bust only is visible. The donor's head makes the panel remarkable: an impressive rustic type, the descendant of the donor on the 'Boulbon' altarpiece (No. 205). (Boulbon is situated on the road from Avignon to Tarascon).

Reproduced: *Labande, pl. XCVI.*

278. SCHOOL OF PROVENCE, ABOUT 1500

ST. MAGDALEN WITH A DONOR. Tarascon, Cathédrale Sainte Marthe

120 : 57 cm.

Part of a retable, but complete, not a fragment and not necessarily connected with St. Michael (No. 277). Of special interest is again the donor, seen in strict profile, who recalls Venetian portraiture (Gentile Bellini, etc.)

Reproduced: *Labande, pl. XCVI.*

279. SCHOOL OF PROVENCE, 1513

RETABLE OF S. ROCH. Tarascon, Cathédrale Sainte Marthe

Each panel 130 : 48 cm. Gold ground.

Three panels: in the centre St. Roch, dated '1513 die 21 decmb.', on the left St. John the Evangelist, on the right St. Laurence. The picture has suffered, particularly the side panels are softened by re-paint. It is nevertheless an important specimen of Provençal 'Alpine' art.

Reproduced: *Labande, pl. XCVIII.*

280. SCHOOL OF PROVENCE, 16TH CENTURY

THE VIRGIN WITH THE ROSARY AND ST. LAURENCE. Avignon, Musée Calvet (No. 5/6)

Two panels, 133 : 58 cm. each. Ornamented gold ground.

Both figures in strict frontal view like geometrical constructions. At the feet of the Virgin a kneeling donor (canon), who can be regarded as the latest descendant of the 'Boulbon' donor's type.

Reproduced: *Labande, pl. XC.*

FIG. 41   ⟨ Cat. No. 152 ⟩

281. JACQUES DURANDI

RETABLE OF ST. MARGARET. Fréjus (Var), Cathedral

223 : 218 cm.

Polyptych consisting of ten parts.

Signed: *Hoc opus fecit fieri dominus Ant(onius) Boneti beneficiarius hujus eccl(es)iae (per magistrum) Jacobu(m) Durandi de Nic(ia).*

This is the only known signed painting by the master, to whom other works have been attributed, e.g. the large Retable of St. John the Baptist in the Museum Masséna, Nice.

The painter is closely dependent on Italian, particularly Tuscan art. His style and quality correspond roughly to, say, Neri di Bicci in Florence.

Reproduced: *Guiffrey Marcel Terrasse, II, pl. 30/31; Barnes, p. 269 (Retable of St. John reprod. p. 449); Doré, 'Art en Provence' 421 (Retable of St. John, 422).*

282. JEAN MIRAILLET (MIRALHETI)

'VIERGE DE MISÉRICORDE'. ON THE PREDELLA: CHRIST APPEARING TO ST. MAGDALEN; PIETÀ; THE THREE MARYS NEAR THE TOMB. Nice, Musée Masséna

259 : 210 cm.

Signed *Hoc pinxit Johnes mirailheti.* Now usually dated about 1425 (*Labande, GBA, 1912, p. 188*).

The picture has suffered and certain parts are repainted, particularly some of the heads. Apparently of purely Italian character, only the predella shows a slightly more personal style, in which one can detect French traces.

Formerly Chapelle de la Confrérie de la Miséricorde, Church of Sainte-Réparate, Nice.

Reproduced: *Labande, pl. XX–XXIII; Guiffrey Marcel Terrasse, II, pl. 9–10; Barnes, p. 270 (text, p. 451); Lemoisne, pl. 65.*

Exhibited: *Nice 1912, No. 29; Nice 1937, 'Les Bréa'* (lent by the Bureau de Bienfaisance, Nice); *Paris 1937, No. 26.*

283. LOUIS BRÉA
PIETÀ; ON THE LEFT ST. MARTIN WITH A BEGGAR; ON THE RIGHT ST. CATHERINE. Nice-Cimiez, Church   PLATE 149

Retable in three parts. 224 : 252 cm.

Signed *Hoc opus fecit fieri condam nobilis M(ar)tinus de Rala cuius executor fuit nobilis Dñs Jacobus Galeani in 1475 die XXV Junii et Ludovicus Brea pinxit.*

This retable is, as far as I can see, the most individual specimen of the entire School of Nice, and it can be included in a book on early French painting with better reasons than the rest of this school. One should note the affinity of the composition with the 'Pietà de Villeneuve' (No. 206). Nevertheless the connection with the Iberian schools, which had to be refuted in the case of the 'Villeneuve' picture, is less remote here, and Italian and Catalan traits match on the whole the French ones.

Barnes (Three French Pietàs, p. 245–265) has drawn an instructive comparative study between the Pietà de Villeneuve, the present Pietà and the Pietà in Sospel (No. 286).

Berenson, Italian Painters of the Renaissance, lists, 1932, p. 111.

Exhibited: *Turin, 1911, No. 550; Nice 1912, No. 42; Nice 1937, 'Les Bréa', No. 1; Paris 1937, No. 10.*

284. LOUIS BRÉA
CRUCIFIXION. Genova, Gall. Communale, Palazzo Bianco

210 : 150 cm.

In the background a landscape with the view of a town.

A work of outstanding quality within this school. It shows strong connections with the School of Milan, but also with Antonello.

Exhibited: *Nice 1937, 'Les Bréa', No. 2 (reprod. Cat., pl. 1).*

285. LOUIS BRÉA
THE PARADISE (OGNI SANTI). Genova, Basilica di Santa Maria di Castello

310 : 220 cm.

The picture is important already by its subject, which is treated in detail in 'The Descent of the Dove' by *Charles Williams (A short History of the Holy Spirit in the Church, 1939, reprod. frontispiece).*

Catalogue Nice 1937, 'Les Bréa', No. 10.

286. SCHOOL OF NICE, 15TH CENTURY
PIETÀ WITH ST. CATHERINE AND ST. NICOLAS. Sospel (Alpes Maritimes), Chapelle des Pénitents Blancs

148 : 180 cm.

One of the 'Three French Pietàs' which Barnes confronts, the other two being the 'Pietà de Villeneuve' (No. 206) and the Pietà of Cimiez (No. 283). Barnes (*p. 245, reprod. p. 255*) stresses the qualities of 'simplicity and dignity' in the Sospel Pietà.

Reproduced: *Guiffrey Marcel Terrasse, II, pl. 6.*

287. SCHOOL OF NICE, LAST QUARTER OF THE 15TH CENTURY
CHRIST AS THE 'MAN OF SORROWS'. Paris, Louvre

51 : 88 cm.

Iconographically a type between the 'Christ de Pitié' and the 'Mise au tombeau'.

Bequest M. Baudin, 1940.

Exhibited: *Paris 1946, No. 17.*

G

287A. FRENCH SCHOOL, ABOUT 1480
DANCE OF DEATH. Le Bar, Parish Church.

36,8 : 73 cm.

Each of the dancers has a little devil standing on his head. On the right three large devils are busy receiving the souls of the deceased.

In a bad state, but of ingenious invention. The subject is a kind of blending of the 'Dance of Death' and the 'Last Judgement'.

This picture which has always been connected with the 'Bréa' School, shows also Burgundian characteristics; one may recall the frescoes of Beaune (No. 233) which for their part show italianizing traits.

Reproduced: *Barnes, p. 450 ; M. Malingue, Les Primitifs Niçois, 1941, p. 132.*

288. SOUTHERN FRENCH SCHOOL, SECOND HALF OF THE 15TH CENTURY
THE DEATH OF THE VIRGIN. Turin, Coll. Conte Em. Balba Bertone

128 : 134 cm.

A remarkable example of Southern French art.

Exhibited: *Turin, 1939, Cat. Tav. 31, Text, p. 51* (the Catalogue suggests a connection with Froment).

289. FRANCO-ITALIAN SCHOOL, ABOUT 1490
'DIEU DE PITIÉ'. Turin, Museo Civico

92 : 169 cm. Cut at the right side.

Christ in the arms of God the Father. Renaissance architecture.

Although the picture is closely akin to the art of Piedmont (Spanzotti), I would rather call it French than Italian.

Reproduced: *Gillet, pl. 63.*

Exhibited: *Turin, 1939, Cat. Tav. 30., Text p. 67; Rome, 1946, No. 6.*

⟨290.⟩ WRONGLY *attributed to the* SOUTHERN FRENCH SCHOOL, *about 1490/1500*

The Virgin of Mercy ('Madone de la Miséricorde'). Saluzzo, Galleria Cavassa

The Virgin is protecting under her mantle Ludovic II de Saluzzo, Viceroy of Naples, his wife Marguerite de Foix, their son Michel-Antoine and their suite.

Attributed to the French School by *Lionello Venturi (Renaissance, May 1919, p. 230–231, with reprod.)* on account of a supposed connection with the 'Coronation' by Enguerrand Charonton (No. 116). In my opinion not French but rather Italian, School of Piedmont.

Exhibited: *Turin 1939, Cat. Tav. 118–119, Text p. 68, No. 6.*

291. JEAN HAY
ECCE HOMO. Brussels, Musées Royaux des Beaux Arts (No. 955)

39 : 30 cm.   FIG. 42-43

An old inscription on the reverse says that the picture was executed in 1494 by Maître Jehan Hay for Jean IV Cueillette, secretary of King Charles VIII of France. The style places the picture between Bourdichon and the Master of Moulins, but nearer to the latter.

Until lately the painter was only known by the present picture and by contemporary literature—Jean Lemaire mentions him in his poem 'La Plainte du Désiré' (1509): 'Et toy Jean Hay, ta noble main chomme elle'. The proposal to identify the painter with the Master of Moulins (see No. 293) although not conclusive must be considered seriously.

292. MASTER OF MOULINS, ABOUT 1480
NATIVITY, WITH THE DONOR CARDINAL JEAN ROLIN. Autun, Museum   PLATES 157–158

55 : 73 cm. (21⅝ : 28¾ in.)

The Virgin, clad in blue, has a white headdress. The donor wears the red Cardinal's robe, a little dog is sitting on the folds of the robe.

Jean Rolin, son of the Chancellor of Burgundy, Nicolas Rolin, was born in Autun in 1408; he was the confessor of Louis XI. Died in 1483. The date of 1480 suggested for the picture is based on the donor's age, who seems to be about 70 years old. It is accordingly the earliest work by the master.

The shepherds in the background show a particularly close connection with Hugo van der Goes.

From the Palais Épiscopal of Autun.

Exhibited: *Paris 1904, No. 103; (Bouchot 1904, pl. LXXXIII); London 1932, No. 67 (Commem. Cat. No. 25, pl. 9); Paris 1937, No. 22.*

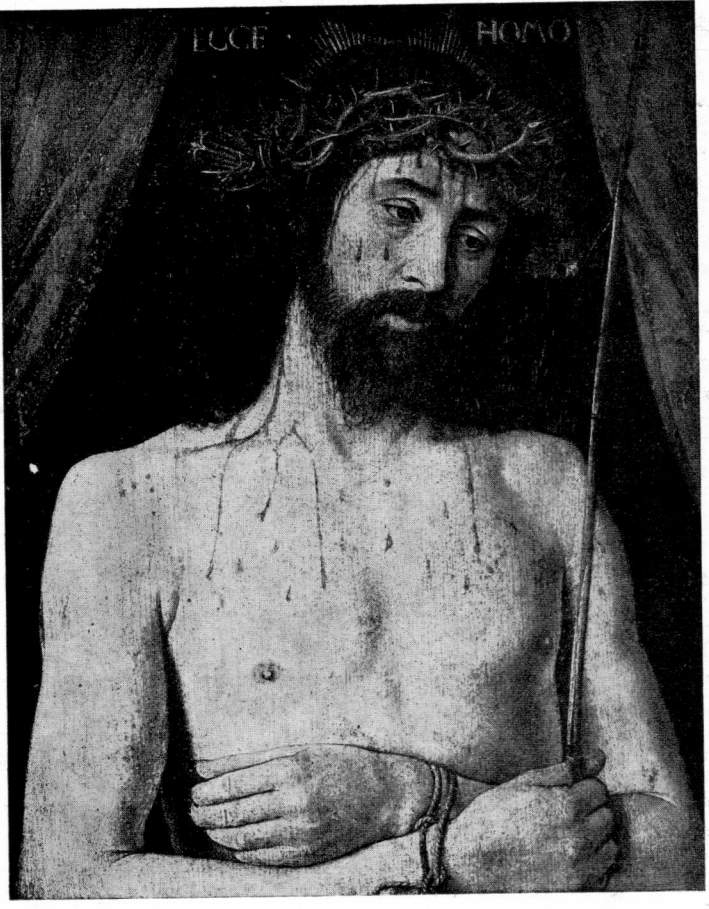

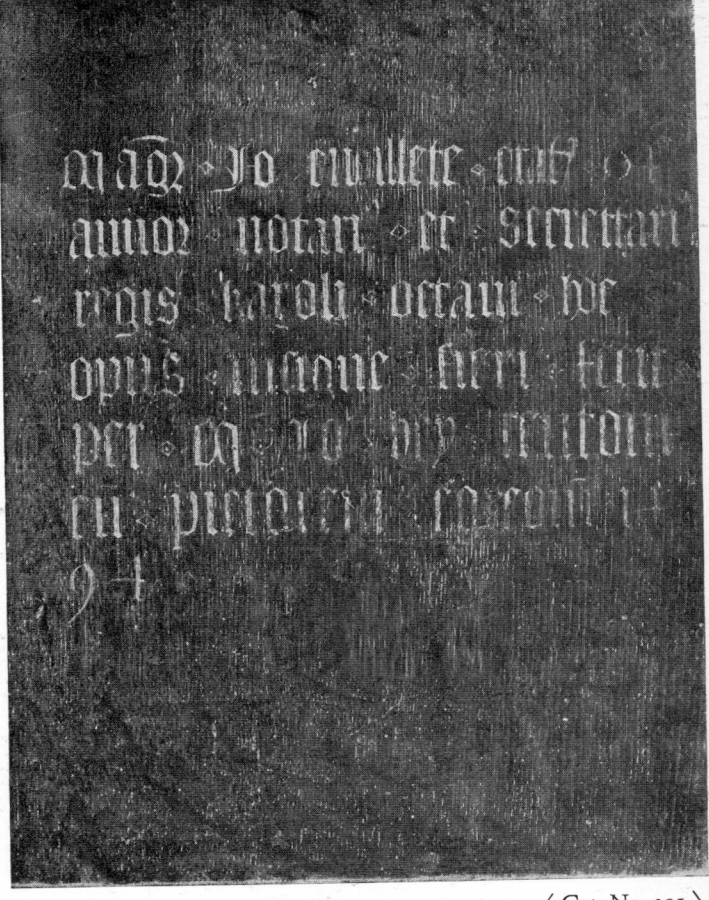

⟨ Cat. No. 291 ⟩

FIG. 42-43

293. MASTER OF MOULINS

TRIPTYCH: MADONNA AND CHILD SURROUNDED BY ANGELS AND
DONORS. Moulins, Cathedral   PLATES 159-163
157 : 283 cm. (61⅞ : 111⅜ in.)

Centre: The Virgin in a blue hermine-lined dress and red mantle is enthroned
before the orb of the sun; her feet rest on the crescent of the moon. Over her head,
two angels are holding the crown; below two angels with a script roll showing
the verse of the Apocalypse, Chapter XII, 1: 'Hec est illa dequa sacra canunt
eulogia sole amicta lunam habens pedibz stelis meruit coronari duodenis.'
Left wing (157 : 63 cm.): Pierre de Bourbon (born in 1439), in ducal state robes,
presented by St. Peter, who bears on his dalmatic the imprese of the Bourbon
family: 'Espérance.' Right wing (157 : 63 cm.): Anne de France, daughter of
Louis XI (born in 1461), in the costume of a Duchess, presented by St. Anne
and accompanied by her young daughter Suzanne (born in 1491, subsequently
married to her kinsman, the Connétable de Bourbon).
On the outside wings the Annunciation, in grisaille.
According to the age of the donors, the triptych can be dated about 1498/1499.
The triptych is the principal work by the great master—formerly called the
'Maître de la Maison de Bourbon'—around which a number of pictures have been
grouped. Although the identification of the master with Jean Perréal had been
supported by such strong champions as de Maulde, Durrieu, Hulin and Bouchot,
recent research has definitely decided against it.
*R. de Maulde la Clavière, Jean Perréal, 1896, p. 86-91; C. Benoit, GBA, XXVII,
1901, p. 66 ff., etc.; Hulin, Cat. crit. 1902.*
Paul Dupieux (Archiviste de l'Allier) has lately (*Les Maîtres de Moulins*, 1946)
made an attempt to date the triptych as late as 1502 and to ascribe it to 'Jean le
Peintre', alias 'Jean Verrier', alias 'Jean Prévost', a stained-glass painter, pupil of
Perréal, who worked for the Bourbon family in Moulins from 1501 to 1503. He
was at the time 70 years old and was, according to Dupieux, assisted by a younger
painter, Jean Richier. The argumentation is by no means conclusive. The affinity,
however, of the triptych to the stained glass windows of Moulins Cathedral

cannot be stressed too strongly, and the colours of the painting have a trans-
parence and glittering lucidity which make it plausible that its author should
also have worked as a 'verrier'.
Another still more recent attempt to identify the master has been made by
M. H. Goldblatt (*The Connoisseur*, June 1948, p. 69-73), who claims to have
found the signature 'J. Hay' on the reverse shutter representing the Virgin of the
'Annunciation' (right side of the Virgin's reading desk). Since Mr. Goldblatt
himself admits that on the detail which he reproduces (p. 70, fig. No. IIa) this
signature has been retouched, its evidence is not perfectly reliable. He further
muddles his case by identifying Jean Hay with 'Jean Clouet the Elder'. Otherwise
the connection of the 'Maître de Moulins' with 'Jean Hay' does not lack probability, and the comparison of the master's types with the 'Suffering Christ' on
the Brussels picture (No. 291), secured for 'Jean Hay' by a trustworthy inscription, shows a reasonable if not overwhelming likeness.
Exhibited: *Paris, Expos. rétrospective, 1900, No. 4545; Paris 1904, No. 112;
London 1932, No. 64 (Commem. Cat. No. 27, pl. 10); Paris 1937, No. 25.*

294. MASTER OF MOULINS, STUDIO

PIERRE II, SIRE DE BEAUJEU, DUC DE BOURBON, PRESENTED BY
ST. PETER. Paris, Louvre (No. 1004)
74 : 66 cm. (with the old frame 84 : 77 cm.).
The frame shows the date: 1488; the Duke is accordingly 49 years old.
Landscape background. Colours: green, purple, red.
The style is definitely that of the Moulins triptych, but the execution is inferior
to that of the works by the master's own hand; the help of studio assistants must
therefore be assumed. The head is of better quality than the rest and nearest to
the Moulins Master himself. A 'Master of 1488' has been tentatively set up by
Benoit (GBA, 1901, II, p. 318 ff.), but only this picture and its companion piece
(No. 295) have so far been assigned to him.

TER OF MOULINS: SAINT AND DONOR. ⟨ Cat. No. 301 ⟩

Acquired in 1842 by Louis-Philippe for the Musée de Versailles; claimed as a 'work of art' for the Louvre in 1870.
Reproduced: *Lemoisne Louvre, pl. 32; Lemoisne, pl. 77; Gillet, pl. 75.*
Exhibited: *Paris 1904, No. 104 (Bouchot 1904, pl. LXXVII); Paris 1946, No. 11.*

295. MASTER OF MOULINS, STUDIO

ANNE DE FRANCE, DAME DE BEAUJEU, DUCHESSE DE BOURBON, WIFE OF PIERRE II, PRESENTED BY ST. JOHN THE EVANGELIST. Paris, Louvre (No. 1005; Don Maciet, 1888)

72 : 51 cm. (the panel has been cut on the right-hand side; the old frame is missing). Landscape background. Colours: red, green, black.
Companion piece to No. 294, of the same quality and execution. Both panels were probably wings of an altarpiece, the centre of which is missing.
Formerly Collection Comte de La Béraudière.
Reproduced: *Réau, pl. 78; Lemoisne, pl. 77; Gillet, pl. 76.*
Exhibited: *Paris 1904, No. 105 (Bouchot 1904, pl. LXXVIII); Paris 1946, No. 12.*

296. MASTER OF MOULINS(?)

CHARLEMAGNE AND ST. LOUIS, KING OF FRANCE. ON THE REVERSE: PIERRE DE BOURBON WITH ST. PETER, ANNE DE BEAUJEU WITH ST. ANNE. London, Wallace Collection (XII-68 and 68A)   FIG. 44–45

FIG. 44–45   ⟨ Cat. No. 26 ⟩

Small diptych of translucent enamel on gold. 4,8 : 3,5 cm.
The donors with their patrons correspond to the wings of the Moulins triptych. Charlemagne is akin to the same personality on the panel of the 'Meeting at the Golden Gate' (No. 298) and it is therefore perhaps not too daring to reconstruct the missing figure, which is supposed to have been his counterpart, by the figure of St. Louis on the present enamel.

297. MASTER OF MOULINS

THE ANNUNCIATION. Chicago, Art Institute (formerly Ryerson Coll.)
73 : 50 cm. (28¾ : 19¾ in.)   PLATE 165
The Virgin wears a dark-blue dress under a red cloak; the very fair-haired angel appears in a green dalmatic lined with pink silk.
Probably the right part of an oblong panel—the traditional winged altar modified to a single picture—showing various scenes; the left-hand extremity was formed by the 'Meeting of St. Joachim and St. Anne' (No. 298).
In perfect state. A characteristic work of the master's late period and without any doubt by his own hand.
Roger Fry, Burl. Mag. IX, 1906, p. 331; *D. C. Rich, Bulletin of the Chicago Art Institute, vol. XXVII, No. 1; Friedlaender, Burl. Mag., October, 1925, p. 187 ff.*
Exhibited: *London, Grafton Galleries, National Loan Exhib., 1909/1910, No. 76; New York 1927, No. 35; Detroit 1928, No. 9; London 1932, No. 63; Chicago 1933, No. 28.*

298. MASTER OF MOULINS

CHARLEMAGNE AND THE MEETING OF ST. JOACHIM AND ST. ANNE AT THE GOLDEN GATE. London, National Gallery (No. 4092)
72 : 59 cm. (28¼ : 23¼ in.)   PLATE 166
The picture has been cut on the right-hand side. The missing figure counterbalancing Charlemagne was probably St. Louis (cf. No. 296). Probably the left

part of a larger panel, the right-hand extremity of which was formed by No. 297. Charlemagne wears a surcoat of gold brocade bearing the eagle of the Holy Roman Empire and the Fleurs-de-Lys of France. His mantle is red, lined and trimmed with hermine. St. Anne is in red with a yellow cap; St. Joachim, in olive-green lined with purple, with a red cap. The architecture is of a pale pink.
Friedlaender, who introduced the picture into literature (*Burl. Mag.,* Oct. 1925, p. 187 ff.), first suggested its connection with the Annunciation (No. 297). He dates the picture about 1495—showing the master in the last phase known to us—and remarks that the tints are 'laid on as in the pattern of a shield or banner'.
The painting is not inferior in quality to the Chicago part, and it is certainly also worthy of the master, but it has been thoroughly cleaned while it was in the Paris trade. This may account for the different aspect of the surface and subsequently for Martin Davies's harsh judgement in the new Nat. Gall. Catalogue (1946, p. 66–68).
Formerly private Collection, France; Hans Tietje Collection, Amsterdam.

299. MASTER OF MOULINS

MADONNA AND CHILD SURROUNDED BY FOUR ANGELS. Brussels, Musées Royaux des Beaux Arts (No. 681)   PLATE 167
38,5 : 29,5 cm. (15¼ : 11¾ in.)
The Virgin in a blue dress and red, blue-lined coat; the Angels colourful in bright red, yellow, etc., the Child particularly pale, modelled without any shades.
Universally accepted and rightly praised as a work by the Master's own hand.
From the Collections R. H. Benson, Henry Willett, Brighton, and Ed. Huybrechts, Antwerp.
Exhibited: *London, Burlington Club, 1902 (Exhibition of Flemish Paintings—there first recognized as a work of the French School); Paris 1904, No. 109; London 1932, No. 65 (Commem. Cat. No. 26, pl. 11); Paris 1937, No. 23.*

300. MASTER OF MOULINS

ST. MARY MAGDALEN AND A FEMALE DONOR. Paris, Louvre (No. 1005 A.)   PLATE 164
55 : 40 cm. (22¾ : 15¾ in.)
Probably left wing of a triptych, the right wing and centre of which are lost.
The arrangement resembles that of the portraits of Pierre and Anne de Beaujeu with their patron Saints (No. 294–295), but the quality is incomparably higher and the execution in this case without doubt by the hand of the master himself. Chief colours: red, green and black; blue is absent.
The personality of the donor has not yet been identified; it is in all probability a princess of the Bourbon family whose Christian name was Madeleine. Réau's suggestion that the picture is the companion piece of 'St. Victor and a Donor' (No. 301) is not convincing.
Formerly Coll. Somzée, Brussels.
Exhibited: *London, New Gallery, 1900, No. 27 (Review by Friedländer, Rep. f. Kw. 1900); Bruges 1902, No. 181; Paris 1904, No. 108.*

301. MASTER OF MOULINS

ST. VICTOR (MAURICE ?) AND A DONOR. Glasgow, Art Gallery and Museum Kelvingrove (No. 203)   COLOUR PLATE P. 237
82 : 48 cm. (22 : 18¾ in.)
The Donor wears a rich cape of crimson velvet and gold brocade; the Saint, in armour and in a dark-purple coat trimmed with fur, has a laurel wreath in his hair. The arms on the Saint's shield have not yet been satisfactorily deciphered, and the donor, probably a prince of the house of France, remains unknown in spite of many suggestions which have been put forward. *Hulin (Notes,* 1932, p. 62/63) believes the Saint to be St. Maurice rather than St. Victor.
Although the style of this famous picture does not perfectly agree with the other paintings attributed to the master, it seems for the time being to be the best choice to leave it within his œuvre, as a work of the latest period.
From the McLellan Collection, Glasgow; Corporation in Glasgow since 1856.
Exhibited: *Bruges 1902, No. 100. Friedlaender,* in his report on the Exhibition (*Rep. f. Kw.* 1903) mentions as the chief result of the exhibition 'that there was towards the end of the 15th century in France a painter great enough to be taken for van der Goes'. *Hulin (Cat. Crit.)* calls the picture the principal work by the Moulins master, about 1510. Cf. *Friedländer IV, p. 77 f.*
When shown in London on various occasions—*Burlington Club 1892, No. 1; New Gallery 1899/1900, No. 51; Guildhall 1906, No. 13; Burlington House 1927, No. 67*—the picture has been honoured by the greatest names of the Flemish School, among which Hugo van der Goes recurs most frequently.
Exhibited as a work by the Master of Moulins: *Paris 1904, No. 106; London 193 No. 68.*

FIG. 46   ⟨ Cat. No. 305 ⟩

302. MASTER OF MOULINS, ABOUT 1485.
PORTRAIT OF CARDINAL CHARLES II OF BOURBON, Munich, Alte Pinakothek (No. 1505)   PLATE 170
Panel, 35 : 27 cm. (11¼ : 10¾ in.)

Charles II, son of Charles I of Bourbon and of Agnes of Burgundy (daughter of Jean Sans Peur and Margaret of Bavaria) born in 1434, died in 1488. He was a Cardinal (since 1476), a remarkable ecclesiastic and clever politician; Louis XI selected him to be godfather to his son Charles VIII. He made his solemn entry as Archbishop in Lyon, on 6th December 1485, and this is the probable date of the portrait, which corresponds to the Master's early style, as represented by the 'Nativity' of Autun (No. 292).

The picture entered the Bavarian Royal Collections in 1817 with the Boisserée Collection.

A 19th-century copy is in Chantilly, Musée Condé, No. 109 (33 : 25 cm.)

303. MASTER OF MOULINS
PORTRAIT OF A YOUNG PRINCESS. New York, Coll. Robert Lehmann
32 : 23 cm. (12⅝ : 9 in.)   PLATE 169

She holds a rosary. In the landscape of the background the view of a castle, tentatively identified as the Château de la Palisse.

According to Durrieu and to Dupont, the sitter is Suzanne de Bourbon, daughter of Pierre de Beaujeu and Anne de France. The portrait, however, does not seem to correspond sufficiently to Suzanne's likeness on the right wing of the Moulins triptych (No. 293). *Hulin (Notes*, 1932) rather thinks of Margaret of Austria, then nominally married to Charles VIII and 'Queen of France'—a suggestion which may be due in great part to Hulin's wish to identify the Moulins Master with Perréal, who was for some time attached to Margaret as her painter.

The affinity of the master to Hugo van der Goes, always noticeable, is particularly striking in this charming portrait, which should be compared with the children on van der Goes' Portinari Altarpiece (Uffizi).

Exhibited: *Paris 1904*, No. 107 (then Coll. M. de Yturbe, Paris).

304. MASTER OF MOULINS
TITLE PAGE OF THE STATUTES OF THE ORDER OF ST. MICHAEL. Paris, Bibliothèque Nationale (Ms. fr. 14363)   PLATE 156
Written about 1494 for Charles VIII (*Bouchot* suggests 1489 as a more probable date).

Saint Michel appears to Charles VIII and to two noblemen of his entourage, Pierre II de Bourbon and (according to Durrieu, probably) Étienne de Vère, one of the most influential advisers to the King.

This is the only miniature so far attributed to the Master of Moulins with certainty—it has even been linked with the Moulins triptych by Dimier, who otherwise wants the whole œuvre of the master to be broken up.

Other miniatures of the Ms. show the hand of a minor illuminator (see No. 133). *C. Benoit, GBA, XXVII,* 1902, *p. 65 f.; Dimier,* 1925, *pl. XXVIII, text p. 42.*
Exhibited: *Paris 1904, No. 175.*

305. MASTER OF MOULINS
HEAD OF A YOUNG WOMAN, IN PROFILE. Collection Mr. Alfred Jowett, Harrogate, Yorks.   FIG. 46
Drawing, pen and ink, 19 : 14,4 cm.

The sheet bears the late and incorrect signature 'Pietro Perugino'.

The drawing shows a marked influence of Hugo van der Goes, but it is certainly not by that master and not Flemish. The attribution to the Master of Moulins, first put forward by Dupont, is convincing. The date would be about 1490. *OMD IX, March* 1935, *pl. 65 (Popham); Dupont, p. 9.*
Exhibited: *Brussels, 1935, No. 41; Paris, De van Eyck à Bruegel, 1935, No. 199.*

306. ATTRIBUTED TO THE MASTER OF MOULINS
PORTRAIT OF THE DAUPHIN CHARLES-ORLAND. Paris, Louvre
The sad-looking child is clad entirely in white. He holds a rosary. 39,7 : 36,8 cm.

The son of Charles VIII and Anne of Brittany, born in 1492, died in 1495. He is here represented at the age of 26 months (1494). The portrait was sent by Anne to her husband; it is mentioned among his baggage which he left behind in his retreat in the Battle of Fornovo. In 1532 it is described as being in the house of 'Messer Andrea di Odoni', Venice ('*Anonimo Morelliano*', *English edition by G. C. Williamson,* 1903, *p.* 101).

The picture has been wrongly ascribed to Bourdichon; it is far nearer to the art of the Moulins Master and may be attributed to the Master himself.

Formerly Coll. de Beistegui, Biarritz; entered the Louvre by donation in 1945.
Reproduced: *Lemoisne, pl. 85 A.; Gillet, pl.* 80
Exhibited: *Paris 1904, No.* 110 (then in the Ayr Collection, London; *Bouchot 1904, pl. LXXXIV*).

307. ATTRIBUTED TO THE MASTER OF MOULINS
PORTRAIT OF A PRAYING CHILD. Paris, Louvre (No. 3159)   PLATE 168
26 : 16 cm. (10 : 6¼ in.) White in white on neutral black ground. In excellent condition.

The name of the Dauphin Charles (second son of Charles VIII, born September 8th, 1496, died 2nd October of the same year) has been proposed, but it is most improbable that the portrayed child should only be one month old.

The picture, certainly painted about 1495 and very near to the portrait of Charles-Orland (No. 306) should also best be assigned to the Moulins Master or at least to his studio.

In the Louvre since 1908.
Exhibited: *Paris 1946, No.* 31.

⟨308.⟩ *Attributed to the MASTER OF MOULINS*
Portrait of a Monk in Prayer. New York, Metropolitan Museum
34,5 : 24 cm.

On blue background. He wears a black cassock with fur border.

The attribution to the master, originally sponsored by M. J. Friedlaender, has not been generally accepted. *Hulin (Notes,* 1932, *p.* 65) rejects it, pointing to the intense clair-obscur and the strong modelling with black shades, which he does not find in agreement with the master's manner. *L. Baldass ('The portraiture of Master Michiel', Burl. Mag., August* 1935) ascribes the picture to 'Michiel' (Michael Sittow), trying to connect it with a small female portrait in Vienna (No. 327); he also stresses the 'full round plastic modelling'.

In my opinion the portrait is not by Michiel and not a work of the Flemish School. I do no more believe it to be a work of the Moulins Master, but I would rather maintain its 'meridional' origin. I see a certain likeness with the 'St.

Anthony' by Gregorio Lopez in the Museum of Lisbon, but the likeness may be superficial and the New York painting is certainly of a higher quality. The picture is not in a perfect state (I had the opportunity of studying it while it was in the Paris trade, with Conte Trotti).
Formerly E. Rosenfeld Collection, New York.
Exhibited: *London 1932, No. 62 (Commem. Cat. No. 30, pl. 9).*

309. SOMETIMES ATTRIBUTED TO THE MASTER OF MOULINS

PORTRAIT OF A MAN. New York, Metropolitan Museum
26 : 20 cm. Arched top.
The sitter is young and beardless with long hair. He wears a dark velvet bonnet with a turned up brim. The very small left hand which is visible is, according to *Jacques (Rep. A., 15th cent. 107),* a modern repaint; there were originally two praying hands, characterizing the sitter as a donor.
The picture is most probably French but neither by nor near the Moulins Master.
Formerly in the Friedsam Collection.
Reproduced: *Jacques, pl. 143 'École de Bourgogne (?) about 1495'.*
Exhibited: *New York 1927, No. 39.*

310. SOMETIMES ATTRIBUTED TO THE MASTER OF MOULINS

PORTRAIT OF A YOUNG MAN HOLDING A COXCOMB. Philadelphia, John G. Johnson Collection (No. 764)
45 : 33 cm. Arched top.
In *Valentiner's Catalogue of the Johnson Collection (Vol. III)* the picture is ascribed to the Moulins Master himself, and this attribution has been retained by *Wescher (Pantheon, Jan. 1938).* The new *Johnson Catalogue (of 1941, p. 47)* lists it merely as 'French ca. 1490–1495'. I agree with this more cautious designation and should like to continue calling the picture French—not Flemish, as had been suggested by *Jacques (Rep. B., 15th cent., 11).* The attribute of a flower is no evidence against French origin—cf. the portrait in St. Louis (No. 337), whose position within the French School has never been doubted.

FIG. 47   ⟨ Cat. No. 314A ⟩

311. SOMETIMES ATTRIBUTED TO THE MASTER OF MOULINS

PORTRAIT OF A YOUNG GIRL HOLDING A PANSY. New York, Coll. S. Guggenheim
29 : 20,5 cm. On red background.
Ascribed to the Moulins Master by W. von Bode and W. R. Valentiner. Friedlaender has connected the picture with the portrait of an elderly woman with a chapelet, formerly in the A. Berg Collection (exhibited New York 1927, No. 36; ill. *Burl. Mag., Oct. 1927).*
I regard this attractive picture, which I had the opportunity of studying closely whilst in Berlin possession, most probably as French about 1485. It has some affinity to the Flemish School, particularly the School of Memling, but certainly no likeness whatever with the 'Master of the Virgo inter Virgines' or with any painter of the Dutch School where *Jacques (Rep. B., 15th cent., 8)* wants to place it.
Reproduced : *Réau, pl. 81.*

⟨*312.*⟩ *Wrongly attributed to the ENTOURAGE OF THE MOULINS MASTER, end of 15th century*
Portrait of a Woman with a White Cap. Chicago, Private Collection
Introduced by *Jacques (Rep. A., 15th cent., 34, reprod. pl. 71)* as 'one of the most authentically French pictures of the 15th century', by a 'Master of the entourage of the Maître de Moulins, probably working in the Bourbonnais'. Jacques mentions, however, that the painting has suffered.
The picture, which I happen to know in different states, is not a portrait, but a fragment of a 'Madonna with Child'. When stripped of all repaints, it showed the sleeping Child, partly cut, lying on the Virgin's breast. Headwear and dress have all been newly arranged about 18 to 20 years ago. In the previous condition, the style of the picture seemed to point to a Westphalian rather than to a French painter, as far as it could be judged at all. In yet another still earlier state it had been attributed to Bernard van Orley.
The picture comes from a noble family in Western Germany.

313. FOLLOWER OF THE MASTER OF MOULINS, END OF THE 15TH CENTURY

THE LIBERAL ARTS. Le Puy-en-Velay, Cathedral   PLATE 172
Frescoes.
Of the seven Liberal Arts which were originally represented, only four remain: 'Music', accompanied by Tubalcain; 'Rhetoric', accompanied by Cicero; 'Logic', accompanied by Aristotle; 'Grammar', accompanied by Priscian.
The types of the four women, who symbolize the arts in question, are related to the types of the Master of Moulins, but the soft colouring is different, and the whole relationship is only sufficient to place these frescoes within the wider orbit of the master—they have to remain anonymous for the time being.
In a thesis, lately presented at the Sorbonne, *Madeleine Huillet d'Istria* attributes the frescoes to Jean Perréal (whom she does not believe to be the Maître de Moulins), mainly relying on the relationship of the four female figures—the 'Muses'—in Le Puy to the statues of the 'Four Virtues' on the tombs of Nantes which were designed by Perréal. She also identifies the 'Muses' and their disciples with famous contemporaries of 'Perréal' *(Arts, 3 septembre, 1948).* The argumentation is so far not conclusive, but one shall have to wait for the publication 'in extenso' which is promised, before passing judgement.
In view of the gradual decay of French panel painting during the rule of Queen Anne, these frescoes deserve in any case special attention.
The subjects may be compared with those of the celebrated 'Liberal Arts' in London and Berlin, attributed to Melozzo da Forlì, to Josse van Ghent or lately to Pedro Berruguete, and certain reminiscences of Melozzo connect the frescoes even stylistically to that circle.
Formerly in the Library of the Cathedral of Le Puy, built by order of Canon Pierre Odin (died in 1502).
Reproduced : *Lemoisne pl. 88 (text p. 108); Bazin No. 49.*

314. FRENCH SCHOOL, ABOUT 1490; FORMERLY ATTRIBUTED TO THE MASTER OF MOULINS

DECAPITATION OF THE FIVE MARTYRS. New York, Brooklyn Museum of Art (formerly Friedsam Collection).
89 : 66 cm.
Certainly not by the Master of Moulins, but possibly French. The rather indistinct style does not give a particular indication as to the region.
Exhibited: *New York 1927, No. 34 (with reprod. in the Catalogue).*

314A. SCHOOL OF TOURAINE, LAST QUARTER OF THE 15TH CENTURY

St. Michael Killing the Dragon. New York, M. Georges Wildenstein FIG. 47

11,1 : 9,5 cm. (4⅜ : 3¾ in.)

Drawing, ink, heightened with white on grey prepared paper.

Design for the plaque suspended from the collar of the Order of St. Michael. The Order was founded at Tours in 1469 by Louis XI. The Statutes of the Order have been illuminated by various artists at different periods—Jean Fouquet illuminated a frontispiece shortly after the foundation of the Order (No. 133), the Master of Moulins painted another one about 1494 (No. 304). For stylistic affinities the present drawing may rather be grouped with the later specimen.

From the Collection of Lord Derwent, Hackness Hall, Yorks.

315. SCHOOL OF TOURAINE, ABOUT 1490

Pietà with St. John and St. Magdalen. Paris, Louvre (No. 996.)

33 : 25 cm. Arched top. Background of greenish damask.

By a distant and somewhat coarse follower of Fouquet who may have worked in the Bourbonnais. *Jacques* (*Rep. A., 15th cent.*, 35) thinks rather of a disciple of the Master of Moulins, with whom I fail to see a connection.

The picture is said to come from the 'Bourbonnais'. Entered the Louvre in 1888, Donation Maciet.

Reproduced: *Barnes, p. 377.*

Exhibited: *Paris 1904, No. 57; Paris, Passion, 1934, No. 161.*

316. SCHOOL OF TOURAINE, ABOUT 1490.

Madonna and Child. Otterloo, Rijksmuseum Kroeller-Mueller

33 : 21 cm. Arched top, original old frame.

On damasked background. Attributed by *Dupont* (*Bulletin des Musées de France, Nov. 1937*) to the same 'Master of the Bourbonnais' who painted the 'Pietà with Sts. John and Magdalen' (No. 315). The connection of the two pictures is obvious.

Sale Frederic Muller, Amsterdam, 28 Nov. 1911, No. 38, *with reprod. in the Sale Catalogue.*

317. SCHOOL OF TOURAINE, ABOUT 1480/1490

St. Martin and the Beggar. Paris, Louvre

The picture is in a rather poor condition; it is probably a fragment.

Jacques (*Rep. A., 15th cent.*, 9) regards it as a late work in the Fouquet tradition.

318. SCHOOL OF TOURAINE, ABOUT 1475

Portrait of King Louis XI (1423–1483). Paris, late Coll. Marquise de Ganay. 22 : 15 cm. (8⅝ : 5⅞ in.) FIG. 12

The King, who seems to be about 50 years old, has a red cap and an orange-coloured doublet with black revers. He wears the order of St. Michael.

Attributed by *Wescher* (*Pantheon, XXI, Jan. 1938, p. 5*) to Bourdichon. In his 'Fouquet' (*p. 81; ann. p. 98; reproduced p. 83, ill. XIV*), Wescher comes back to this attribution; he hints, however, at the possibility that the author may be Jean Colombe, who represented Louis rather similarly (although at a more youthful age) in the Dedication miniature of his 'Livre des douze perilz d'enfer'. Neither of the two attributions seems to me absolutely convincing.

Formerly Coll. G. de Montbrison, Château de St. Roch.

Exhibited: *Paris 1904, No. 53.*

319. JEAN BOURDICHON, ABOUT OR SHORTLY BEFORE 1494

Triptych: Madonna between the two St. Johns; in the Lunette: The Crucifixion (centre), St. Michael with the Devil and St. George with the Dragon. Naples, Museo Nazionale PLATE 155

In the background of the Crucifixion a landscape on the borders of the Loire, with Tours, the Cathedral, the Church of St. Julien, the Castle, etc. Among the colours, a greyish green violet and brown predominate.

First rightly ascribed to Bourdichon by *Dupont, Un triptyque de Jean Bourdichon au Musée de Naples, Mon. Piot, 1935, p. 179 ff., pl. XI.*

This is the only easel painting given to Bourdichon with full success, its style corresponding exactly to the ascertained late miniatures of the master.

Dupont suggests that the triptych may be a commission by Ferdinand I of Aragon, King of Naples, for whom Bourdichon executed the 'Heures d' Aragon', or a present made by Charles VIII to Ferdinand of Aragon. As Ferdinand died in 1494, the triptych was probably executed about or shortly before this date.

Formerly Chartreuse de San Martino, Naples.

Wescher (*Fouquet, p. 86, ill. 71*) also places the triptych rather late, next to Bourdichon's 'Heures de Charles d'Angoulême' (No. 323). He explains the divergence of style between the Naples triptych and the Triptyque de Loches—which he also ascribes to Bourdichon—by the difference of epoch, the Naples picture being about 10 years later.

Reproduced: *Venturi, VII, 4, ill. p. 159 and p. 161, text p. 146; Dupont, p. 51.*

320. ASCRIBED TO JEAN BOURDICHON

Virgin in Prayer. Formerly Riga, Collection L. Michelson

Ascribed to Bourdichon by *Dupont, Mon. Piot, 1935, p. 185, fig. 4.*

Reproduced: *Dupont, p. 64.*

321. JEAN BOURDICHON

'Les Heures d'Anne de Bretagne'. Paris, Bibliothèque Nationale (Ms. lat. 9474)

29,9: 19,5 cm.

Commissioned by Anne of Brittany, Queen of France (wife of Louis XII) about 1500; finished in 1507.

An order for payment for the illumination of these very sumptuous 'Hours' has been recorded 'A notre cher et bien aimé Jean Bourdichon painctre et valet de chambre de Monseigneur', signed by the Queen in Blois on 14th March 1507. The book is thus secured for Bourdichon's mature style and must be taken as a starting point for all other attributions to him.

L. Delisle, Les grandes Heures d'Anne de Bretagne et l'atelier de Jean Bourdichon, Paris 1913; Verve, vol. IV, Nos. 14 and 15, Paris 1946 (with introduction by Emile Mâle; review by F. Wormald, Burl. Mag., August 1947, p. 231).

Exhibited: *Paris 1904, Ms. No. 178; London 1932, No. 752 e (Commem. Cat., No. 952); Paris 1937, Ms. No. 190.*

321A. JEAN BOURDICHON

The Four Stages of Society. Formerly Amiens, Coll. Jean Masson

Four miniatures on vellum, 15,1 : 15 cm. each (6 : 5⅞ in.) PLATES 151–154

(*a*) The Primitive man (the troglodyte); (*b*) The poor man; (*c*) The artisan; (*d*) The rich man.

Exhibited: *Paris 1904, No. 125 (Bouchot 1904, Pl. XCV).*

322. ASCRIBED TO JEAN BOURDICHON ABOUT 1505

Portrait of Anne de Bretagne, Queen of France. Paris, Private Collection

Inscribed: ANNA BIS REGINA FR.

Attributed to the master by *Sterling* (*p. 85, fig. 91, note 83*) on the analogy with the 'Grandes Heures d'Anne de Bretagne' (No. 321).

Reproduced: *Jacques, pl. 146 (Rep. A., 15th cent., 16).*

323. JEAN BOURDICHON, ABOUT 1495

'Les Heures de Charles d'Angoulême'. Paris, Bibliothèque Nationale (Ms. lat. 1173)

Several of the miniatures of this manuscript are by the hand of Bourdichon. Charles d'Angoulême died in 1497; the manuscript should be dated rather late.

L. Delisle, Grandes Heures d'Anne de Bretagne, p. 64; Wescher, Fouquet, ill. 72.

Exhibited: *Paris 1937, Ms. No. 191.*

324. JEAN BOURDICHON, FORMERLY ASCRIBED TO FOUQUET

Madonna, in a Border adorned with Flowers (Aquilejas). The Hague, Royal Library (Ms. 74, G. 37, vol. II, fol. 1 verso)

This page, inserted in a Book of Hours, has mostly been ascribed to Fouquet himself or to his studio. It should rather be regarded as a work by Bourdichon, cf. the 'Madonna' on the 'Adoration of the Magi' in Bourdichon's 'Heures de Charles d'Angoulême' (No. 323), the 'Madonna' of the Altarpiece in Naples (No. 319), etc.

In the context of Bourdichon's works, the 'Madonna with Aquilejas' is a distinguished specimen, showing the master's descent from Fouquet.

A. W. Byvanck, Les principaux Manuscrits à peinture de la Bibliothèque Royale, Paris 1924, Pl. XXVII; Perls, Fouquet, p. 83. ill. 46.

FIG. 48   ⟨ Cat. No. 331 ⟩

⟨325.⟩ *Wrongly attributed to JEAN BOURDICHON*
Portraits of a Man and his Wife, praying. Formerly New York, Mortimer
L. Schiff Collection

19 : 12,7 cm. each. Probably donors (fragments?) from a larger altarpiece.
The portrait of the man is on green background, that of the woman on red.
Certainly not French, but in the manner of the Flemish 'Master of the Magdalen
Legend', about 1510.
From the Collection of Prince Borosselski, Warsaw.
Reproduced: '*Renaissance*' 1927, p. 443; *Sale Catalogue of the Schiff Collection*,
Christies, June 24, 1939, lot 59.
Exhibited: *New York 1927, No. 33; Chicago 1934, No. 5; Paris 1937, No. 9.*

⟨326.⟩ *Wrongly attributed to the MASTER OF MOULINS*
Portraits of Jean, Count of Egmond, and his Wife, Madeleine de Wardemberghe
New York, Metropolitan Museum (formerly Friedsam Collection)

41 : 24 cm. each
The sitters have been identified after the drawings in the 'Recueil d'Arras',
where the male portrait is inscribed 'Jehan premier Comte d'Egmont'.
Not French, but by the 'Master of Alkmaar' (*Friedlaender, X, No. 59, pl. XXXI*).
Exhibited: *New York 1927, Nos. 37/38.*

⟨327.⟩ *Attributed to the FRENCH SCHOOL, beginning of the 16th century*
(formerly attributed to the MASTER OF MOULINS)
Portrait of a Woman with White Headdress. Paris, Louvre (Gift Walter Gay)

20 : 15 cm.
The portrait bears the device of the sitter *X. tout. X. bien.*
There exists another version, less well known but of finer quality, in the
Kunsthistorisches Museum, Vienna (formerly Coll. Benda).
The sitter has been tentatively identified with various princely personages, so
far without success. (*G. Glück, Burl. Mag. LXIII, 1933, p. 107.*)
The connection with the Master of Moulins, which had formerly been suggested
does not stand. *L. Baldass (Burl. Mag., August 1935)* has put forward the pro-
position in regard to the Vienna version that the painter might be 'Maître
Michiel' (lately identified with Michel Sithium or Sittow, painter to Queen
Isabelle the Catholic; cf. *Pr. Jhb.*, 1940, and *Winkler, Pantheon, XVI*). Baldass
detects in this portrait the French source of Michiel's art. In my opinion the
picture is in fact better placed in the semi-Flemish context than in the French
School proper, but it does not seem to me characteristic of 'Michiel'.
Reproduced: *Lemoisne, Louvre, pl. 39* ('Ecole Française' about 1514); *Barnes*,
p. 305.
Exhibited: *Paris 1904, No. 113; Paris 1937, No. 32.*

328. SCHOOL OF TOURAINE, 16TH CENTURY

PORTRAIT OF KING LOUIS XI IN PROFILE. New York, Brooklyn
Museum (formerly Friedsam Collection)

37 : 27 cm.
The King wears a hat with a brim over a red skull cap and the order of St.
Michael.
The picture is a later 16th century copy of a lost original which must have been
executed about 1475. It is reported to have been in the Gaignières Collection in
the 17th century.
A replica is in the Musée Ariana, Geneva.
Reproduced: *Sterling, fig. 185; Bazin, ill. 2; H. Bouchot, 'Deux portraits de Louis
XI', GBA, 1903; Réau, GBA, Janv. 1926, p. 8.*
Exhibited: *Paris 1904, No. 102 (then Coll. Baron Vitta, Paris); New York 1927,
No. 12.*

329. FRENCH SCHOOL, ABOUT 1495

'L'HOMME À LA CANNE'. Santa Barbara, Cal., Coll. Arthur Sachs
Portrait of a man wearing the order of the Toison d'or, his hands resting on a
cane.
Assigned by Dupont to a master of the School of Tours whom he calls the
'Maître à la Canne' and to whom he attributes another picture as a companion
piece—the portrait of a woman holding a flower (Vienna, Kunsthistorisches
Museum).
Since both pictures are not in a perfect state of preservation it is not easy to settle
the question. The male portrait is in any case a late 15th century specimen of
French courtly art; the female one looks in its present condition more like an
archaizing ancestral portrait than like a work of the same epoch.
Both pictures reproduced: *Dupont, p. 62/63;* 'L'homme à la canne' reprod.:
Sterling, fig. 187; Jacques, pl. 145.
Exhibited: *Detroit, 1928.*

330. FRENCH SCHOOL, ABOUT 1500

'LA DAME AUX PENSÉES'. Paris, Louvre (No. 1000 A.)   PLATE 173
36 : 26 cm. (14¼ : 10 in.)
Portrait of a lady on a background strewn with pansies.
Blue dress over a red velvet underdress. She wears a medallion with a representa-
tion of St. John the Baptist (her name was probably Jeanne). In her left hand a
scroll with the device: *De quoilque non vede yo my recorde.*
Old frame ornamented with pansies and myosotis and with the letters 'S' and 'E'.
Bouchot 1904, pl. XCVIII.

331. ATTRIBUTED TO JEAN PERRÉAL

PORTRAIT OF PIERRE SALA. London, British Museum (Ms. Stowe 955,
fol. 17)   FIG. 48
This portrait appears in a volume of love poems by Sala, 'Énigmes' ('Emblesmes
et Devises d'Amour'), further illustrated by 11 representations of allegorical
scenes in the courtly costumes of the time about 1500. Whereas the other miniatures show the average style of the period, the Sala portrait is of outstanding
quality and execution, with abundant use of gold. It is set on red fonds, in a
painted frame.
The portrait is secured as the likeness of Sala by an inscription on the back:
*Cet de vray le Portret de Pierre Sala Mestre Hotelle chez le Roy avec des énigmes quil
avoit fet a sa metresse . . . .*
Sala, a native of Lyon, was equerry to Charles VIII and confidential adviser to the
royal family. He was the intimate friend of the painter Jean Perréal, to whom he
dedicated his book '*De l'Amitié*'.
The present 'Énigmes' were dedicated to the beautiful young widow Marguerite
Bulliond, who was to become Sala's wife.
Since the identification of Perréal with the Maître de Moulins can now be regarded as discarded, 'Perréal' may rather be the author of the 'Sala' portrait
which would thereby become the starting point for a group of closely correlated
portraits. Several of these portraits have been ascribed to the so-called 'Master of
Charles VIII'—a somewhat incoherent construction which would then have to
be definitely broken off. The 'Sala' had already been ascribed to 'Perréal' by
Durrieu in 1919 ('*Les relations de Lionardo da Vinci avec le peintre français Jean
Perréal*', *Études Italiennes 1ère année*, published by '*L'Union intellectuelle Franco-
Italienne*', 1919, p. 152; *Perls (AdA, Mars 1935)* had proposed the attribution to
the 'Maître de Charles VIII' which was taken up by *Sterling (p. 143, fig. 182).*

332. ATTRIBUTED TO JEAN PERRÉAL
PORTRAIT OF LOUIS XII OF FRANCE. Windsor Castle, H.M. the King
30,4 : 22,9 cm. PLATE 173
King Louis is represented as a middle-aged man. He wears a black cap on his long hair. The golden chain of the Order of St. Michael hangs over a brocaded dress. The face is pale, the background peacock-blue.
After the picture had been exhibited with the *King's Pictures* (London 1946/1947, No. 138) it has been successfully cleaned. The cleaning has considerably improved the quality, reducing the size, recovering the original background and revealing a hand which had been hidden by repaints.
Lionel Cust (Burl. Mag. IX, September 1911 p. 127) had already proposed the name of Jean Perréal for the picture and *Jacques Dupont,* who published it after the recent cleaning *(Burl. Mag. September 1947, p. 235 ff; frontispiece)* strengthens the attribution by convincing arguments. The picture comes from the collection of King Henry VIII (Inventory of Henry VIII, of 1543), brother of the princess Mary Tudor, whose portrait Perréal was commissioned to paint for his master Louis XII in 1514. It is likely that he painted a portrait of Louis himself about the same time. It is further known that Perréal made a portrait of Louis in 1499, in the beginning of that monarch's reign *(G. Lebel, 'Quelques précisions sur l'œuvre du peintre Jean Perréal', Société des Antiquaires de France, April 1939).*

332A. ATTRIBUTED TO JEAN PERRÉAL
TWO PORTRAITS. Chantilly, Musée Condé
(*a*) PORTRAIT OF PHILIPPE DE LA PLATIÈRE, SEIGNEUR DES BORDES, DIT BOURDILLON
Drawing, silver point heightened with gold, 20 : 13 cm.
The sitter was born about 1465, died in 1499, equerry to the King.

(*b*) PORTRAIT OF LOUIS DE LUXEMBOURG, COMTE DE LIGNY (died in 1503).
Drawing, silver point, 20 : 13,7 cm.
The style goes well together with the 'Sala' portrait (No. 331). Jean Lemaire, in his poem 'Temple d'honneur et de vertus', dedicated to the Comte de Ligny (whose secretary he was at the time) praises particularly the art of Perréal, 'a second Appelles'—a connection which leads again into the same circle.
Both portraits were formerly in the Collections Wellesley and Duc d'Aumale.
Reproduced: *Lavallée, pl. XXVII; Chantilly, Musée Condé (1933) Nos. 1–2; Perls AdA 1935 (as 'Maître de Charles VIII').*
Exhibited: *École des Beaux-Arts 1879, No. 286.*

333. ATTRIBUTED TO THE SO-CALLED MASTER OF CHARLES VIII, ABOUT 1491/1492
TWO PORTRAITS, SUPPOSED TO REPRESENT CHARLES VIII AND ANNE DE BRETAGNE. Paris, Bibliothèque Nationale (Fonds lat. 1190)
The portraits, enclosed in the binding of a manuscript, are not miniatures on vellum, but small paintings on panel, although obviously executed by a miniaturist.
Perls (AdA, Mars 1935, p. 95–99) has grouped a number of portraits around these pictures under the temporary designation 'Maître de Charles VIII' (see No. 331). While several portraits of this group seem to fit well together, the present pictures are not necessarily connected with them.
Dupont (Bulletin de l'Histoire de la Société d'Art Français, 1936, II, p. 186–189) contests the identification of the sitters with the King and his consort. The female portrait shows in fact no likeness with the buxom young lady (attributed to Bourdichon, No. 322) secured as 'Anne de Bretagne' by an old inscription, and the male portrait is also fairly different from the various more or less authenticated portraits of the King.
From the Gaignières Collection.
First published by *Bouchot, Gaz. archéologique, XIII, 1888, p. 103*
Exhibited: *Paris 1904, Ms. No. 170 (Bouchot 1904, pl. LXXXVII).*

334. FRENCH SCHOOL, END OF THE 15TH CENTURY
PORTRAIT OF A MAN WITH A BIG NOSE. Fonthill, Coll. J. Morrison
22 : 16 cm. Gold background.
He wears a puce-coloured doublet with ermine collar.
According to the London Catalogue of 1932 the sitter is perhaps Charles VIII.
Exhibited: *London 1932, No. 78 (Commem. Cat. No. 12, pl. 14).*

335. FRENCH SCHOOL, END OF THE 15TH CENTURY
MAN WITH A BIG NOSE. Formerly Berlin art trade 32 : 22,5 cm.
The picture obviously represents the same sitter as the Morrison portrait (No. 334) and might therefore also be regarded as a portrait of King Charles VIII. Both pictures must be considered when drawing up a list of the portraits by Perréal.

336. FRENCH SCHOOL, BEGINNING OF THE 16TH CENTURY
PORTRAIT OF GUILLAUME DE MONTMORENCY. Lyon, Museum
37 : 26 cm.
He wears a black cap and holds his gloves in his hand; on his doublet the order of St. Michael.
Guillaume, Seigneur de Montmorency, first baron of France, was Councillor to three Kings: Charles VIII, Louis XII, and François Ier; he died in 1531.
Guillaume is apparently the 'Monsieur de Montmorency' to whom Louis XII writes from Italy in 1507, asking him to send him his 'visages pourtraits par Jehan de Paris . . . pour montrer aux dames de par deçà . . .' The idea that 'Jehan de Paris' (i.e. Perréal) was also the author of the present portrait presents itself, although the connection with the other portraits here ascribed to Perréal (Nos. 331–332A) is not striking.
Reprod. *Sterling, ill. 194.*
Exhibited: *Paris 1904, No. 148.*
There exists another version in the Louvre (No. 1007A; 39 : 29 cm.), showing the sitter bareheaded, with praying hands; on the background the inscription: APLA . . . NOS. The Louvre version comes from the Church of St. Martin de Montmorency, which Guillaume reconstructed in 1525.
Reproduced: *Lemoisne, Louvre, pl. 41, Réau, pl. 91.*
Exhibited: *Paris 1946, No. 37.*

337. FRENCH SCHOOL, ABOUT 1515
PORTRAIT OF A MAN HOLDING A FLOWER. St. Louis, City Art Museum
36 : 26 cm.
Over the head a scroll with the device *Fol desir nous abuze.*
The picture has lately been cleaned and has become more colourful; it is in very good state. This is one of the portraits that lead in a straight line to the style of Jean Clouet.
Formerly Coll. E. Richtenberger.
Reproduced: *Jacques, pl. 149; cf. GBA, August, 1904, p. 133; Les Arts, 1904, No. 28, p. 44.*
Exhibited: *Paris 1904, No. 145 ('Jean Clouet'); New York 1927, No. 47.*

⟨338.⟩ Attributed to the FRENCH SCHOOL, about 1510
Madonna enthroned between two Angels, St. Louis and St. Margaret. Ince Blundell Hall (Lancashire), Coll. Weld Blundell
122 : 107 cm.
The Virgin sits under a canopy on which are the arms of Burgundy; the Child is playing with a goldfinch. St. Louis wears a blue mantle with golden lilies, St. Margaret has a dove on her shoulder and the dragon under her feet (this monster has also been regarded as the 'Tarasque', which would point to a representation of St. Martha).
The kneeling figures have been identified with various personages. On the copy made by Antoine de Succa in the beginning of the 17th century (pen and ink drawing) they have already been regarded as portraits—they bore first an inscription 'saint Louis' and 'Marguerite de Provence', which were later replaced by 'Louis XI roy de France' and 'Charlotte de Savoye, la 2e femme de Louis XI'. *Weale (Burl. Mag. IX, p. 239, with reprod.)* calls the man Louis XII—which would correspond better to the date of the painting. I see neither a necessity to suspect portraits under the guise of the Saints, nor to look for the models among members of the royal family of France exclusively.
The composition shows a strong influence of Jan van Eyck; Madonna and Child are copied (with variations) from the 'van der Paele Madonna' in Bruges.
Weale and *Roger Fry (Burl. Mag., IX, p. 331)* consider the picture to be French. I agree with *Hulin (Notes 1932)* who calls it Flemish about 1510 or 1515.
From the Abbaye de Tronchiennes-lez-Gand (Ordre des Prémontrés).
Described in the *Ince Blundell Catalogue of 1803, No. 190; Waagen, Art Treasures in Great Britain, 1857, III, p. 249.*
Exhibited: *London, Guildhall, 1906, No. 60; London 1932, No. 50 a.*

BIOGRAPHICAL NOTES ON THE PAINTERS

PIÈTRE ANDRÉ

Mentioned in 1455 as court painter of Duke Charles of Orléans; worked in Tours and in Blois. Since 1484 painter to Charles's eldest son, Louis of Orléans, who later became King Louis XII.

His name has been connected with the *Madonna of the Melun Diptych*, No. 123.

JEAN D'ARBOIS

A painter from the Franche-Comté, who worked in Lombardy and later, in 1373, entered the service of Duke Philippe the Bold of Burgundy. He is supposed to have painted the *Retable of Besançon*, No. 4.

JEAN DE BANDOL (BONDOL), ALSO CALLED JEAN (HENNEQUIN) OF BRUGES   FIG. 3

Since 1368 in the service of King Charles V. 'Peintre et valet de chambre du roi' in 1379. Louis I, Duke of Anjou, commissioned him about 1375 to draw the cartoons for the tapestries of the *Apocalypse of Angers*. No. 5.

ANDRÉ BEAUNEVEU   PLATES 13–14

A native of Valenciennes (Hainault). Painter, illuminator and sculptor ('tailleur d'images'). Worked in 1374 on the *Funeral Monument of Louis de Mâle* in Courtrai. For King Charles V he executed the *Funeral Statues* in the Abbey of S. Denis near Paris, several of which are preserved. Mentioned as being in the service of Duke Jean de Berri at Mehun-sur-Yèvre in 1390. Died between 1403 and 1413.

No. 42; cf Nos. 31, 32, 47, 48.

HENRI BELLECHOSE   PLATE 20

Born in Brabant, lived in Burgundy, mostly at Dijon. In 1415 he succeeded Malouel as court painter to the Dukes of Burgundy. Between 1416 and 1425 he worked for Jean sans Peur and afterwards for Philippe le Bon at the Chartreuse de Champmol, the Palace of Dijon, and other ducal castles. Died at Dijon between 1440 and 1444.

Of his works for the Chartreuse, the *S. Denis* has been identified: No. 54. Cf. Nos. 52, 53, 55.

JEAN BOURDICHON   PLATES 151–155

Born about 1457; resident at Tours. From 1478 onwards he worked for Louis XI, and was appointed 'peintre du roi et valet' in 1484, soon after the accession of Charles VIII, under the regency of Anne de Beaujeu. Went on working for Charles VIII, Louis XII and Anne de Bretagne, and for François Ier. Died in 1521.

His chief documented work are the *Heures d'Anne de Bretagne*, No. 321. Nos. 319–320, and 321A–324 are attributed to him with good reasons. Cf. Nos. 147, 318, 325.

LOUIS (LUDOVICO) BRÉA   PLATE 149

A native of Nice. His earliest signed retable, the *Pietà*, is dated 1475. He died, probably at a high age, between 1522 and 1523. Worked at Nice, Taggia, Montalto, Monaco, etc. Collaborated with the Lombard painter Vincenzo Foppa in 1490. His sons, François and Antoine, continued in his manner. Nos. 283–285.

MELCHIOR BROEDERLAM

Born at Ypres, where he lived most of his life. From 1381 onwards he worked for Louis de Mâle, Count of Flanders. Since 1385 'peintre et valet de chambre' to Philippe the Bold, Duke of Burgundy. In Paris

between 1390 and 1393. Last mentioned in 1409. Commissioned in 1392 to paint the shutters of an *Altarpiece for the Chartreuse de Champmol,* which he delivered in 1399, No. 18. Ascribed to him are Nos. 19 and 20.

JEAN CHAPUS (CHAPUIS, CAPUS)

Born probably in Avignon as a son of the draper and merchant Jean Chapus of Chambéry. Citizen and resident of Aix, mentioned at Chambéry in 1440/41. Worked for King René of Anjou (documents of 1437 and 1448) and possibly also for Duke Amédée of Savoy, a grandson of Jean de Berri.

He has been tentatively identified with the painter of the *Retable of the Annunciation of Aix*, Nos. 91–94.

ENGUERRAND CHARONTON (QUARTON)   PLATES 62–68;
     FIG. 16

Born in the diocese of Laon about 1410. Worked at Avignon between 1447 and 1461.

Two of his documented works are preserved: the *Madone de la Miséricorde*, painted for the Cadard family in 1452, and the large *Coronation of the Virgin*, painted for the priest Jean de Montagnac in 1454. Nos. 116 and 117; cf. Nos. 118, 119, 290.

BARTHÉLÉMY DE CLERC

Of Flemish origin. Worked at Tarascon from 1447 onwards for King René of Anjou. Appointed 'peintre et valet de chambre du roi' before 1449. Active in Provence and Anjou until his death about 1476.

As he is reported to have been the king's favourite artist, he has been identified—not convincingly—with the René Master, the illuminator of the *Cueur d'amours espris* and of other manuscripts.

Nos. 102–105.

JACQUES COËNE

A native of Bruges. In Paris 1398. In 1399 he was called to Milan, where he worked on the plans for the Cathedral. By 1401 he was back in France and worked for Duke Philippe the Bold of Burgundy. He is supposed to have died about 1415.

Coëne has been plausibly identified with the illuminator known as the Master of the Hours of the Maréchal de Boucicaut, Nos. 36–38.

NICCOLÒ ANTONIO COLANTONIO   FIG. 29 and 33

Born at Naples. He is reported to have learnt the 'art of painting in the manner of Flanders' from King René of Anjou between 1438 and 1442. According to tradition he was the teacher of Antonello da Messina.

Of his documented works, the *St. Jerome* of 1436 and the *Altarpiece of San Vincenzo Ferrero* in the Church of San Pietro Martire at Naples, painted between 1456 and 1465, have been identified. Nos 97 and 98. Colantonio has been suggested as the possible author of the altarpiece of the Master of the Annunciation of Aix, Nos. 91–94, cf. Nos. 95, 96, 100.

JEAN COLOMBE

A relative of the sculptor Michel Colombe. Worked in Bourges, and became 'maître' before 1470. For some time a 'familier et enlumineur de livres' of the court of Savoy, he was commissioned by Charles I of Savoy to complete the *Limbourg Hours* of Chantilly (finished in 1485). Died in 1529.

No. 65.

JACQUES DALIWE (D'ALIWES, D'ALIVE)   PLATES 23–24

Known by his signature as the author of a *Sketch Book* executed about 1430, No. 75.

NICOLAS DIPRE (D'YPRES), CALLED D'AMIENS

First mentioned at Avignon in 1495; lived there until his death about 1531/32. Was commissioned to paint 'des histoires' on the occasion of the entry of the papal legate in Carpentras in 1508. A fragment of an *Altarpiece* for St. Siffrein, Carpentras, of 1499, has been claimed as his work. No. 266; cf. Nos. 267–270.

JACQUES DURANDI

Born probably about 1410. Active mostly at Nice; at Marseille in 1450. Died before 1469.
One signed work by him is preserved, No. 281.

JEAN FOUQUET   PLATES 69–90; FIG. 31, 32

Born at Tours about 1420. Supposed to have passed his apprenticeship in Paris. Between 1443 and 1447 he went to Italy; in Rome he painted a *Portrait of Pope Eugenius IV;* he probably visited Florence also. After his return to Tours he married, took over his father's house in 1448 and began to work for King Charles VII and his entourage. In 1461 he coloured the king's death mask and prepared the festive arrangements (which were not carried out) for the entry of the new king, Louis XI. He worked for the Order of St. Michael, which was instituted by Louis in 1469, and designed the cartoons for the royal tomb in 1474. In 1475 he was appointed 'peintre du roy'. He died at Tours in 1481 or shortly before. The identification of the painter Jean Fouquet with the 'clerc de la diocèse de Tours' of the same name, the son of a priest and an unmarried woman (proposed by Abbé Yves de Raulin and accepted by Perls) is open to doubt; it rests on a letter, dated 8 August 1449, from Pope Nicholas V to 'Johanni Fouquet Juniori clerico Turonensis diocesis', in which the Pope acknowledges receipt of an application made by the 'clerc' for dispensation from his illegitimacy.
Wescher's suggestion that Fouquet may have accompanied the French delegation which was sent to Rome in 1446 to negotiate between France and the Popes has much to recommend it, particularly as Jean Jouvenel des Ursins, a future patron of Fouquet's, was a member of that delegation.
Documented works: miniatures of the *Antiquités Judaïques*, No. 129.
Ascribed with good reasons: Nos. 120–128, and 130–137.
Attributed: Nos. 138–144; cf. No. 317, 324.

NICOLAS FROMENT   PLATES 117–130; FIG. 22

Born at Uzès in Languedoc. Mentioned from 1450 to 1490; active at Avignon between 1468 and 1472. Painter to King René of Anjou. Two documented works by him are preserved: the *Altarpiece* in Florence, signed and dated 1461, and the *Altar of the Burning Bush*, of 1475/76, Nos. 214 and 216. Attributed to him or to his studio and school: Nos. 215, 217–218, 220 and 222–223; cf. No. 219, 221, 224–227, 288.

GIRARD D'ORLÉANS   FIG. 11

Court painter and 'valet de chambre' to King Jean II le Bon. Reported to have followed the king into his captivity in England shortly after 1356. Died in Paris in 1361.
The *Portrait of Jean le Bon* has been ascribed to him, without cogency, No. 1.

HAINCELIN (HAENSLEIN) DE HAGUENAU

Probably of Alsatian origin. Worked for the royal court in Paris; executed several commissions for Queen Isabeau de Bavière in 1403. Together with Jacques Coëne, he illuminated a Bible for Philippe the Bold in 1404. From 1409 to 1415, he was 'enlumineur et valet de chambre' to Louis of France, Duke of Guyenne, son of King Charles VI. He has been tentatively identified, first, with the studio that executed the

illuminations of the *Gaston Phébus* (Paris, Bibliothèque Nationale, Ms. fr. 616), the *Térence des Ducs* (Bibliothèque de l'Arsénal,) etc., and more recently with the Master of the Duke of Bedford, Nos. 76–79.

JEAN HAY (HEY)   FIGS. 42, 43

Mentioned by Jean Lemaire (*La Plainte du Désiré, 1509*) as one of his most distinguished contemporaries, together with Leonardo, Gentile Bellini, Perugino and 'Jehan de Paris' (i.e. Perréal). A trustworthy inscription on the back of the master's only documented picture calls him 'egregius teutonicus' (probably referring to a Flemish origin) and states that the picture was painted in 1494 for a secretary to King Charles VIII. No. 291.
Hay has recently been identified with the 'Master of Moulins' (Nos. 292–307), on the evidence of a signature, supposed to have been found on No. 293.

JACQUEMART DE HESDIN   PLATES 21–22

Mostly resident at Bourges. Painter to the Duke of Berri since 1384. He worked for the Duke probably until his death, about 1410/11, when his place was taken by the brothers de Limbourg.
Two documented works by him are preserved: the *Très belles Heures*, of Brussels, executed shortly before 1402, and the *Grandes Heures*, finished in 1409. Nos. 43 and 46.
Attributed to him Nos. 44 and 45; cf. No. 47.

JACQUES IVERNY (D'YVERNI)   PLATES 33–34

A native of Avignon. He worked in Piedmont and was commissioned, about 1420, to paint an *Altarpiece for the Family of the Marquis of Ceva*, No. 83.
Frescoes, also in Piedmont, have been ascribed to him, No. 84.

JEAN D'ORLÉANS

Son of Girard d'Orléans. Court painter to Jean le Bon after Girard's death, painter to Charles V since 1364, to Charles VI, and to the Duke of Berri since 1369. Mentioned until 1420.
He has been credited with the *Parement de Narbonne,* No. 2.

ADENOT (ADENET) LESCUYER

Active at Angers as a miniature painter. Illuminated a manuscript for Jeanne de Laval, wife of King René, in 1457. Worked until *c.* 1471.
He has been tentatively identified, without success, with the Master of the *Grandes Heures de Rohan*, No. 86.

JOSSE LIEFERINXE

Born at Denguiers in the diocese of Cambrai. Active in Marseille since 1493, and in Avignon. Was commissioned in 1497 to execute an *Altarpiece* for the priors of the 'Luminaire de S. Sébastien' of Notre-Dame des Accoules in Marseilles, in collaboration with the painter Bernardino Simondi of Piedmont. Died between 1505 and 1508.
He has been identified with the Master of St. Sebastian, Nos. 258–264

PAUL (POL) DE LIMBOURG   PLATES 27–29, 31–32; FIG. 13

Worked in collaboration with his brothers Jean (Hennequin) and Herman (Hermant). The three Limbourgs were probably nephews of the painter Jean Malouel, natives of Gelders like him, and their surname was also Malouel (Maelwel). They worked for the Dukes of Burgundy, John the Fearless and Philippe the Bold, about 1402/03. Later on they were in the service of the Duke of Berri, and from 1411 onwards were his court painters in succession to Jacquemart de Hesdin. Paul died shortly after 1416; his brothers, who survived him, died before 1434.
Documented works are Nos. 65 and 66.
Ascribed to them Nos. 67–69.

JEAN MALOUEL (MAELWEL)   PLATES 18, 20
A native of Gelders. He was painter to Isabeau de Bavière (1396 in Paris), and court painter to the Dukes of Burgundy from 1397 onwards as the successor of Jean de Beaumetz. He worked for Philippe the Bold (five *Altarpieces for the Chartreuse de Champmol*, 1398) and for John the Fearless. He died in Paris on 12 March 1419.
Nos. 52–54; cf. No. 51.

SIMON MARMION   PLATES 99–104
Born probably at Amiens, where he is mentioned between 1449 and 1454. Later he worked mainly at Valenciennes, where he is reported to have lived from 1458 until his death in 1489. Guicciardini and Lemaire praise him as the 'prince d'enluminure'.
The identification of Marmion with the master who painted the *retable of St. Bertin*, some other panels, and a great number of miniatures can be regarded as conclusive.
Nos. 170–189; cf. Nos. 190–202.

JEAN MIRAILLET (MIRALHETI)
Born at Montpellier, active at Nice. In Marseilles 1432–44. Died before 8 Oct. 1457.
A signed retable by him, the *Madone de la Miséricorde* has been preserved, No. 282.

JEAN PERRÉAL (JEAN DE PARIS)   PLATE 173; FIG. 48
Born about 1455, often mentioned between 1485 and 1529. Resided in Lyon since 1483. Court painter to the Bourbon family; executed decorations for the entry of Cardinal Charles of Bourbon into Lyon in 1485, was employed as a confidential agent by Anne de Beaujeu in 1487. Later in the service of Charles VIII, Louis XII and François Ier. Accompanied Louis XII to Italy repeatedly between 1499 and 1505. Drafted the model for the *Tombs of the Cathedral of Nantes* on the order of Anne de Bretagne. Worked on the *Tombs of Brou* (1509–1512), which were commissioned by Marguerite d'Autriche. In 1514 he came to London on behalf of Louis XII to supervise the new dresses of the princess Mary Tudor who was to be Queen of France and to paint her portrait. Died in 1530, probably in Paris.
Perréal has for a long time been wrongly identified with the Master of Moulins. Attempts to assign a new 'œuvre' to him are just on their way.
Nos. 331–332A; cf. Nos. 313, 336.

JEAN POYET
Miniature painter in Tours, first mentioned in 1483. Worked on the decorations for the entry of Queen Anne de Bretagne in 1491. Has been wrongly credited with the *Grandes Heures d'Anne de Bretagne*. No. 321; cf. No. 147.

PIERRE SPICRE (SPIC, SPICKER)
Probably born in Dijon as son of the stained-glass painter Guillaume Spicre. First mentioned in 1470. Commissioned to paint a retable for the Cathedral of Lausanne in 1473. Drew the cartoons for the tapestry *Life of the Virgin* in Notre-Dame de Beaune (1474). Died before June 1478.

The painter has been connected with the mural paintings executed for Cardinal Rolin at Beaune in 1470/71, and with other frescoes. He has been identified—unconvincingly—with the painter of cartoons ('patrons') Pierre Fiéret in Tournai and more recently with the Master of S. Jean de Luz. Nos. 233 and 234; cf. No. 235.

PIERRE VILLATTE, CALLED MALEBOUCHE   PLATE 62
Born in the diocese of Limoges. In 1452 in Avignon, working in connection with Enguerrand Charenton. No. 117; cf. No. 206.

MASTER OF THE ANNUNCIATION OF AIX
          PLATES 40–53; COLOUR PLATE P. 29
No. 91–96; cf. Nos. 97–100; 275.   FIG. 14

MASTER OF THE DUKE OF BEDFORD   FIG. 10
Nos. 76–79.

MASTER OF THE HOURS OF THE MARÉCHAL DE BOUCICAUT   PLATE 7; FIG. 9
Nos. 36–38; cf. No. 39.

MASTER OF CHARLES VIII
No. 333; cf. 331–332A.

MASTER OF ST. GILES   PLATES 135–138; COLOUR PLATE P. 25
Nos. 239–248; cf. Nos. 249 and 250.   FIG. 40

MASTER OF HEILIGENKREUZ
Nos. 58 and 59.

MASTER OF SAINT-JEAN DE LUZ   PLATES 131 and 132
No. 235.

MASTER OF MOULINS   PLATES 156–170; FIG. 23, 44–46
          COLOUR PLATE P. 237
Nos. 292–307. cf. Nos. 291, 308–314A, 326, 327.

MASTER OF THE PIETÀ OF ST. GERMAIN
Nos. 251–255; cf. No. 256.

RENÉ MASTER (MASTER OF THE CUER D'AMOURS ESPRIS)   PLATES 54–58
Nos. 102–105; cf. No. 143.

MASTER OF THE GRANDES HEURES DE ROHAN
          COLOUR PLATE P. 17; PLATES 36–42
Nos. 86–90

MASTER OF ST. SEBASTIAN   PLATES 143–148
Nos. 258–264; cf. No. 265.

MASTER OF THE ALTARPIECE OF THE LIFE OF THE VIRGIN   PLATES 139–142
Nos. 267–270; cf. No. 266.

INDEX OF PLACES

AIX-EN-PROVENCE, Musée
Salome, 256

Musée Paul Arbaud
Crucifixion, 110, Pl. 61

Cathédrale Saint-Sauveur
The Burning Bush (Froment), 216, Pl. 126–130, Fig. 22
St. Mitre (School of Froment), 223, Pl. 125

Église de la Madeleine
The Annunciation (Master of Aix), 91, Pl. 43–46, Fig. 14

Private Collection
Retable of St. Robert (School of Froment), 222

AMIENS, Musée de Picardie
Puy d'Amiens of 1499, 159
Christ Blessing, 160
Angel of the Annunciation, 164
St. Joachim and St. Anne, 168

Coll. Jean Masson (formerly)
The Four Stages of Society (Bourdichon), 321A, Pl. 151–154

AMSTERDAM, Rijksmuseum
Still Life (Master of Aix), 94, Pl. 50, Colour Pl. p. 29
Dionysius the Areopagite, 275, Pl. 174

Coll. Proehl
Woman with Fruit Still Life, 145, Fig. 35

Frederik Muller
The Pérussis Altarpiece (attrib. to Froment), 224

Goudstikker (formerly)
Virgin and Child (Marmion), 176

ANGERS, Museum of Tapestries
'L'Apocalypse d'Angers' (Jean Bandol and Nic. Bataille), *Tapestries,* 5, Fig. 3

ANTWERP, Musée Royal des Beaux-Arts
Virgin and Child (Fouquet), 123, Pl. 74
Pietà (Master of St. Sebastian), 261

Musée Mayer van den Bergh
Nativity, Resurrection, St. Christopher (attrib. to Broederlam), 19
Small Tabernacle, 21

AUTUN, Musée
Nativity with Cardinal Rolin (Master of Moulins), 292, Pl. 157–158

Cathédrale
Frescoes (attrib. to Pierre Spicre), 234

AVIGNON, Musée Calvet
'Le Bienheureux Pierre de Luxembourg', 106, Pl. 59
St. Catherine and Lazarus (School of Avignon), 107
Saint Siffrein (attrib. to Froment), 218
'Fons Pietatis', 229
St. Michael, The Annunciation (Master of St. Sebastian), 262, Pl. 145, 143
The Adoration, with a Knight and a Bishop, 273, Pl. 150
'Le Retable de Venasque', 274
The Virgin and St. Laurence, 280

BALTIMORE, Walters Art Gallery
Annunciation, Crucifixion and Baptism of Christ (attrib. to Broederlam), 20
St. Sebastian and the Plague-Stricken (Master of St. Sebastian), 259, Pl. 147

LE BAR, Parish Church
Dance of Death, 287A

BASLE, Oeffentliche Kunstsammlung
Virgin and Child, *Drawing,* 17, Pl. 15

BEAUNE (Côte d'Or), Église Notre-Dame (Chap. Saint-Léger)
Frescoes (attrib. to Pierre Spicre), 233

BERLIN, Deutsches Museum
Diptych, 7, Pl. 19
The Trinity, Triptych, 29
The Childhood of Christ, 30
The Coronation of the Virgin, 49, Pl. 6
Étienne Chevalier and St. Stephen (Fouquet), 122, Pl. 73
The Altarpiece of St. Bertin (Marmion), 170, Pl. 103–104, Fig. 19
St. Jerome (Master of St. Giles), 241

Kupferstichkabinett
Guillaume Jouvenel des Ursins, *Drawing* (Fouquet), 127, Pl. 71
The Transfiguration of Christ, *Drawing* (Froment), 215, Pl. 117
'Le Mortifiement de la Vaine Plaisance,' *Illuminated Ms.* (René Master), 105

Staatliche Bibliothek
Sketch Book (Jacques Daliwe), 75, Pl. 23–24

Schlossmuseum (formerly)
Believers and Unbelievers, *Enamel* (Fouquet), 125, Pl. 90

Private Collection (formerly)
Pietà, with a praying monk, 10, Fig. 25

Art Trade (formerly)
Portrait of Charles VIII (?) (attrib. to Perréal), 335

BESANÇON, Musée
Retable de Besançon (attrib. to Jean d'Arbois), 4

BLARICUM, Coll. Kleiweg de Zwaan
Virgin and Child (Marmion), 178

BONN, Provinzialmuseum
Wings with Saints (attrib. to the Master of the Maréchal de Boucicaut), 39

BOSTON, MASS., Museum of Fine Arts
Virgin and Child, 26
Portrait of a Man (attrib. to the Master of St. Giles), 250

BOURGES, Hôtel Jacques Cœur
'Les Anges de Bourges', *Frescoes,* 114, Fig. 4

BRUNSWICK, Herzog Anton Ulrich Museum
The Pool of Bethesda, *Drawing* (Rohan Master), 90, Pl. 36

BRUSSELS, Musées Royaux des Beaux-Arts
The Prophet Jeremiah; Noli me tangere (Master of Aix) 92, Pl. 48, 51–52
The Betrayal of Christ (Master of St. Giles), 243, Pl. 137
The Marriage of the Virgin (Master of St. Sebastian), 263, Pl. 144
Ecce Homo (Jean Hay), 291, Fig. 42–3
Virgin and Child (Master of Moulins), 299, Pl. 167

Bibliothèque Royale
Les Très Belles Heures du Duc de Berri, *Miniatures* (Jacquemart de Hesdin), 46, Pl. 21–22
Le Pontificale de Sens, *Illuminated Ms.* (Marmion), 173

BUDAPEST, Coll. Delmar (formerly)
The Marriage of St. Catherine (Master of Heiligenkreuz), *see* 59

CAMBRIDGE, Fitzwilliam Museum
The Cambridge Hours (Rohan Master), 88

CAROMB, Parish Church
St. George, 213, Pl. 115–116

CARPENTRAS, Museum
St. Joachim and Anne at the Golden Gate (attrib. to Nicolas Dipre), 266
St. Anthony, 272

Cathédrale Saint-Siffrein
Triptych: The Coronation, with Sts. Siffrein and Michael, 119

La Chaise-Dieu (Haute-Loire), Church
    The Dance of Death, *Frescoes*, 115, Fig. 20–21

Chantilly, Musée Condé
    The Virgin of Mercy (Charonton and Villatte), 117, Pl. 62, Fig. 16
    'La Châsse de Sainte-Perpétue' (attrib. to Marmion), 199
    Portraits of a Man and his Wife (Master of St. Giles), 247, Pl. 138
    Portraits of Philippe de la Platière and Louis Comte de Ligny, *Drawings* (attrib. to Perréal), 332A
    Les Très Riches Heures du Duc de Berri, *Illuminated Ms.* (Limbourg), 65, Pl. 28–29, 31–32, Fig. 2
    Les Heures d'Étienne Chevalier, 40 Miniatures from an *Illuminated Ms.* (Fouquet), 130, Pl. 70, 75–78

Chicago, Ill., Art Institute
    'Le Retable de Thuison', 169, Pl. 105–106
    The Entombment of Christ (attrib. to the Master of the Pietà of Saint-Germain), 255
    The Annunciation (Master of Moulins), 297, Pl. 165
  Private Collection
    Portrait of a Woman with a White Cap, 312

Cleveland, Ohio, Museum of Art
    St. Louis of Toulouse, 56
    Death of the Virgin (Master of Heiligenkreuz), 59
    Portrait of a Man (Colantonio), 98, Fig. 33

Cologne, Wallraf Richartz Museum
    The Holy Kinship (School of Amiens ?), 166

Copenhagen, Museum
    Head of an old Man (attrib. to the Master of Aix), 96

Dessau, Museum
    St. Christopher, *Drawing*, 73

Detroit, Coll. Julius H. Haas
    St. Robert de Molesmes, 230

Dijon, Musée
    'Le Retable de Champmol' (Broederlam), 18
    Christ on the Cross, 238

Dresden, Print Room
    Series of Planets, *Drawings*, 70, Pl. 30
    An Aquatic Tournament, *Drawing*, 70A

Dublin, National Gallery of Ireland
    St. Jerome and his Disciples, 100

Erlangen, Universitätsbibliothek
    View of a Gothic Cathedral, *Drawing*, 74

Fénis nr. Aosta (Piedmont), Chapel of the Castle
    Frescoes, 85

Florence, Museo Nazionale, Palazzo del Bargello
    'Large Bargello Diptych', 6, Pl. 1–3, Fig. 24
    'Small Bargello Diptych', 15, Pl. 16, Fig. 27
  Galleria degli Uffizi
    Triptych (Nicolas Froment), 214, Pl. 118–124

Fonthill, Coll. J. Morrison
    The Man with a big nose (Charles VIII ?) (attrib. to Perréal), 334

Fréjus (Var), Cathedral
    Retable of St. Margaret (Durandi), 281

Genova, Galleria Communale
    Crucifixion (Louis Bréa), 284
  Santa Maria di Castello
    The Paradise (Louis Bréa), 285

Glasgow, Art Gallery
    Adoration of the Child (attrib. to Colantonio), 212, Fig. 30
    St. Victor (St. Maurice ?) and a Donor (Master of Moulins), 301, Colour Pl. p. 237

Guy's Cliff, Warwick, Coll. J. H. Percy (formerly)
    Legend of a Saint, 152, Fig. 41

The Hague, Royal Library
    Virgin and Child, *Miniature* (Bourdichon), 324
  Late A. W. Volz Coll.
    Portrait of a Man, 237

Harrogate, Yorks., Coll. Alfred Jowett
    Head of a Young Woman, *Drawing* (Master of Moulins), 305, Fig. 46

Hartford, Conn., Wadsworth Atheneum
    Pietà, 231, Fig. 38

Ince Blundell Hall, Lanc., Coll. Weld Blundell
    Madonna with St. Louis and St. Margaret, 338

Joigny (Yonne), Église S. Jean
    St. Anne with the Virgin and Child (Master of St. Giles,), 249

Laon, Musée
    Apostles and Prophets; The Angel of the Annunciation (Rohan Master), 89, Pl. 41–42

Leningrad, Hermitage
    Head of a Man, *Drawing* (Fouquet), 128
  Library
    Grandes Chroniques de S. Denis, *Illuminated Ms.* (Marmion), 172

Loches, Église S. Antoine
    'Le Triptyque de Loches' (School of Fouquet), 147, Pl. 95

London, National Gallery
    The Holy Trinity (Entourage of the Master of St. Lambert), 28
    The Wilton Diptych, 31
    Parts of the Altarpiece of St. Bertin (Marmion), 171, Pl. 99–100
    St. Clement with a Donor (Marmion), 182
    Virgin with Child and Saints (attrib. to Mazerolles), 191
    Two Scenes from the Legend of St. Giles (Master of St. Giles), 239, Pl. 135–136
    Charlemagne and the Meeting at the Golden Gate (Master of Moulins), 298, Pl. 166
  British Museum
    The Betrayal of Christ, *Drawing* (attrib. to Paul de Limbourg), 69, Pl. 35
    The Bedford Hours, *Illuminated Ms.*, (Master of the Duke of Bedford), 78, Fig. 10
    Book of Hours, *Illuminated Ms.*, (Miniaturist of King René), 101, Fig. 8, and p. 5
    David Praying, *Miniature* from the Hours of Étienne Chevalier (Fouquet), 130
    Book of Hours (Marmion), *Illuminated Ms.*, 174, Pl. 101–102
    Portrait of Pierre Sala, *Miniature* (Perréal), 331, Fig. 48
    Shield of Parade, 202, Pl. 96
  Wallace Collection
    Small *Enamel* Diptych (attrib. to the Moulins Master), 296, Fig. 44–45
  Westminster Abbey
    King Richard II, 32
  Coll. Viscount Bearsted
    St. Michael, *Miniature* from the Hours of Étienne Chevalier (Fouquet), 130
  Coll. Mrs. Gutekunst
    Statue of the Virgin, *Drawing*, 13
  Coll. Henry Oppenheimer (formerly)
    Rider on a Rearing Horse, *Drawing*, 72
  Private Collection
    The Lamentation over Christ (School of Touraine), 150
  Durlacher Brs. (formerly)
    Jacob's Dream; Gideon and the Fleece, 221

Lubeck, Museum
    The Resurrection (Master of the Pietà of S. Germain), 253

LUCERNE, Coll. Chillingworth (formerly)
Bearing of the Cross, with Donors (Master of the Pietà of S. Germain), 254

LUGANO, Coll. Schloss Rohoncz
Virgin and Child (Marmion), 183
Female Donor with Patron-Saint (Marmion), 184

LYON, Musée
Bearing of the Cross (Master of the Pietà of S. Germain), 252
Death of the Virgin; Coronation of the Virgin (School of the Rhône), 265
Guillaume de Montmorency, 336

LE MANS, Musée Hôtel de Tessé
Four Panels (School of Touraine), 149

MANTA, Castello (Piedmont)
Frescoes, 84, Pl. 33–34

MARSEILLE, Musée Grobet-Labadié
St. Bernardin's Vision and Two Donors, 198, Pl. 60
Coll. Comte Demandolx-Dedons
Head of a Monk (Fouquet), 137
Two panels from an Altarpiece, 156
The Marriage of the Virgin (Master of the Altarpiece of the Life of the Virgin), 267, Pl. 140

MERION, Pa., Barnes Foundation
The Presentation in the Temple, 23
The Circumcision, 257

MONTPELLIER, Musée Fabre
The Resurrection with St. Catherine and Donors, 201
Coll. d'Albénas (formerly)
Virgin and Child (attrib. to Marmion), 190

MOULINS, Musée
Triptych (School of Touraine), 148, Pl. 94
Cathedral
The Moulins Triptych (Master of Moulins), 293, Pl. 159–163, Fig. 22

MUNICH, Alte Pinakothek
Cardinal Charles II of Bourbon (Master of Moulins), 302, Pl. 170
Staatsbibliothek
Boccaccio, Illuminated Ms. (Fouquet), 131, Pl. 81
Private Collection (formerly)
Death of a Saint (Master of Heiligenkreuz), 59

NAPLES, Museo Nazionale
St. Jerome (Colantonio), 97, Fig. 29
Wings to an Adoration of the Kings (attrib. to Froment), 227
Triptych (Bourdichon), 319, Pl. 155

NEW YORK, Metropolitan Museum
Virgin and Child (formerly Coll. G. Blumenthal), 151
Altarpiece of 1451, 155
The Martyrdom of Two Saints (Studio of Marmion), 189
A Monk in Prayer (attrib. to the Master of Moulins), 308
Portrait of a Young Man (attrib. to the Master of Moulins), 309
Portraits of Jean of Egmont and his Wife (Master of Alkmaar), 326
Brooklyn Museum of Art
Decapitation of Five Martyrs (formerly Friedsam Coll.), 314
King Louis XI (formerly Friedsam Coll.), 328
Pierpont Morgan Library
Adoration of the Magi; Death of the Virgin, 25
Sketch Book, 47
Frick Collection
Virgin and Child, 62
Pietà with a Donor, 210, Pl. 114
Coll. Miss Helen Frick
Pietà, see 210, Fig. 37

Coll. E. Garbaty
Legend of St. Benedict (attrib. to Marmion), 193
Coll. W. Goldmann
Dunois, Bastard of Orléans (attrib. to Fouquet), 141
Coll. S. Guggenheim
Portrait of a Young Girl (attrib. to the Moulins Master), 311
Late Otto H. Kahn Coll.
St. George (attrib. to Marmion), 200
Mogmar Art Foundation (formerly)
St. Jerome and his Disciples, 100
Coll. Robert Lehman
'Vespers of the Holy Spirit', Miniature from the Hours of Étienne Chevalier (Fouquet), 130
Portrait of a Young Lady with a Hénin, 153
Portrait of a Lady in Profile, 154
Lamentation over Christ (Marmion), 188
Virgin and Child (Master of St. Giles), 245
Portrait of a Young Princess (Master of Moulins), 303, Pl. 169
Coll. John Rockefeller, jun.
Hugues de Rabutin and his Wife (Master of S. Jean de Luz), 235, Pl. 131–132
Late Mortimer Schiff Coll.
Madonna and Saints, 61
Portraits of a Man and his Wife, 325
Late Lord Duveen Coll.
A Papal Legate, Drawing (attrib. to Fouquet), 139, Pl. 92
J. Seligmann (formerly)
Abraham and Melchisedek (attrib. to Marmion), 196
Georges Wildenstein Coll.
Memorial of St. Veranus, Miniature from the Hours of Étienne Chevalier (Fouquet), 130
Two Scenes from the Legend of S. Remi (Master of St. Giles), 240, Colour Pl. p. 25, Fig. 40
St. Michael killing the Dragon, Drawing, 314A, Fig. 47

NICE, Musée Masséna
Retable of St. John (attrib. to Durandi), see 281
Virgin of Mercy (Miralhet), 282

NICE-CIMIEZ, Church
Pietà with St. Martin and St. Catherine (Louis Bréa), 283, Pl. 149

NOUANS (Indre et Loire), Parish Church
'La Pietà de Nouans' (Fouquet), 136, Pl. 85–88

OTTERLOO, Rijksmuseum Kroeller-Muller
Virgin and Child (School of Touraine), 316

OXFORD, Ashmolean Museum
Scenes of Court Life, Drawing, 48
Pietà, 197

PARIS, Musée du Louvre
King Jean le Bon, 1, Fig. 11
'Le Parement de Narbonne', 2, Fig. 26
'Small circular Pietà', 8, Pl. 4, 175
The Entombment, 9, Pl. 5
The 'Cardon Polyptych', 22
The 'Madone aux Églantines', 24
The Virgin with the Writing Desk, 27
Christ Carrying the Cross (School of Avignon), 33, Pl. 9
'Le Retable de Thouzon', 34
Virgin and Child (formerly C. de Beistegui Coll.), 51, Pl. 25
'Large circular Pietà', 53, Pl. 18
S. Denis (attrib. to Bellechose), 54, Pl. 20
Life of St. George, 55
Four Panels of the Martyrdom of St. George, 57
Votive picture of Jean Juvénal des Ursins and his family, 112
The Presentation in the Temple, with Donors, 113
Charles VII (Fouquet), 120, Pl. 69
Guillaume Jouvenel des Ursins (Fouquet), 126, Pl. 72

PARIS, Musée du Louvre
  The Man with a Glass of Wine (formerly attrib. to Fouquet), 144, Fig. 36
  'Le Retable du Parlement de Paris', 157
  'Le Sacerdoce de la Vierge', 158, Pl. 97
  The Mass of St. Gregory, 167
  Legend of St. Helena (Marmion), 175
  Virgin and Child (Marmion), 179
  Margaret of York (attrib. to Marmion; formerly Gay Coll.), 192
  The Altarpiece of Boulbon, 205, Pl. 107, 111
  'La Pietà de Villeneuve-lès-Avignon', 206, Pl. 108–110, 112
  St. Jerome (School of Avignon), 207
  Sts. Jerome, Augustine and Ambrose (formerly Coll. Cte. Demandolx-Dedons), 211
  'Le Diptyque des Matheron' (attrib. to Froment), 217, Fig. 7
  The Raising of Lazarus (formerly attrib. to Froment), 219
  Virgin and Child (Master of St. Giles), 246
  Pietà (Master of the Pietà of Saint-Germain), 251
  The Adoration of the Child (Master of St. Sebastian), 264
  The Man of Sorrows (School of Nice), 287
  Pierre Duc de Bourbon and St. Peter (Master of Moulins, Studio), 294
  Anne de Beaujeu, Duchesse de Bourgogne, and St. John (Master of Moulins, Studio), 295
  Mary Magdalen and a Donatrix (Master of Moulins), 300, Pl. 164
  The Dauphin Charles-Orland (Master of Moulins; formerly Beistegui Coll.), 306
  Portrait of a Praying Child (attrib. to the Master of Moulins), 307, Pl. 168
  Pietà with Sts. John and Mary Magdalen (School of Touraine), 315
  St. Martin and the Beggar (School of Touraine), 317
  Woman with a white headdress (attrib. to Michiel), 327
  'La Dame aux Pensées', 330, Pl. 171
  Guillaume de Montmorency, see 336
  Death, Assumption and Coronation of the Virgin, Drawing, 11, Pl. 8
  Four Apostles, Drawings, 12
  A Lady with a Dog and a Falcon, Drawing, 40, Pl. 12
  Three Young Ladies, Drawing, 60
  Study for a 'Pleurant' (formerly Gay Coll.), Drawing, 71
  St. Martin and St. Margaret, Miniatures from the Hours of Étienne Chevalier (Fouquet), 130, Pl. 82
  'Histoire Ancienne et Faits des Romains', Four Miniatures (Fouquet), 132
  Self-Portrait of Jean Fouquet, Enamel, 124, Pl. 89
  'The Offering of the Heart', Tapestry, 41, Pl. 11
Musée des Arts Décoratifs
  The Last Judgement (Master of the Duke of Bedford), 76
Musée de Cluny
  A Bishop's Mitre, 3
  Coronations of King David and Louis XII (Puy d'Amiens), 161
  Madonna in a Church (Puy d'Amiens), 162
  The Madonna of the Wheat, 163
  Four Wings with the Apostles (School of Amiens), 165
  'La Pietà de Tarascon', 209, Pl. 113
  Pietà with Donors, Enamel (School of the so-called Monvaerni), 232, Fig. 39
Musée Jacquemart-André
  'Les Heures du Maréchal de Boucicaut', Illuminated Ms., 36
  Mater Dolorosa (attrib. to Charonton), 118
Bibliothèque Nationale
  Dedication Miniature (Master of the Hours of the Maréchal de Boucicaut), 38, Fig. 9
  Psalter, Illuminated Ms. (André Beauneveu), 42, Pl. 13–14
  'Les Grandes Heures du Duc de Berri', Illuminated Ms. (Jacquemart de Hesdin), 43
  'Les Petites Heures du Duc de Berri', Illuminated Ms. (Jacquemart de Hesdin), 44
  Portrait of Louis II of Anjou, Water Colour Drawing, 63, Pl. 26

St. Jerome in his Study, Drawing (Paul de Limbourg), 67, Fig. 13
'Le Bréviaire de Salisbury', Illuminated Ms. (Master of the Duke of Bedford), 77
'Les Grandes Heures de Rohan', Illuminated Ms. (Rohan Master), 86, Pl. 37–40, Colour Pl. p. 17
'Les Heures des Ducs d'Anjou', Illuminated Ms. (Rohan Master), 87, Fig. 5
Hours of Louis de Savoie, Illuminated Ms., 99
'Le Livre des Tournois du Roi René', Illuminated Ms. (René Master), 104
Portrait of Agnes Sorel, Drawing, see 123
'Les Antiquités Judaïques', Illuminated Ms. (Fouquet), 129, Pl. 79, 83
St. Anne with the Three Marys, Miniature from the Hours of Étienne Chevalier (Fouquet), 130, Colour Pl. p. 213
Frontispiece Miniature of the Statutes of the Order of St. Michael (Fouquet), 133, Pl. 84
'Les Grandes Chroniques de France', Illuminated Ms. (Fouquet), 134, Pl. 80
Portrait of Henri le Navigateur, Miniature (Portuguese School), 146
Frontispiece, Miniature of the Statutes of the Order of St. Michael (Master of Moulins), 304, Pl. 156
'Les Heures d'Anne de Bretagne', Illuminated Ms. (Bourdichon), 321
'Les Heures de Charles d'Angoulême', Illuminated Ms. (Bourdichon), 323
Two Portraits, formerly supposed to represent Charles VIII and Anne de Bretagne, 333
Coll. Henri Chalandon
  Crucifixion with a Carthusian Monk, 50
  The Annunciation (School of Provence), 276
Coll. Comtesse Durrieu
  Head of the Virgin; Santa Facies, 111
  'Les Heures de la Dame de Baudricourt' Illuminated Ms. (attrib. to Fouquet), 135
Coll. L. A. Gaboriaud (formerly)
  The Crucifixion, 228
Late Marquise de Ganay Coll.
  King Louis XI (attrib. to Bourdichon), 318, Fig. 12
Coll. Heugel
  Portrait of a Man (School of Touraine), 142, Pl. 93
Late Martin Le Roy Coll.
  The Angers Hours, Illuminated Ms. (Rohan Master) see 89
Coll. Baron Maurice de Rothschild
  'Les Très Belles Heures de Notre-Dame du Duc de Berri', Illuminated Ms. (J. de Hesdin), 45
  'Les Heures d'Ailly', Illuminated Ms. (Limbourg), 66
Private Collections
  Virgin and Child with Saints and Donors (School of Provence), 225
  The Presentation of the Virgin (Master of the Altarpiece of the Life of the Virgin), 269, Pl. 141
  Portrait of Anne de Bretagne (attrib. to Bourdichon), 322

PHILADELPHIA, John G. Johnson Collection
  St. Jerome and a Donor (Marmion), 181, Pl. 98
  The Crucifixion (Marmion), 185
  Christ Before Caiphas (School of Marmion), 195
  Portrait of a Man (attrib. to the Froment Entourage), 220
  The Legend of St. Sebastian, Four Panels (Master of St. Sebastian), 258, Pl. 146, 148
  Young Man with Coxcomb (attrib. to the Master of Moulins), 310

POITIERS, Musée
  Two Saints and a Cardinal in Adoration (School of Avignon), 108

LE PUY-EN-VELAY, Musée Crozatier
  'La Vierge Protectrice', 80
Cathedral
  The Liberal Arts, Frescoes, 313, Pl. 172

RIGA, Private Collection (formerly)
  Virgin in Prayer (Bourdichon), 320

RIPAILLE, Château, Coll. Engel-Gros (formerly)
    The Rich Man and the Poor Lazarus (Master of the Heures du Maréchal de Boucicaut), 37, Pl. 7

ROME, Galleria Corsini
    The Crucifixion (Marmion), 186

    Palazzo Venezia
    Pilgrims Worshipping the Relics of a Saint (Master of St. Sebastian), 260

    Private Collection
    The Crucifixion (Master of the Altarpiece of the Life of the Virgin), 270, Pl. 142

ROTTERDAM, Boymans Museum (formerly F. Koenigs Coll.)
    Statue of a Youthful King, *Drawing*, 14
    Architectural Framework, *Drawing* (Limbourg), 68
    Standing Man, *Drawing* (Master of Aix), 95, Pl. 53
    Young Man in Prayer before an Altar, *Drawing*, 204

SAINT-FLORET (Puy-de-Dôme), Église du Chastel
    Virgin and Donors, *Fresco*, 82

SAINT LOUIS, U.S.A., City Art Museum
    Portrait of a Man holding a Flower, 337

SAINT-MAXIMIN, Église des Dominicains
    Retable of the Four Saints, 271

SALUZZO, Galleria Cavassa
    The Virgin of Mercy, 290

SANTA BARBARA, Cal., Coll. Arthur Sachs
    The Annunciation, 16, Pl. 17
    Man in a Turban (attrib. to Fouquet), 138
    'L'Homme à la Canne', 329

SOSPEL (Alpes Maritimes), Chapelle des Pénitents Blancs
    Pietà with Sts. Catherine and Nicolas (School of Nice), 286

STRASBOURG, Museum
    Mater Dolorosa and Christ (Marmion), 187

STUTTGART-OBERLENNINGEN, Coll. H. Scheufelen
    Virgin and Child (Marmion), 180

TARASCON, Cathédrale Sainte-Marthe
    St. Michael, 277
    Mary Magdalen with a Donor, 278
    Retable of St. Roch, 279

TROYES (Aube), Musée
    Pietà (attributed to Malouel or Bellechose), 52, Fig. 28

TURIN, Galleria Sabauda
    Triptych (Iverny), 83

    Museo Civico
    'Dieu de Pitié', 289

    Coll. Conte Emilio Balba-Bertone
    The Death of the Virgin, 288

UPSALA, Library
    Courtiers and Ladies, *Drawing*, 70B

VADUZ, Fürst of Liechtenstein
    Figure of a Young Man, *Drawing* (attrib. to Fouquet), 140, Fig. 32
    Portrait of a Man, of 1456, 143, Pl. 91

VERCELLI, Museo Borgogna (Istituto di Belle Arti)
    Pietà, 210A

VIENNA, Kunsthistorisches Museum
    The Annunciation; The Marriage of St. Catherine (Master of Heiligenkreuz), 58
    Portrait of a woman with a white headdress (attrib. to Michiel), *see* 327

    Graphische Sammlung, Albertina
    Head of a Man, *Drawing*, 208

    Staatsbibliothek
    'Le Cuer d'Amours Espris', *Illuminated Ms.* (René Master), 102, Pl. 54–58
    The Legend of Theseus, *Illuminated Ms.* (René Master), 103

VIERHOUTEN, Coll. van Beuningen
    The Prophet Isaiah; St. Mary Magdalen (Master of Aix), 93, Pl. 47, 49
    St. Jerome in his Study, 109
    Portrait of a Young Man (Burgundian School), 203
    The Flight into Egypt; The Presentation in the Temple (Master of St. Giles), 242

VILLENEUVE-LÈS-AVIGNON, Hospice
    The Coronation of the Virgin (Charonton), 116, Pl. 63–68

WASHINGTON, National Gallery
    Profile Portrait of a Lady, 64, Pl. 27

WINDSOR CASTLE, H.M. THE KING
    Book of Hours, *Illuminated Ms.* (Master of the Duke of Bedford), 79
    Portrait of Louis XII (Perréal), 332, Pl. 173

WINTERTHUR, Coll. Dr. Oscar Reinhart
    Portrait of Philippe le Beau (Master of St. Giles), 248

WORCESTER, Mass., Art Museum
    'Le Bienheureux Pierre de Luxembourg' presenting a Donor to the Virgin, 35, Pl. 10
    'Le Christ de Pitié' (attrib. to Froment), 226
    Claude de Toulongeon and Guillemette de Vergy (Burgundian School), 236, Pl. 133–134

YPRES, Hôtel de Ville
    Votive Picture of Yolande Belle, 81

ZUG (Switzerland), Coll. Abegg
    St. Christopher and a Saint Bishop (Master of St. Giles), 244

ZURICH, Private Collection
    Virgin and Child (Marmion), 177
    The Adoration of the Magi (Master of the Altarpiece of the Life of the Virgin), 268, Pl. 139

ENGLAND, Private Collection
    Portrait of a Young Man (attrib. to Marmion), 194

LOST
    Portrait of Pope Eugene IV (Fouquet), 121

TABLE OF PATRONS
AND ARTISTS

MAP OF FRANCE
IN THE XV CENTURY

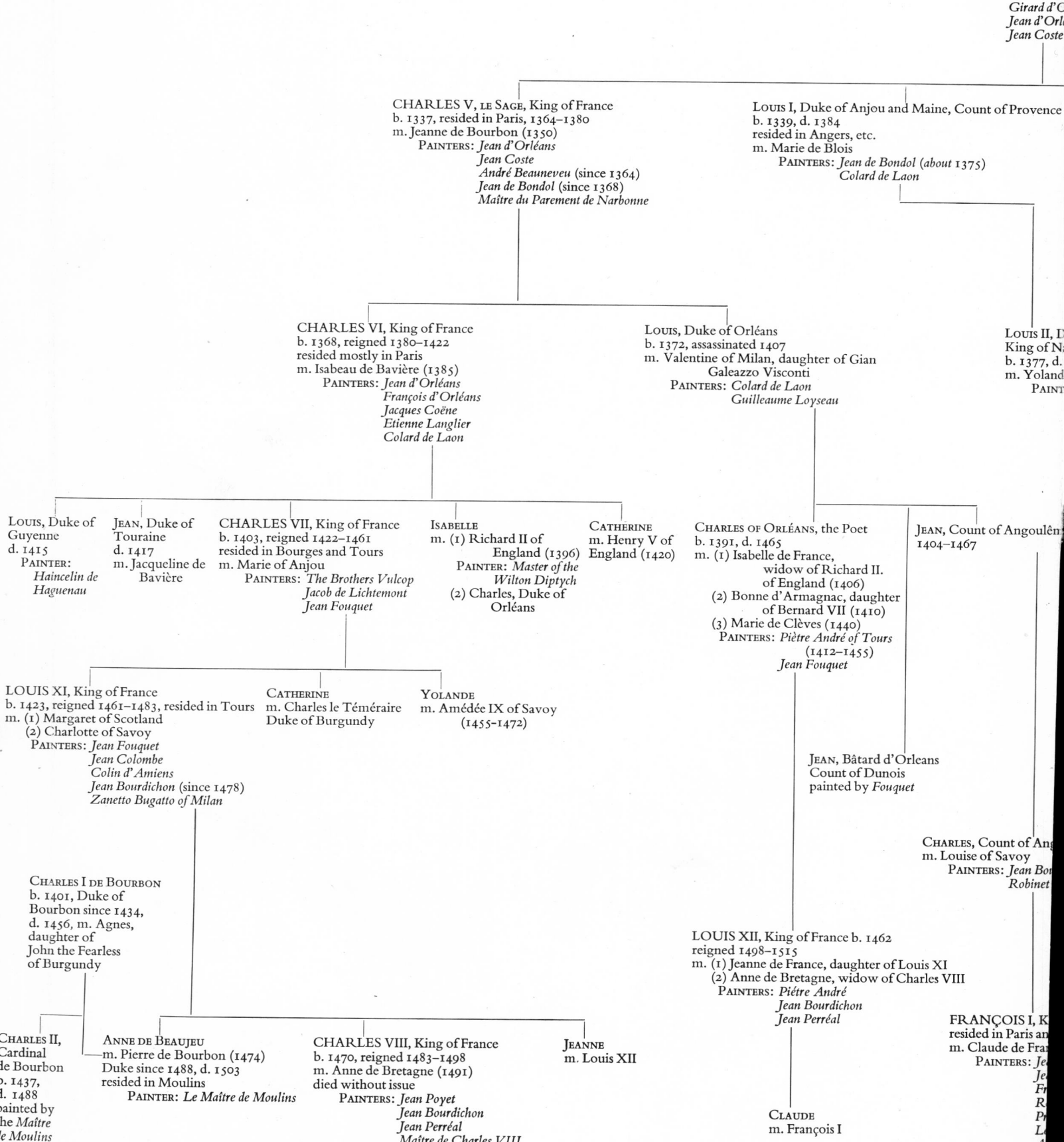

JEAN II, LE BON, King of
b. 1310, resided in Paris, 13
married (1) Bonne de Luxe
(2) Jeanne de Boulo
PAINTERS: *Evrard d'Orléan*
Girard d'Orléar
Jean d'Orléans
Jean Coste

CHARLES V, LE SAGE, King of France
b. 1337, resided in Paris, 1364–1380
m. Jeanne de Bourbon (1350)
PAINTERS: *Jean d'Orléans*
Jean Coste
André Beauneveu (since 1364)
Jean de Bondol (since 1368)
Maître du Parement de Narbonne

LOUIS I, Duke of Anjou and Maine, Count of Provence
b. 1339, d. 1384
resided in Angers, etc.
m. Marie de Blois
PAINTERS: *Jean de Bondol (about 1375)*
Colard de Laon

CHARLES VI, King of France
b. 1368, reigned 1380–1422
resided mostly in Paris
m. Isabeau de Bavière (1385)
PAINTERS: *Jean d'Orléans*
François d'Orléans
Jacques Coëne
Etienne Langlier
Colard de Laon

LOUIS, Duke of Orléans
b. 1372, assassinated 1407
m. Valentine of Milan, daughter of Gian
Galeazzo Visconti
PAINTERS: *Colard de Laon*
Guilleaume Loyseau

LOUIS II, Duke of
King of Naples a
b. 1377, d. 1417 i
m. Yolande d'A
PAINTER: *M*

LOUIS, Duke of
Guyenne
d. 1415
PAINTER:
*Haincelin de
Haguenau*

JEAN, Duke of
Touraine
d. 1417
m. Jacqueline de
Bavière

CHARLES VII, King of France
b. 1403, reigned 1422–1461
resided in Bourges and Tours
m. Marie of Anjou
PAINTERS: *The Brothers Vulcop*
Jacob de Lichtemont
Jean Fouquet

ISABELLE
m. (1) Richard II of
England (1396)
PAINTER: *Master of the
Wilton Diptych*
(2) Charles, Duke of
Orléans

CATHERINE
m. Henry V of
England (1420)

CHARLES OF ORLÉANS, the Poet
b. 1391, d. 1465
m. (1) Isabelle de France,
widow of Richard II.
of England (1406)
(2) Bonne d'Armagnac, daughter
of Bernard VII (1410)
(3) Marie de Clèves (1440)
PAINTERS: *Piètre André of Tours
(1412–1455)*
Jean Fouquet

JEAN, Count of Angoulêm
1404–1467

LOUIS XI, King of France
b. 1423, reigned 1461–1483, resided in Tours
m. (1) Margaret of Scotland
(2) Charlotte of Savoy
PAINTERS: *Jean Fouquet*
Jean Colombe
Colin d'Amiens
Jean Bourdichon (since 1478)
Zanetto Bugatto of Milan

CATHERINE
m. Charles le Téméraire
Duke of Burgundy

YOLANDE
m. Amédée IX of Savoy
(1455-1472)

JEAN, Bâtard d'Orleans
Count of Dunois
painted by *Fouquet*

CHARLES, Count of An
m. Louise of Savoy
PAINTERS: *Jean Bo*
Robinet

CHARLES I DE BOURBON
b. 1401, Duke of
Bourbon since 1434,
d. 1456, m. Agnes,
daughter of
John the Fearless
of Burgundy

LOUIS XII, King of France b. 1462
reigned 1498–1515
m. (1) Jeanne de France, daughter of Louis XI
(2) Anne de Bretagne, widow of Charles VIII
PAINTERS: *Piétre André*
Jean Bourdichon
Jean Perréal

CHARLES II,
Cardinal
de Bourbon
b. 1437,
d. 1488
painted by
the *Maître
de Moulins*

ANNE DE BEAUJEU
m. Pierre de Bourbon (1474)
Duke since 1488, d. 1503
resided in Moulins
PAINTER: *Le Maître de Moulins*

CHARLES VIII, King of France
b. 1470, reigned 1483–1498
m. Anne de Bretagne (1491)
died without issue
PAINTERS: *Jean Poyet*
Jean Bourdichon
Jean Perréal
Maître de Charles VIII

JEANNE
m. Louis XII

CLAUDE
m. François I

FRANÇOIS I, K
resided in Paris an
m. Claude de Fra
PAINTERS: *Je*
Je
Fr
R
Pr
L
A

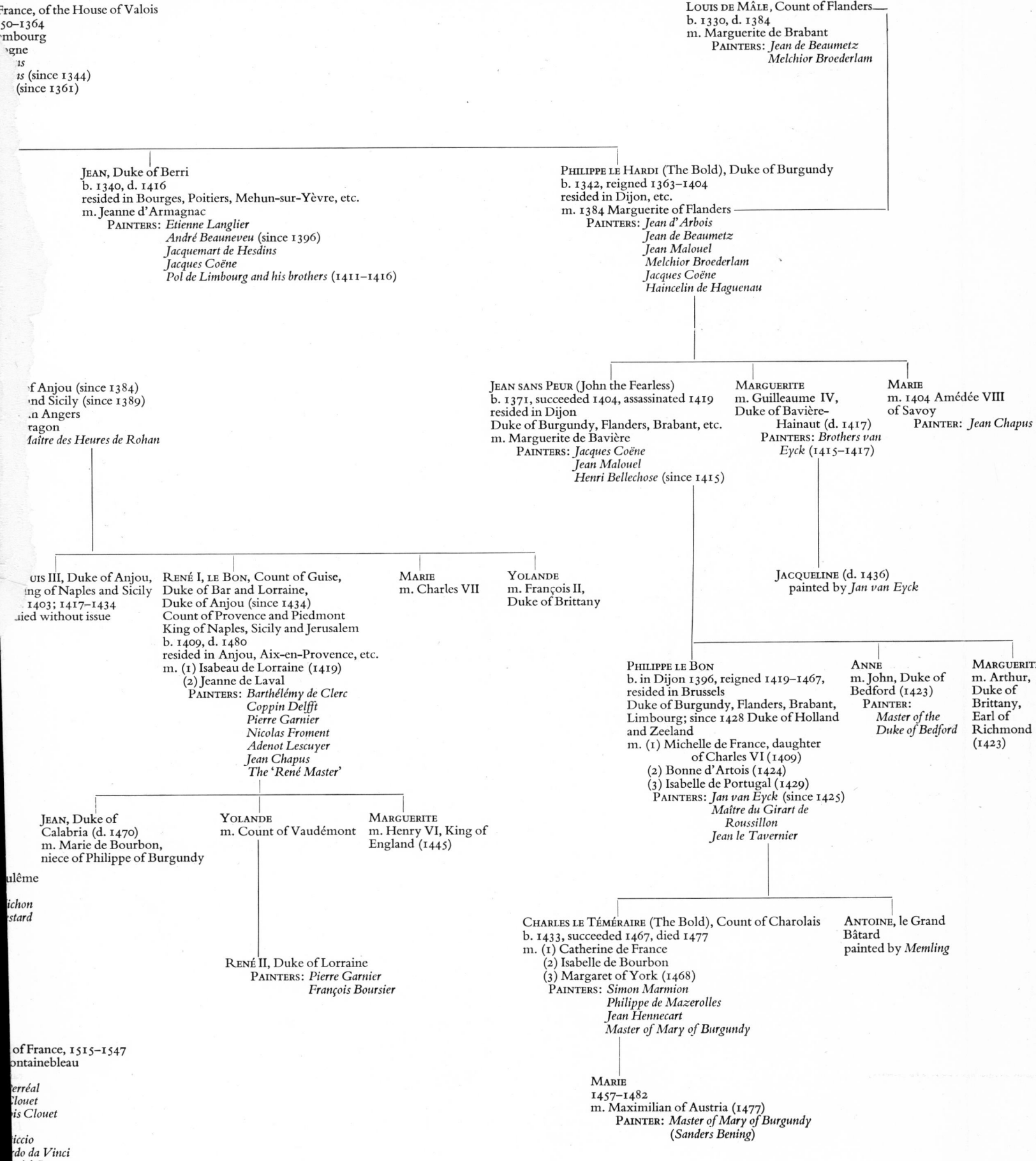

France, of the House of Valois
,50–1364
mbourg
gne
1s
1s (since 1344)
(since 1361)

LOUIS DE MÂLE, Count of Flanders
b. 1330, d. 1384
m. Marguerite de Brabant
PAINTERS: *Jean de Beaumetz*
Melchior Broederlam

JEAN, Duke of Berri
b. 1340, d. 1416
resided in Bourges, Poitiers, Mehun-sur-Yèvre, etc.
m. Jeanne d'Armagnac
PAINTERS: *Etienne Langlier*
André Beauneveu (since 1396)
Jacquemart de Hesdins
Jacques Coëne
Pol de Limbourg and his brothers (1411–1416)

PHILIPPE LE HARDI (The Bold), Duke of Burgundy
b. 1342, reigned 1363–1404
resided in Dijon, etc.
m. 1384 Marguerite of Flanders
PAINTERS: *Jean d'Arbois*
Jean de Beaumetz
Jean Malouel
Melchior Broederlam
Jacques Coëne
Haincelin de Haguenau

f Anjou (since 1384)
nd Sicily (since 1389)
n Angers
ragon
Maître des Heures de Rohan

JEAN SANS PEUR (John the Fearless)
b. 1371, succeeded 1404, assassinated 1419
resided in Dijon
Duke of Burgundy, Flanders, Brabant, etc.
m. Marguerite de Bavière
PAINTERS: *Jacques Coëne*
Jean Malouel
Henri Bellechose (since 1415)

MARGUERITE
m. Guilleaume IV,
Duke of Bavière-
Hainaut (d. 1417)
PAINTERS: *Brothers van
Eyck* (1415–1417)

MARIE
m. 1404 Amédée VIII
of Savoy
PAINTER: *Jean Chapus*

UIS III, Duke of Anjou,
ng of Naples and Sicily
1403; 1417–1434
ied without issue

RENÉ I, LE BON, Count of Guise,
Duke of Bar and Lorraine,
Duke of Anjou (since 1434)
Count of Provence and Piedmont
King of Naples, Sicily and Jerusalem
b. 1409, d. 1480
resided in Anjou, Aix-en-Provence, etc.
m. (1) Isabeau de Lorraine (1419)
    (2) Jeanne de Laval
PAINTERS: *Barthélémy de Clerc*
Coppin Delfft
Pierre Garnier
Nicolas Froment
Adenot Lescuyer
Jean Chapus
The '*René Master*'

MARIE
m. Charles VII

YOLANDE
m. François II,
Duke of Brittany

JACQUELINE (d. 1436)
painted by *Jan van Eyck*

PHILIPPE LE BON
b. in Dijon 1396, reigned 1419–1467,
resided in Brussels
Duke of Burgundy, Flanders, Brabant,
Limbourg; since 1428 Duke of Holland
and Zeeland
m. (1) Michelle de France, daughter
        of Charles VI (1409)
    (2) Bonne d'Artois (1424)
    (3) Isabelle de Portugal (1429)
PAINTERS: *Jan van Eyck* (since 1425)
*Maître du Girart de
Roussillon*
Jean le Tavernier

ANNE
m. John, Duke of
Bedford (1423)
PAINTER:
*Master of the
Duke of Bedford*

MARGUERITE
m. Arthur,
Duke of
Brittany,
Earl of
Richmond
(1423)

JEAN, Duke of
Calabria (d. 1470)
m. Marie de Bourbon,
niece of Philippe of Burgundy

YOLANDE
m. Count of Vaudémont

MARGUERITE
m. Henry VI, King of
England (1445)

ulême

ichon
stard

RENÉ II, Duke of Lorraine
PAINTERS: *Pierre Garnier*
François Boursier

CHARLES LE TÉMÉRAIRE (The Bold), Count of Charolais
b. 1433, succeeded 1467, died 1477
m. (1) Catherine de France
    (2) Isabelle de Bourbon
    (3) Margaret of York (1468)
PAINTERS: *Simon Marmion*
Philippe de Mazerolles
Jean Hennecart
Master of Mary of Burgundy

ANTOINE, le Grand
Bâtard
painted by *Memling*

of France, 1515–1547
ontainebleau

erréal
Clouet
is Clouet

iccio
rdo da Vinci
a del Sarto

MARIE
1457–1482
m. Maximilian of Austria (1477)
PAINTER: *Master of Mary of Burgundy*
(*Sanders Bening*)

MEDIAEVAL
FRANCE